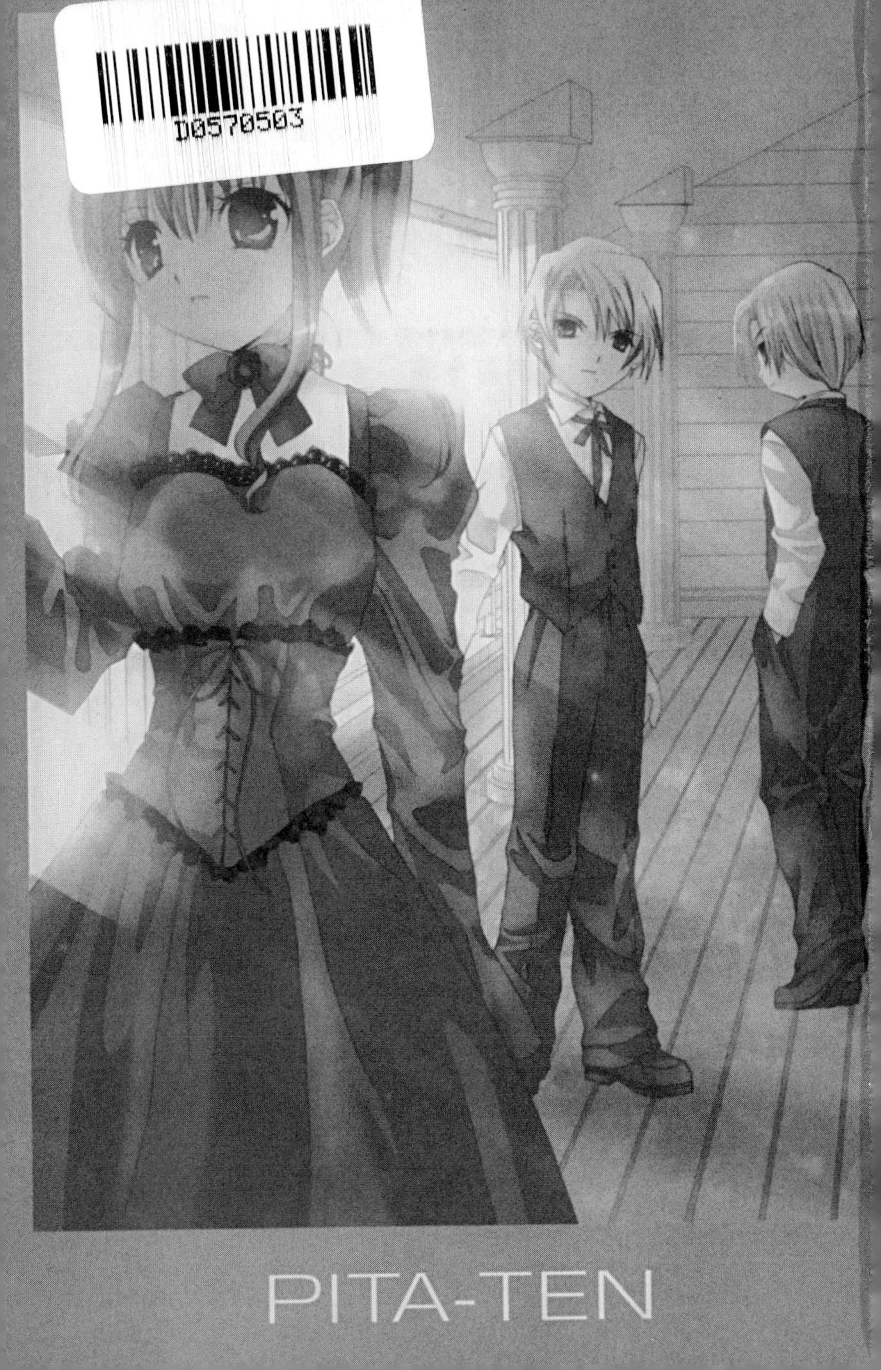

PITA-TEN

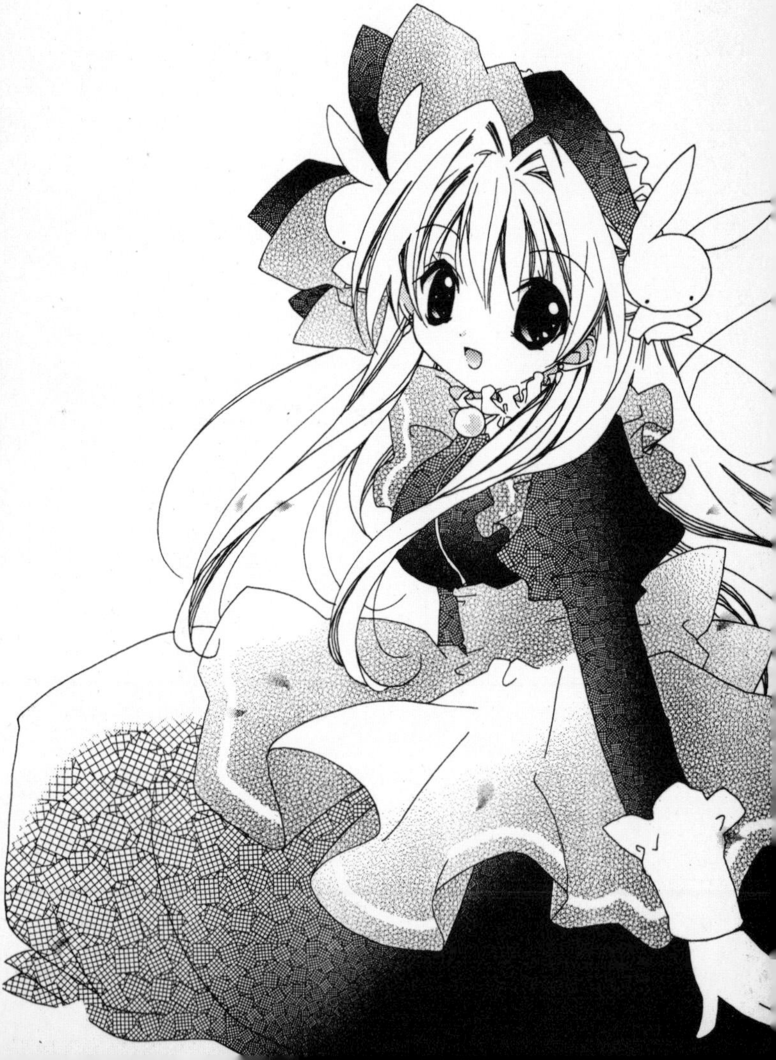

Volume 6

by
Koge-Donbo

HAMBURG // LONDON // LOS ANGELES // TOKYO

Pita-Ten Vol. 6
Created by Koge-Donbo

Translation - Nan Rymer
English Adaptation - Adam Arnold
Copy Editor - Peter Ahlstrom
Retouch and Lettering - Abelardo Bigting
Production Artist - Louis Csontos
Cover Design - Raymond Makowski

Editor - Paul Morrissey
Digital Imaging Manager - Chris Buford
Pre-Press Manager - Antonio DePietro
Production Managers - Jennifer Miller and Mutsumi Miyazaki
Art Director - Matt Alford
Managing Editor - Jill Freshney
VP of Production - Ron Klamert
President and C.O.O. - John Parker
Publisher and C.E.O. - Stuart Levy

A  Manga

TOKYOPOP Inc.
5900 Wilshire Blvd. Suite 2000
Los Angeles, CA 90036

E-mail: info@TOKYOPOP.com
Come visit us online at www.TOKYOPOP.com

© 2002 Koge-Donbo. All rights reserved. No portion of this book may be
First published in Japan in 2002 reproduced or transmitted in any form or by any means
by Media Works Inc.,Tokyo, Japan. without written permission from the copyright holders.
English publication rights arranged This manga is a work of fiction. Any resemblance to
through Media Works Inc. actual events or locales or persons, living or dead, is
English text copyright © 2004 TOKYOPOP Inc. entirely coincidental.

ISBN: 1-59182-632-2

First TOKYOPOP printing: November 2004
10 9 8 7 6 5 4 3 2 1
Printed in the USA

Contents

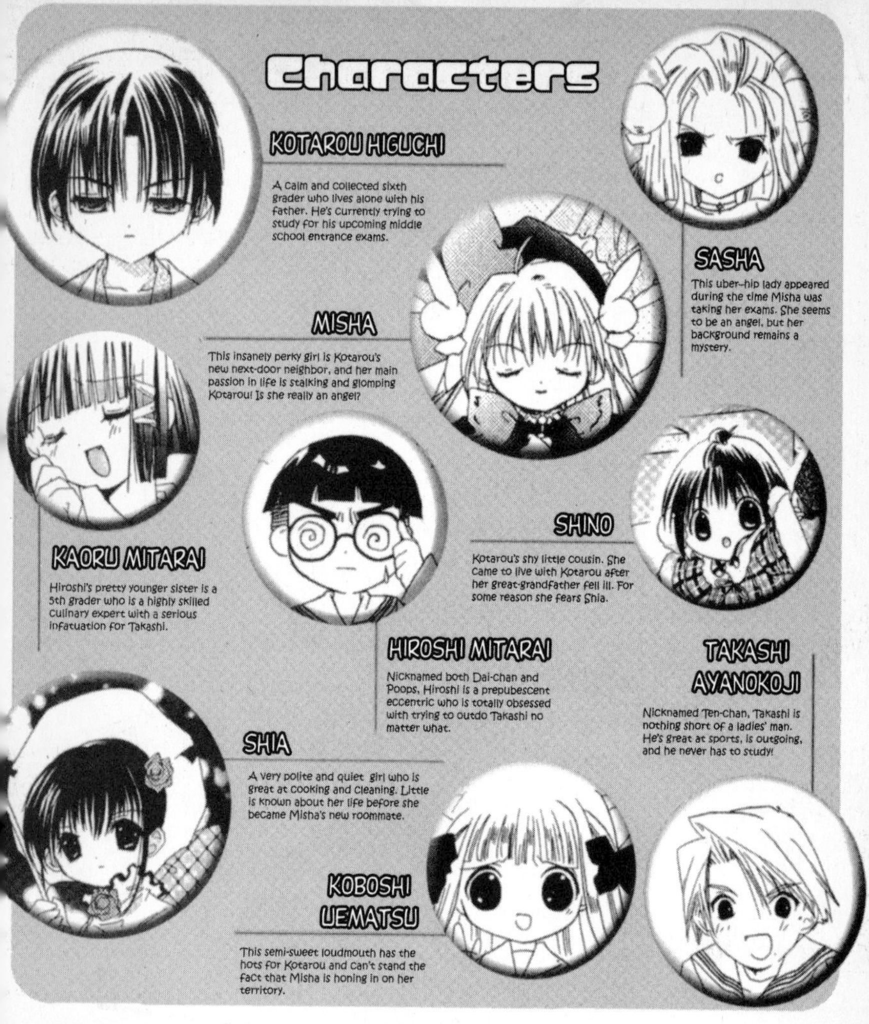
Characters
KOTAROU HIGUCHI
A calm and collected sixth grader who lives alone with his father. He's currently trying to study for his upcoming middle school entrance exams.
SASHA
This uber-hip lady appeared during the time Misha was taking her exams. She seems to be an angel, but her background remains a mystery.
MISHA
This insanely perky girl is Kotarou's new next-door neighbor, and her main passion in life is stalking and glomping Kotarou! Is she really an angel?
KAORU MITARAI
Hiroshi's pretty younger sister is a 5th grader who is a highly skilled culinary expert with a serious infatuation for Takashi.
SHINO
Kotarou's shy little cousin. She came to live with Kotarou after her great-grandfather fell ill. For some reason she fears Shia.
HIROSHI MITARAI
Nicknamed both Dai-chan and Poops, Hiroshi is a prepubescent eccentric who is totally obsessed with trying to outdo Takashi no matter what.
TAKASHI AYANOKOJI
Nicknamed Ten-chan, Takashi is nothing short of a ladies' man. He's great at sports, is outgoing, and he never has to study!
SHIA
A very polite and quiet girl who is great at cooking and cleaning. Little is known about her life before she became Misha's new roommate.
KOBOSHI UEMATSU
This semi-sweet loudmouth has the hots for Kotarou and can't stand the fact that Misha is honing in on her territory.

The Story Until Now:

Quiet elementary school student Kotarou Higuchi is worse off than most kids. His mother died in a traffic accident and his workaholic father is never at home. This leaves Kotarou struggling to make it to school on time, cook his own meals and keep up with his studies.

Yet, his so-called normal life has thrown him a curveball in the form of a mysterious angel named Misha, who has not only moved in next door to him, but has made it her life's work to chase after, "abuse" and glomp onto Kotarou. Not long after her appearance, *another* strange girl by the name of Shia ends up becoming Misha's new roommate!

Just as Kotarou manages to adjust to his topsy-turvy new life, he suffers a mysterious coma after Shia steals a kiss from him. By the time Misha manages to return Kotarou from the brink of an unending slumber, Shia has already fled, her whereabouts unknown.

Shortly thereafter, Kotarou is informed of his maternal great-grandfather's deteriorating health and rushes to his mother's home. There he is miraculously reunited with Shia as reality blurs and fate begins to reveal a tangled image of the past.

Lesson 32
How to Peek Into an Unknown Time: Part 2

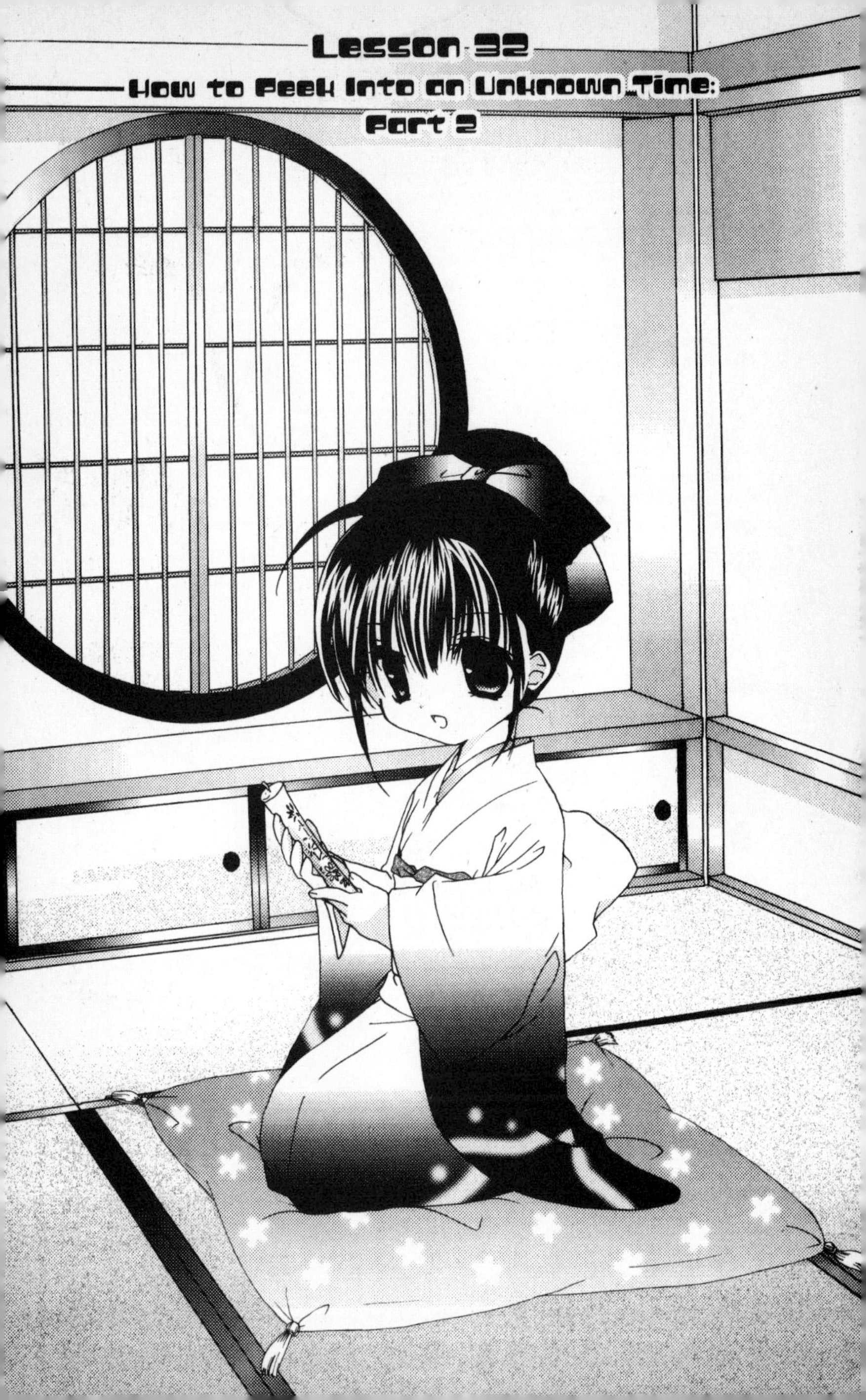

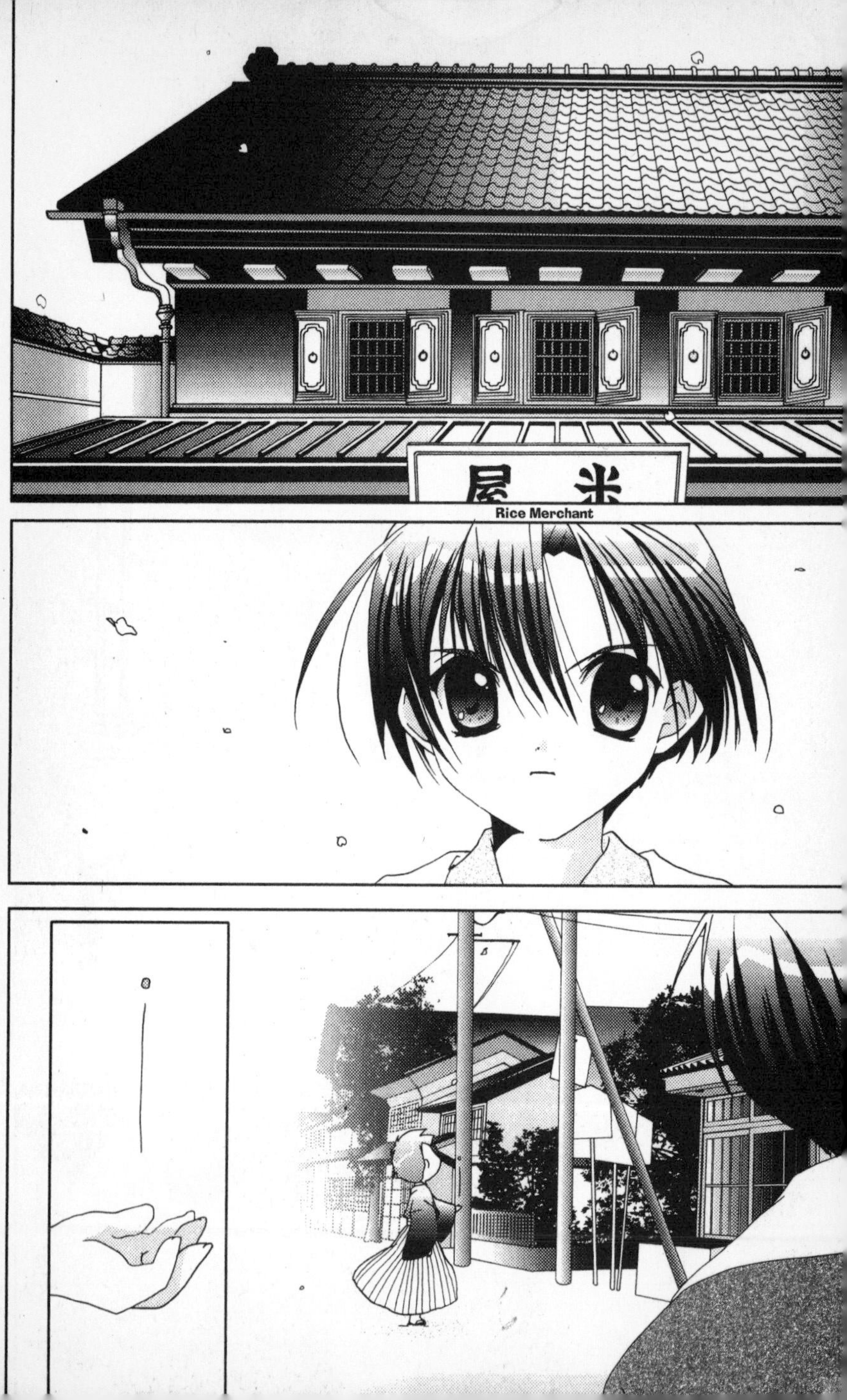
米屋
Rice Merchant

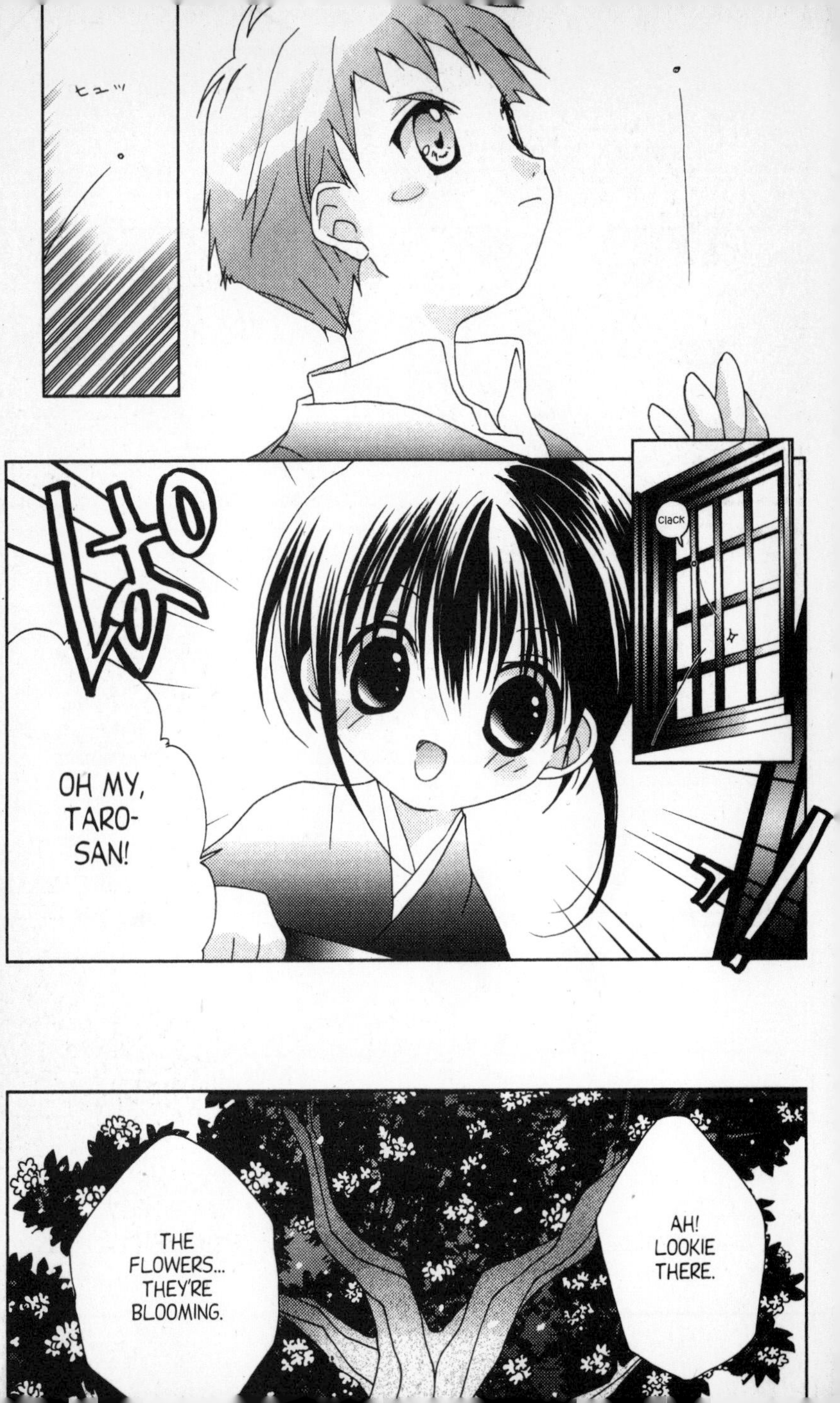
ヒュッ
Clack
ぱっ
OH MY, TARO-SAN!
AH! LOOKIE THERE.
THE FLOWERS... THEY'RE BLOOMING.

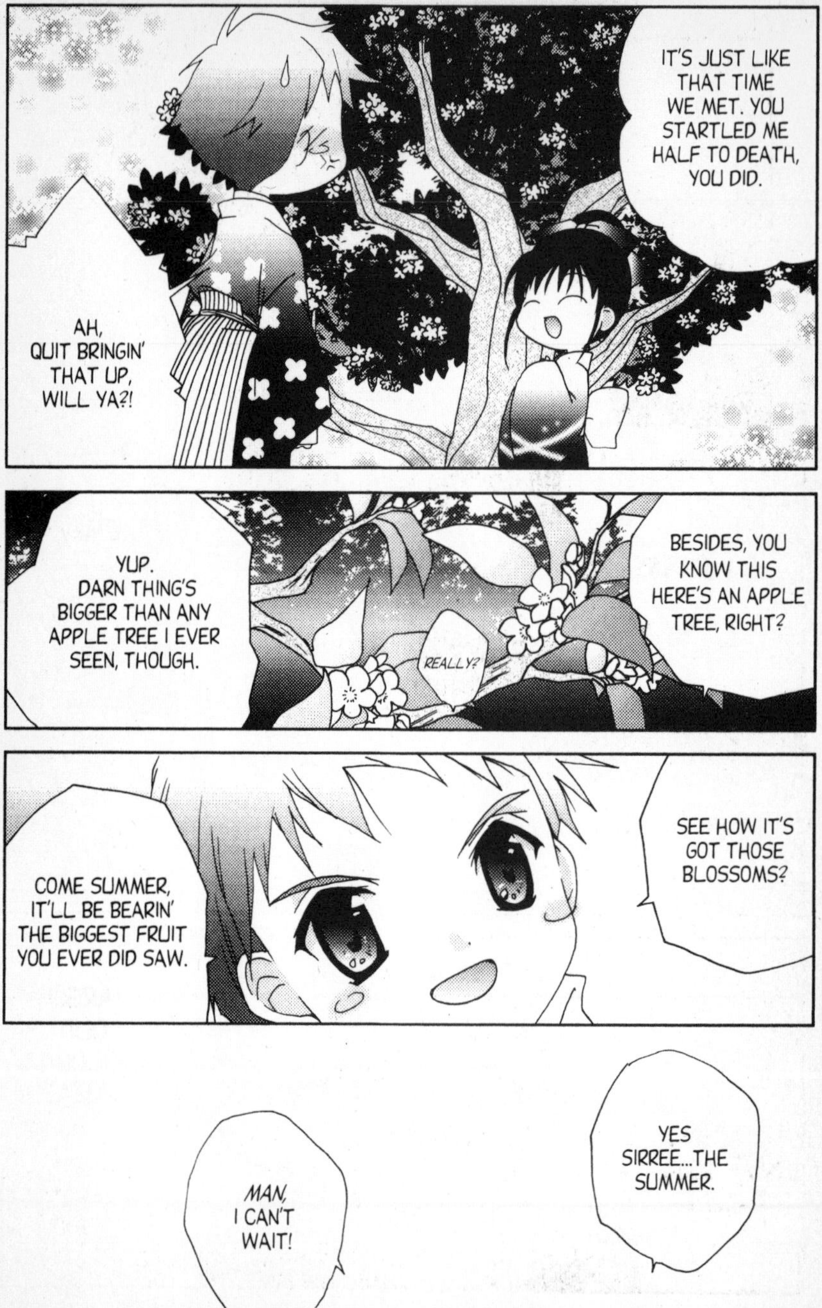
IT'S JUST LIKE THAT TIME WE MET. YOU STARTLED ME HALF TO DEATH, YOU DID.
AH, QUIT BRINGIN' THAT UP, WILL YA?!
BESIDES, YOU KNOW THIS HERE'S AN APPLE TREE, RIGHT?
REALLY?
YUP. DARN THING'S BIGGER THAN ANY APPLE TREE I EVER SEEN, THOUGH.
SEE HOW IT'S GOT THOSE BLOSSOMS?
COME SUMMER, IT'LL BE BEARIN' THE BIGGEST FRUIT YOU EVER DID SAW.
YES SIRREE...THE SUMMER.
MAN, I CAN'T WAIT!

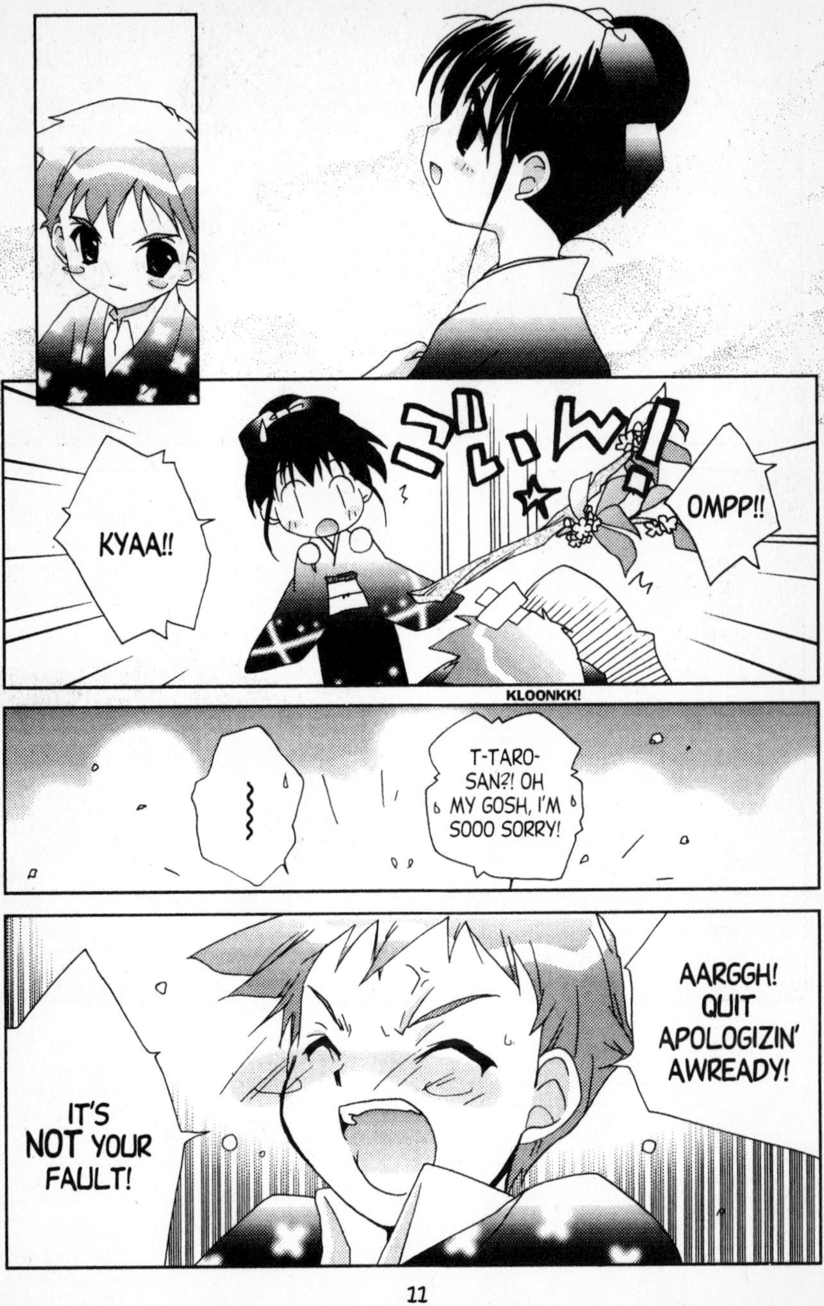
OMPP!!
ごぃん!
KYAA!!
KLOONKK!
T-TARO-SAN?! OH MY GOSH, I'M SOOO SORRY!
AARGGH! QUIT APOLOGIZIN' AWREADY!
IT'S NOT YOUR FAULT!

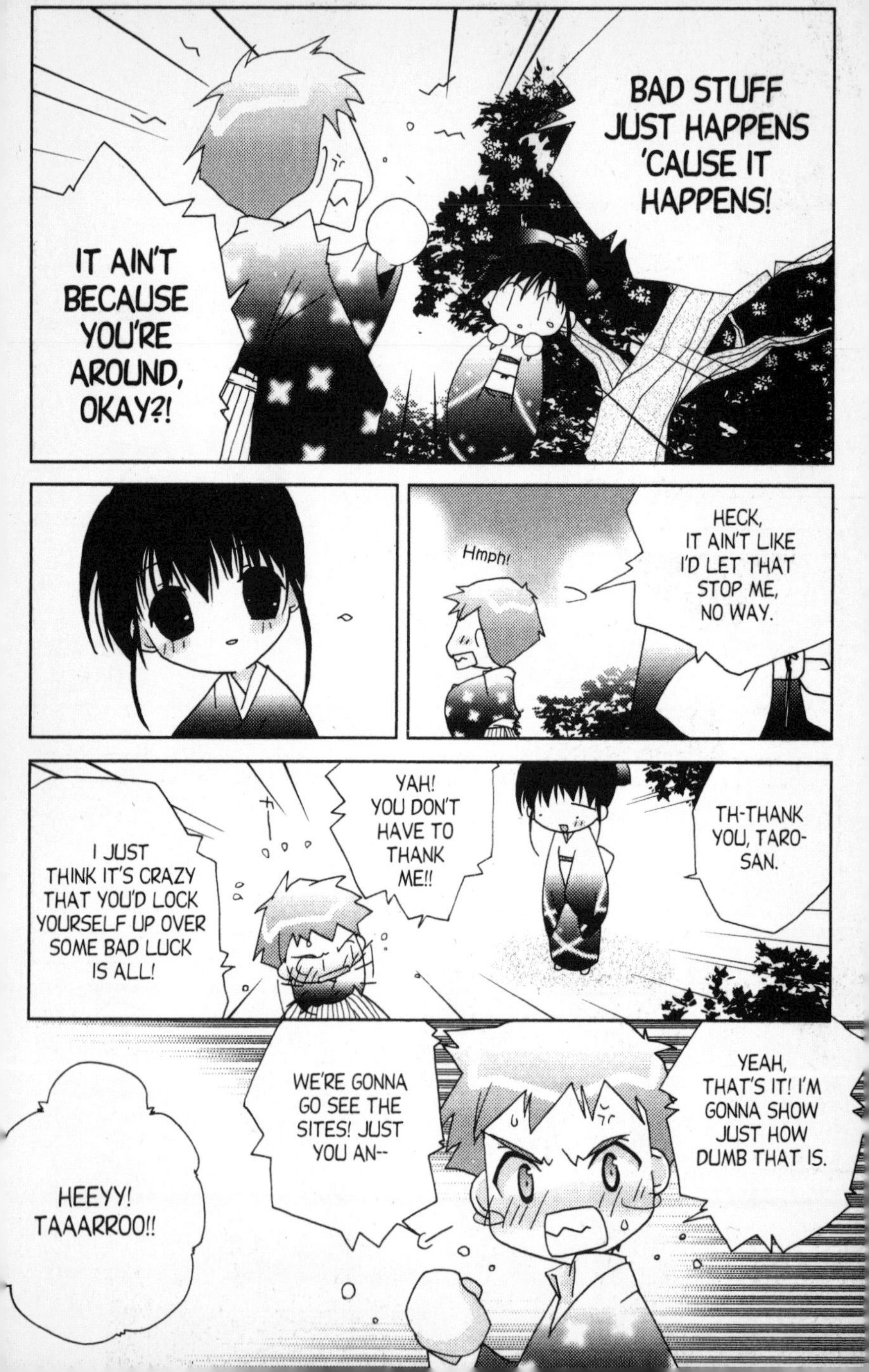
BAD STUFF JUST HAPPENS 'CAUSE IT HAPPENS!
IT AIN'T BECAUSE YOU'RE AROUND, OKAY?!
HECK, IT AIN'T LIKE I'D LET THAT STOP ME, NO WAY.
Hmph!
TH-THANK YOU, TARO-SAN.
YAH! YOU DON'T HAVE TO THANK ME!!
I JUST THINK IT'S CRAZY THAT YOU'D LOCK YOURSELF UP OVER SOME BAD LUCK IS ALL!
YEAH, THAT'S IT! I'M GONNA SHOW JUST HOW DUMB THAT IS.
WE'RE GONNA GO SEE THE SITES! JUST YOU AN--
HEEYY! TAAARROO!!

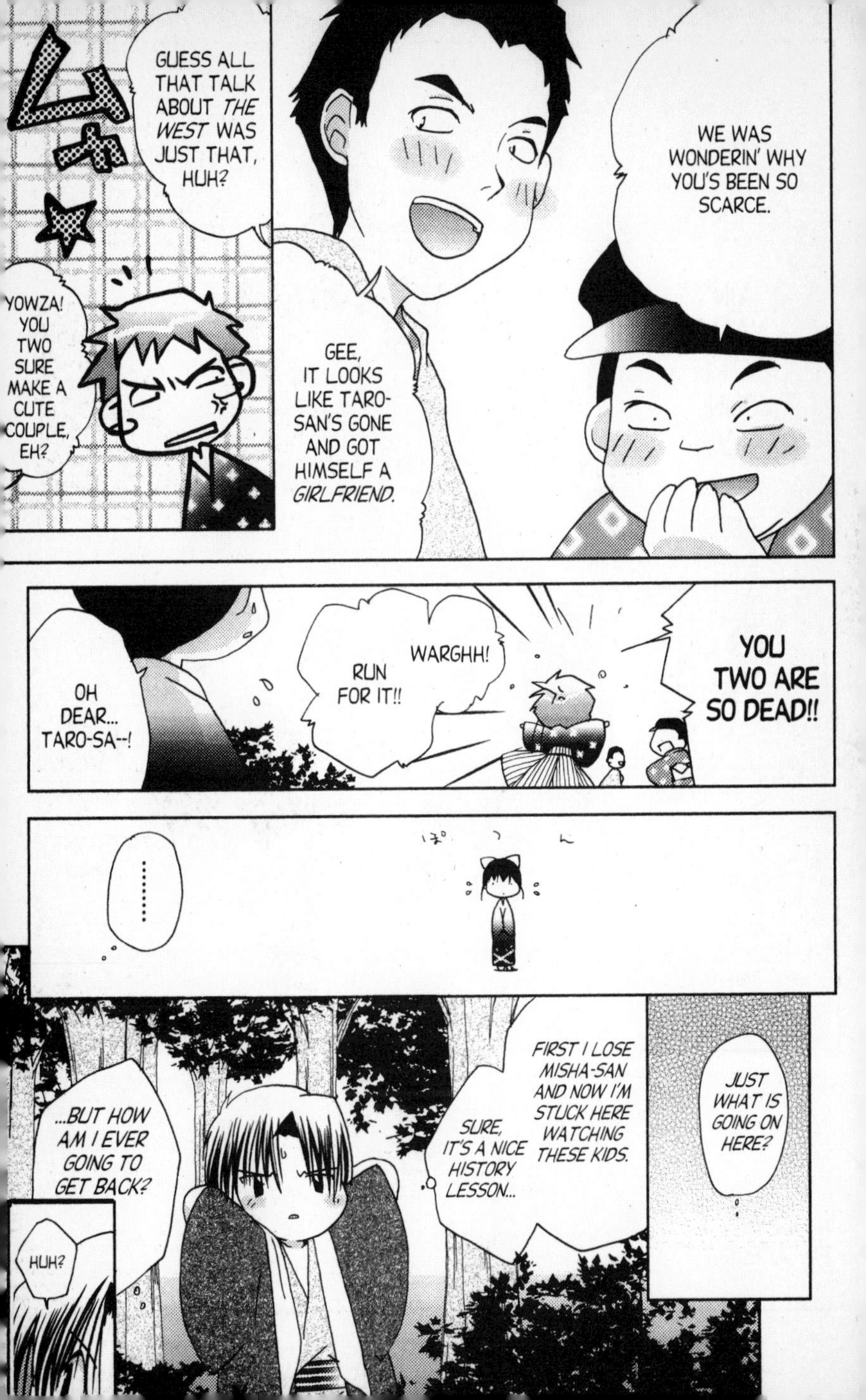
WE WAS WONDERIN' WHY YOU'S BEEN SO SCARCE.
GEE, IT LOOKS LIKE TARO-SAN'S GONE AND GOT HIMSELF A *GIRLFRIEND*.
GUESS ALL THAT TALK ABOUT *THE WEST* WAS JUST THAT, HUH?
ムッ
YOWZA! YOU TWO SURE MAKE A CUTE COUPLE, EH?
YOU TWO ARE SO DEAD!!
WARGHH!
RUN FOR IT!!
OH DEAR... TARO-SA--!
ぽつん
......
JUST WHAT IS GOING ON HERE?
FIRST I LOSE MISHA-SAN AND NOW I'M STUCK HERE WATCHING THESE KIDS.
SURE, IT'S A NICE HISTORY LESSON...
...BUT HOW AM I EVER GOING TO GET BACK?
HUH?

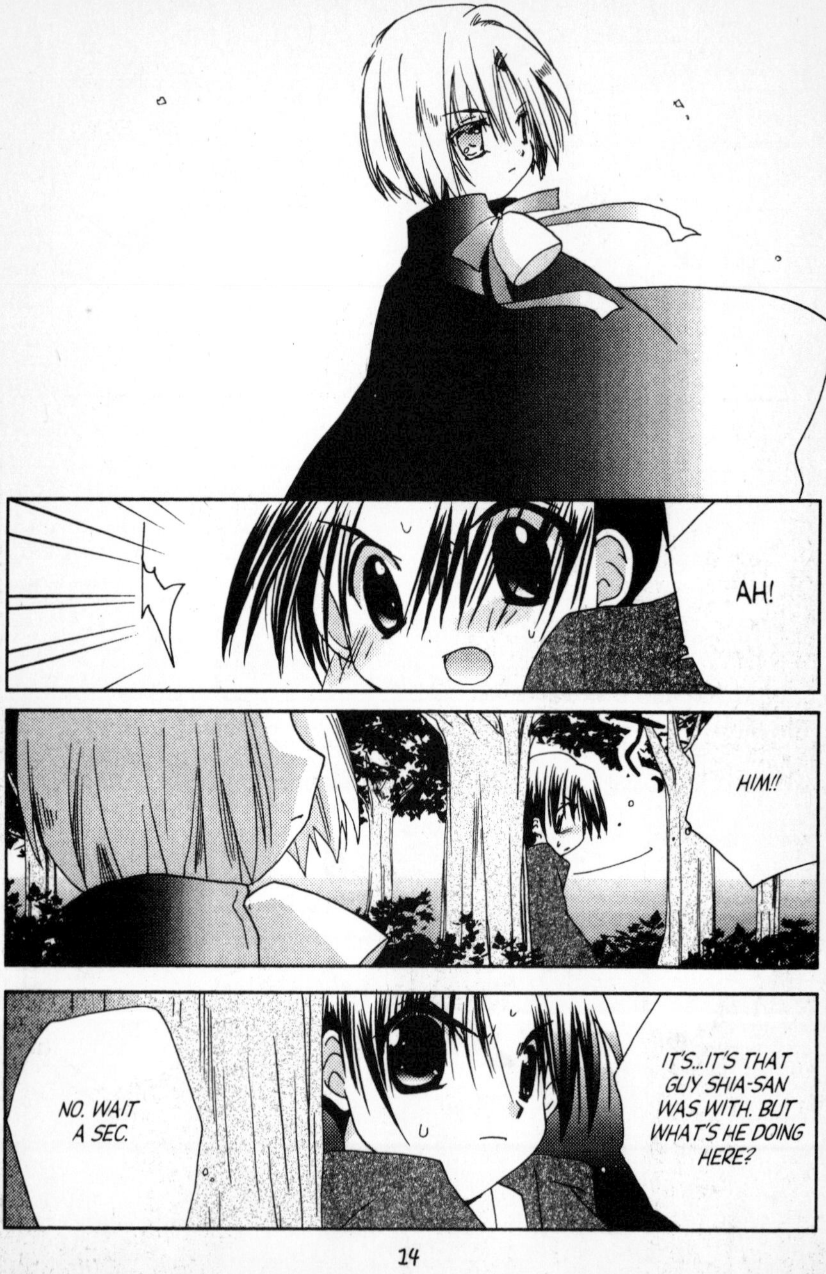
AH!
HIM!!
IT'S...IT'S THAT GUY SHIA-SAN WAS WITH. BUT WHAT'S HE DOING HERE?
NO. WAIT A SEC.

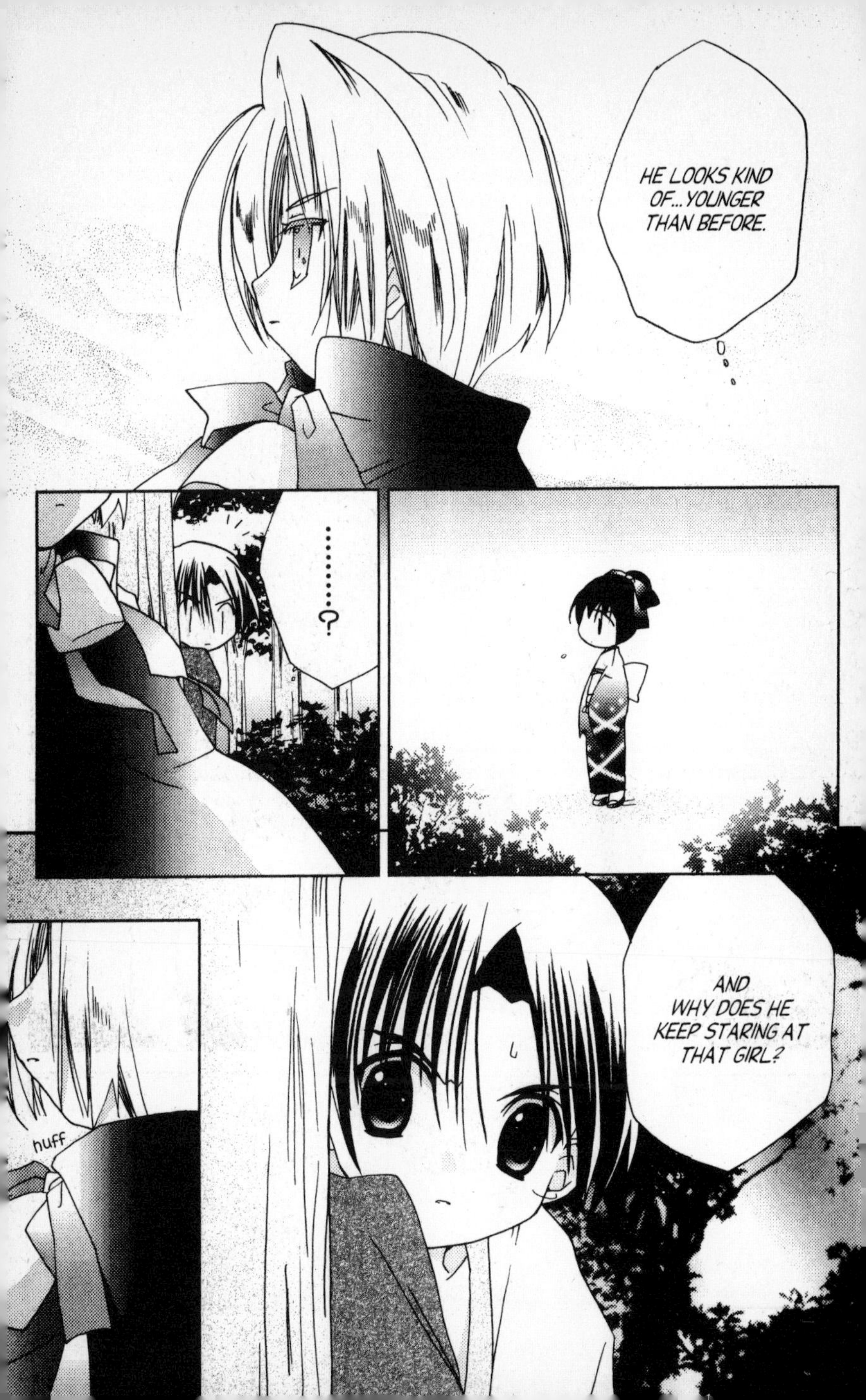
HE LOOKS KIND OF... YOUNGER THAN BEFORE.
......?
AND WHY DOES HE KEEP STARING AT THAT GIRL?
huff

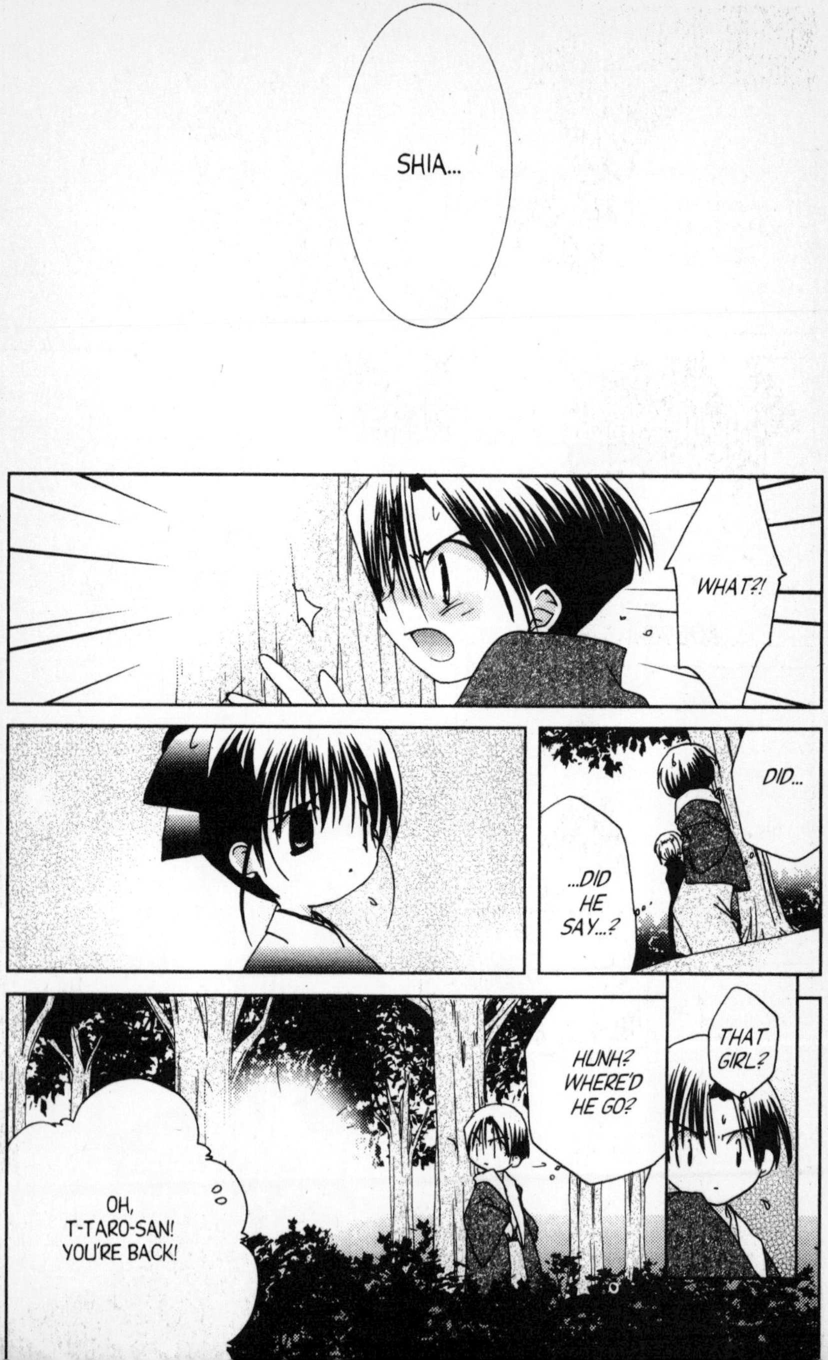
SHIA...
WHAT?!
DID...
...DID HE SAY...?
THAT GIRL?
HUNH? WHERE'D HE GO?
OH, T-TARO-SAN! YOU'RE BACK!

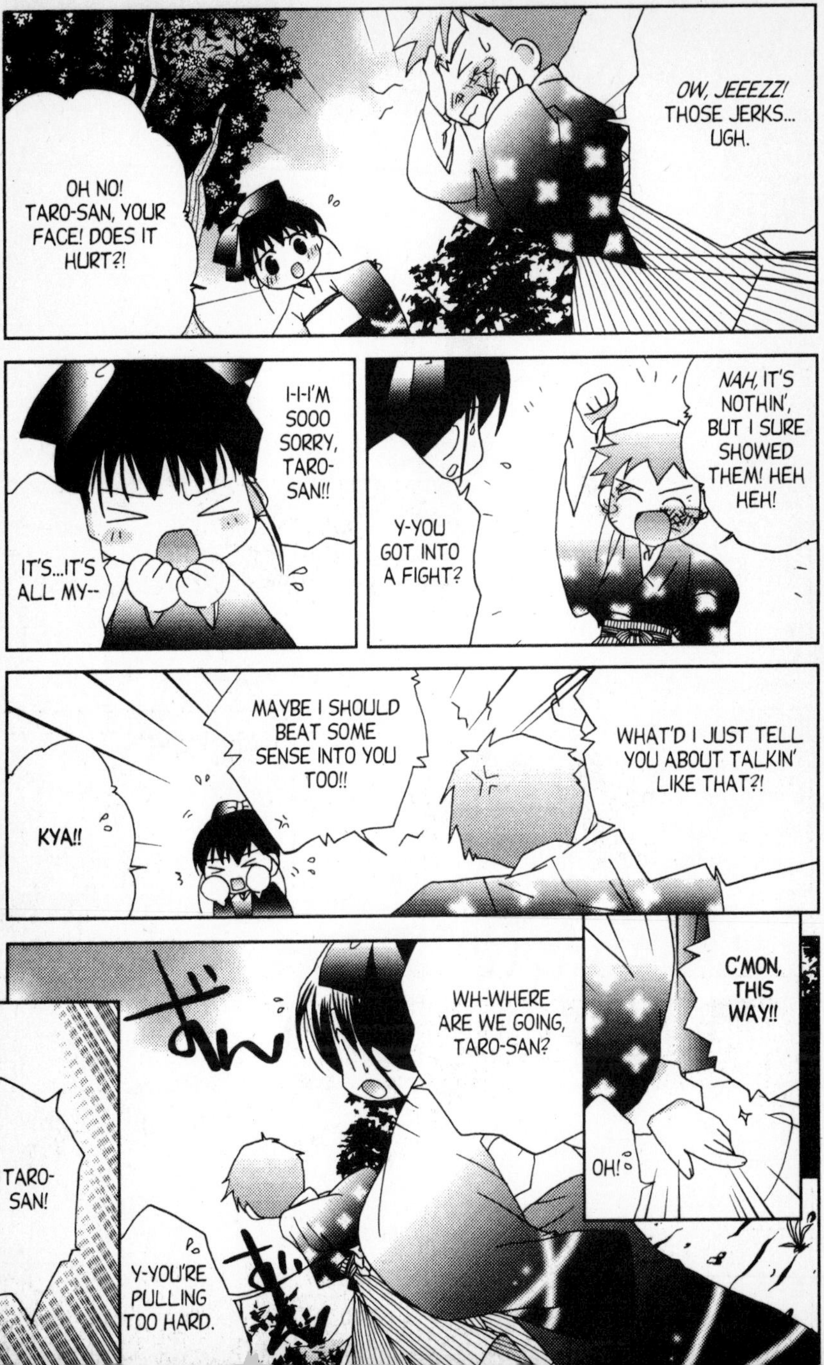
OW, JEEEZZ! THOSE JERKS... UGH.
OH NO! TARO-SAN, YOUR FACE! DOES IT HURT?!
NAH, IT'S NOTHIN', BUT I SURE SHOWED THEM! HEH HEH!
Y-YOU GOT INTO A FIGHT?
I-I-I'M SOOO SORRY, TARO-SAN!!
IT'S...IT'S ALL MY--
WHAT'D I JUST TELL YOU ABOUT TALKIN' LIKE THAT?!
MAYBE I SHOULD BEAT SOME SENSE INTO YOU TOO!!
KYA!!
C'MON, THIS WAY!!
OH!
WH-WHERE ARE WE GOING, TARO-SAN?
Y-YOU'RE PULLING TOO HARD.
TARO-SAN!

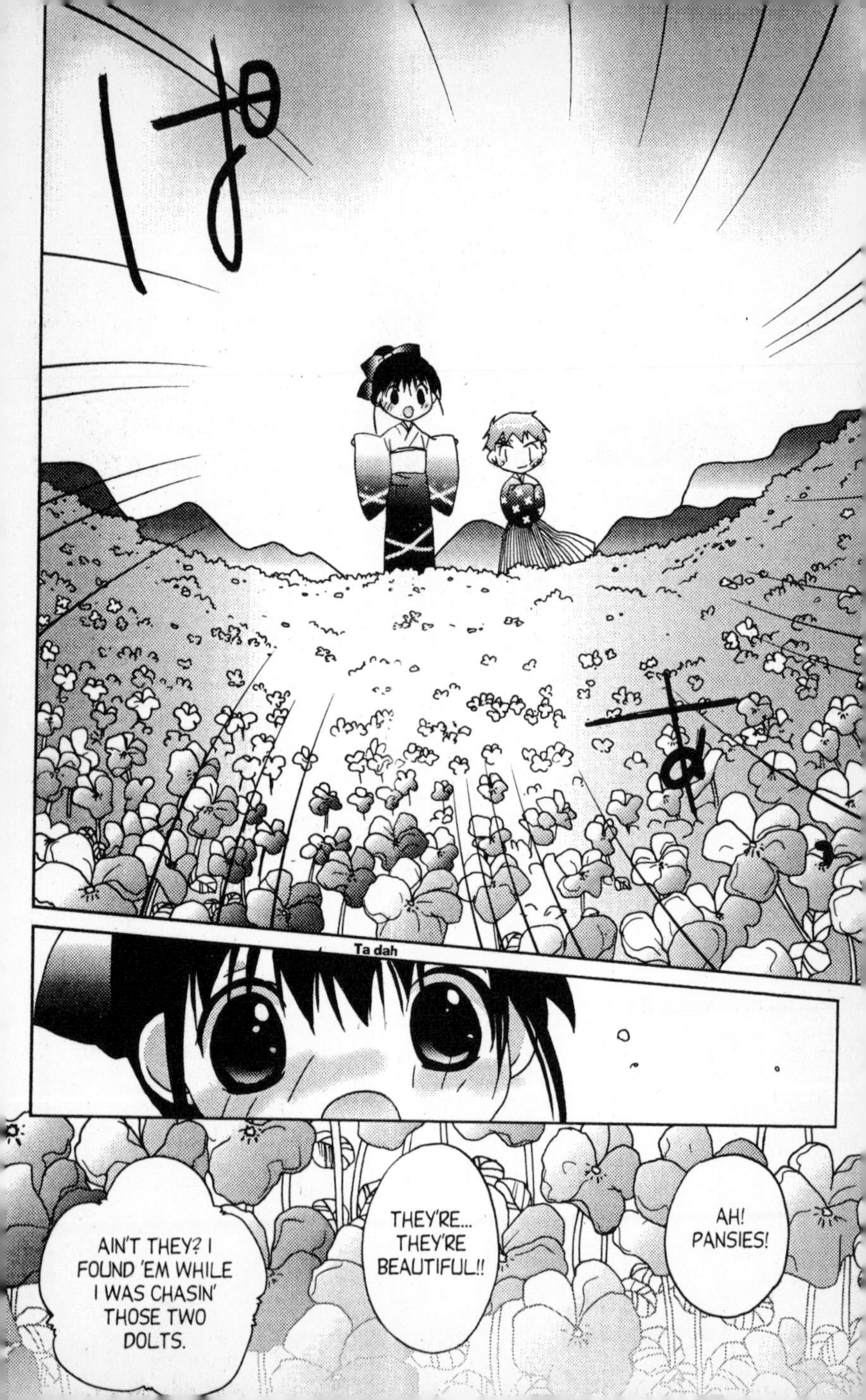
Ta dah
AH! PANSIES!
THEY'RE... THEY'RE BEAUTIFUL!!
AIN'T THEY? I FOUND 'EM WHILE I WAS CHASIN' THOSE TWO DOLTS.

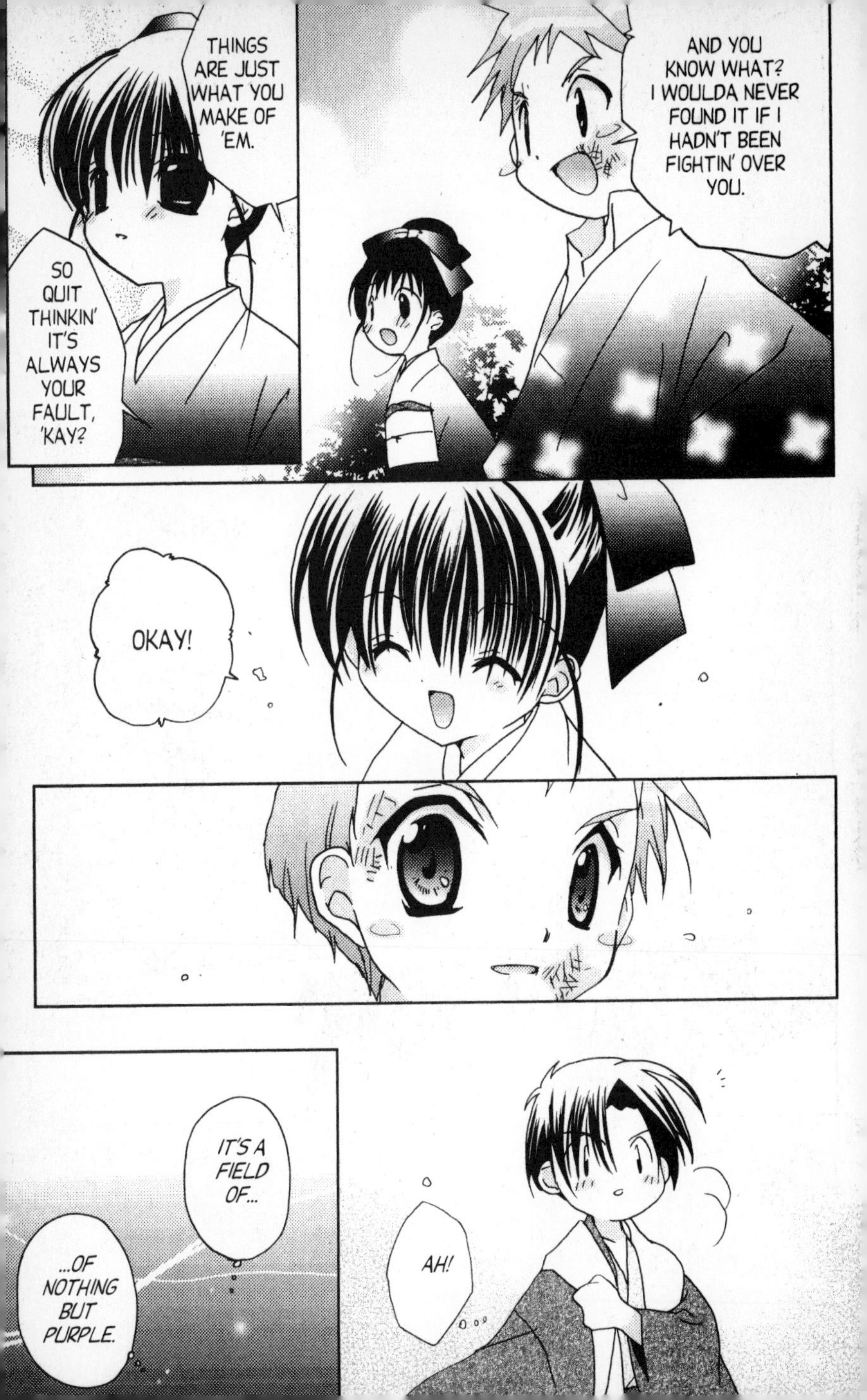
AND YOU KNOW WHAT? I WOULDA NEVER FOUND IT IF I HADN'T BEEN FIGHTIN' OVER YOU.
THINGS ARE JUST WHAT YOU MAKE OF 'EM.
SO QUIT THINKIN' IT'S ALWAYS YOUR FAULT, 'KAY?
OKAY!
AH!
IT'S A FIELD OF...
...OF NOTHING BUT PURPLE.

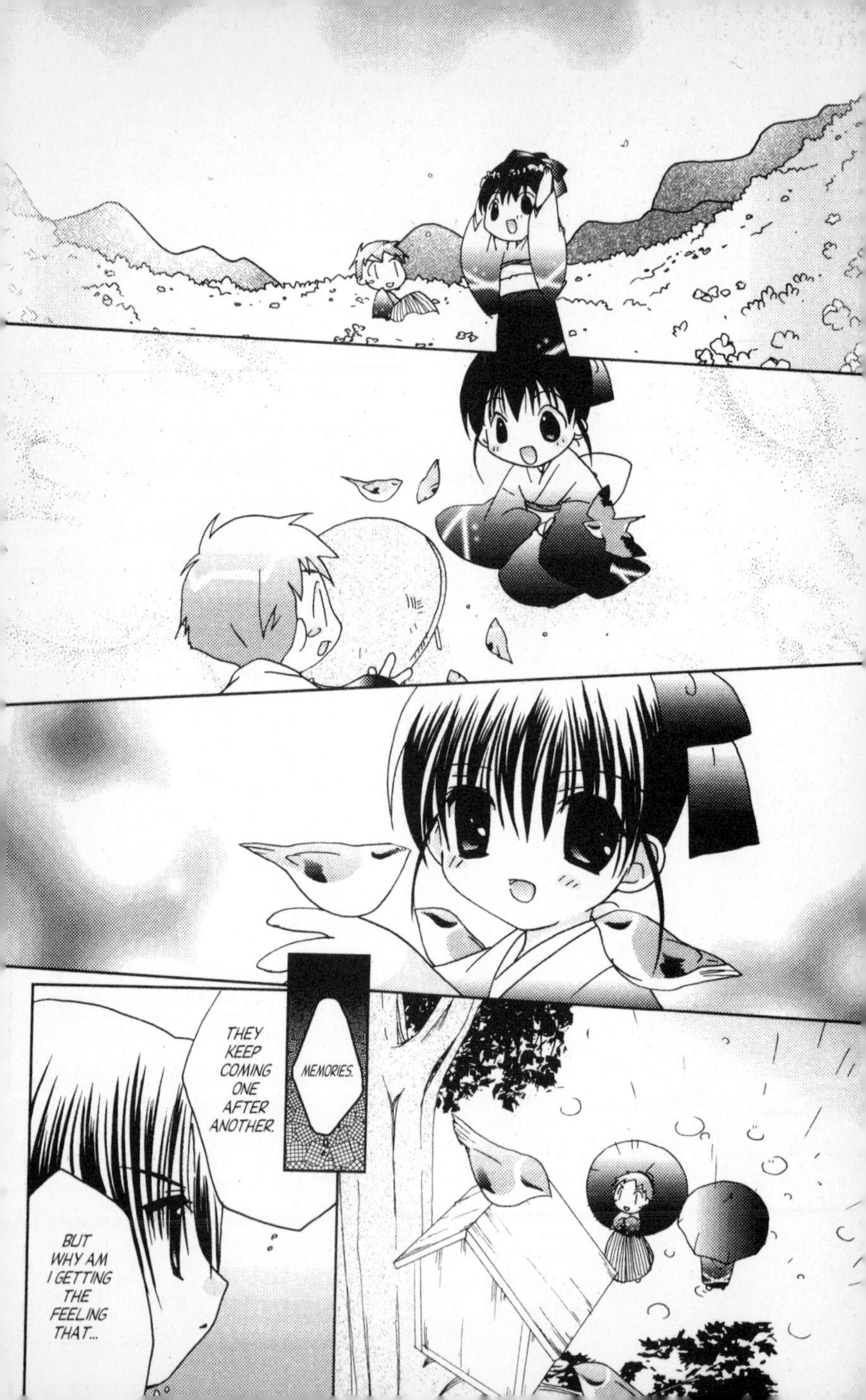
MEMORIES.
THEY KEEP COMING ONE AFTER ANOTHER.
BUT WHY AM I GETTING THE FEELING THAT...

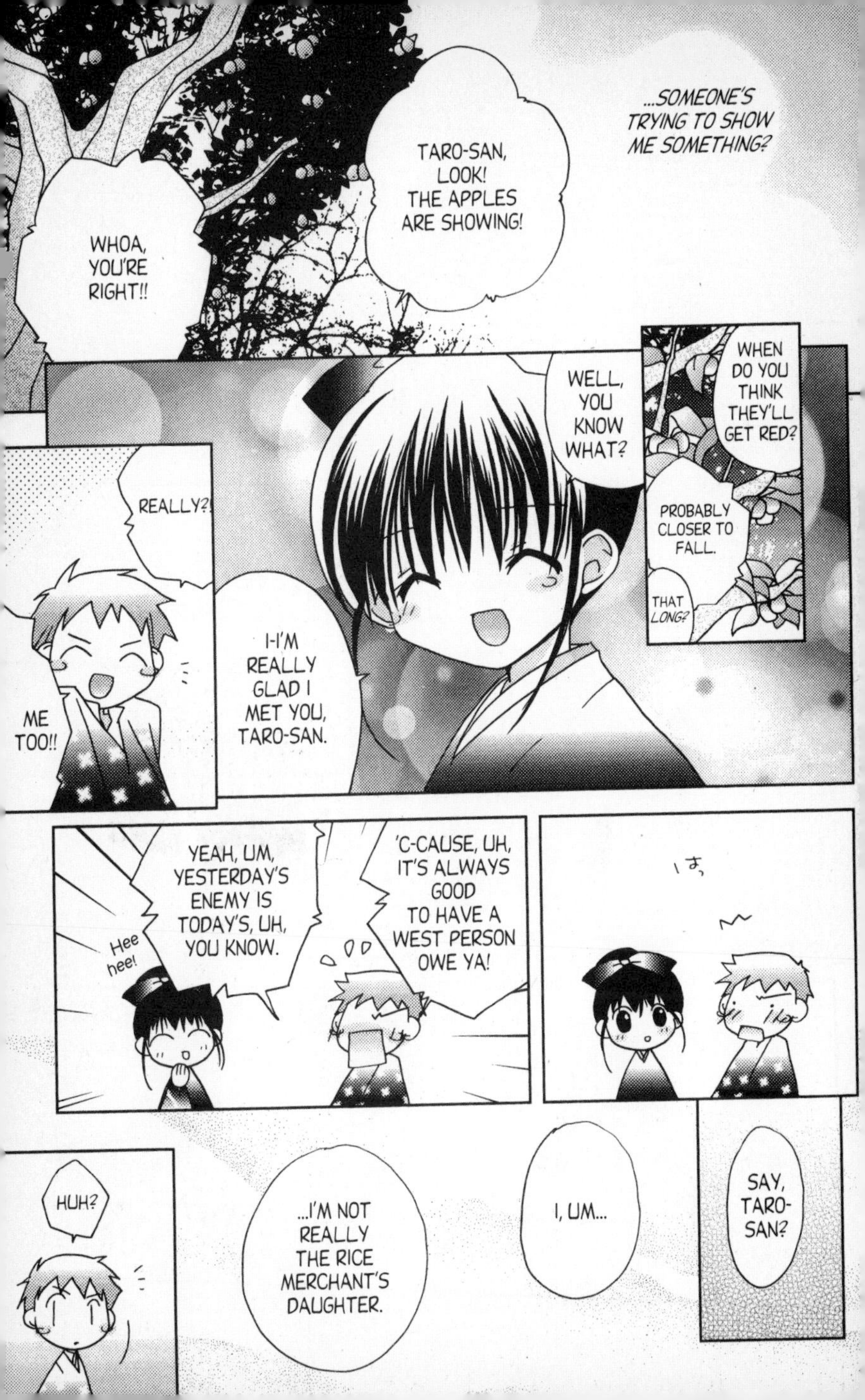
...SOMEONE'S TRYING TO SHOW ME SOMETHING?
TARO-SAN, LOOK! THE APPLES ARE SHOWING!
WHOA, YOU'RE RIGHT!!
WHEN DO YOU THINK THEY'LL GET RED?
PROBABLY CLOSER TO FALL.
THAT *LONG?*
WELL, YOU KNOW WHAT?
I-I'M REALLY GLAD I MET YOU, TARO-SAN.
REALLY?!
ME TOO!!
はっ
'C-CAUSE, UH, IT'S ALWAYS GOOD TO HAVE A WEST PERSON OWE YA!
YEAH, UM, YESTERDAY'S ENEMY IS TODAY'S, UH, YOU KNOW.
Hee hee!
SAY, TARO-SAN?
I, UM...
...I'M NOT REALLY THE RICE MERCHANT'S DAUGHTER.
HUH?

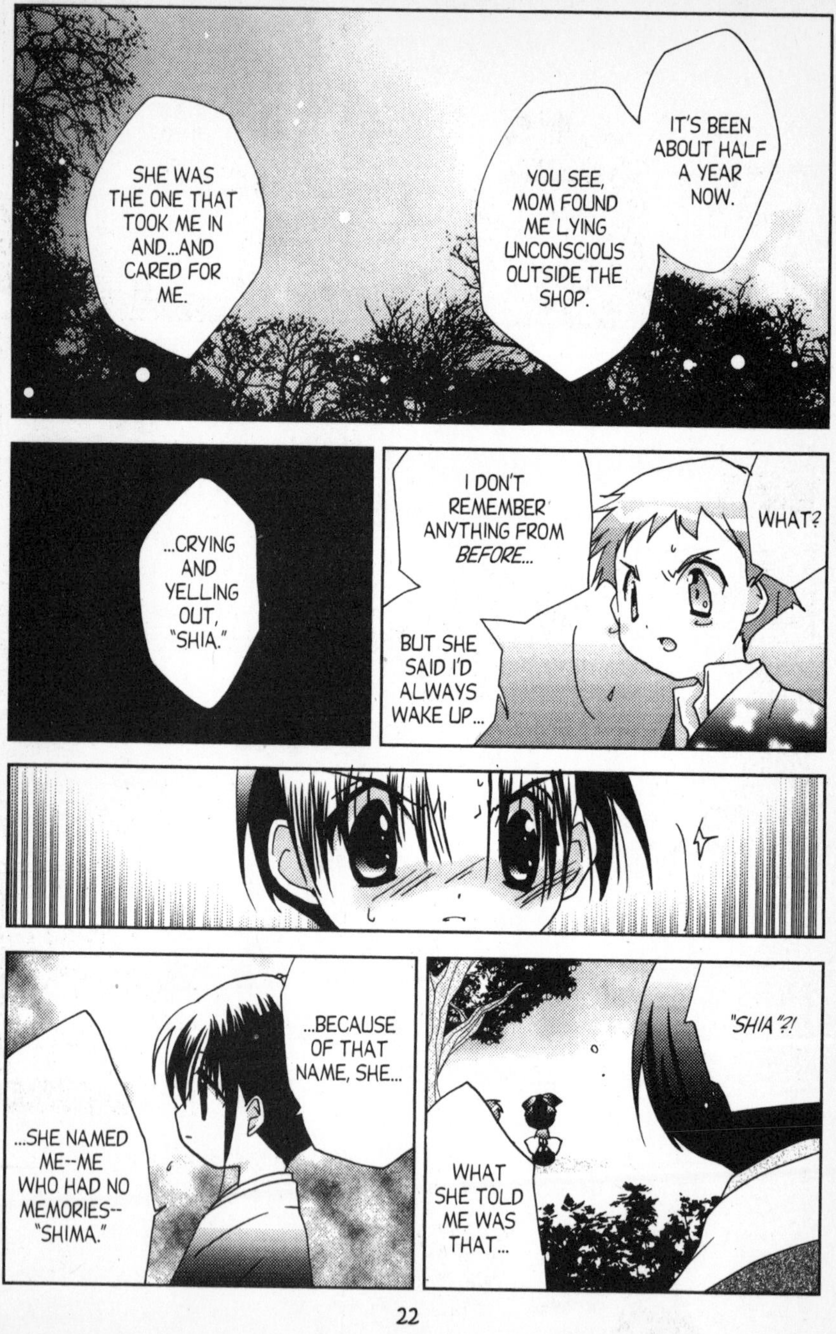
IT'S BEEN ABOUT HALF A YEAR NOW.
YOU SEE, MOM FOUND ME LYING UNCONSCIOUS OUTSIDE THE SHOP.
SHE WAS THE ONE THAT TOOK ME IN AND...AND CARED FOR ME.
WHAT?
I DON'T REMEMBER ANYTHING FROM *BEFORE*...
BUT SHE SAID I'D ALWAYS WAKE UP...
...CRYING AND YELLING OUT, "SHIA."
"SHIA"?!
WHAT SHE TOLD ME WAS THAT...
...BECAUSE OF THAT NAME, SHE...
...SHE NAMED ME--ME WHO HAD NO MEMORIES--"SHIMA."

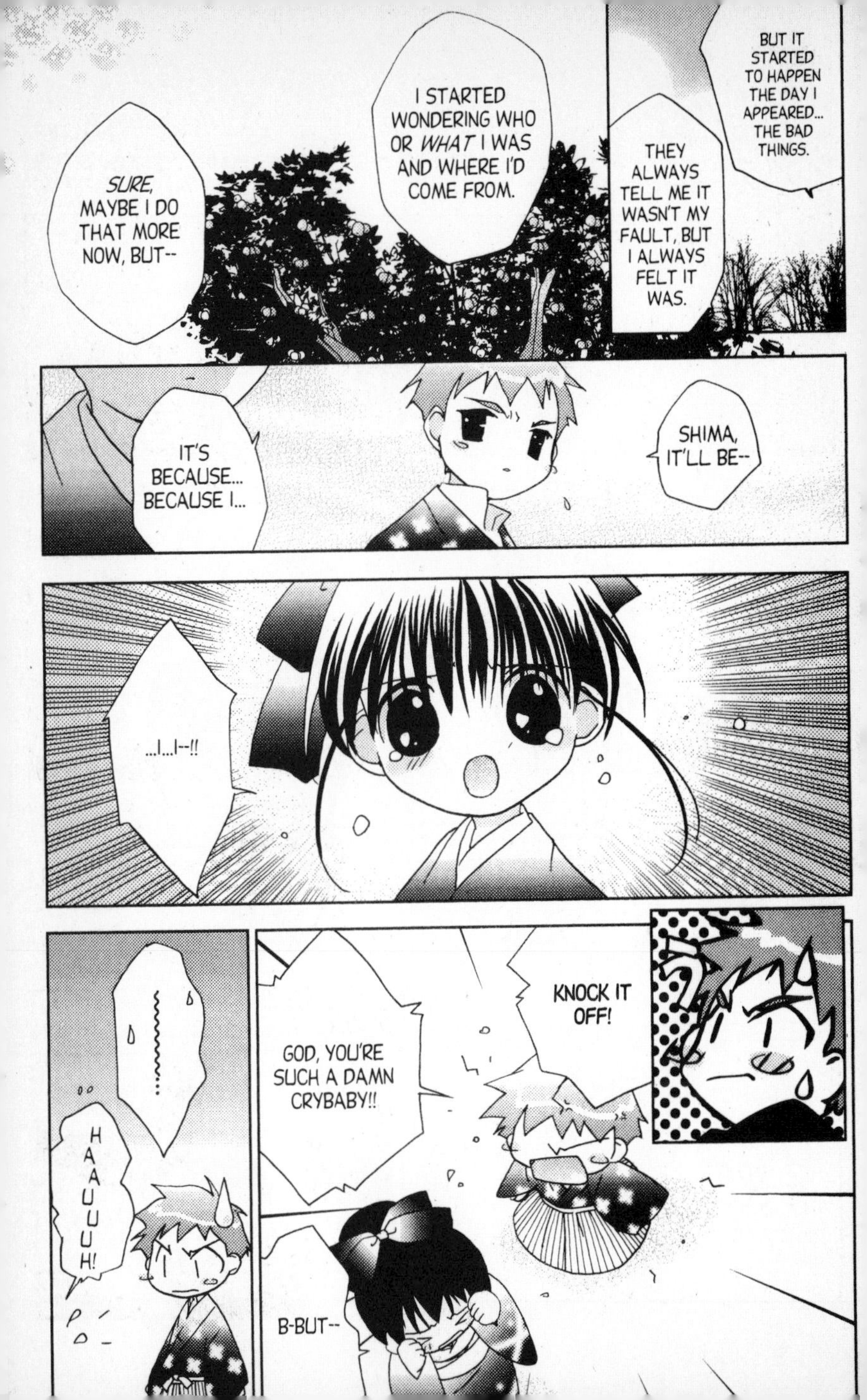
BUT IT STARTED TO HAPPEN THE DAY I APPEARED... THE BAD THINGS.
THEY ALWAYS TELL ME IT WASN'T MY FAULT, BUT I ALWAYS FELT IT WAS.
I STARTED WONDERING WHO OR *WHAT* I WAS AND WHERE I'D COME FROM.
SURE, MAYBE I DO THAT MORE NOW, BUT--
SHIMA, IT'LL BE--
IT'S BECAUSE... BECAUSE I...
...I...I--!!
KNOCK IT OFF!
GOD, YOU'RE SUCH A DAMN CRYBABY!!
B-BUT--
......
HAAUUUH!

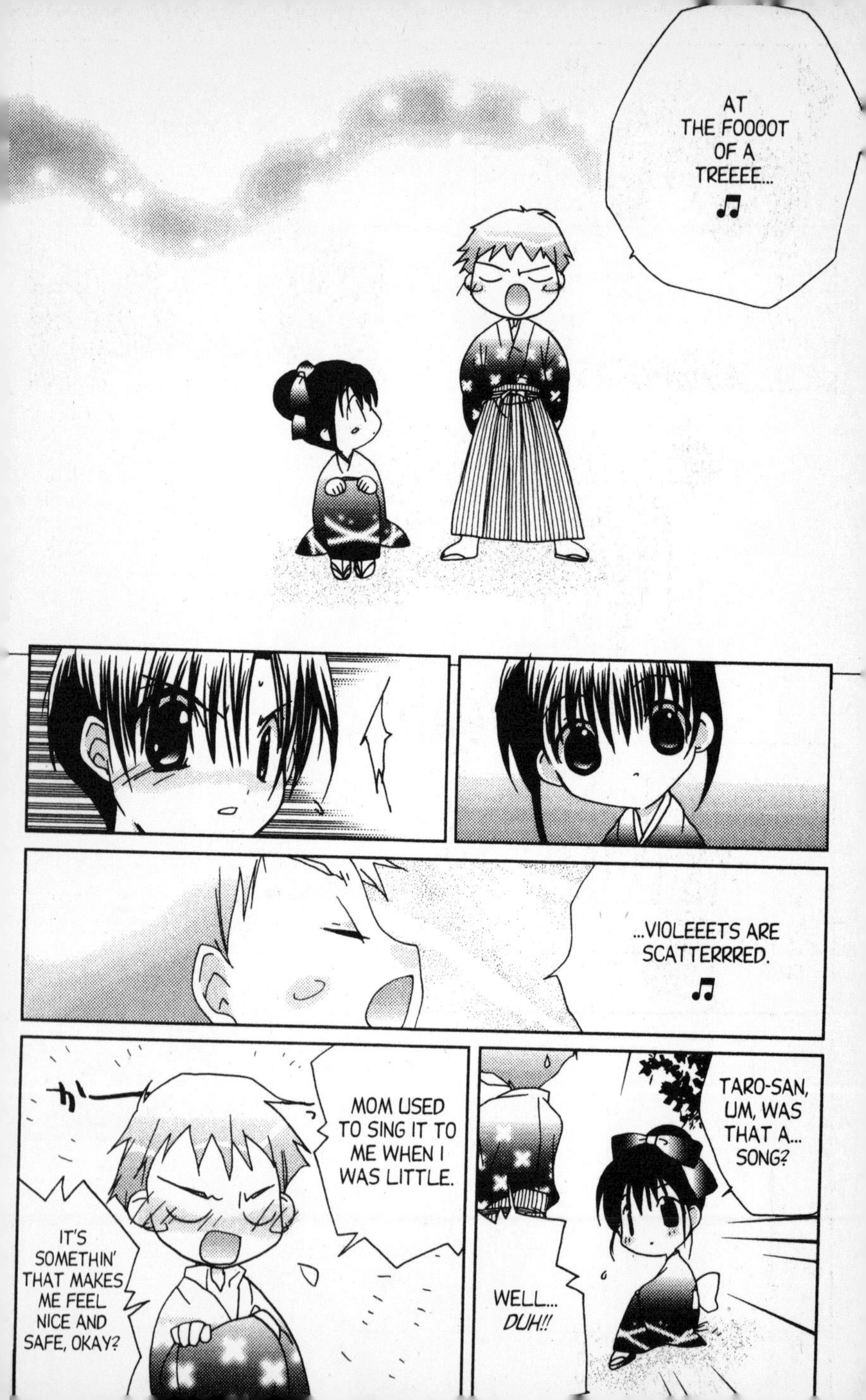
AT THE FOOOOT OF A TREEEE... ♫
...VIOLEEETS ARE SCATTERRRED. ♫
TARO-SAN, UM, WAS THAT A... SONG?
WELL... DUH!!
かー
MOM USED TO SING IT TO ME WHEN I WAS LITTLE.
IT'S SOMETHIN' THAT MAKES ME FEEL NICE AND SAFE, OKAY?

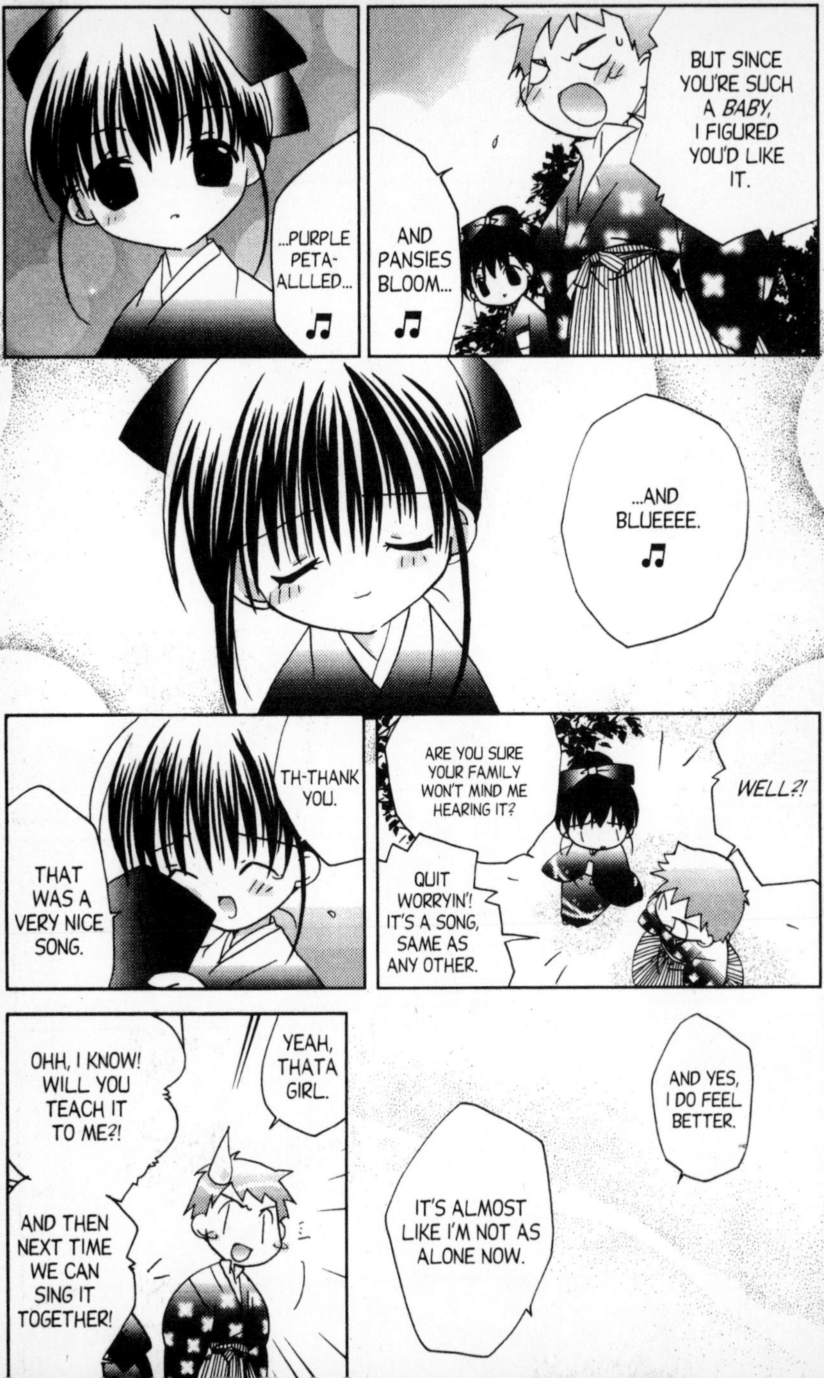
BUT SINCE YOU'RE SUCH A *BABY*, I FIGURED YOU'D LIKE IT.
AND PANSIES BLOOM... ♫
...PURPLE PETA-ALLLED... ♫
...AND BLUEEEE. ♫
WELL?!
ARE YOU SURE YOUR FAMILY WON'T MIND ME HEARING IT?
QUIT WORRYIN'! IT'S A SONG, SAME AS ANY OTHER.
TH-THANK YOU.
THAT WAS A VERY NICE SONG.
AND YES, I DO FEEL BETTER.
IT'S ALMOST LIKE I'M NOT AS ALONE NOW.
YEAH, THATA GIRL.
OHH, I KNOW! WILL YOU TEACH IT TO ME?!
AND THEN NEXT TIME WE CAN SING IT TOGETHER!

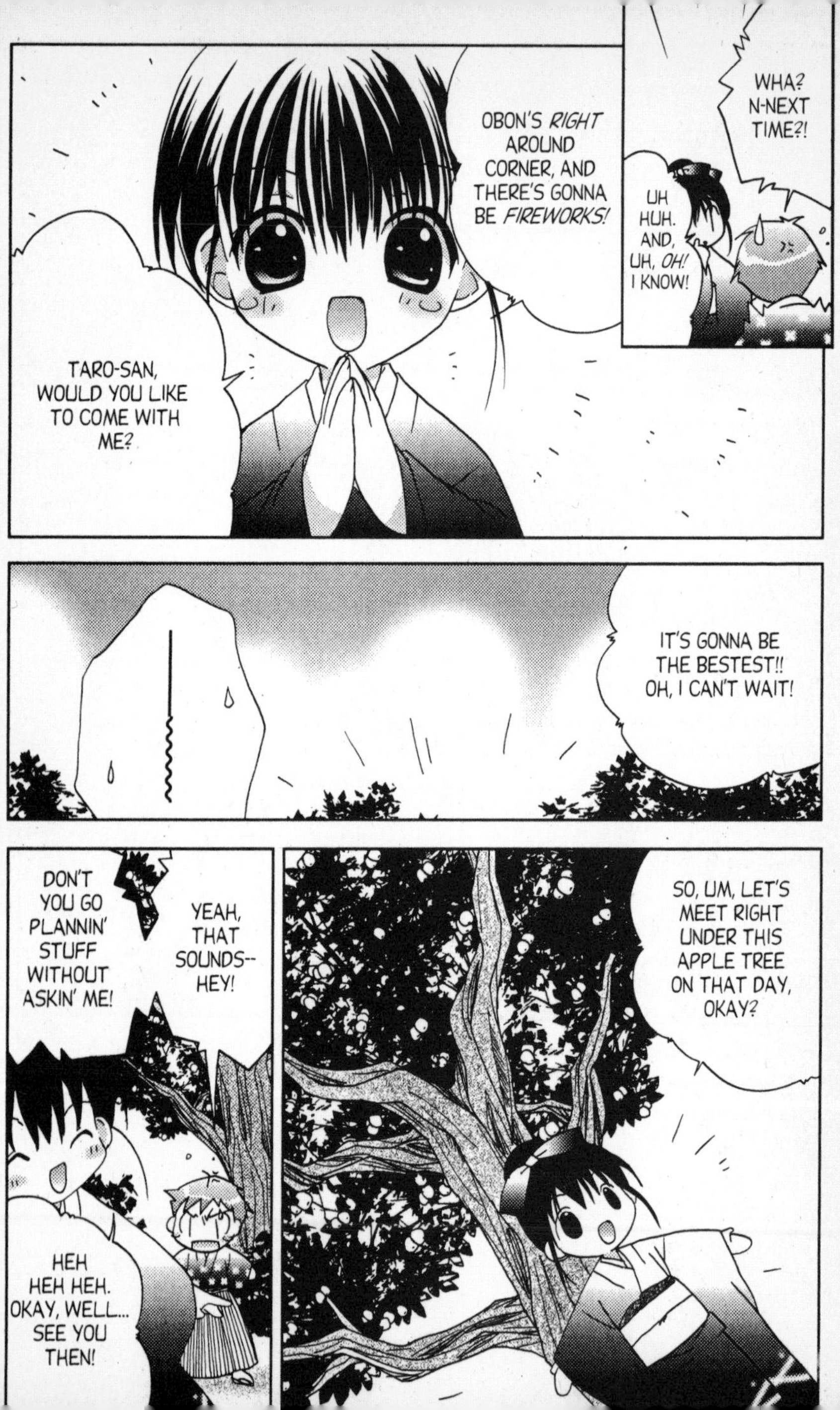
WHA? N-NEXT TIME?!
UH HUH. AND, UH, *OH!* I KNOW!
OBON'S *RIGHT* AROUND CORNER, AND THERE'S GONNA BE *FIREWORKS!*
TARO-SAN, WOULD YOU LIKE TO COME WITH ME?
IT'S GONNA BE THE BESTEST!! OH, I CAN'T WAIT!
SO, UM, LET'S MEET RIGHT UNDER THIS APPLE TREE ON THAT DAY, OKAY?
YEAH, THAT SOUNDS-- HEY!
DON'T YOU GO PLANNIN' STUFF WITHOUT ASKIN' ME!
HEH HEH HEH. OKAY, WELL... SEE YOU THEN!

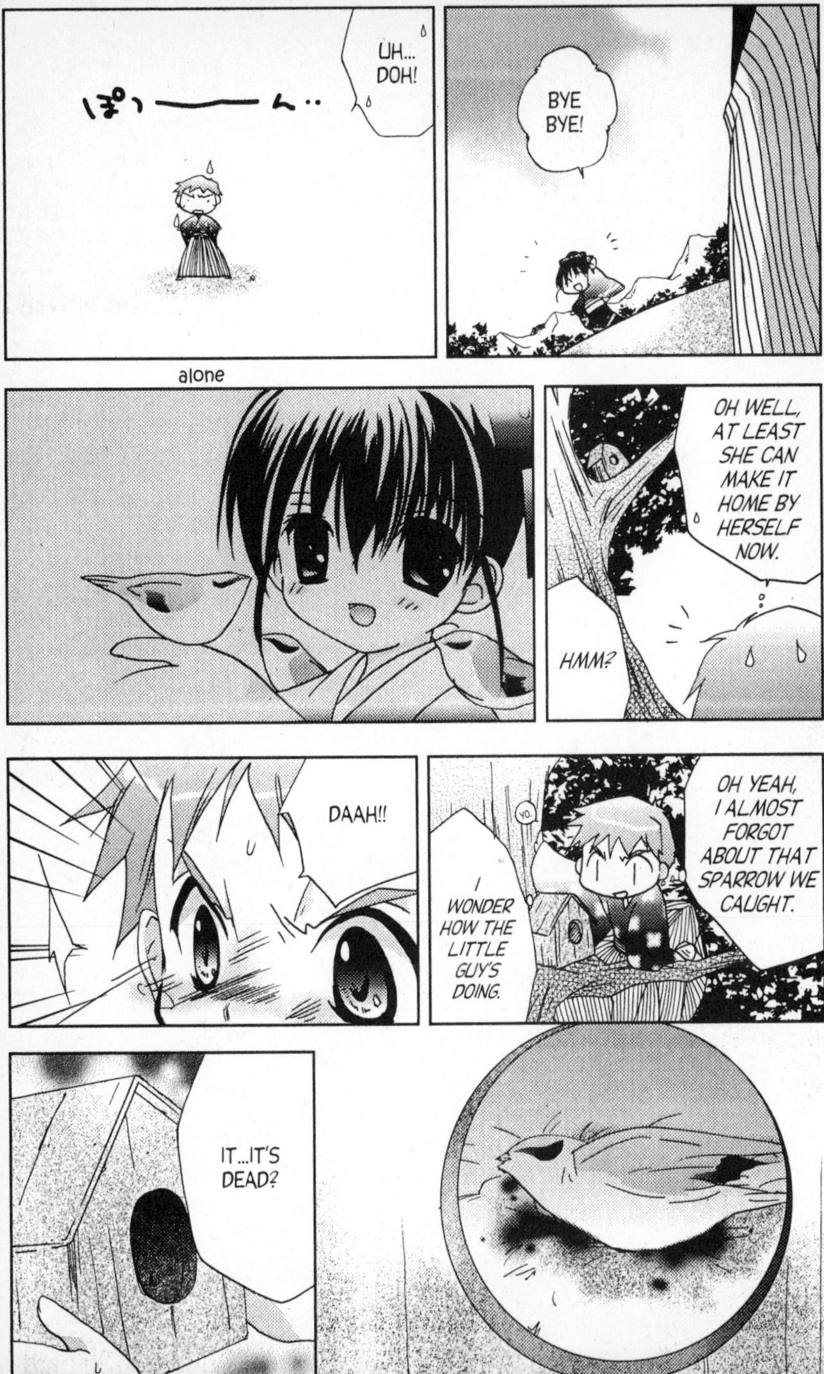
BYE BYE!
UH... DOH!
ぽつーーーん‥
alone
OH WELL, AT LEAST SHE CAN MAKE IT HOME BY HERSELF NOW.
HMM?
OH YEAH, I ALMOST FORGOT ABOUT THAT SPARROW WE CAUGHT.
YO.
I WONDER HOW THE LITTLE GUY'S DOING.
DAAH!!
IT...IT'S DEAD?

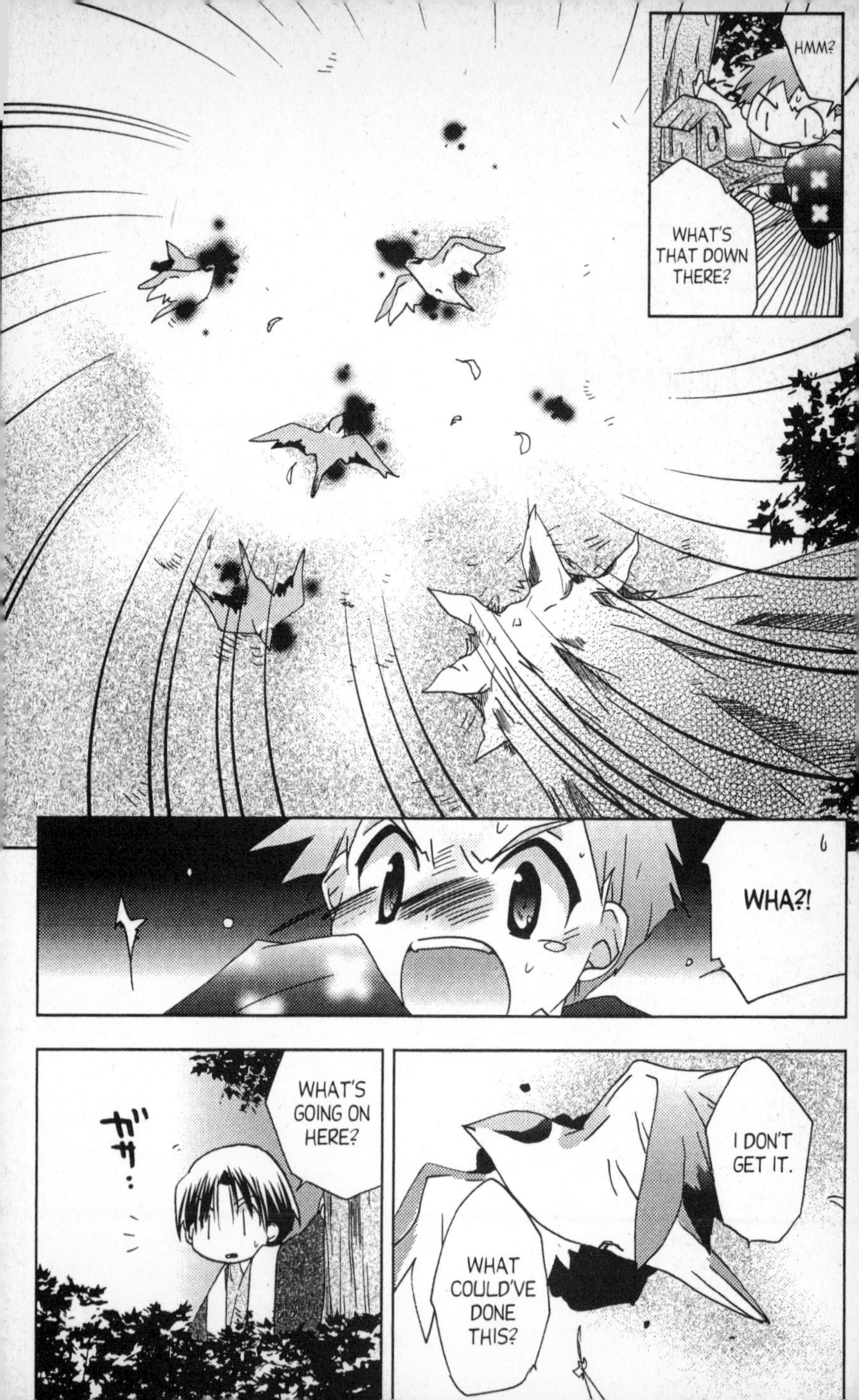
HMM?
WHAT'S THAT DOWN THERE?
WHA?!
I DON'T GET IT.
WHAT COULD'VE DONE THIS?
WHAT'S GOING ON HERE?
ガサ..

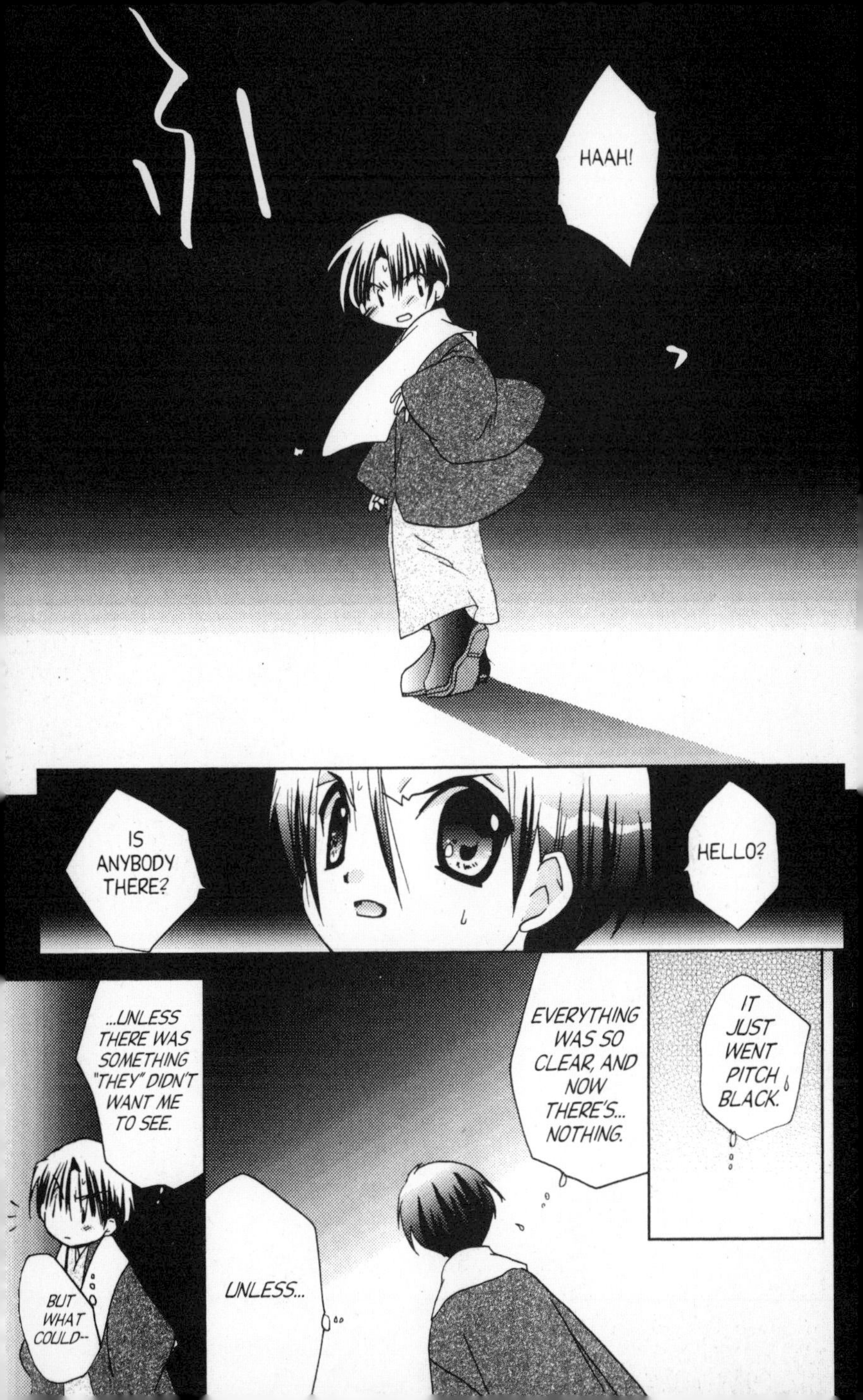
HAAH!
HELLO?
IS ANYBODY THERE?
IT JUST WENT PITCH BLACK.
EVERYTHING WAS SO CLEAR, AND NOW THERE'S... NOTHING.
UNLESS...
...UNLESS THERE WAS SOMETHING "THEY" DIDN'T WANT ME TO SEE.
BUT WHAT COULD--

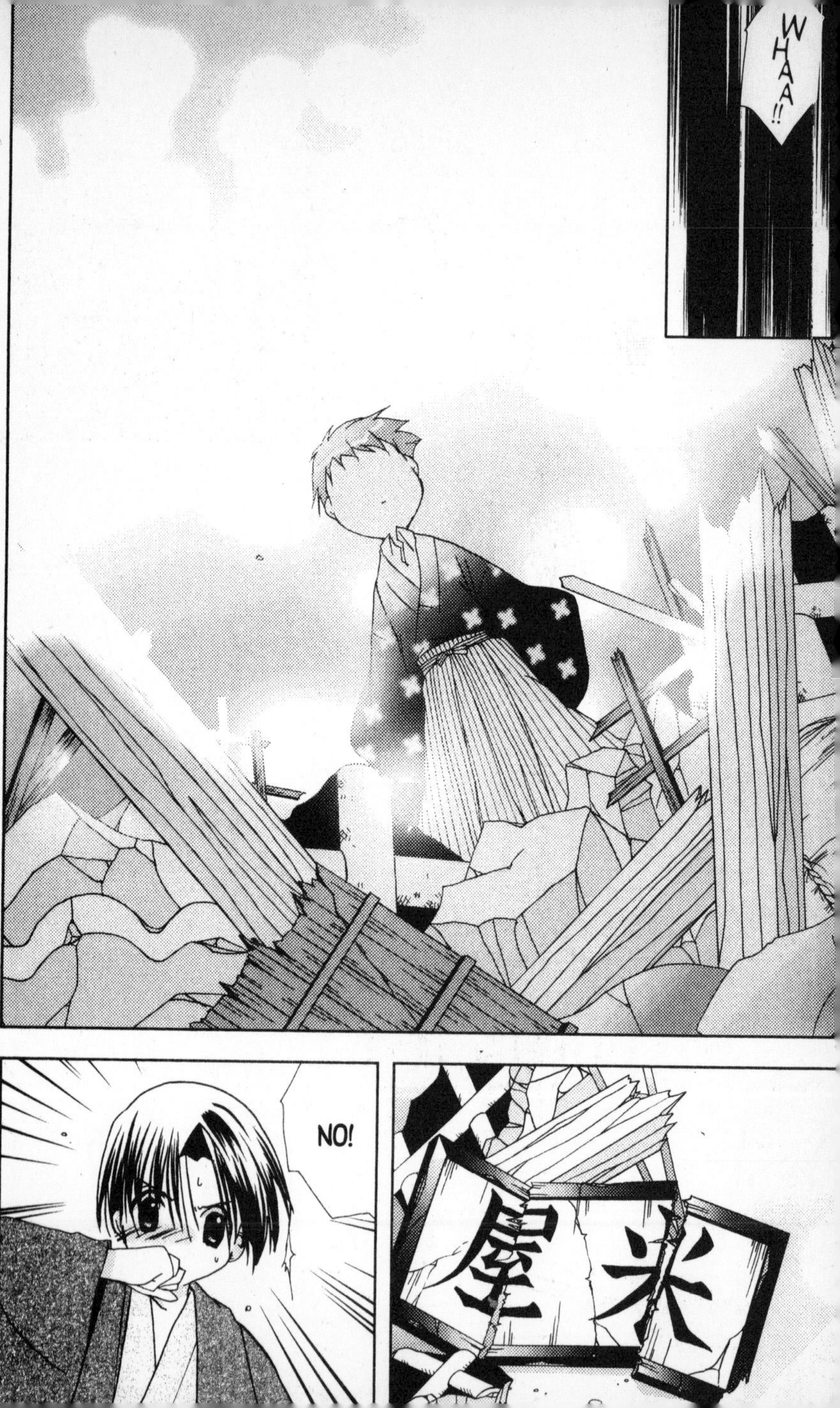
WHAA!!
米屋
NO!

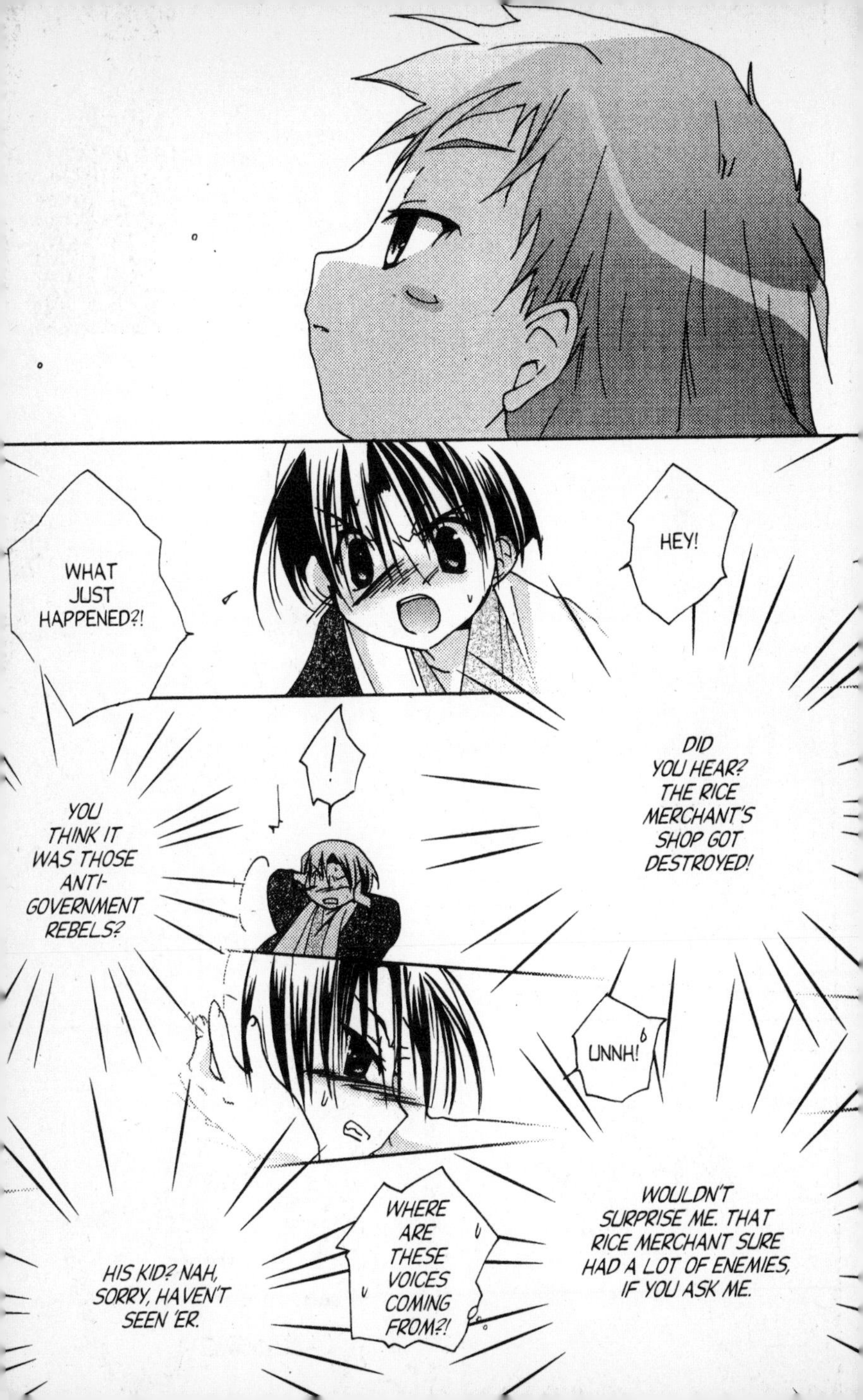
HEY!
WHAT JUST HAPPENED?!
!
DID YOU HEAR? THE RICE MERCHANT'S SHOP GOT DESTROYED!
YOU THINK IT WAS THOSE ANTI-GOVERNMENT REBELS?
UNNH!
WOULDN'T SURPRISE ME. THAT RICE MERCHANT SURE HAD A LOT OF ENEMIES, IF YOU ASK ME.
WHERE ARE THESE VOICES COMING FROM?!
HIS KID? NAH, SORRY, HAVEN'T SEEN 'ER.

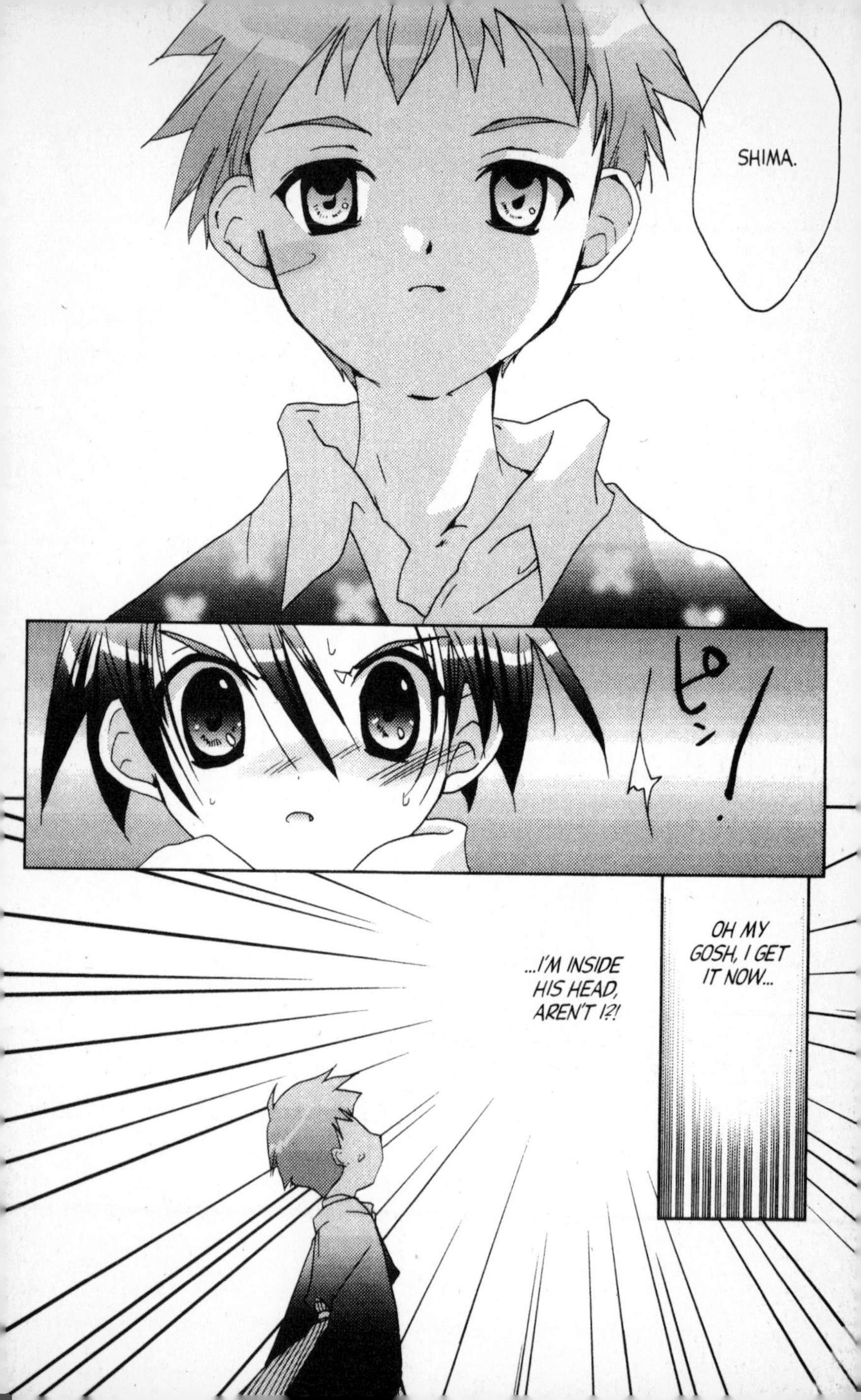
SHIMA.
OH MY GOSH, I GET IT NOW...
...I'M INSIDE HIS HEAD, AREN'T I?!

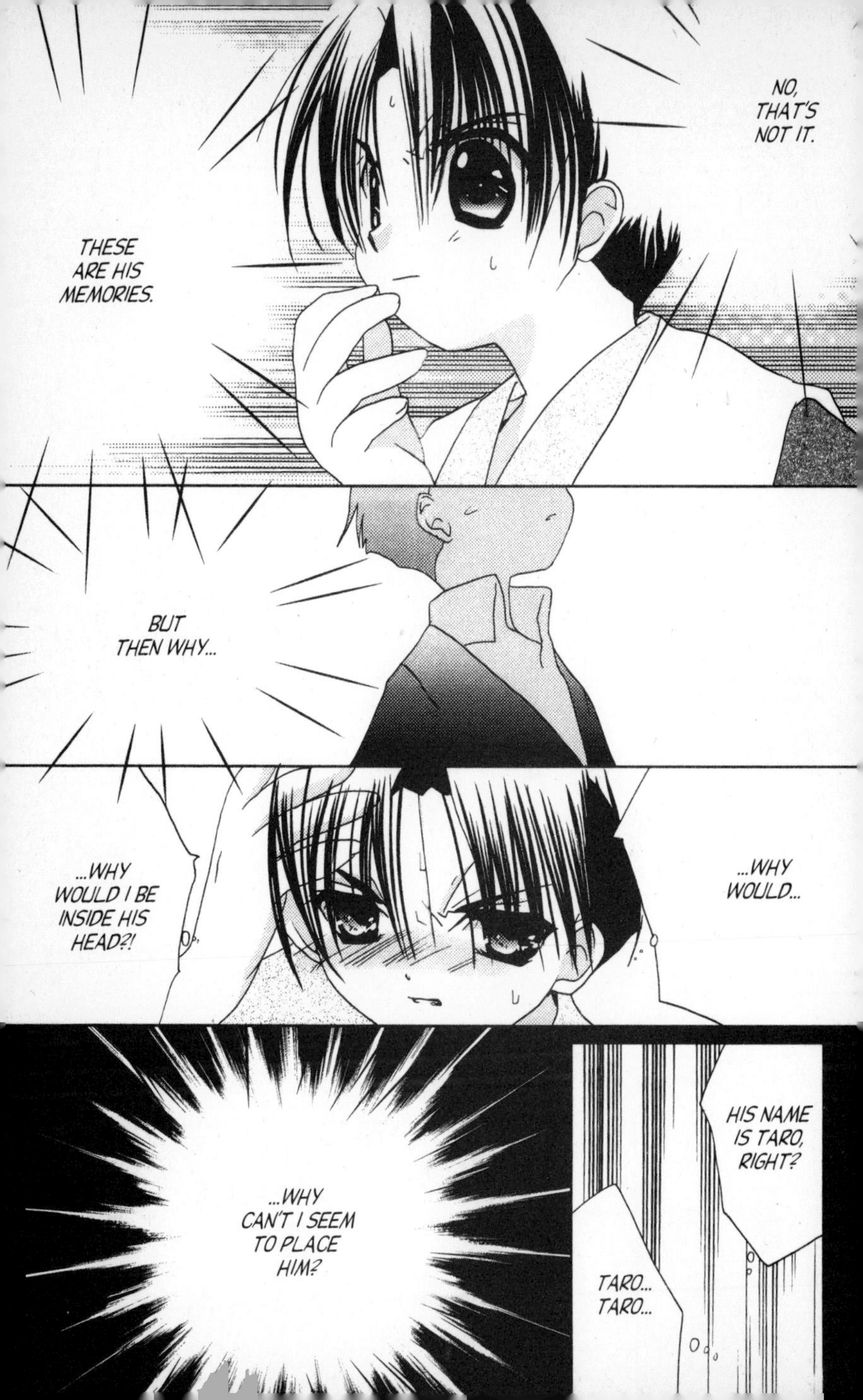
NO, THAT'S NOT IT.
THESE ARE HIS MEMORIES.
BUT THEN WHY...
...WHY WOULD...
...WHY WOULD I BE INSIDE HIS HEAD?!
HIS NAME IS TARO, RIGHT?
TARO... TARO...
...WHY CAN'T I SEEM TO PLACE HIM?

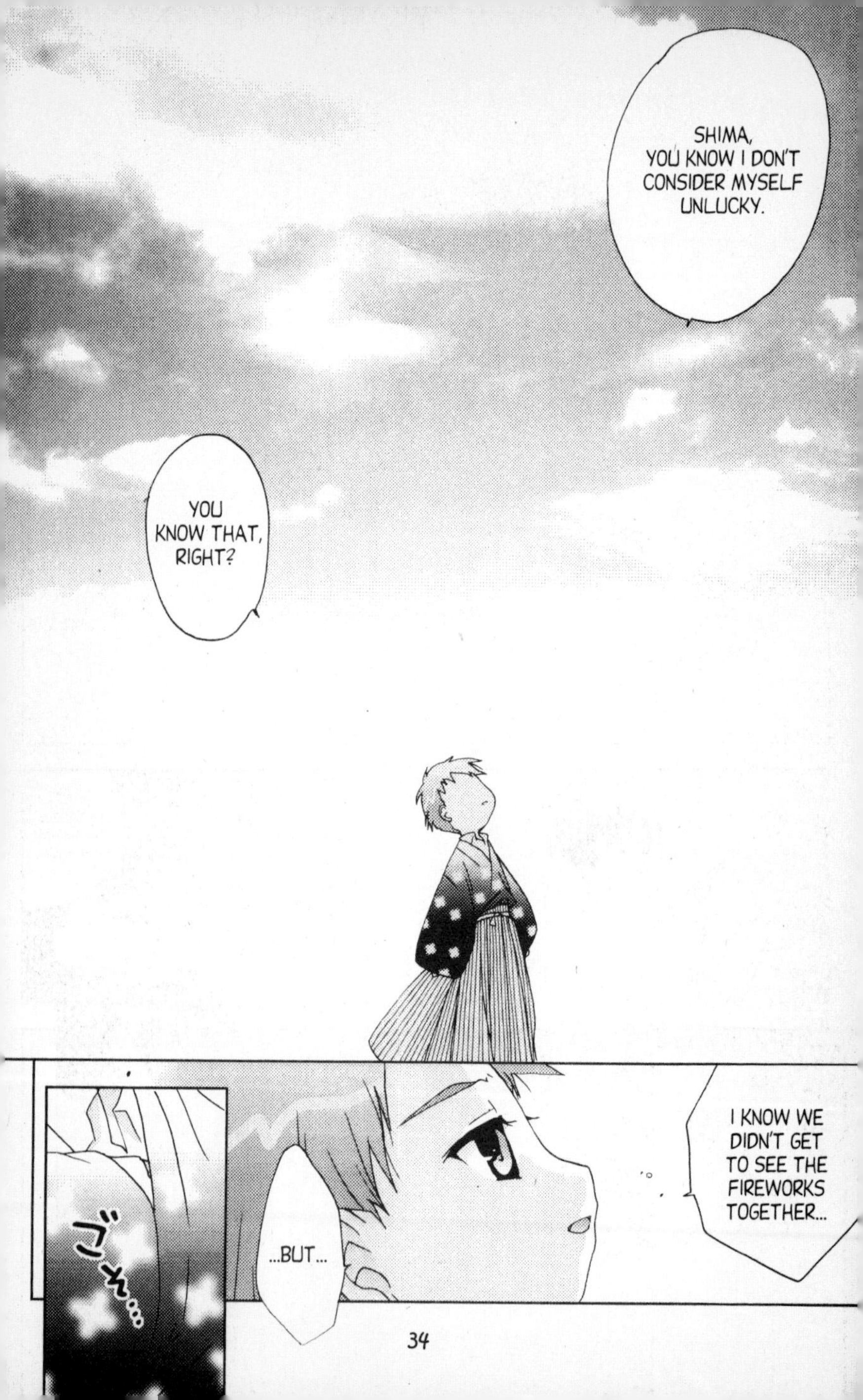
SHIMA, YOU KNOW I DON'T CONSIDER MYSELF UNLUCKY.
YOU KNOW THAT, RIGHT?
I KNOW WE DIDN'T GET TO SEE THE FIREWORKS TOGETHER...
...BUT...
ごそ…

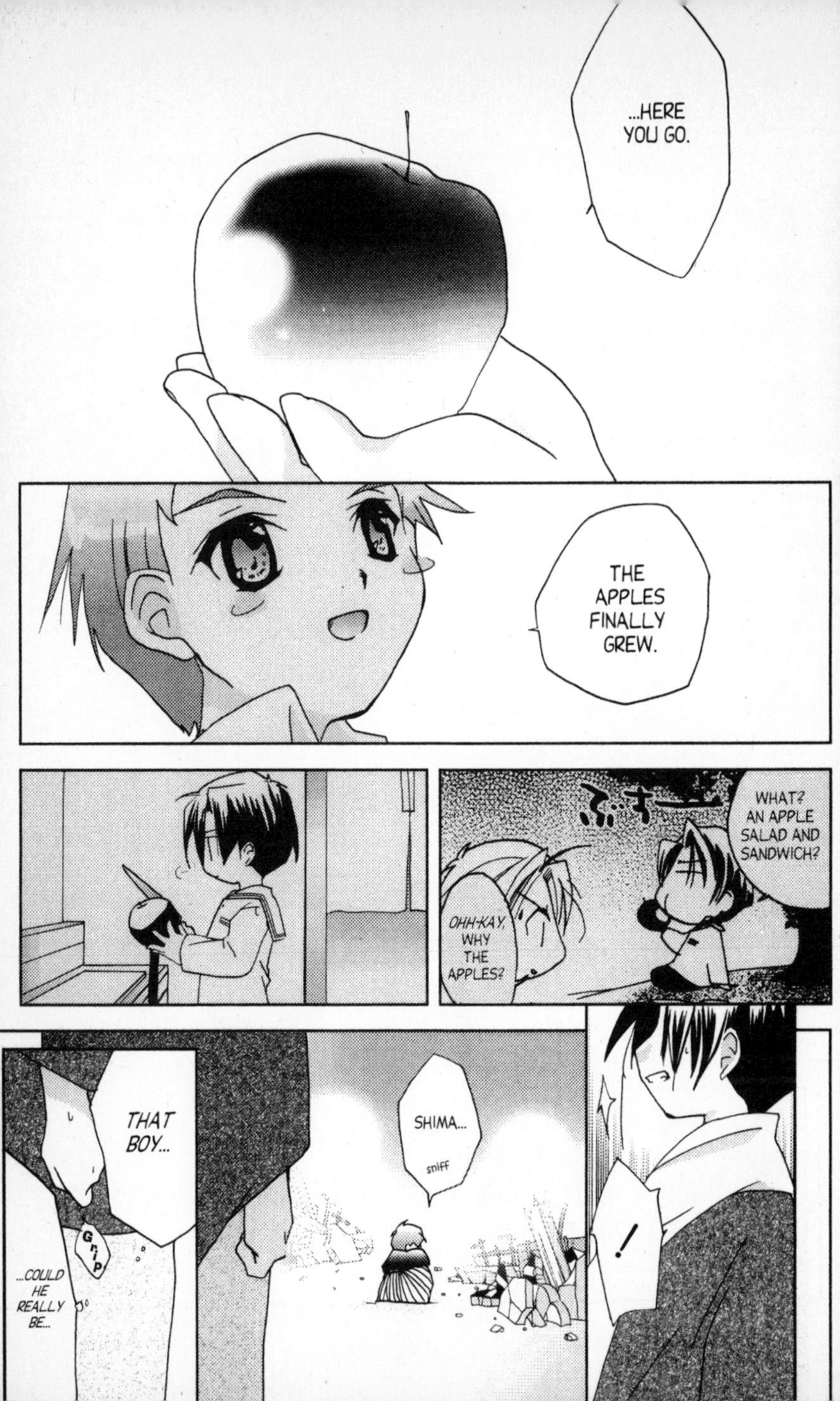
...HERE YOU GO.
THE APPLES FINALLY GREW.
WHAT? AN APPLE SALAD AND SANDWICH?
OHH-KAY, WHY THE APPLES?
!
SHIMA...
sniff
THAT BOY...
Grip
...COULD HE REALLY BE...

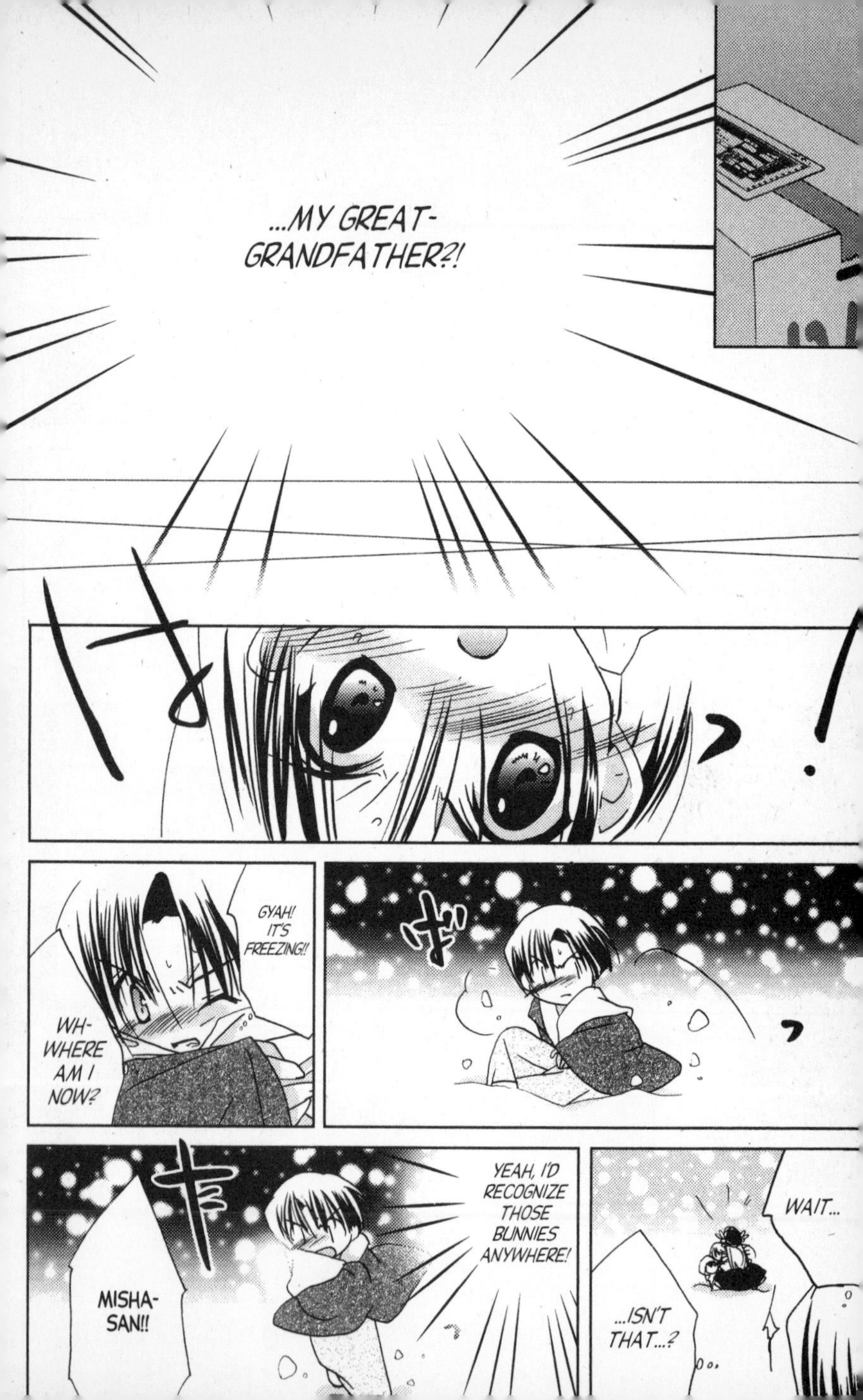
...MY GREAT-GRANDFATHER?!
はっ!
GYAH! IT'S FREEZING!!
WH- WHERE AM I NOW?
WAIT...
...ISN'T THAT...?
YEAH, I'D RECOGNIZE THOSE BUNNIES ANYWHERE!
MISHA-SAN!!

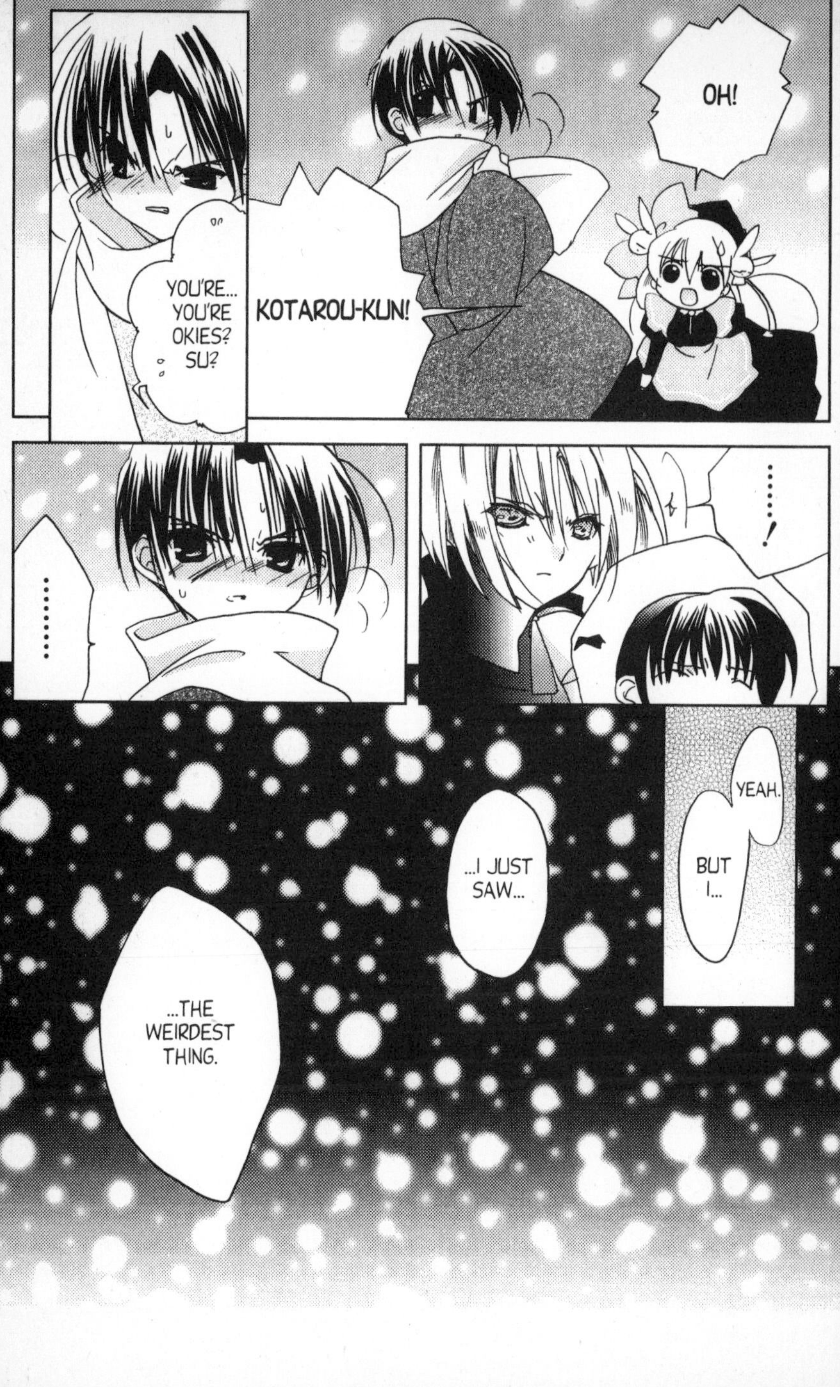
OH!
KOTAROU-KUN!
YOU'RE... YOU'RE OKIES? SU?
......!
....
YEAH.
BUT I...
...I JUST SAW...
...THE WEIRDEST THING.

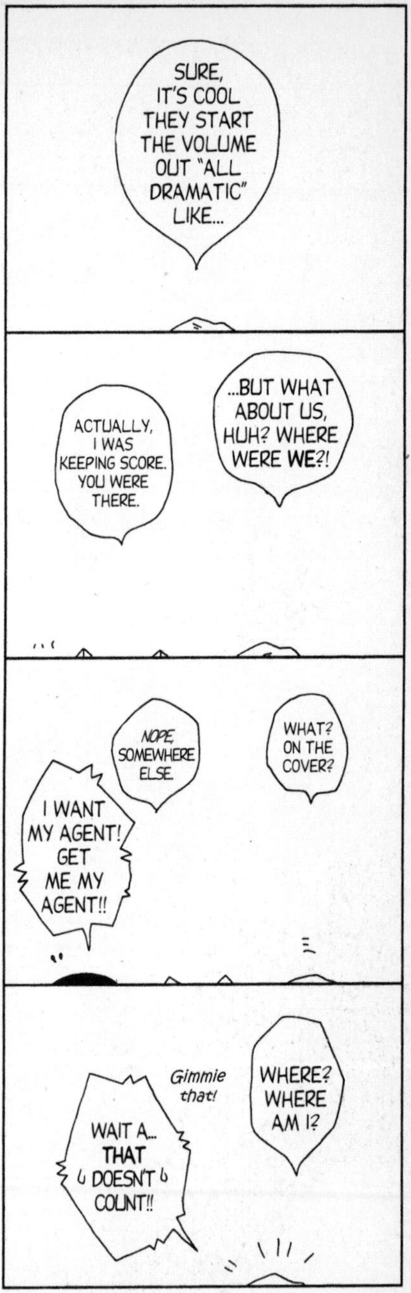
SURE, IT'S COOL THEY START THE VOLUME OUT "ALL DRAMATIC" LIKE...
...BUT WHAT ABOUT US, HUH? WHERE WERE **WE**?!
ACTUALLY, I WAS KEEPING SCORE. YOU WERE THERE.
WHAT? ON THE COVER?
NOPE, SOMEWHERE ELSE.
I WANT MY AGENT! GET ME MY AGENT!!
WHERE? WHERE AM I?
Gimmie that!
WAIT A... **THAT** DOESN'T COUNT!!

Lesson 33

How to Find What You're Looking For: Part 1

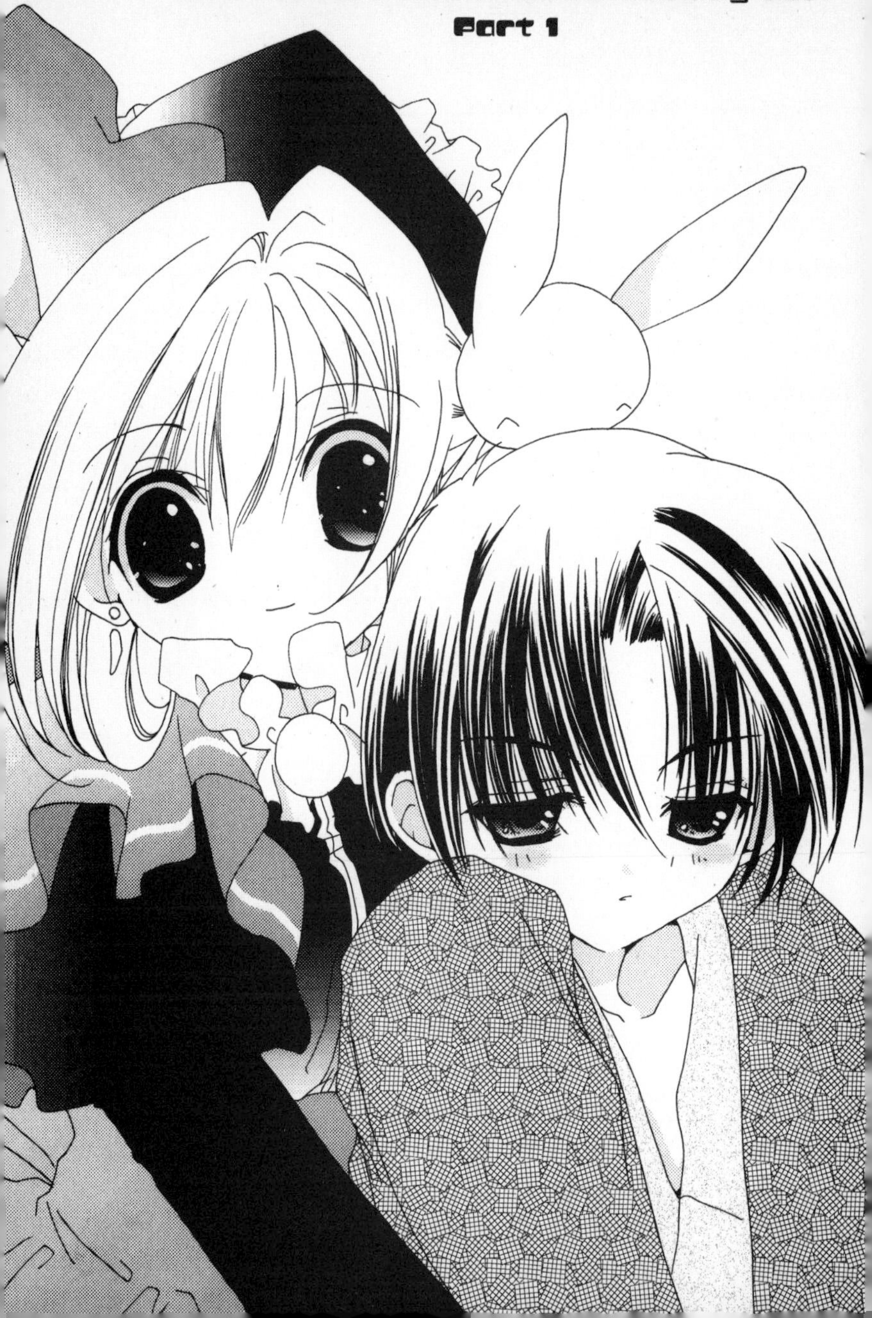

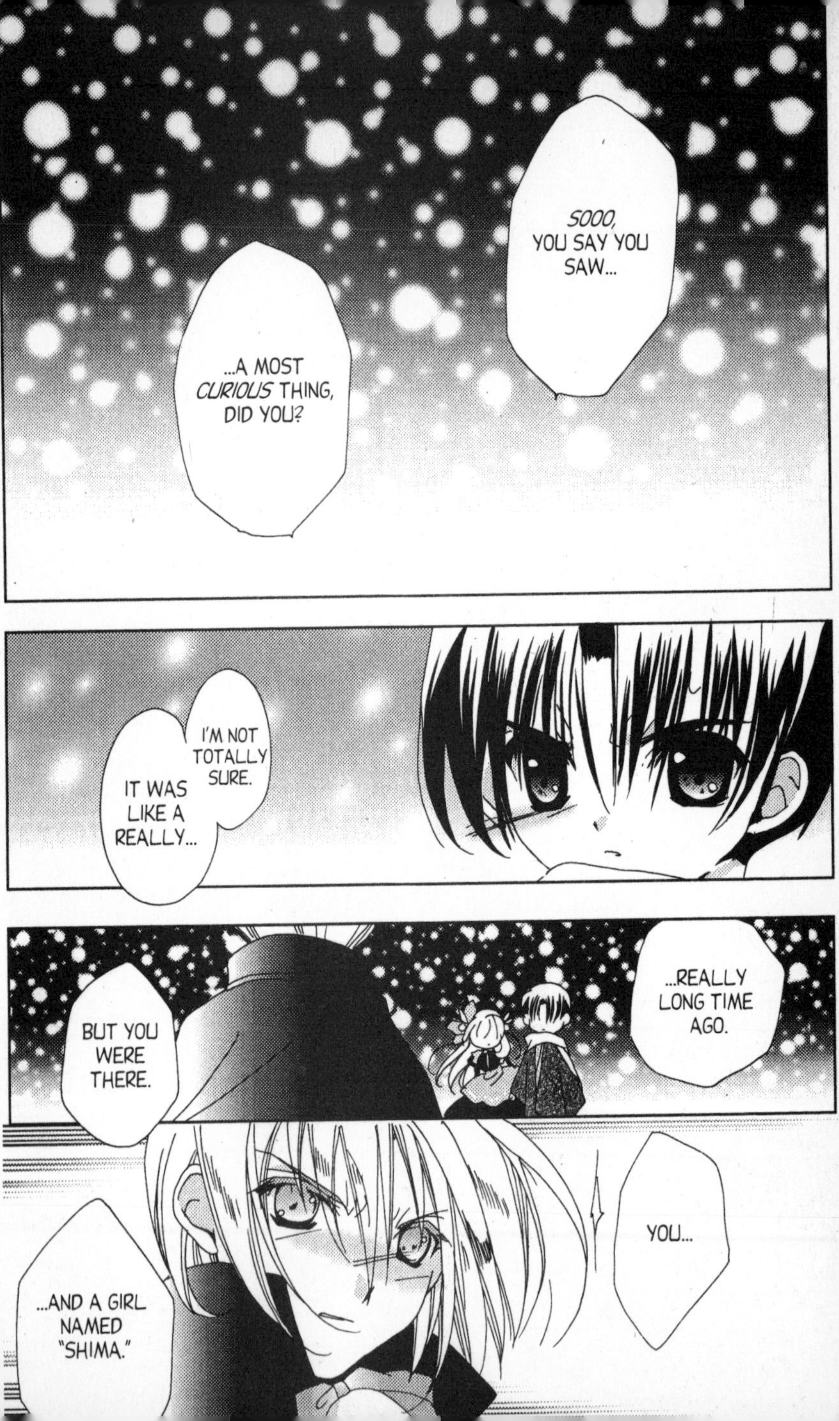
SOOO, YOU SAY YOU SAW...
...A MOST CURIOUS THING, DID YOU?
I'M NOT TOTALLY SURE.
IT WAS LIKE A REALLY...
...REALLY LONG TIME AGO.
BUT YOU WERE THERE.
YOU...
...AND A GIRL NAMED "SHIMA."

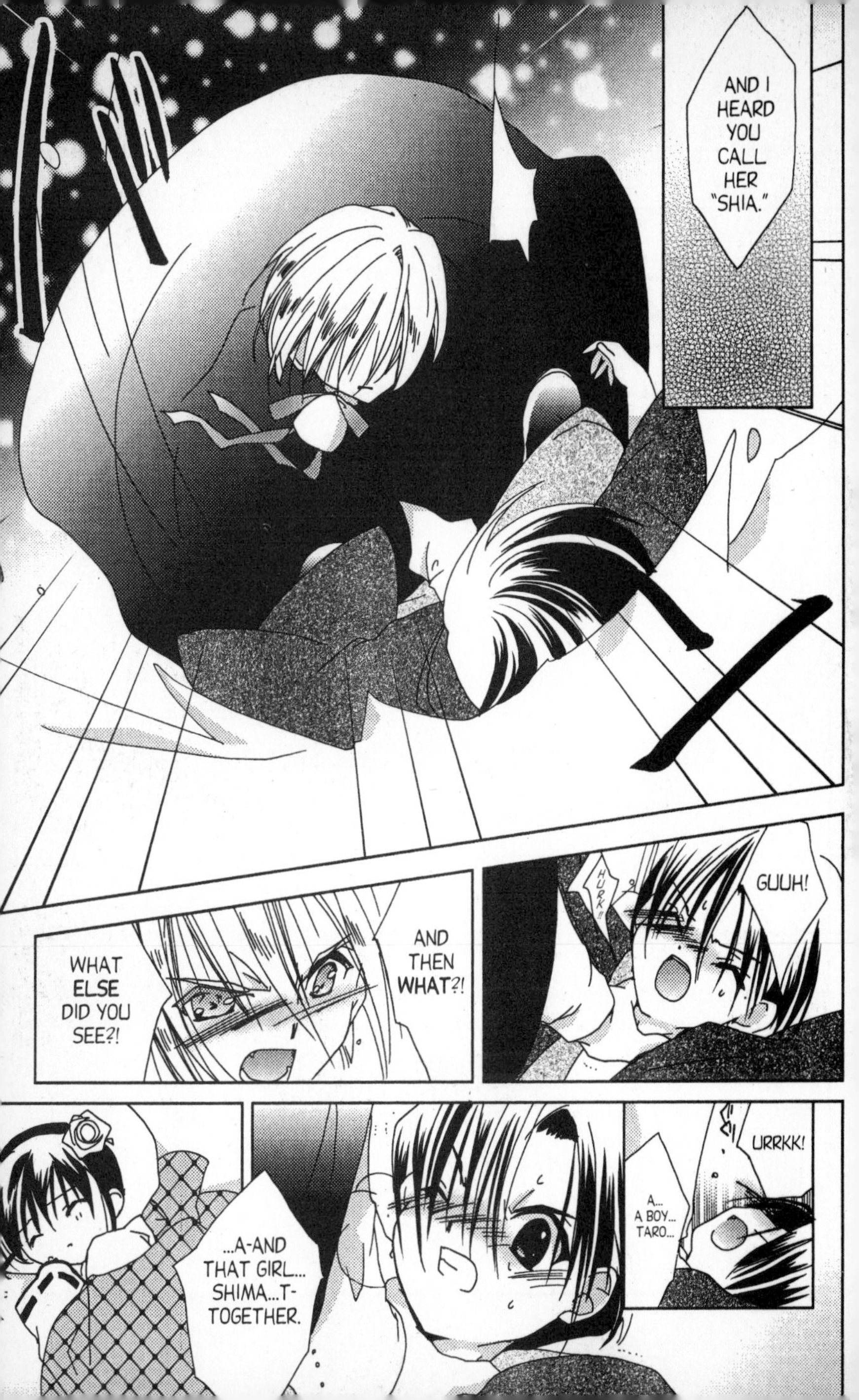
AND I HEARD YOU CALL HER "SHIA."
HURK!!
GUUH!
AND THEN WHAT?!
WHAT ELSE DID YOU SEE?!
URRKK!
A... A BOY... TARO...
...A-AND THAT GIRL... SHIMA...T-TOGETHER.

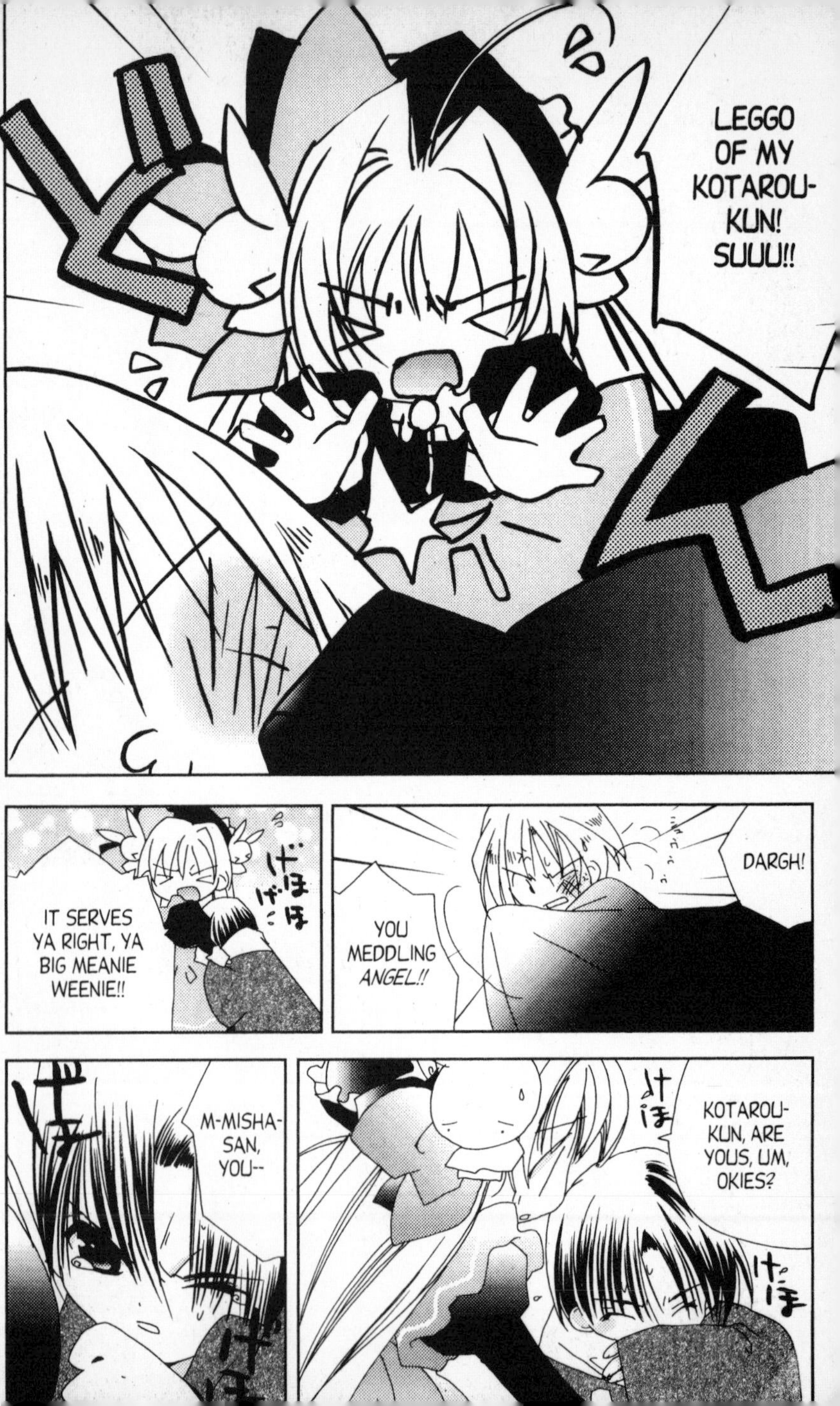
LEGGO OF MY KOTAROU-KUN! SUUU!!
DARGH!
YOU MEDDLING *ANGEL!!*
げほげほ
IT SERVES YA RIGHT, YA BIG MEANIE WEENIE!!
けほ
KOTAROU-KUN, ARE YOUS, UM, OKIES?
けほ
M-MISHA-SAN, YOU--

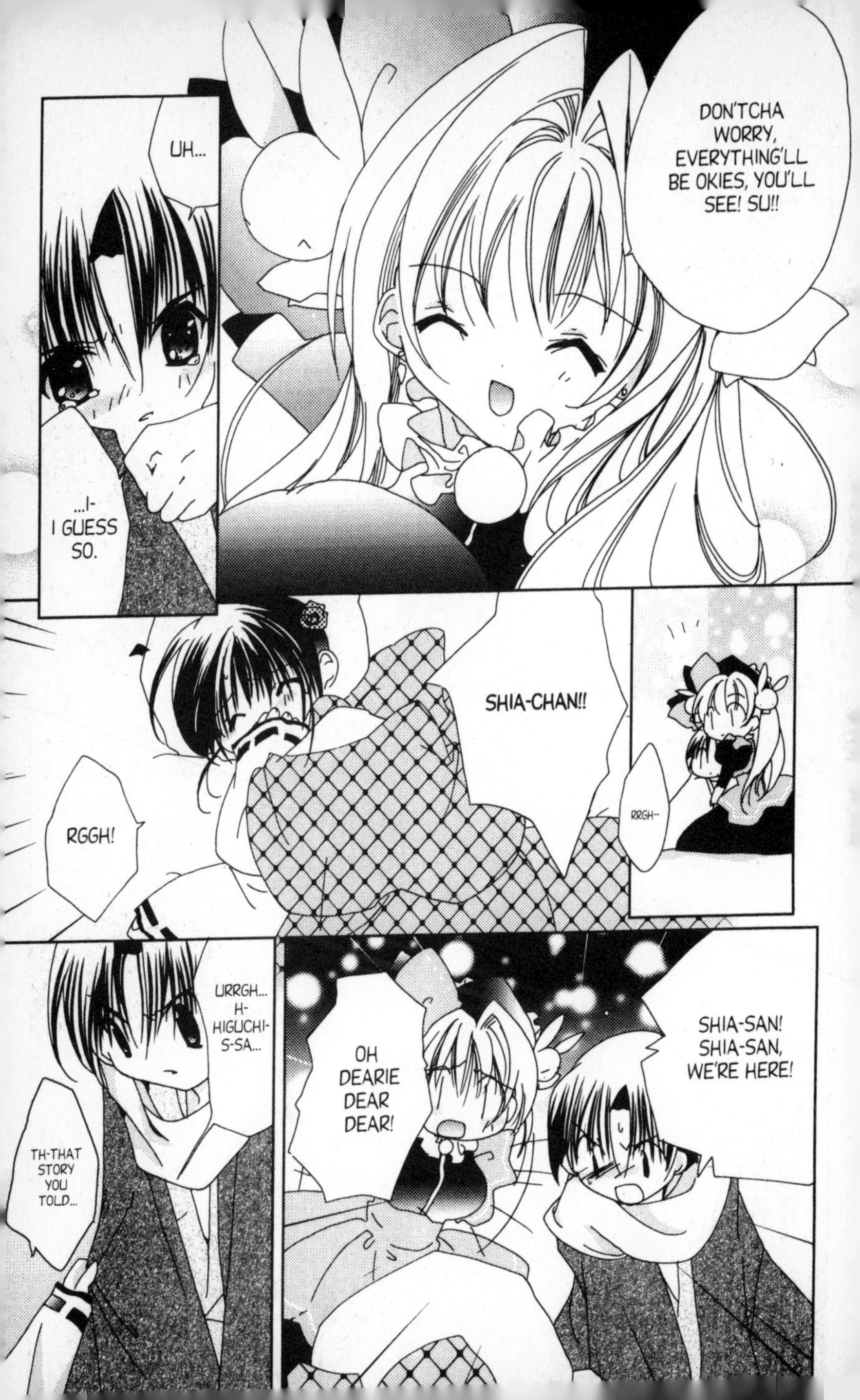
DON'TCHA WORRY, EVERYTHING'LL BE OKIES, YOU'LL SEE! SU!!
UH...
...I- I GUESS SO.
RRGH--
SHIA-CHAN!!
RGGH!
SHIA-SAN! SHIA-SAN, WE'RE HERE!
OH DEARIE DEAR DEAR!
URRGH... H-HIGUCHI-S-SA...
TH-THAT STORY YOU TOLD...

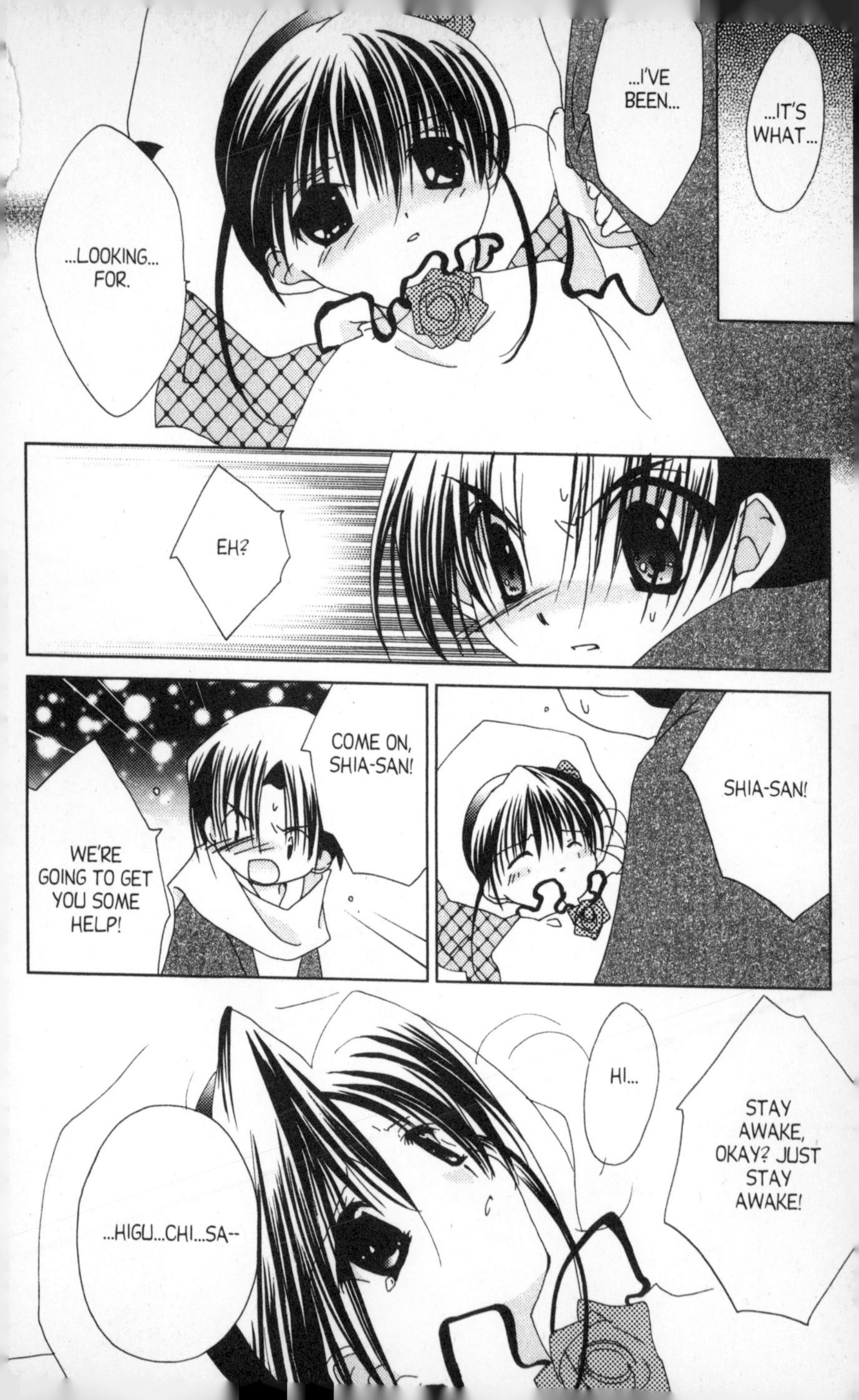
...IT'S WHAT...
...I'VE BEEN...
...LOOKING... FOR.
EH?
SHIA-SAN!
COME ON, SHIA-SAN!
WE'RE GOING TO GET YOU SOME HELP!
STAY AWAKE, OKAY? JUST STAY AWAKE!
HI...
...HIGU...CHI...SA--

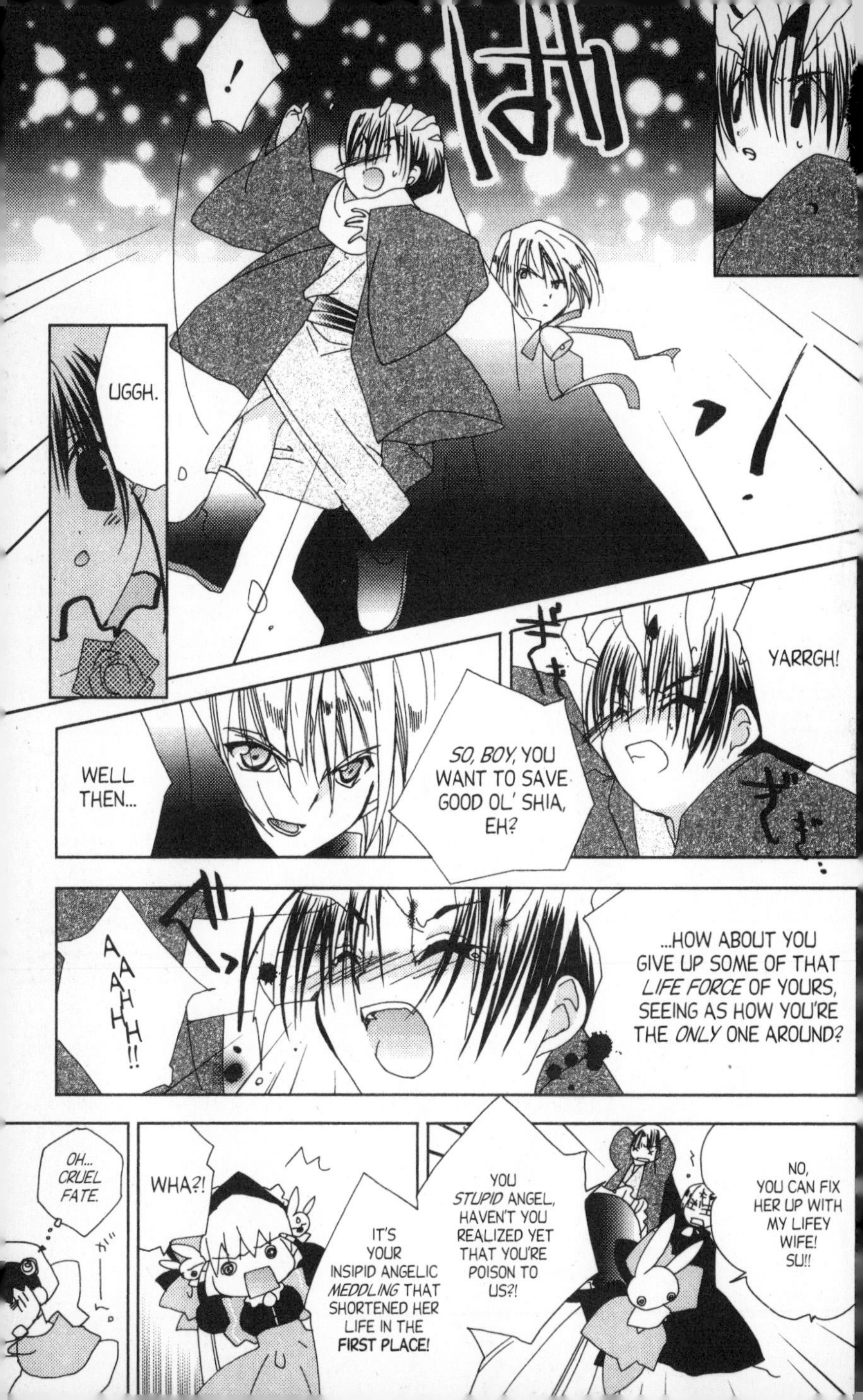
!
はっ
UGGH.
YARRGH!
SO, BOY, YOU WANT TO SAVE GOOD OL' SHIA, EH?
WELL THEN...
...HOW ABOUT YOU GIVE UP SOME OF THAT *LIFE FORCE* OF YOURS, SEEING AS HOW YOU'RE THE *ONLY* ONE AROUND?
AAAHHH!!
NO, YOU CAN FIX HER UP WITH MY LIFEY WIFE! SU!!
YOU *STUPID* ANGEL, HAVEN'T YOU REALIZED YET THAT YOU'RE POISON TO US?!
IT'S YOUR INSIPID ANGELIC *MEDDLING* THAT SHORTENED HER LIFE IN THE **FIRST PLACE!**
WHA?!
OH... CRUEL FATE.

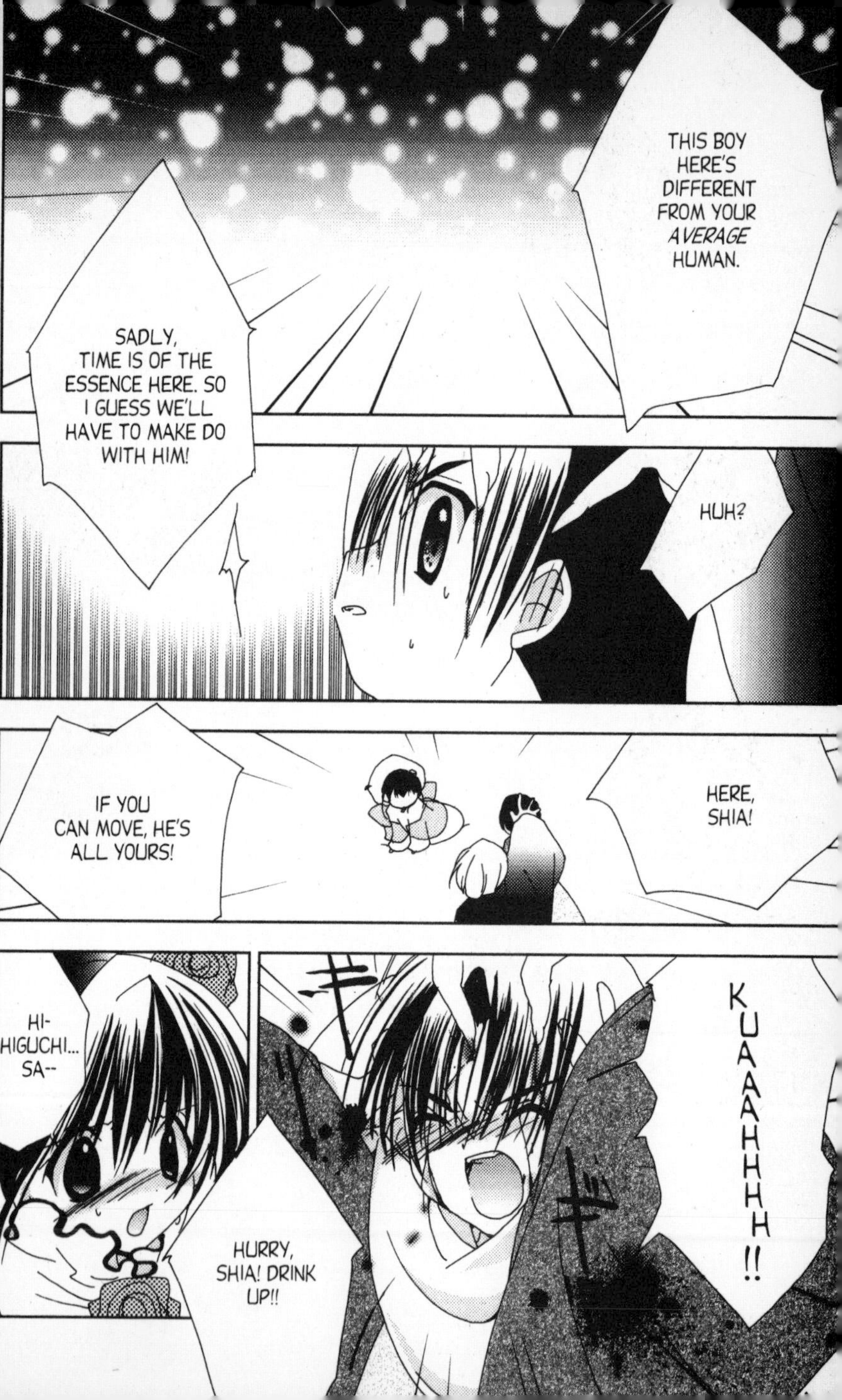
THIS BOY HERE'S DIFFERENT FROM YOUR *AVERAGE* HUMAN.
SADLY, TIME IS OF THE ESSENCE HERE. SO I GUESS WE'LL HAVE TO MAKE DO WITH HIM!
HUH?
HERE, SHIA!
IF YOU CAN MOVE, HE'S ALL YOURS!
KUAAAHHHH!!
HURRY, SHIA! DRINK UP!!
HI- HIGUCHI... SA--

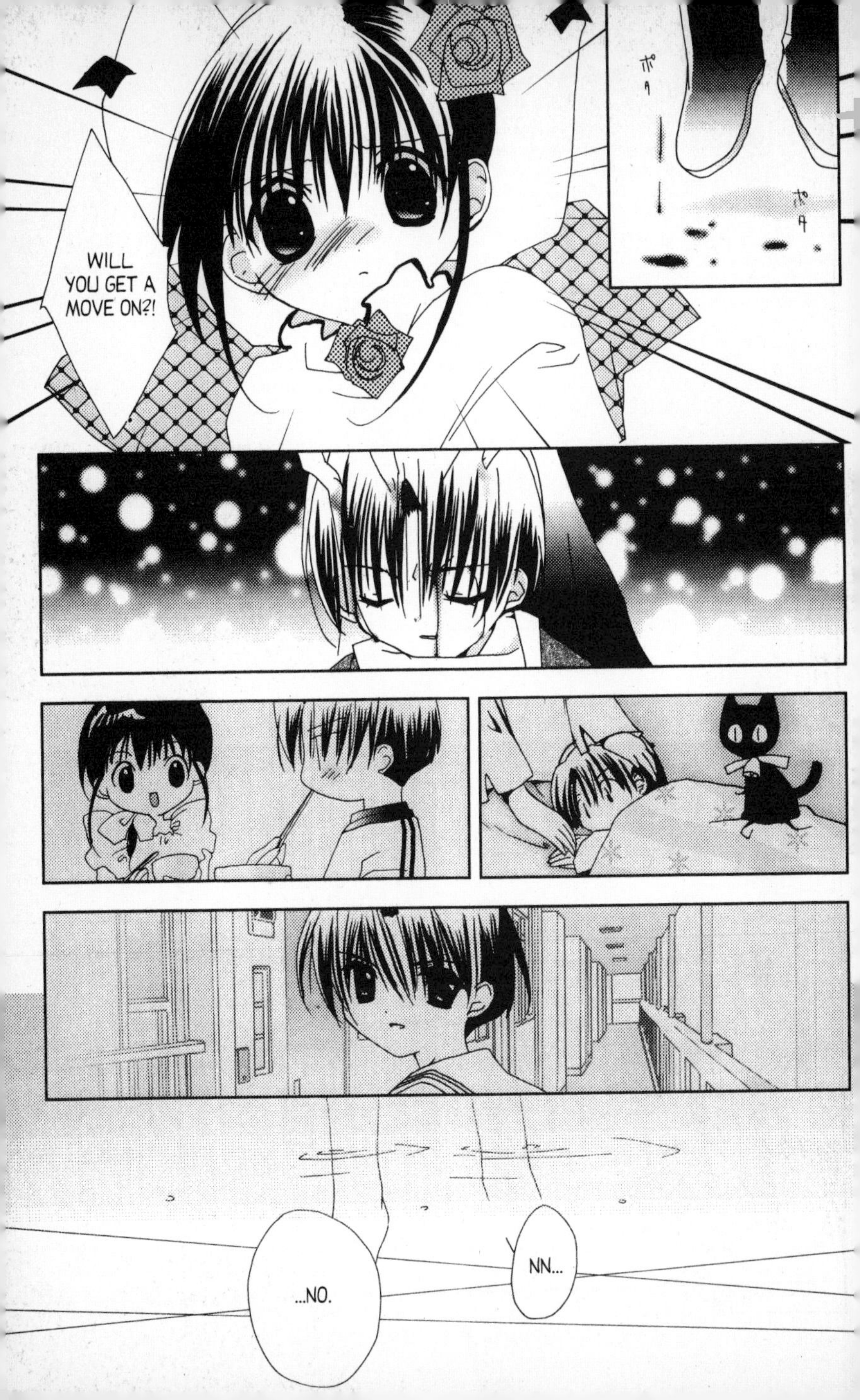
ポタ
ポタ
WILL YOU GET A MOVE ON?!
NN...
...NO.

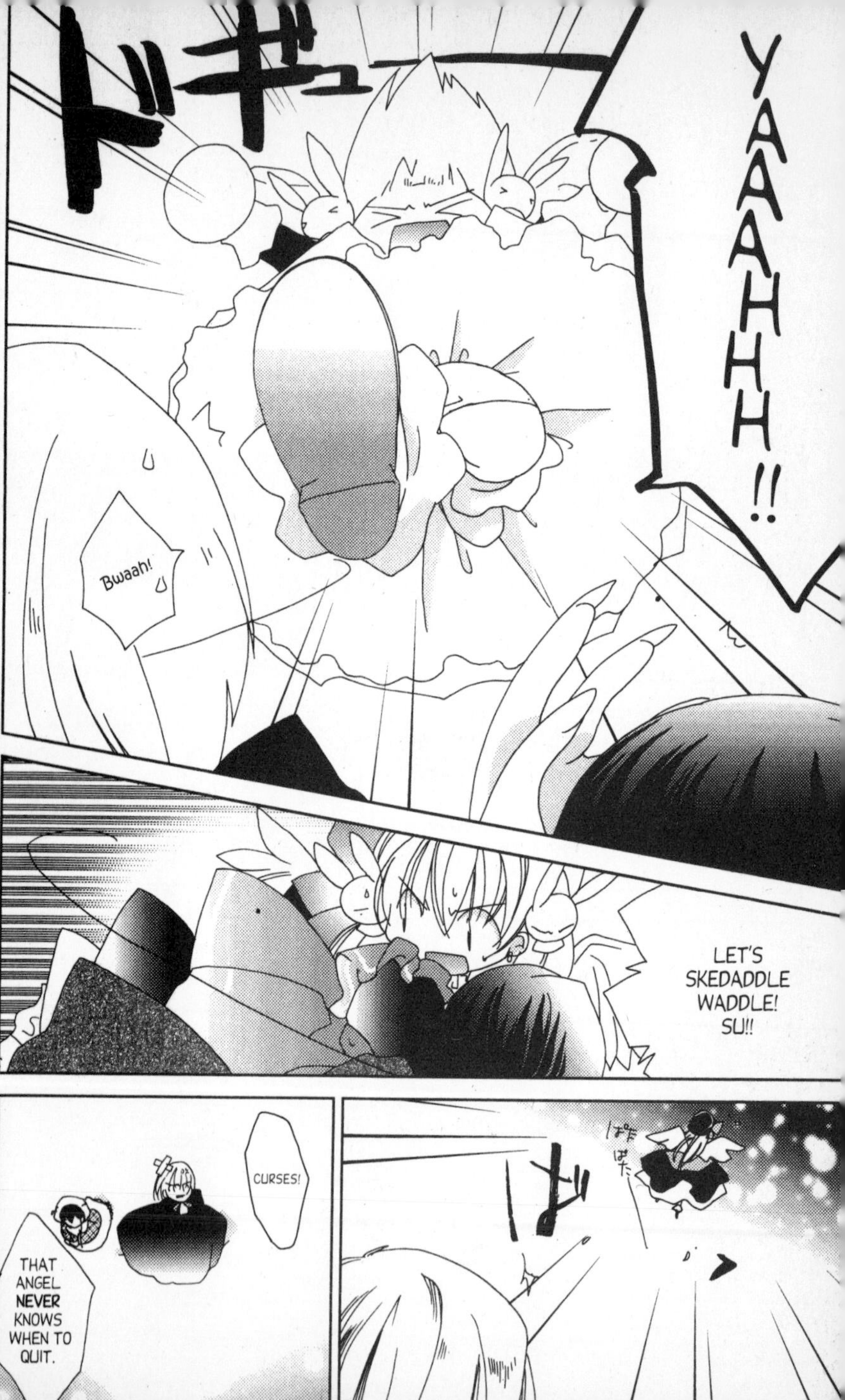
ドギュー
YAAAHH!!
Bwaah!
LET'S SKEDADDLE WADDLE! SU!!
ぱたぱた
CURSES!
THAT ANGEL **NEVER** KNOWS WHEN TO QUIT.

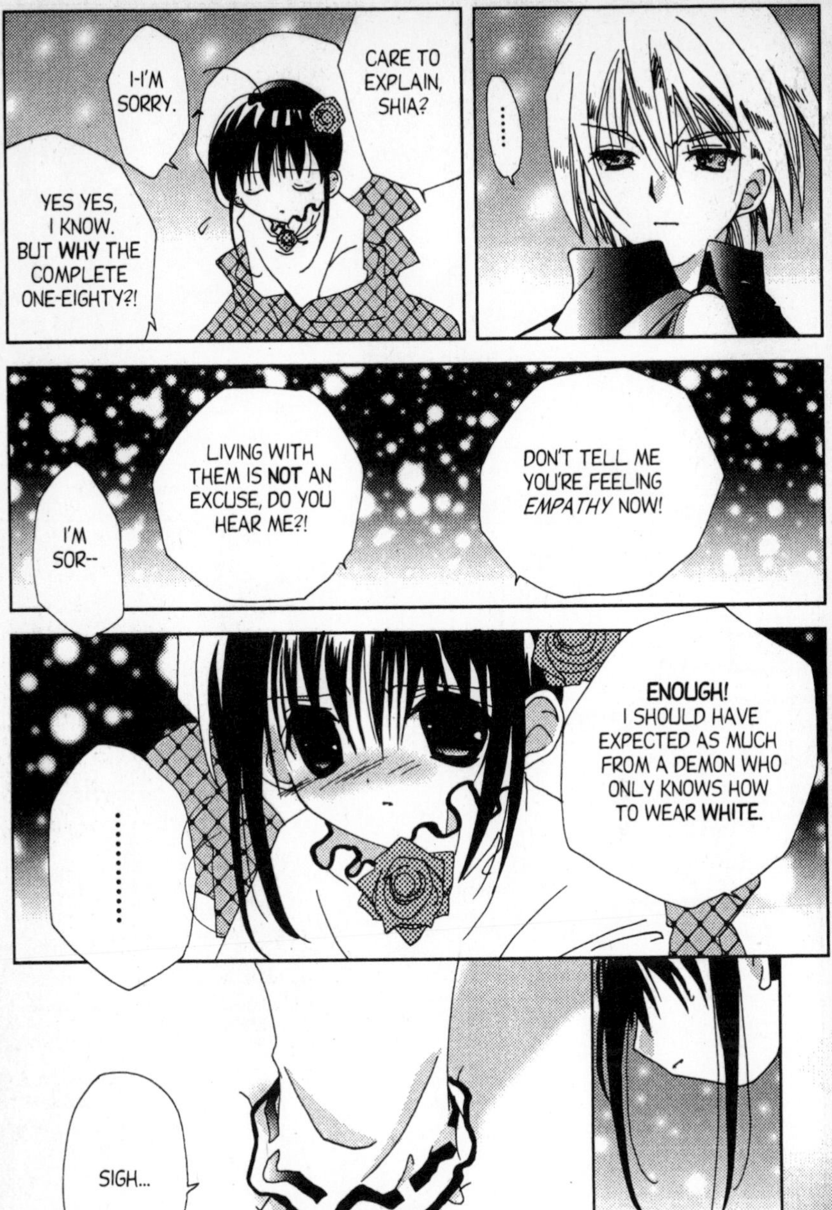
......
CARE TO EXPLAIN, SHIA?
I-I'M SORRY.
YES YES, I KNOW. BUT WHY THE COMPLETE ONE-EIGHTY?!
DON'T TELL ME YOU'RE FEELING EMPATHY NOW!
LIVING WITH THEM IS NOT AN EXCUSE, DO YOU HEAR ME?!
I'M SOR--
ENOUGH! I SHOULD HAVE EXPECTED AS MUCH FROM A DEMON WHO ONLY KNOWS HOW TO WEAR WHITE.
....
SIGH...

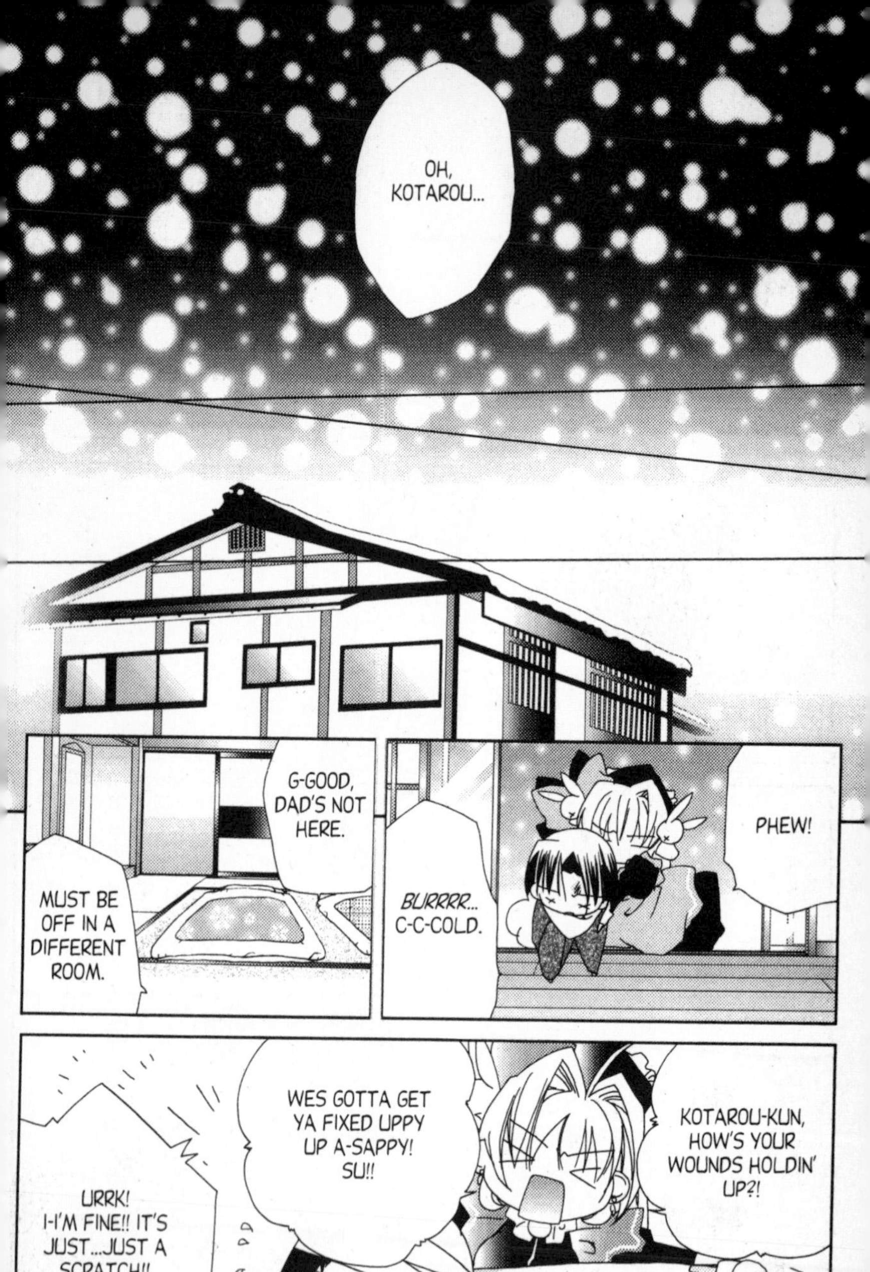
OH, KOTAROU...
PHEW!
BURRRR... C-C-COLD.
G-GOOD, DAD'S NOT HERE.
MUST BE OFF IN A DIFFERENT ROOM.
KOTAROU-KUN, HOW'S YOUR WOUNDS HOLDIN' UP?!
WES GOTTA GET YA FIXED UPPY UP A-SAPPY! SU!!
URRK! I-I'M FINE!! IT'S JUST...JUST A SCRATCH!!

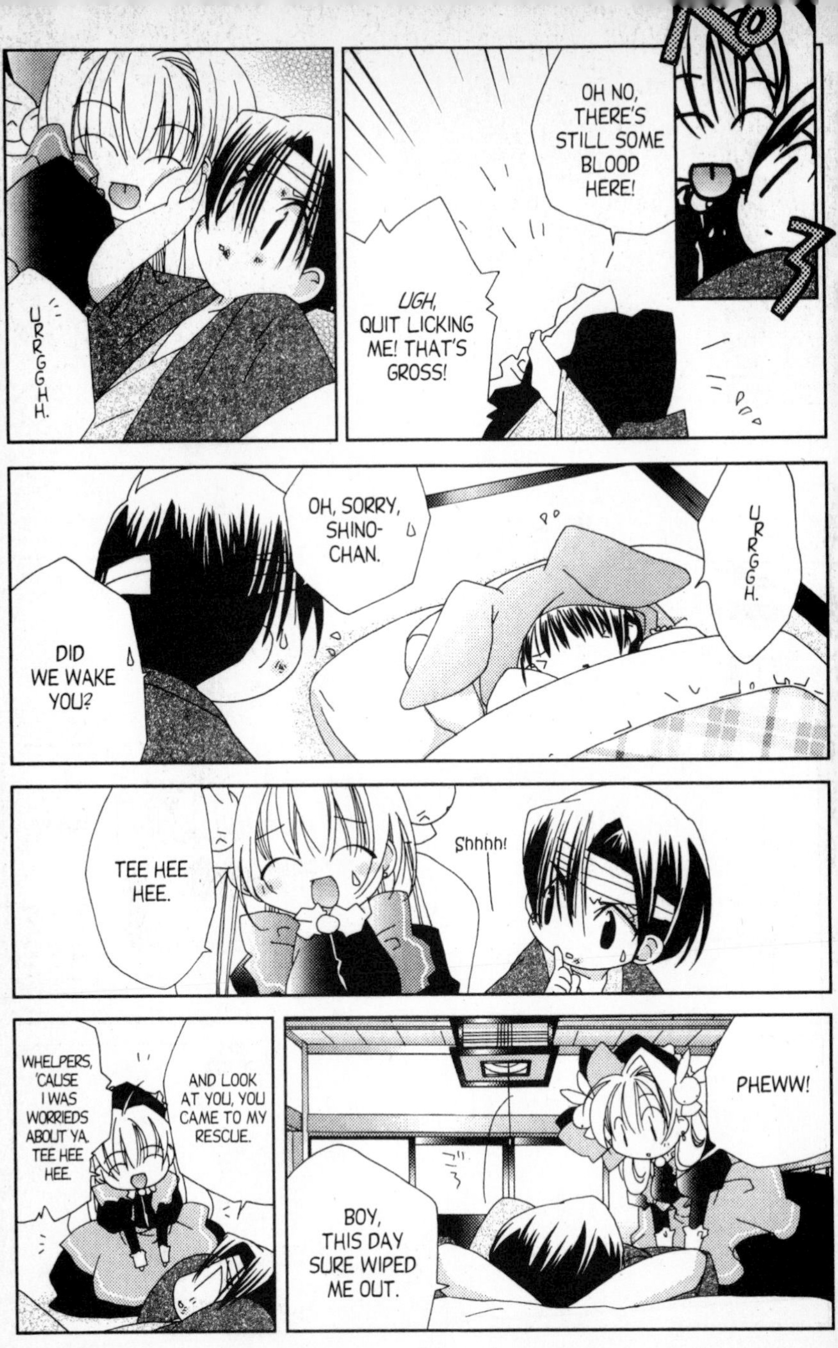
OH NO, THERE'S STILL SOME BLOOD HERE!
UGH, QUIT LICKING ME! THAT'S GROSS!
URRGGH.
URRGGH.
OH, SORRY, SHINO-CHAN.
DID WE WAKE YOU?
Shhhh!
TEE HEE HEE.
PHEWW!
BOY, THIS DAY SURE WIPED ME OUT.
AND LOOK AT YOU, YOU CAME TO MY RESCUE.
WHELPERS, 'CAUSE I WAS WORRIEDS ABOUT YA. TEE HEE HEE.

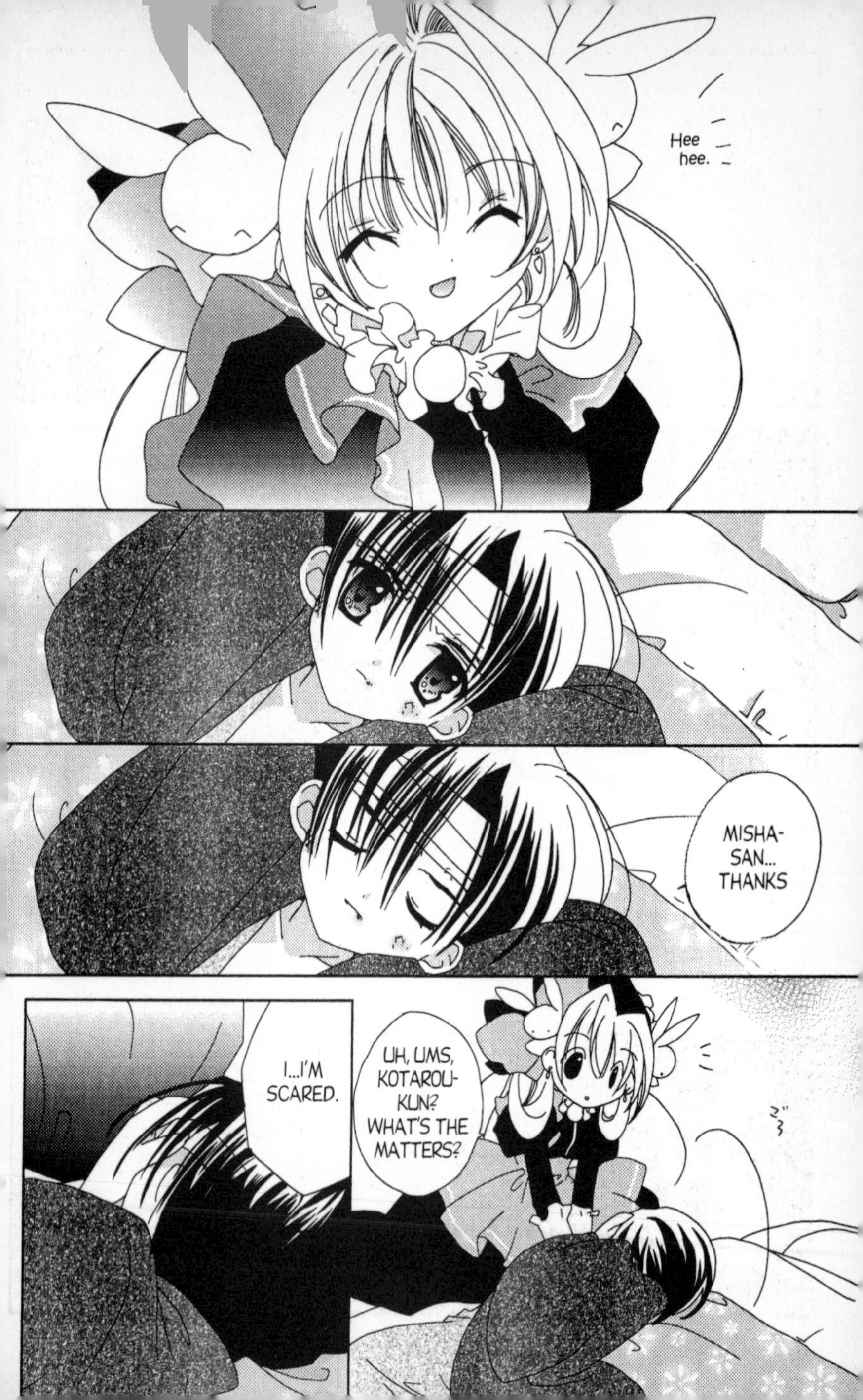
Hee hee.
MISHA-SAN... THANKS
UH, UMS, KOTAROU-KUN? WHAT'S THE MATTERS?
I...I'M SCARED.

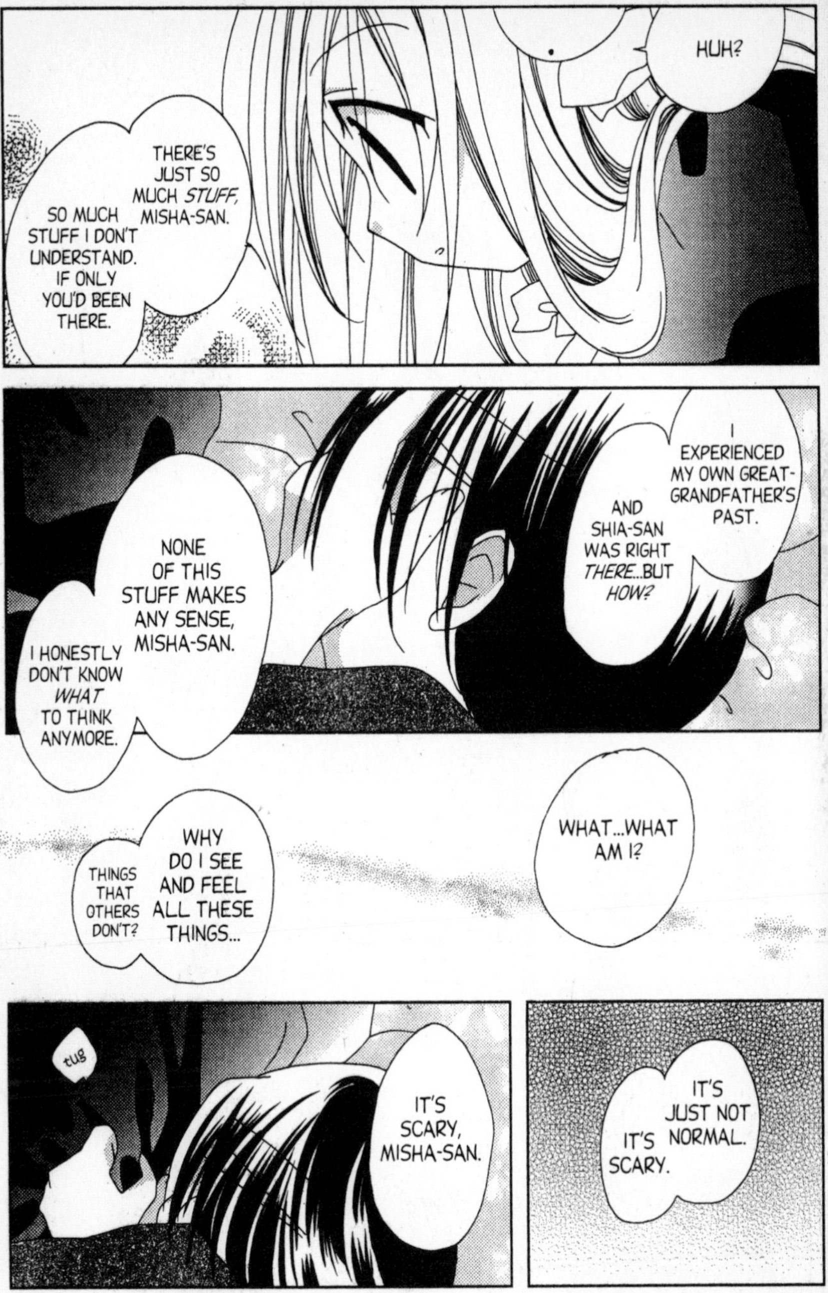
HUH?
THERE'S JUST SO MUCH *STUFF,* MISHA-SAN.
SO MUCH STUFF I DON'T UNDERSTAND. IF ONLY YOU'D BEEN THERE.
I EXPERIENCED MY OWN GREAT-GRANDFATHER'S PAST.
AND SHIA-SAN WAS RIGHT *THERE*...BUT *HOW?*
NONE OF THIS STUFF MAKES ANY SENSE, MISHA-SAN.
I HONESTLY DON'T KNOW *WHAT* TO THINK ANYMORE.
WHAT...WHAT AM I?
WHY DO I SEE AND FEEL ALL THESE THINGS...
THINGS THAT OTHERS DON'T?
IT'S JUST NOT NORMAL.
IT'S SCARY.
IT'S SCARY, MISHA-SAN.
tug

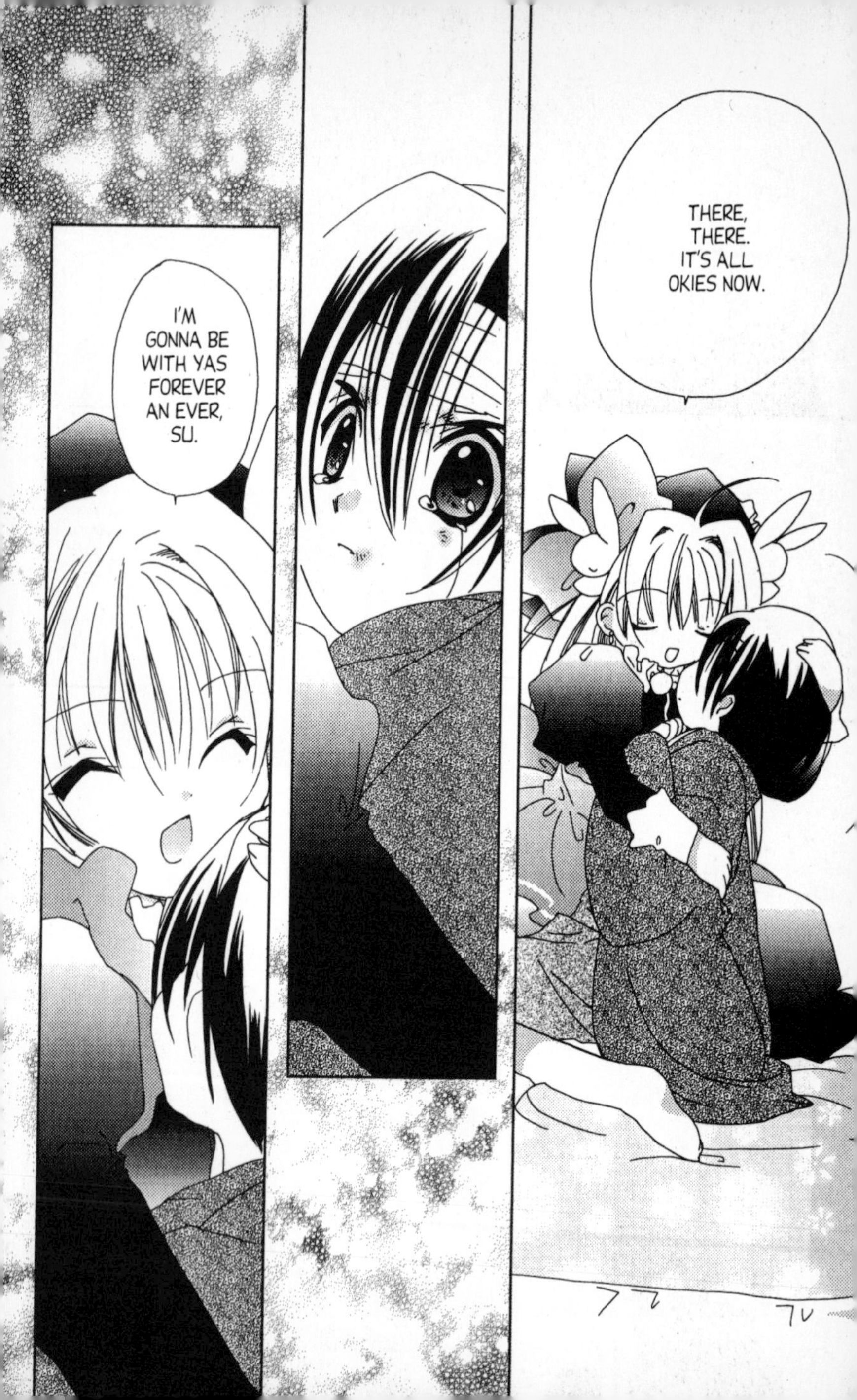
THERE, THERE. IT'S ALL OKIES NOW.
I'M GONNA BE WITH YAS FOREVER AN EVER, SU.

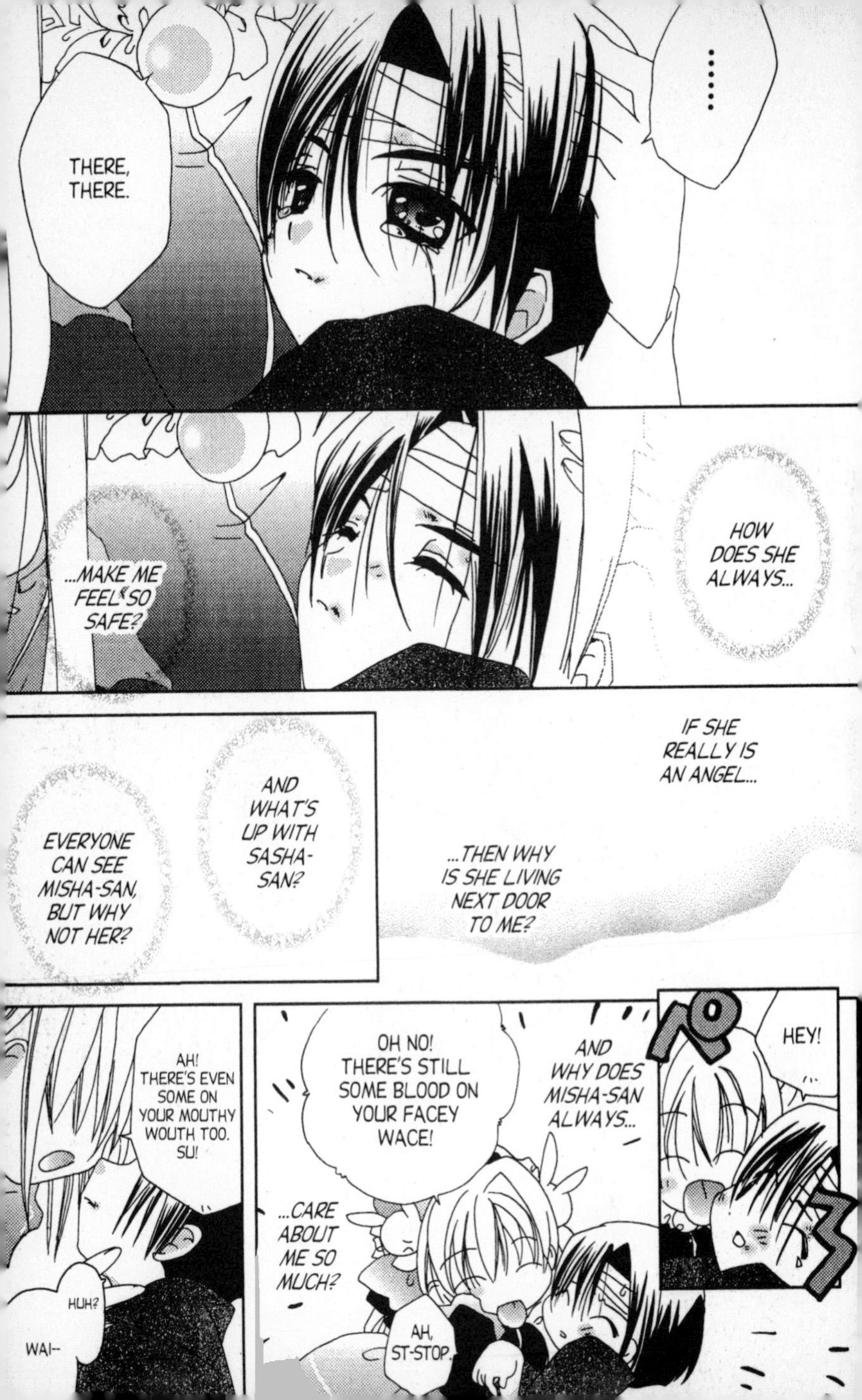
......
THERE, THERE.
HOW DOES SHE ALWAYS...
...MAKE ME FEEL SO SAFE?
IF SHE REALLY IS AN ANGEL...
...THEN WHY IS SHE LIVING NEXT DOOR TO ME?
AND WHAT'S UP WITH SASHA-SAN?
EVERYONE CAN SEE MISHA-SAN, BUT WHY NOT HER?
HEY!
AND WHY DOES MISHA-SAN ALWAYS...
OH NO! THERE'S STILL SOME BLOOD ON YOUR FACEY WACE!
...CARE ABOUT ME SO MUCH?
AH, ST-STOP.
AH! THERE'S EVEN SOME ON YOUR MOUTHY WOUTH TOO. SU!
HUH?
WAI--

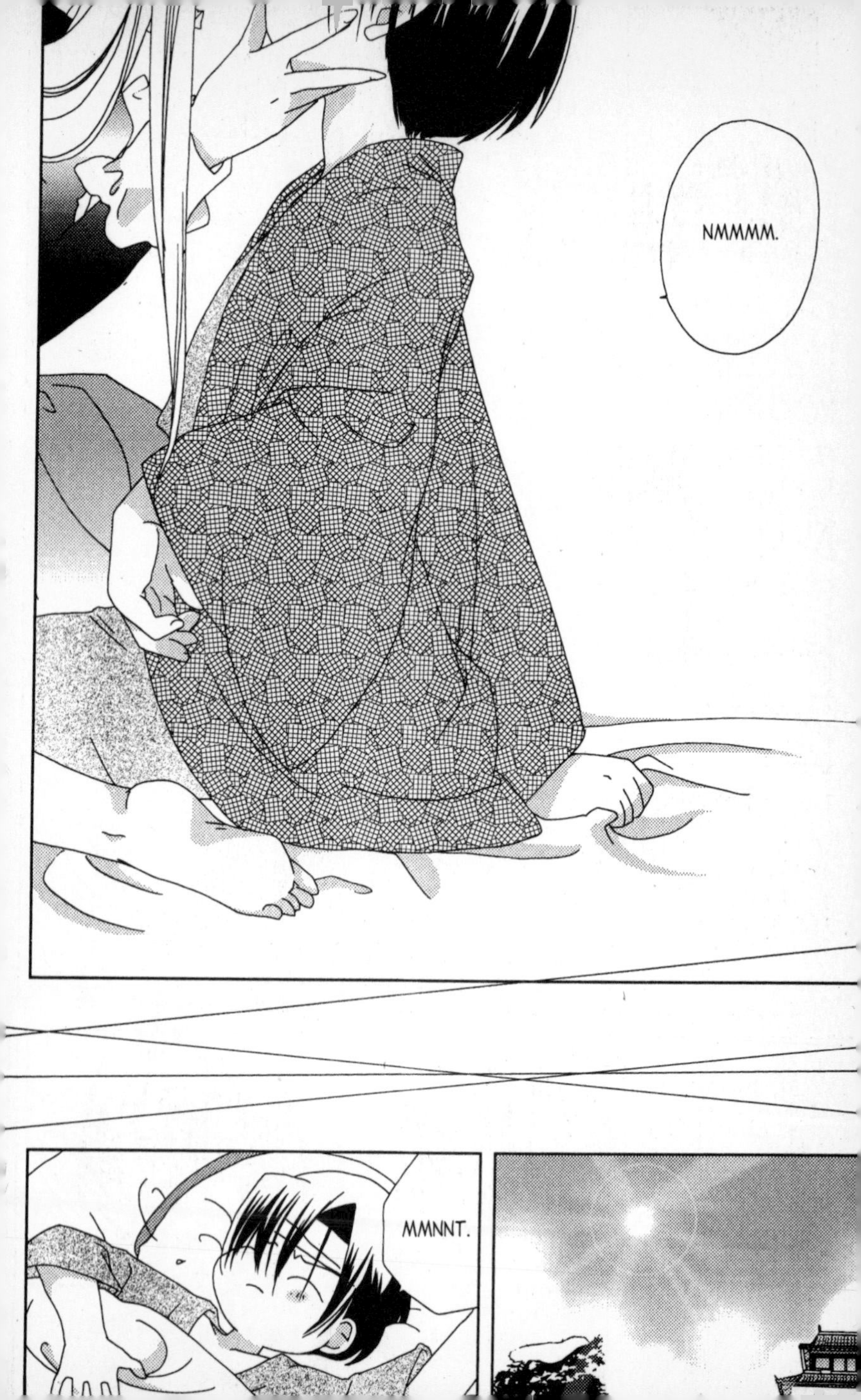
NMMMM.
MMNNT.

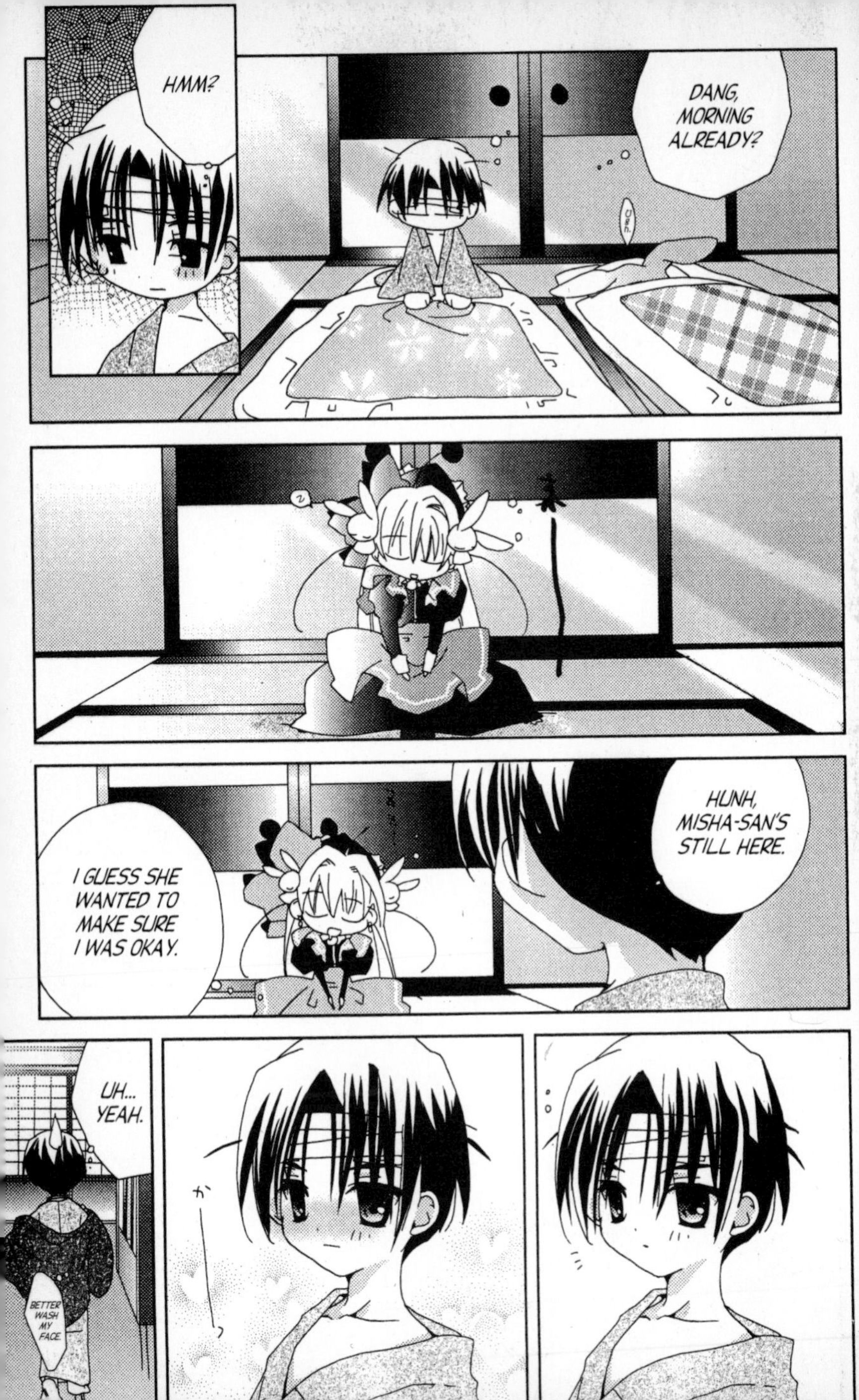
DANG, MORNING ALREADY?
Ugh.
HMM?
HUNH, MISHA-SAN'S STILL HERE.
I GUESS SHE WANTED TO MAKE SURE I WAS OKAY.
か―っ
UH... YEAH.
BETTER WASH MY FACE.

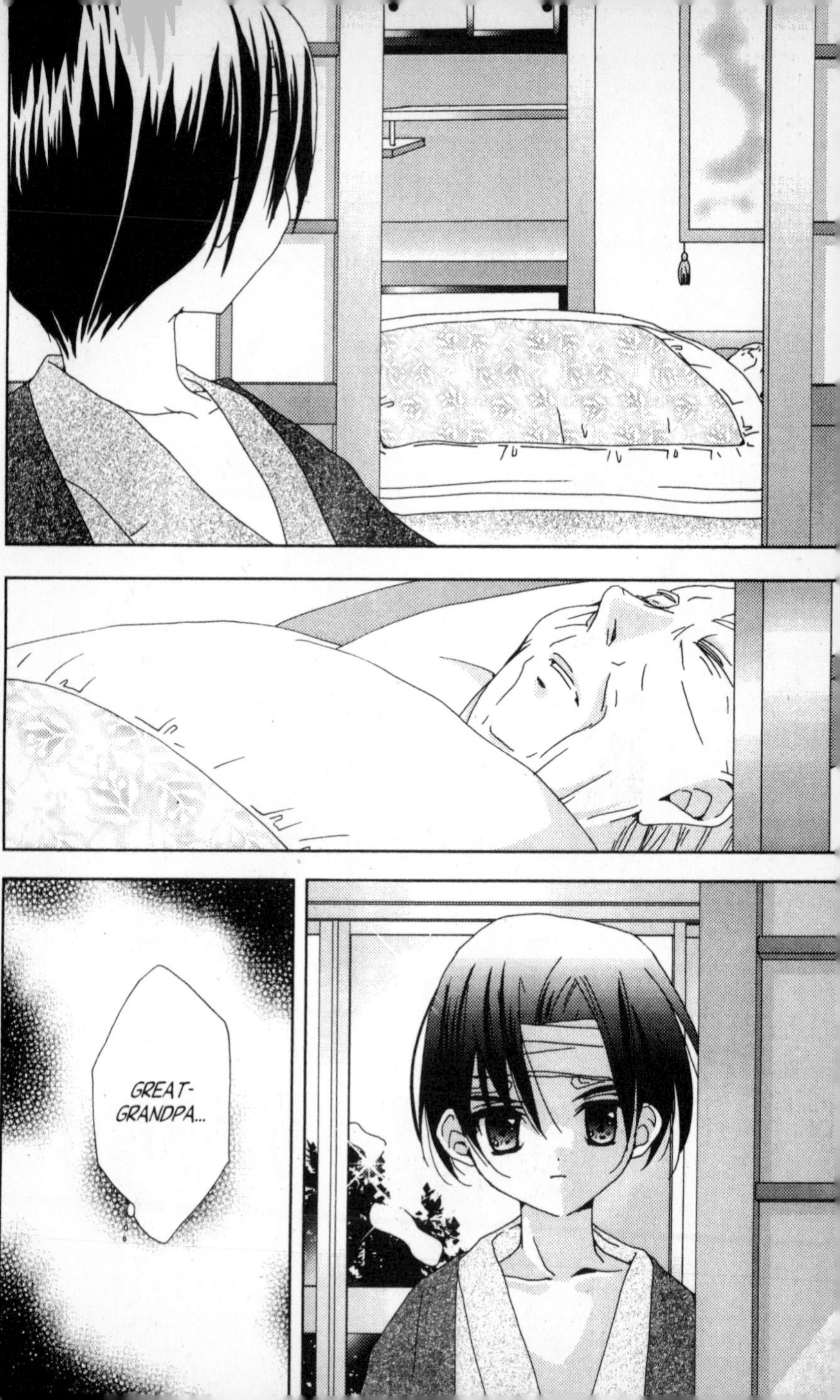
GREAT-GRANDPA...

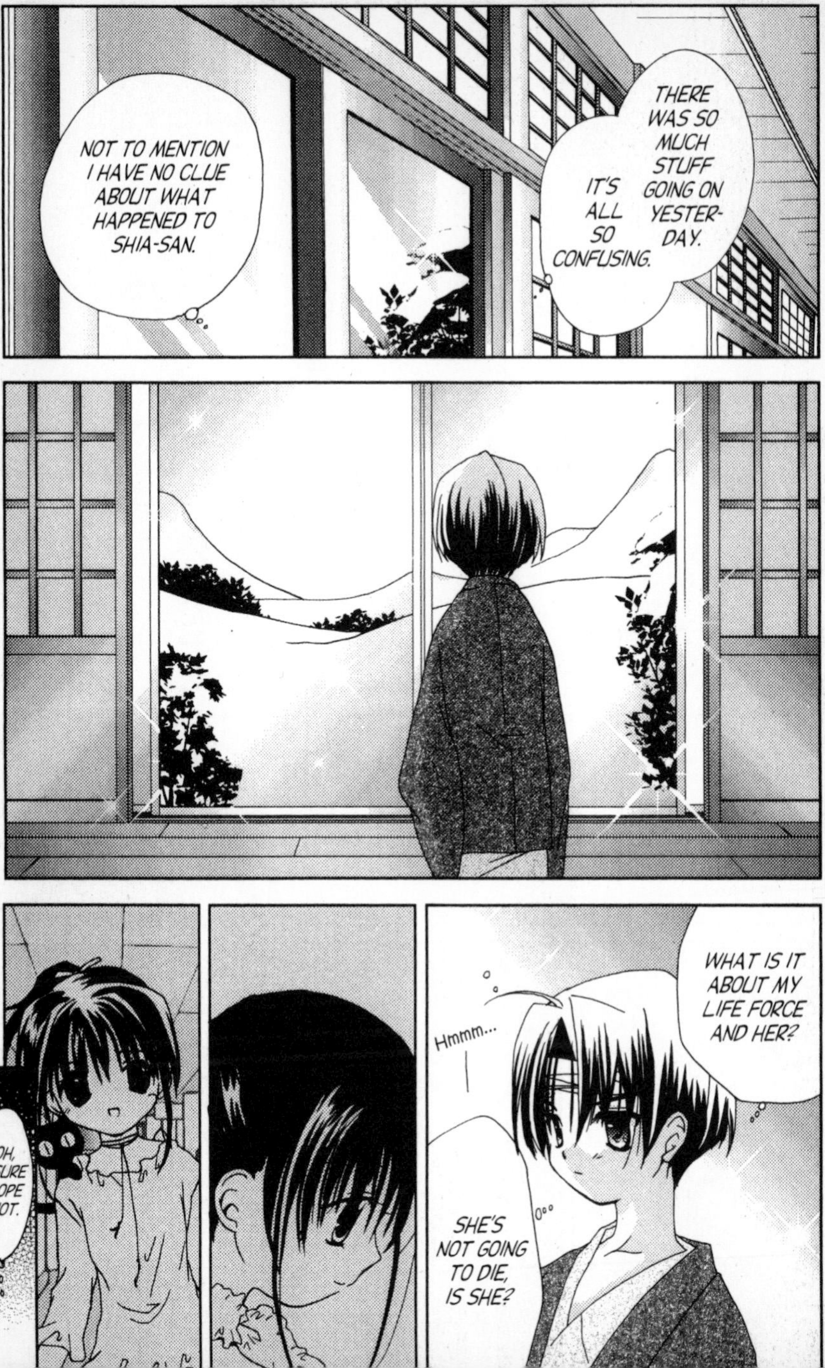
THERE WAS SO MUCH STUFF GOING ON YESTER-DAY.
IT'S ALL SO CONFUSING.
NOT TO MENTION I HAVE NO CLUE ABOUT WHAT HAPPENED TO SHIA-SAN.
WHAT IS IT ABOUT MY LIFE FORCE AND HER?
Hmmm...
SHE'S NOT GOING TO DIE, IS SHE?
OH, I SURE HOPE NOT.

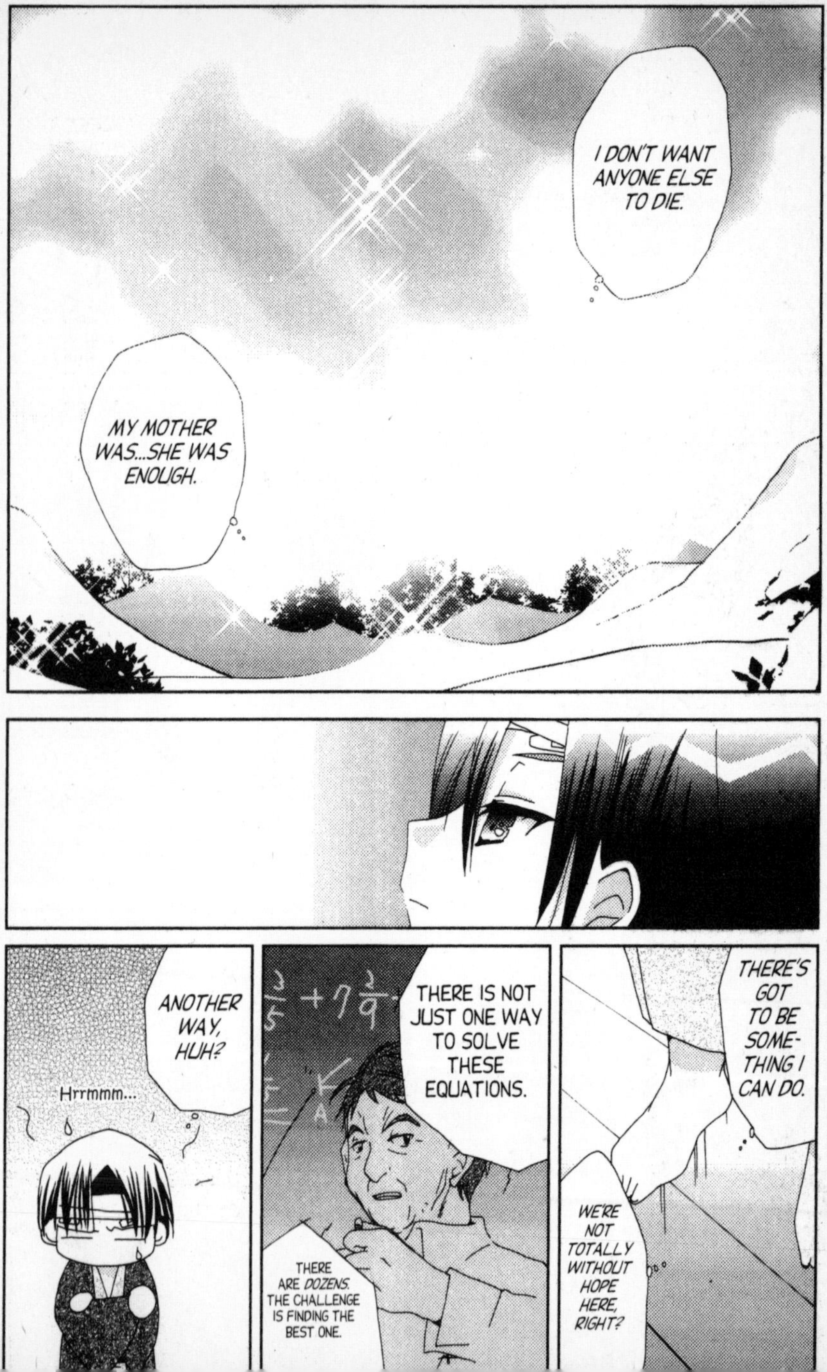
I DON'T WANT ANYONE ELSE TO DIE.
MY MOTHER WAS...SHE WAS ENOUGH.
THERE'S GOT TO BE SOME-THING I CAN DO.
WE'RE NOT TOTALLY WITHOUT HOPE HERE, RIGHT?
THERE IS NOT JUST ONE WAY TO SOLVE THESE EQUATIONS.
THERE ARE DOZENS. THE CHALLENGE IS FINDING THE BEST ONE.
ANOTHER WAY, HUH?
Hrrmmm...

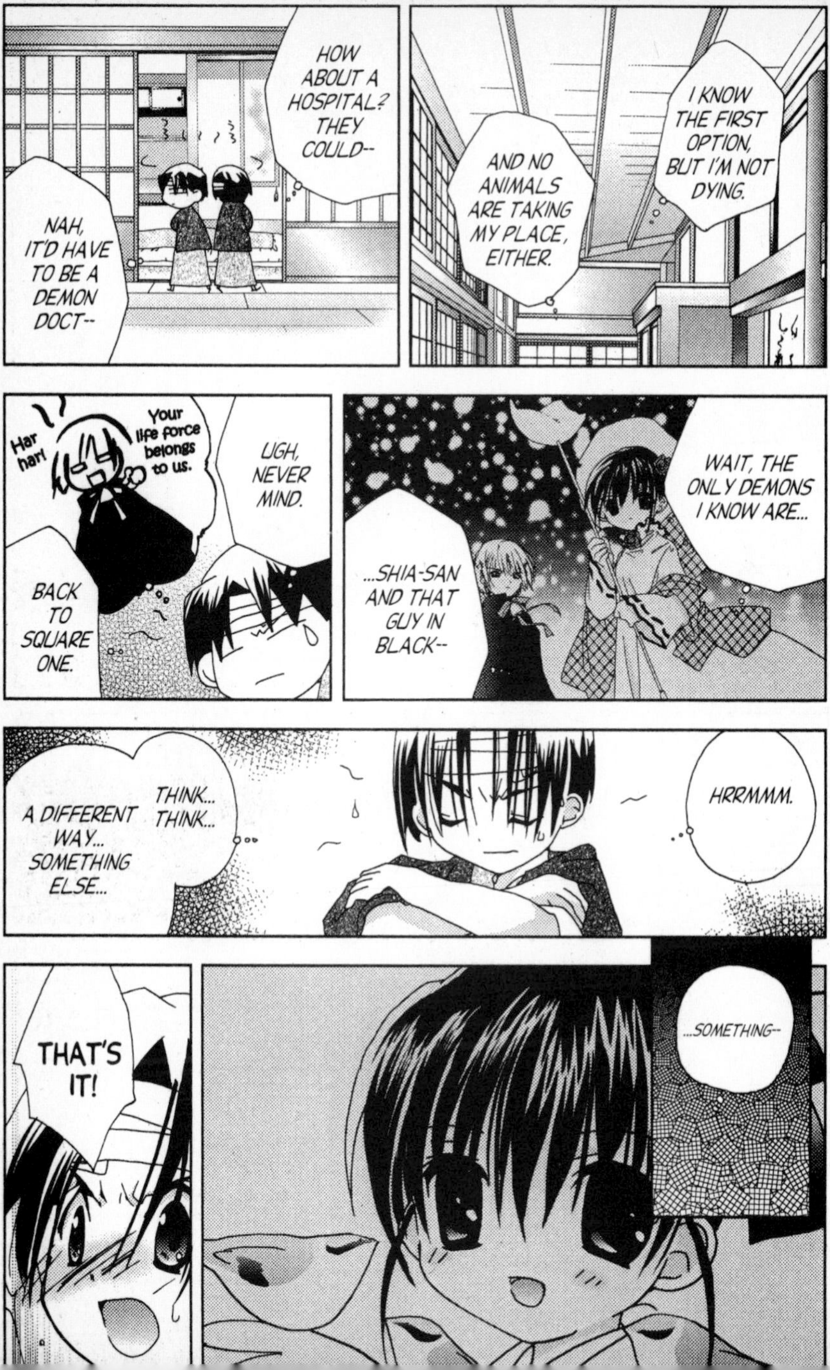
I KNOW THE FIRST OPTION, BUT I'M NOT DYING.
AND NO ANIMALS ARE TAKING MY PLACE, EITHER.
HOW ABOUT A HOSPITAL? THEY COULD--
NAH, IT'D HAVE TO BE A DEMON DOCT--
WAIT, THE ONLY DEMONS I KNOW ARE...
...SHIA-SAN AND THAT GUY IN BLACK--
UGH, NEVER MIND.
Your life force belongs to us.
Har har!
BACK TO SQUARE ONE.
HRRMMM.
THINK... THINK...
A DIFFERENT WAY... SOMETHING ELSE...
...SOMETHING--
THAT'S IT!

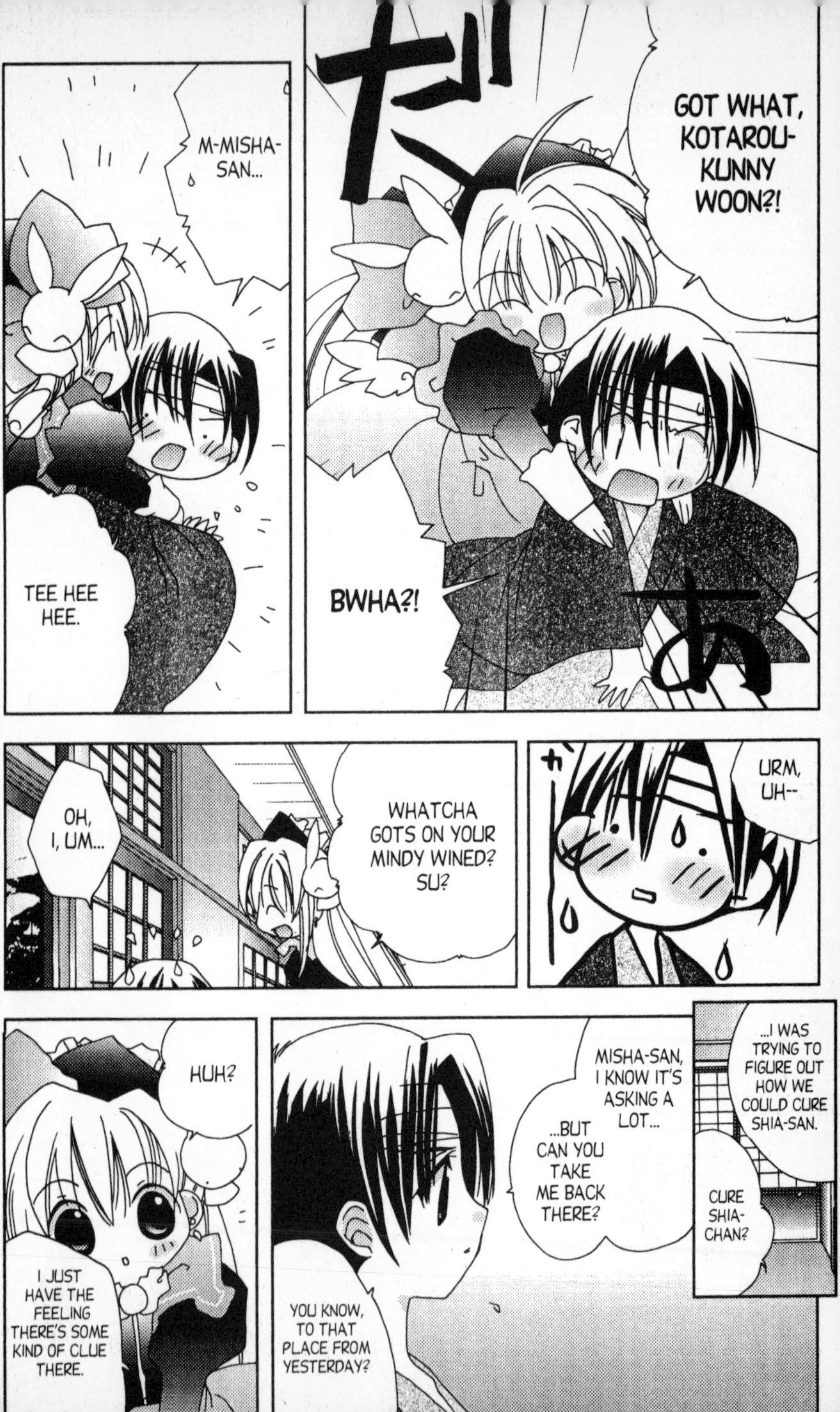
GOT WHAT, KOTAROU-KUNNY WOON?!
BWHA?!
M-MISHA-SAN...
TEE HEE HEE.
URM, UH--
WHATCHA GOTS ON YOUR MINDY WINED? SU?
OH, I, UM...
...I WAS TRYING TO FIGURE OUT HOW WE COULD CURE SHIA-SAN.
CURE SHIA-CHAN?
MISHA-SAN, I KNOW IT'S ASKING A LOT...
...BUT CAN YOU TAKE ME BACK THERE?
YOU KNOW, TO THAT PLACE FROM YESTERDAY?
HUH?
I JUST HAVE THE FEELING THERE'S SOME KIND OF CLUE THERE.

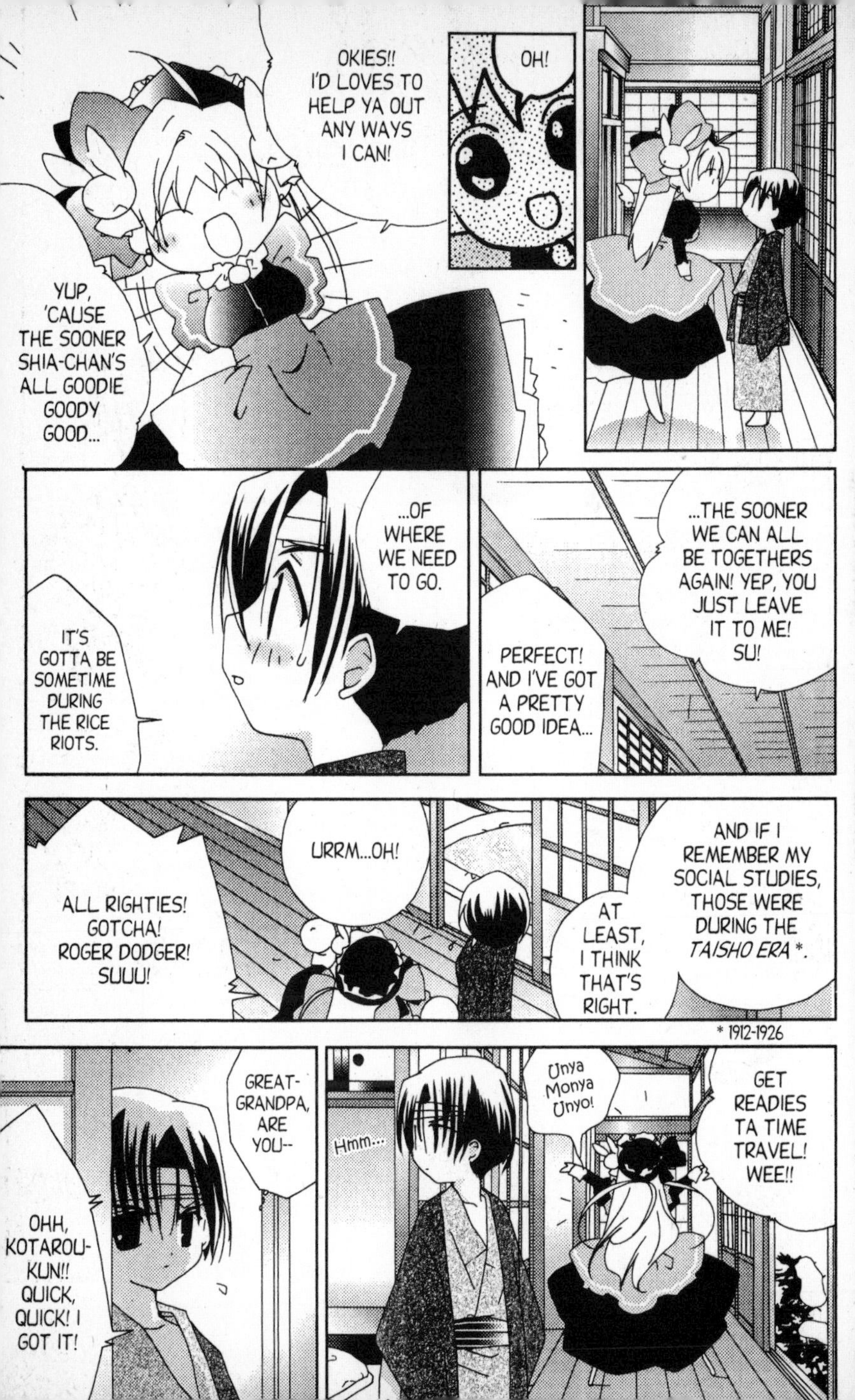
OH!
OKIES!! I'D LOVES TO HELP YA OUT ANY WAYS I CAN!
YUP, 'CAUSE THE SOONER SHIA-CHAN'S ALL GOODIE GOODY GOOD...
...THE SOONER WE CAN ALL BE TOGETHERS AGAIN! YEP, YOU JUST LEAVE IT TO ME! SU!
PERFECT! AND I'VE GOT A PRETTY GOOD IDEA...
...OF WHERE WE NEED TO GO.
IT'S GOTTA BE SOMETIME DURING THE RICE RIOTS.
AND IF I REMEMBER MY SOCIAL STUDIES, THOSE WERE DURING THE *TAISHO ERA* *.
AT LEAST, I THINK THAT'S RIGHT.
URRM...OH!
ALL RIGHTIES! GOTCHA! ROGER DODGER! SUUU!
GET READIES TA TIME TRAVEL! WEE!!
Unya Monya Unyo!
Hmm...
GREAT-GRANDPA, ARE YOU--
OHH, KOTAROU-KUN!! QUICK, QUICK! I GOT IT!

* 1912-1926

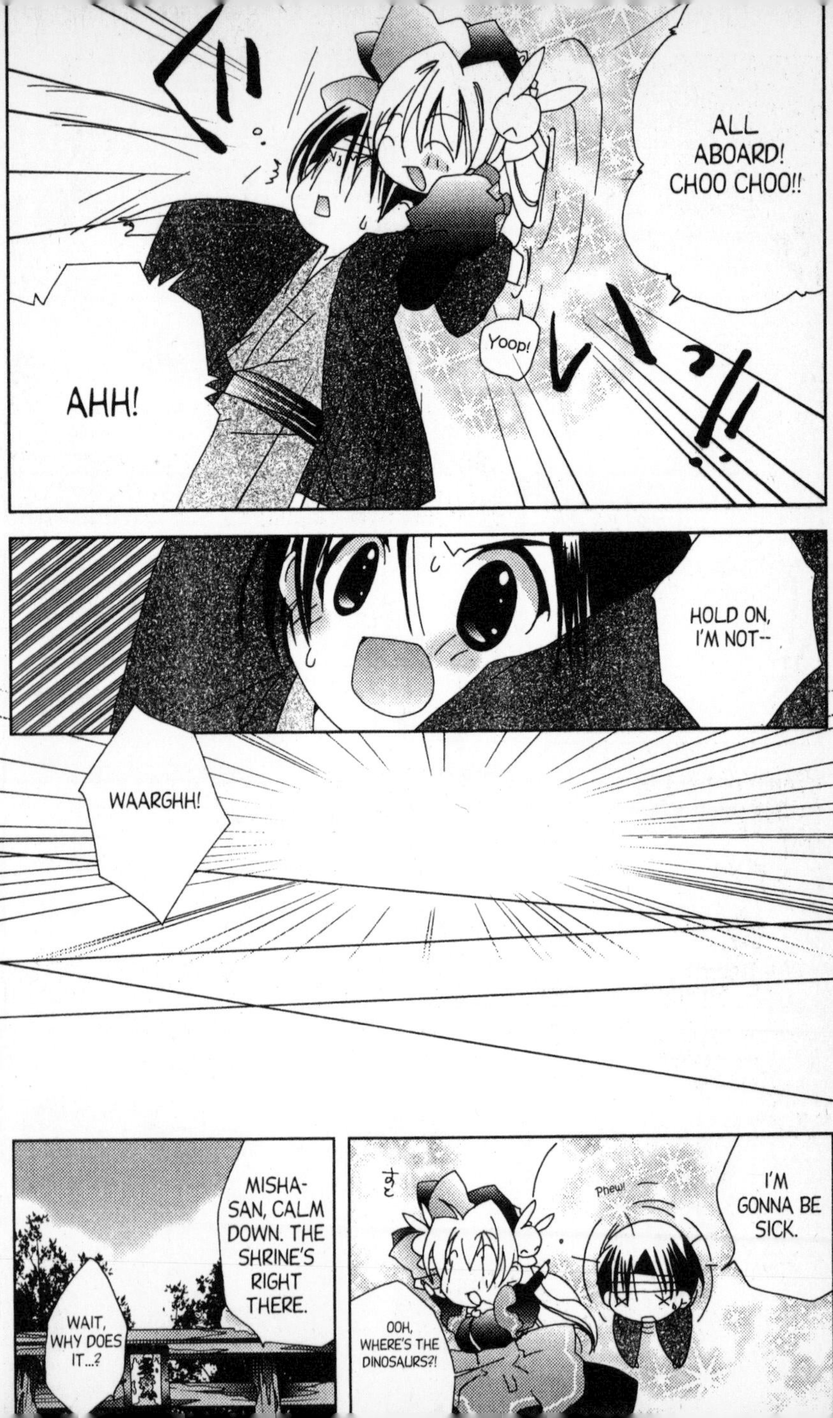
ALL ABOARD! CHOO CHOO!!
Yoop!
AHH!
HOLD ON, I'M NOT--
WAARGHH!
I'M GONNA BE SICK.
Phew!
OOH, WHERE'S THE DINOSAURS?!
MISHA-SAN, CALM DOWN. THE SHRINE'S RIGHT THERE.
WAIT, WHY DOES IT...?

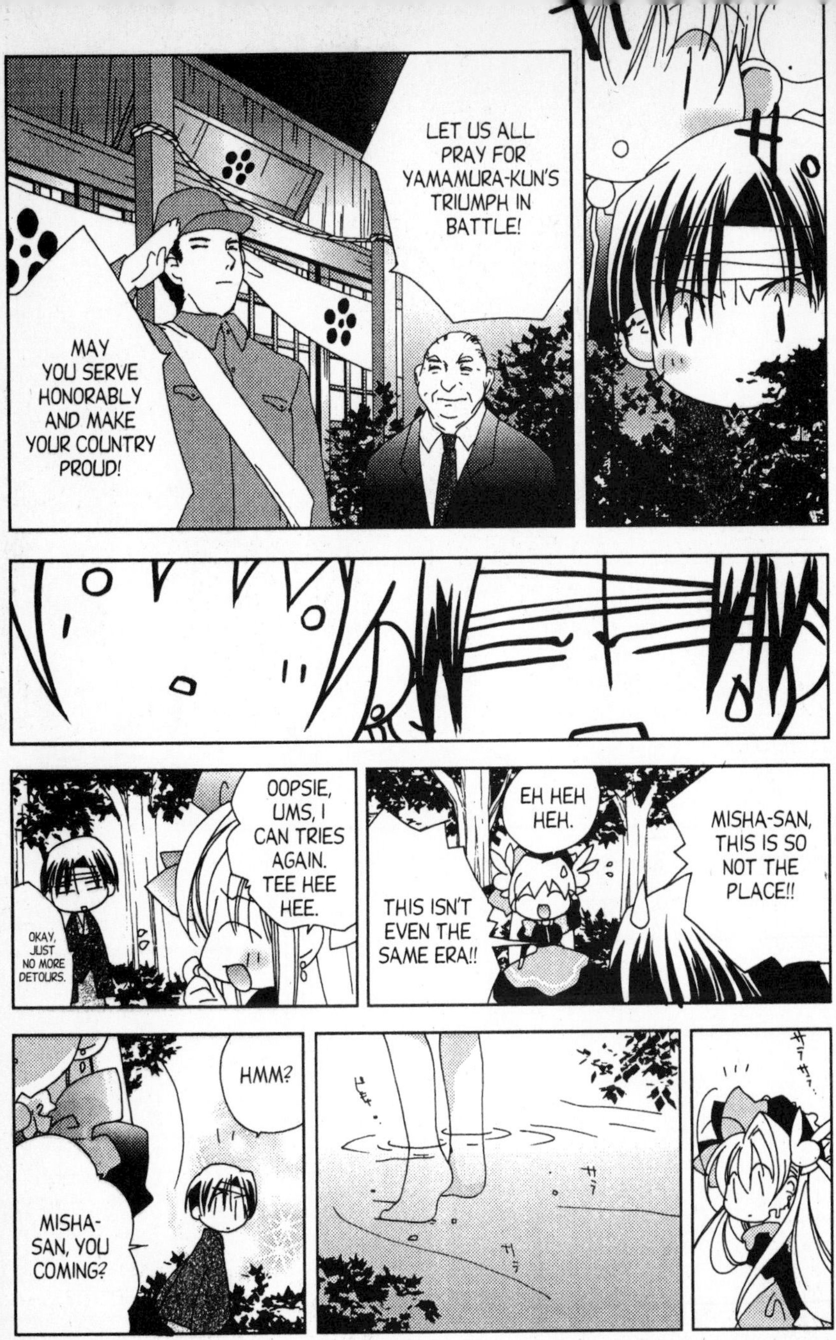
LET US ALL PRAY FOR YAMAMURA-KUN'S TRIUMPH IN BATTLE!
MAY YOU SERVE HONORABLY AND MAKE YOUR COUNTRY PROUD!
MISHA-SAN, THIS IS SO NOT THE PLACE!!
EH HEH HEH.
THIS ISN'T EVEN THE SAME ERA!!
OOPSIE, UMS, I CAN TRIES AGAIN. TEE HEE HEE.
OKAY, JUST NO MORE DETOURS.
HMM?
MISHA-SAN, YOU COMING?

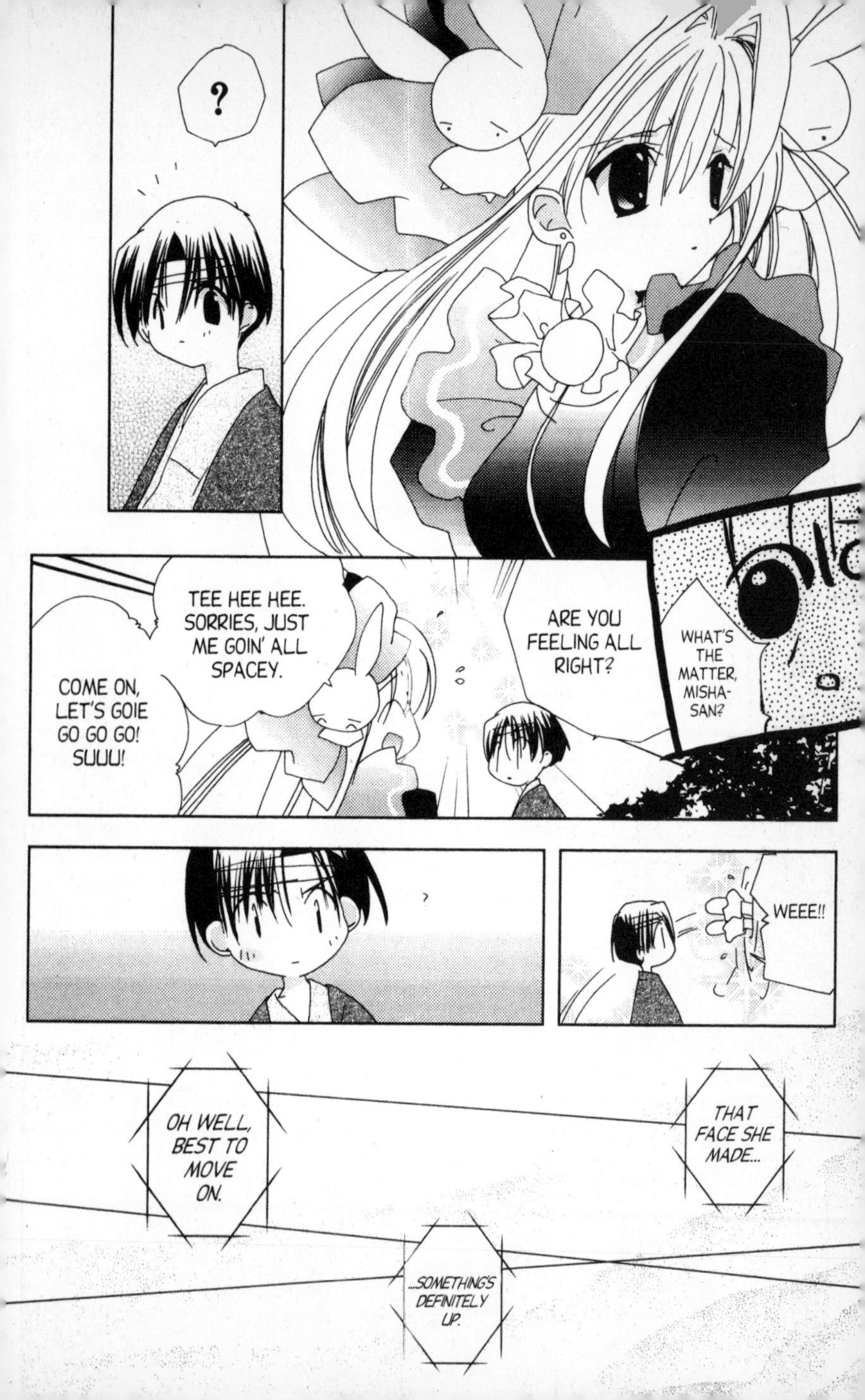
?
WHAT'S THE MATTER, MISHA-SAN?
ARE YOU FEELING ALL RIGHT?
TEE HEE HEE. SORRIES, JUST ME GOIN' ALL SPACEY.
COME ON, LET'S GOIE GO GO GO! SUUU!
WEEE!!
?
THAT FACE SHE MADE...
OH WELL, BEST TO MOVE ON.
...SOMETHING'S DEFINITELY UP.

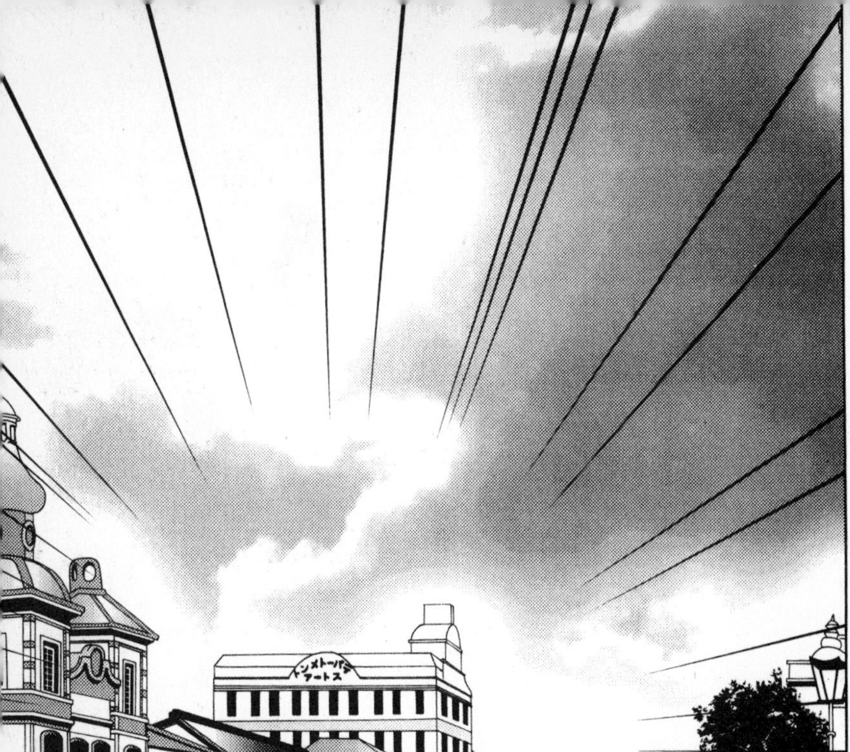
トンメトーパデ
アートス
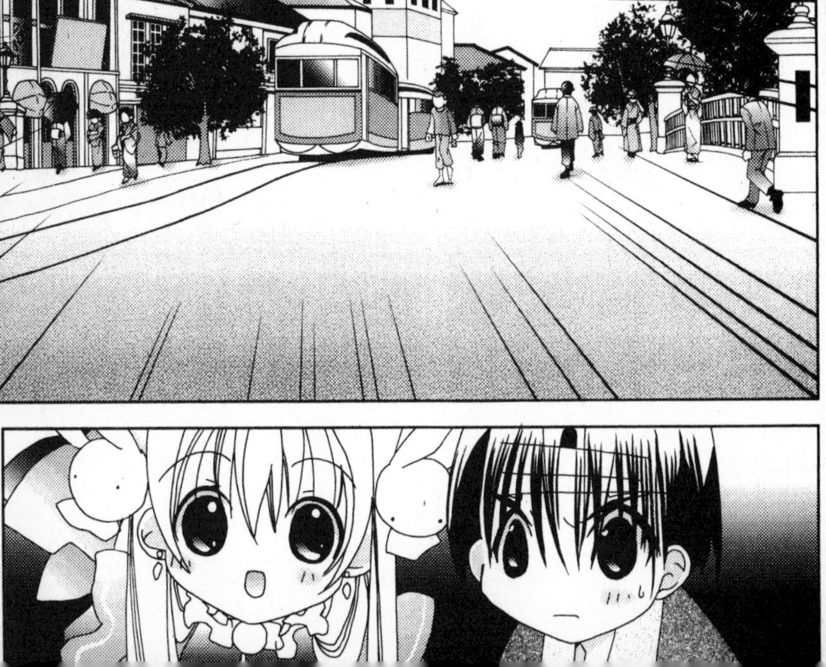

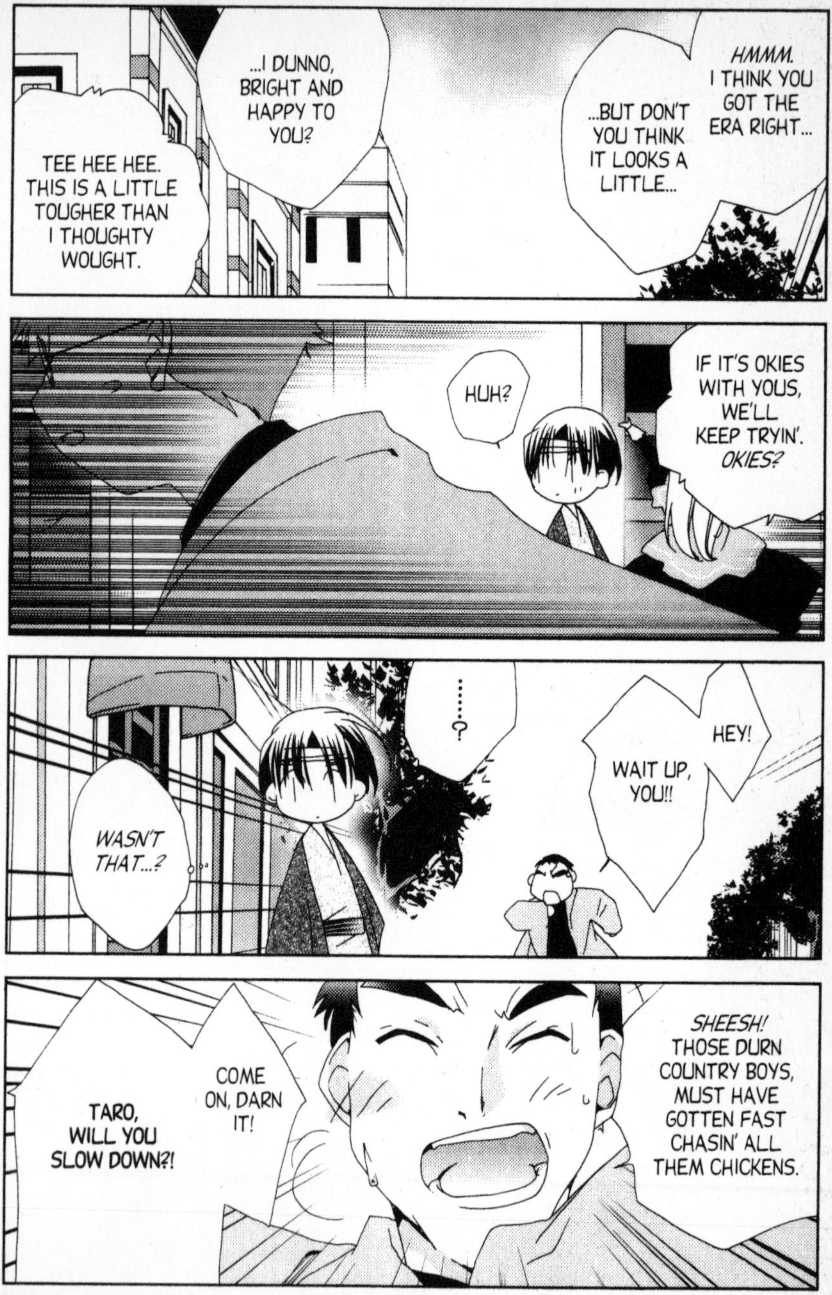

HMMM. I THINK YOU GOT THE ERA RIGHT...
...BUT DON'T YOU THINK IT LOOKS A LITTLE...
...I DUNNO, BRIGHT AND HAPPY TO YOU?
TEE HEE HEE. THIS IS A LITTLE TOUGHER THAN I THOUGHTY WOUGHT.
IF IT'S OKIES WITH YOUS, WE'LL KEEP TRYIN'. *OKIES?*
HUH?
HEY!
WAIT UP, YOU!!
......?
WASN'T THAT...?
SHEESH! THOSE DURN COUNTRY BOYS, MUST HAVE GOTTEN FAST CHASIN' ALL THEM CHICKENS.
COME ON, DARN IT!
TARO, WILL YOU SLOW DOWN?!

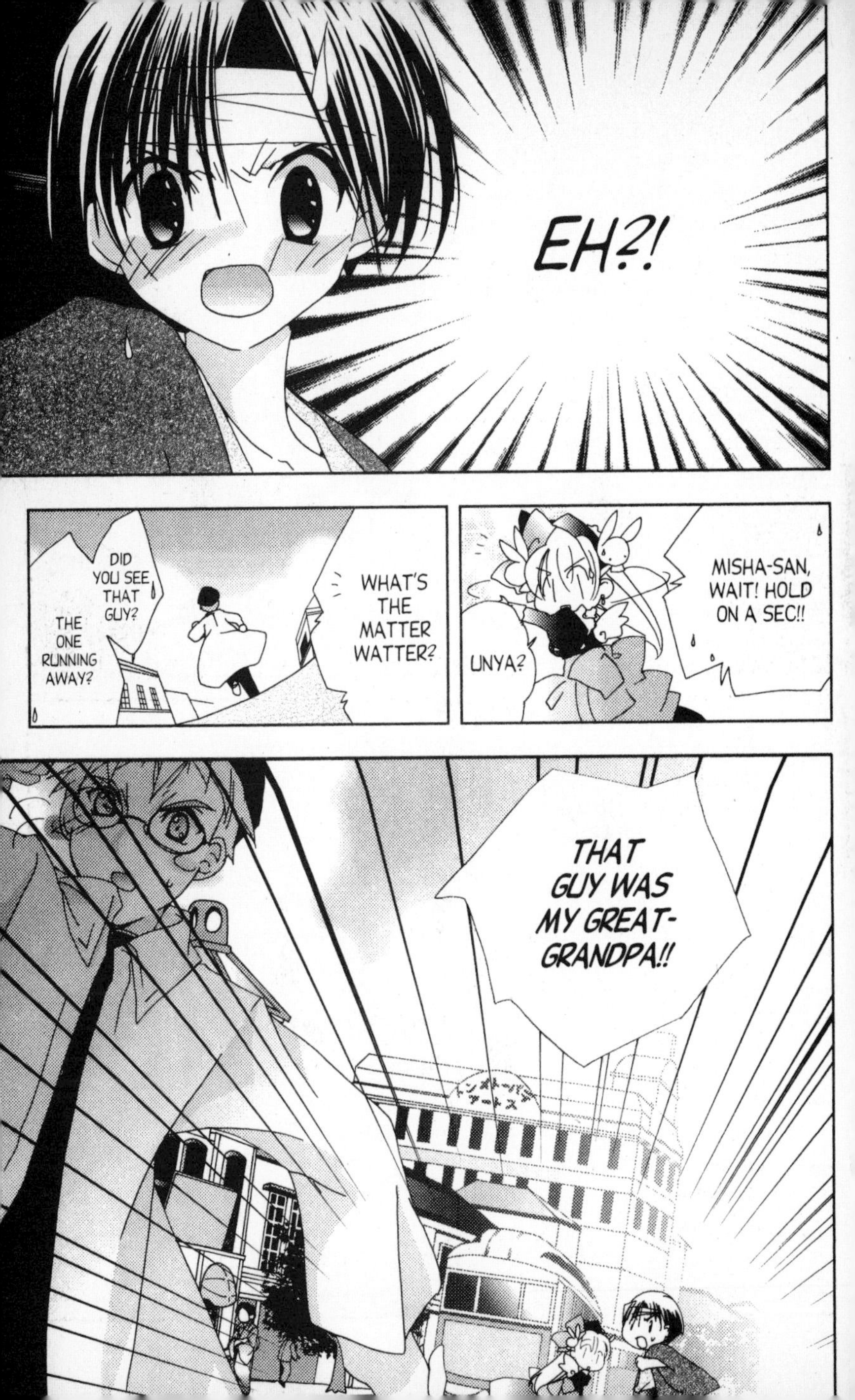
EH?!
MISHA-SAN, WAIT! HOLD ON A SEC!!
UNYA?
WHAT'S THE MATTER WATTER?
DID YOU SEE THAT GUY?
THE ONE RUNNING AWAY?
THAT GUY WAS MY GREAT-GRANDPA!!

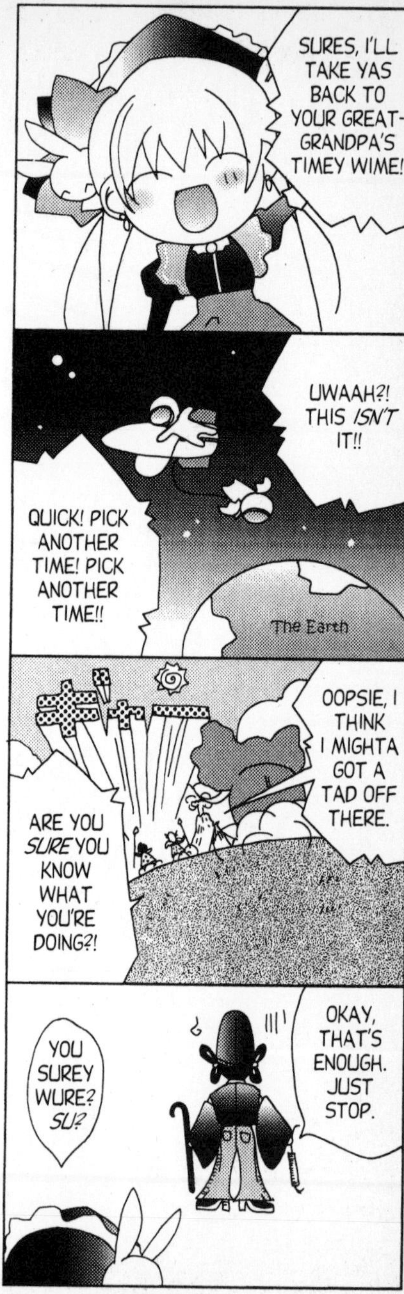
SURES, I'LL TAKE YAS BACK TO YOUR GREAT-GRANDPA'S TIMEY WIME!
UWAAH?! THIS *ISN'T* IT!!
QUICK! PICK ANOTHER TIME! PICK ANOTHER TIME!!
The Earth
OOPSIE, I THINK I MIGHTA GOT A TAD OFF THERE.
ARE YOU *SURE* YOU KNOW WHAT YOU'RE DOING?!
OKAY, THAT'S ENOUGH. JUST STOP.
YOU SUREY WURE? *SU?*

Lesson 34

How to Find What You're Looking For: Part 2

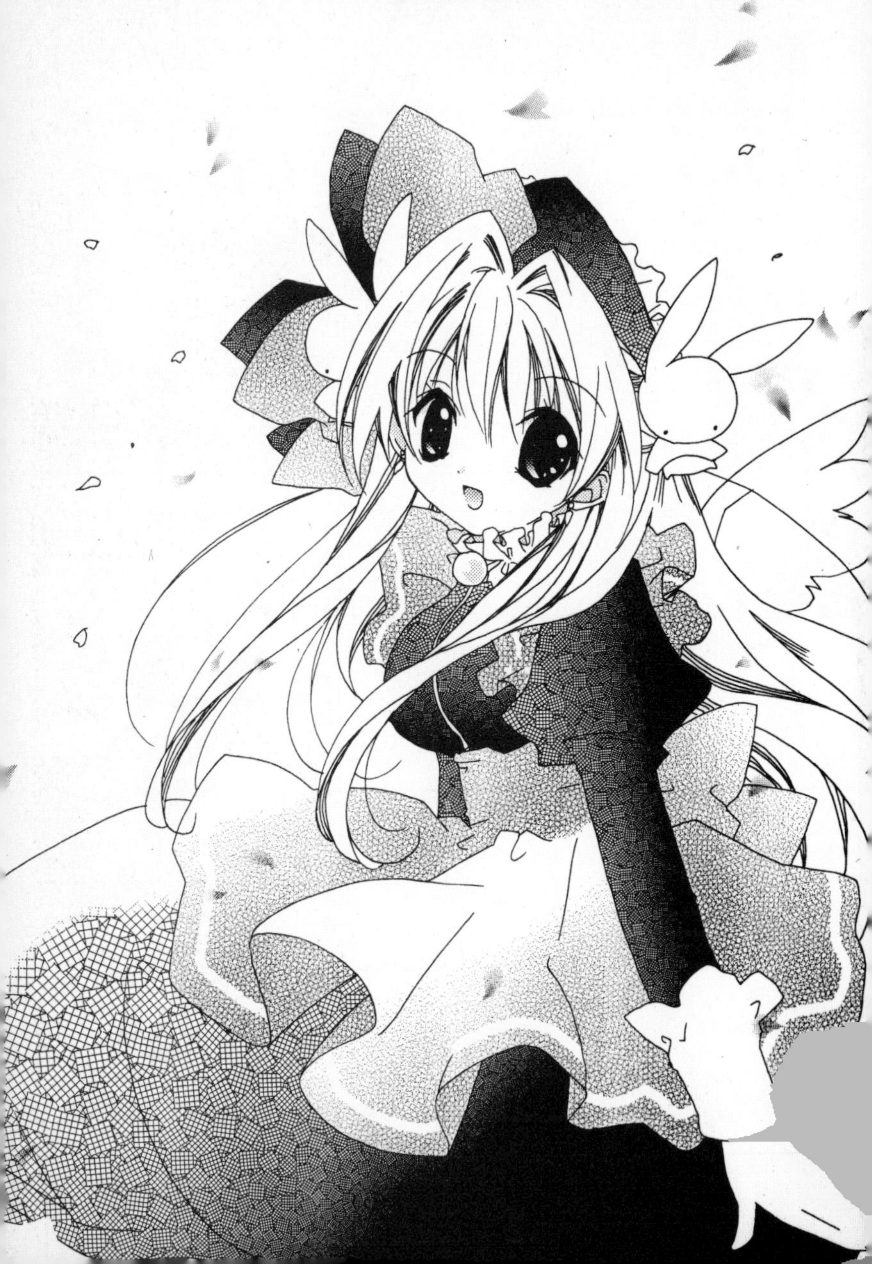

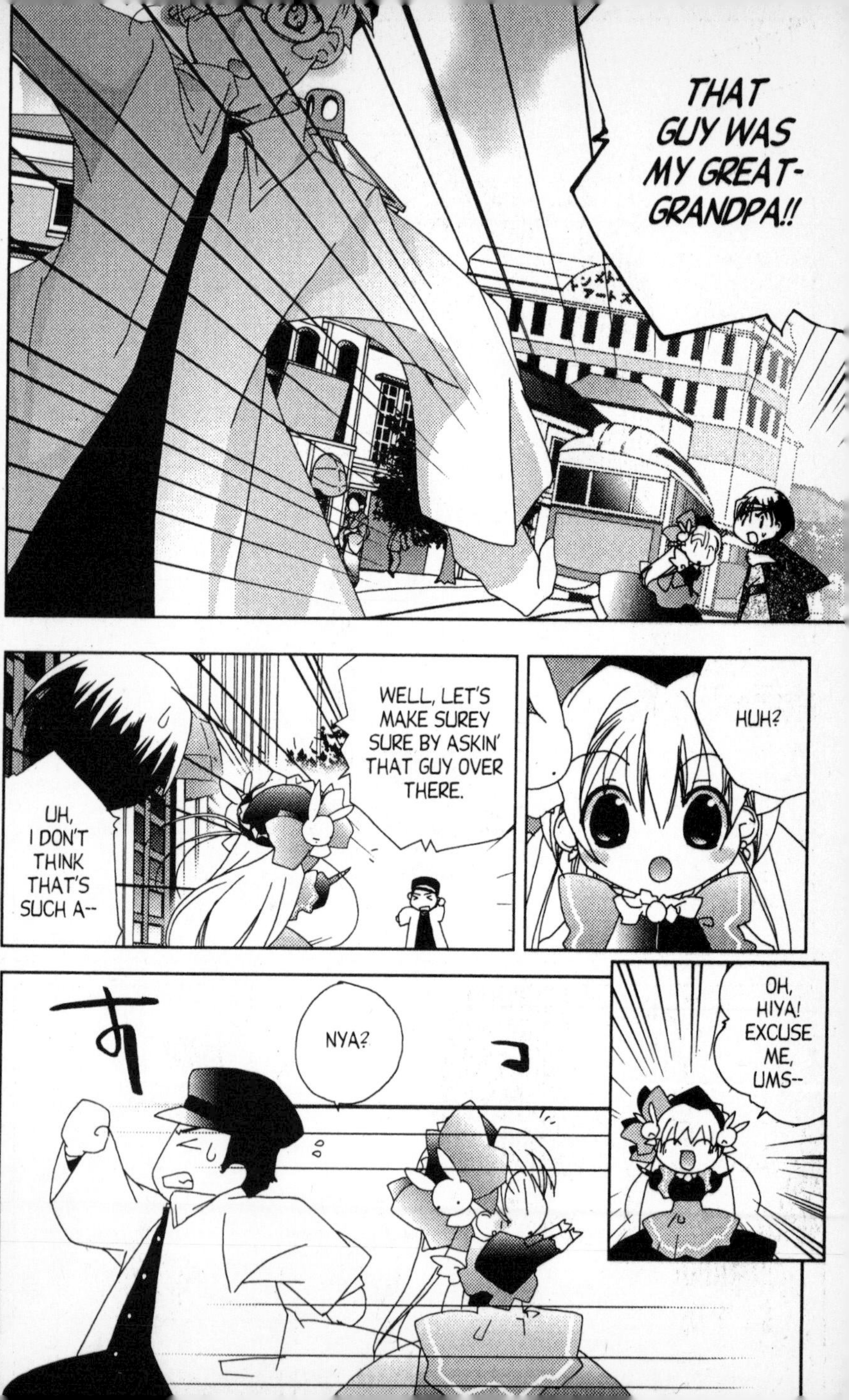
THAT GUY WAS MY GREAT-GRANDPA!!
HUH?
WELL, LET'S MAKE SUREY SURE BY ASKIN' THAT GUY OVER THERE.
UH, I DON'T THINK THAT'S SUCH A--
OH, HIYA! EXCUSE ME, UMS--
NYA?
あ
コ

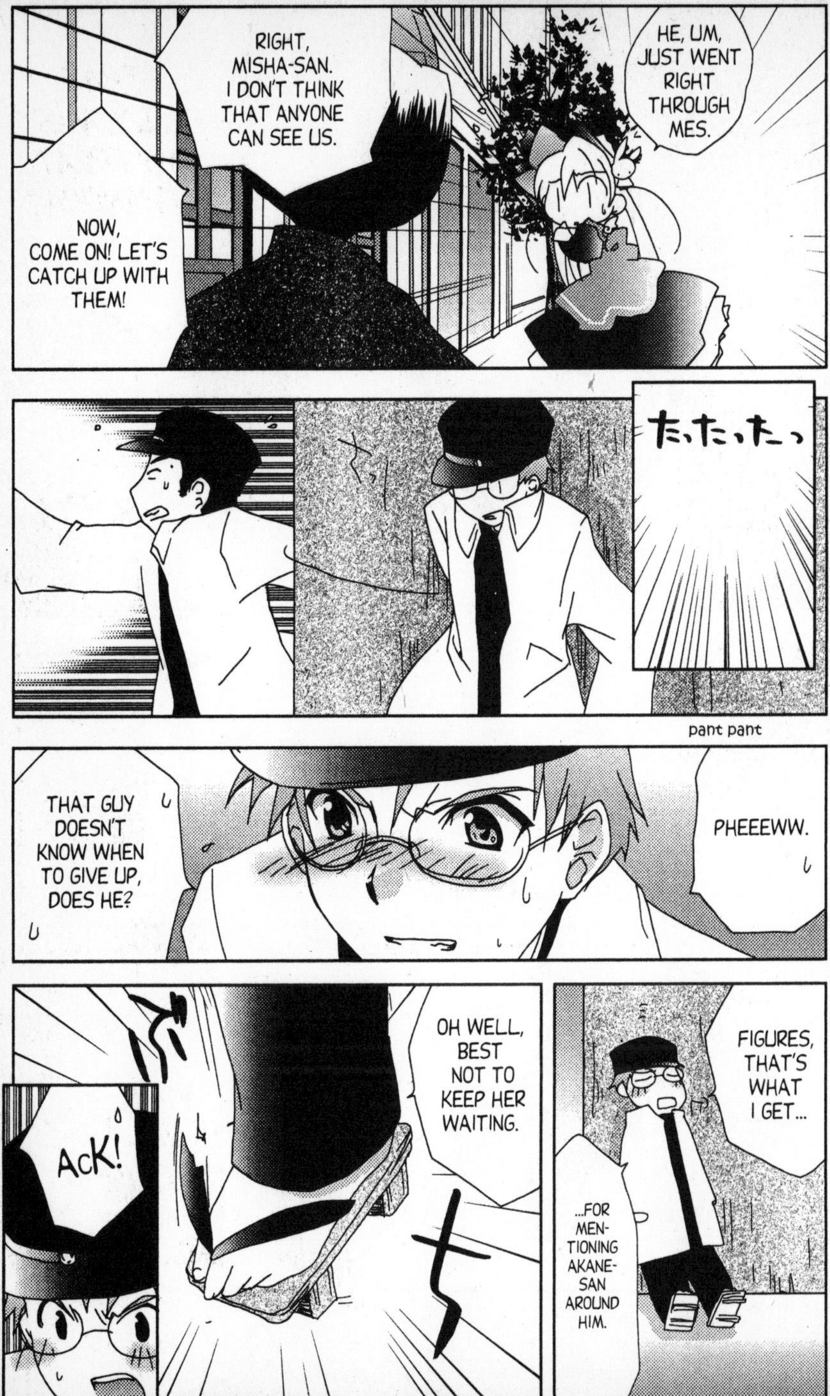
HE, UM, JUST WENT RIGHT THROUGH MES.
RIGHT, MISHA-SAN. I DON'T THINK THAT ANYONE CAN SEE US.
NOW, COME ON! LET'S CATCH UP WITH THEM!
たったったっ
pant pant
PHEEEWW.
THAT GUY DOESN'T KNOW WHEN TO GIVE UP, DOES HE?
FIGURES, THAT'S WHAT I GET...
...FOR MENTIONING AKANE-SAN AROUND HIM.
OH WELL, BEST NOT TO KEEP HER WAITING.
AcK!

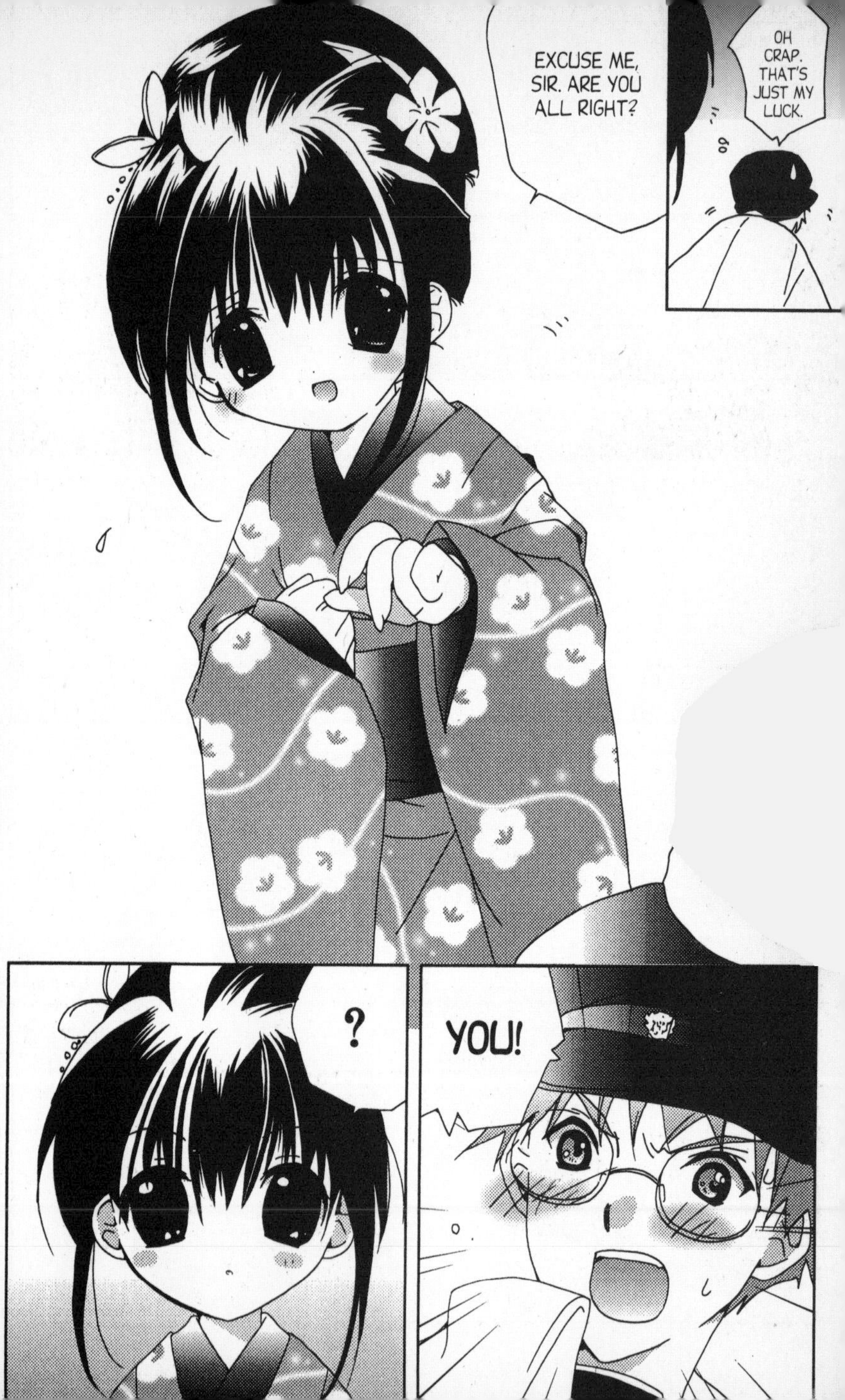
OH CRAP. THAT'S JUST MY LUCK.
EXCUSE ME, SIR. ARE YOU ALL RIGHT?
YOU!
?

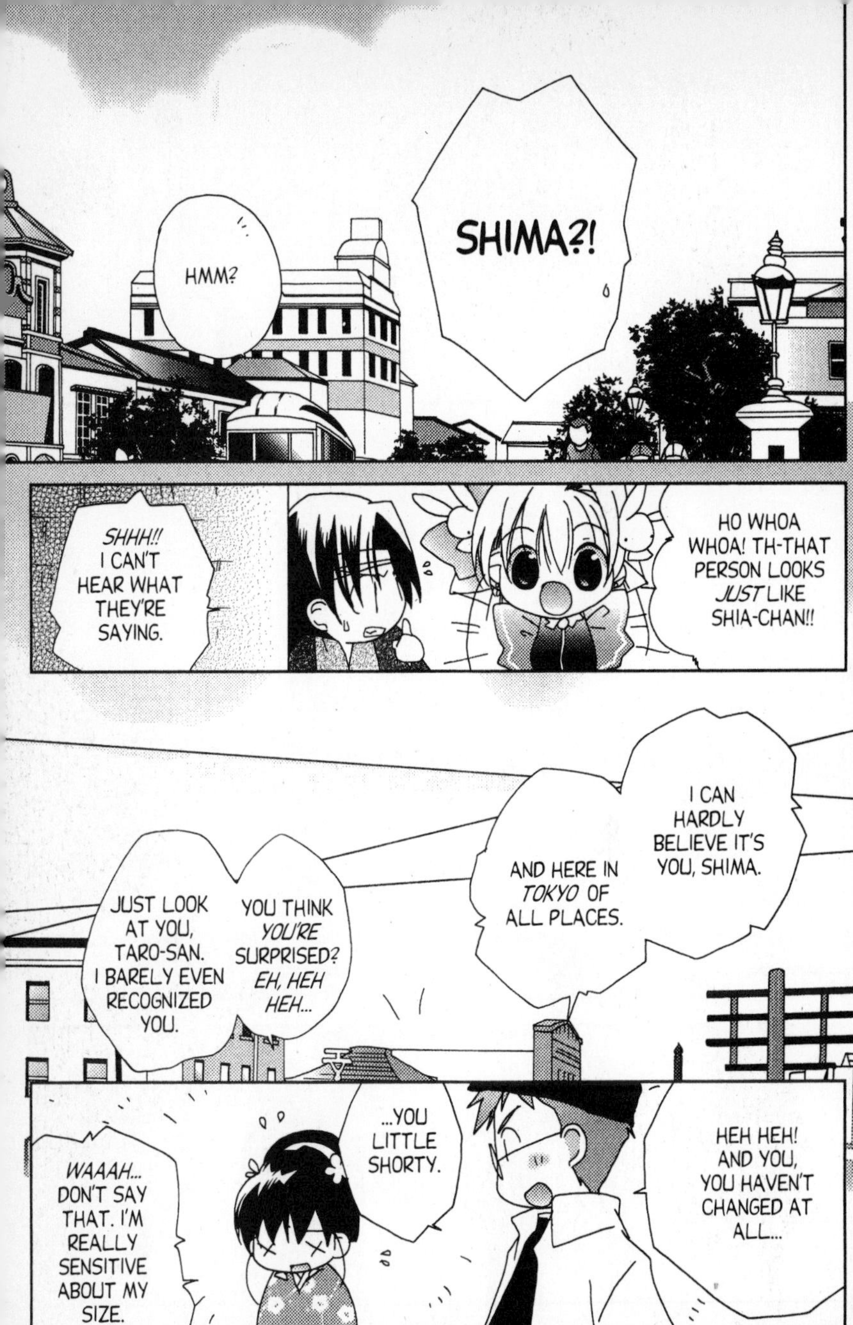
SHIMA?!
HMM?
HO WHOA WHOA! TH-THAT PERSON LOOKS *JUST* LIKE SHIA-CHAN!!
SHHH!! I CAN'T HEAR WHAT THEY'RE SAYING.
I CAN HARDLY BELIEVE IT'S YOU, SHIMA.
AND HERE IN *TOKYO* OF ALL PLACES.
YOU THINK *YOU'RE* SURPRISED? *EH, HEH HEH...*
JUST LOOK AT YOU, TARO-SAN. I BARELY EVEN RECOGNIZED YOU.
HEH HEH! AND YOU, YOU HAVEN'T CHANGED AT ALL...
...YOU LITTLE SHORTY.
WAAAH... DON'T SAY THAT. I'M REALLY SENSITIVE ABOUT MY SIZE.

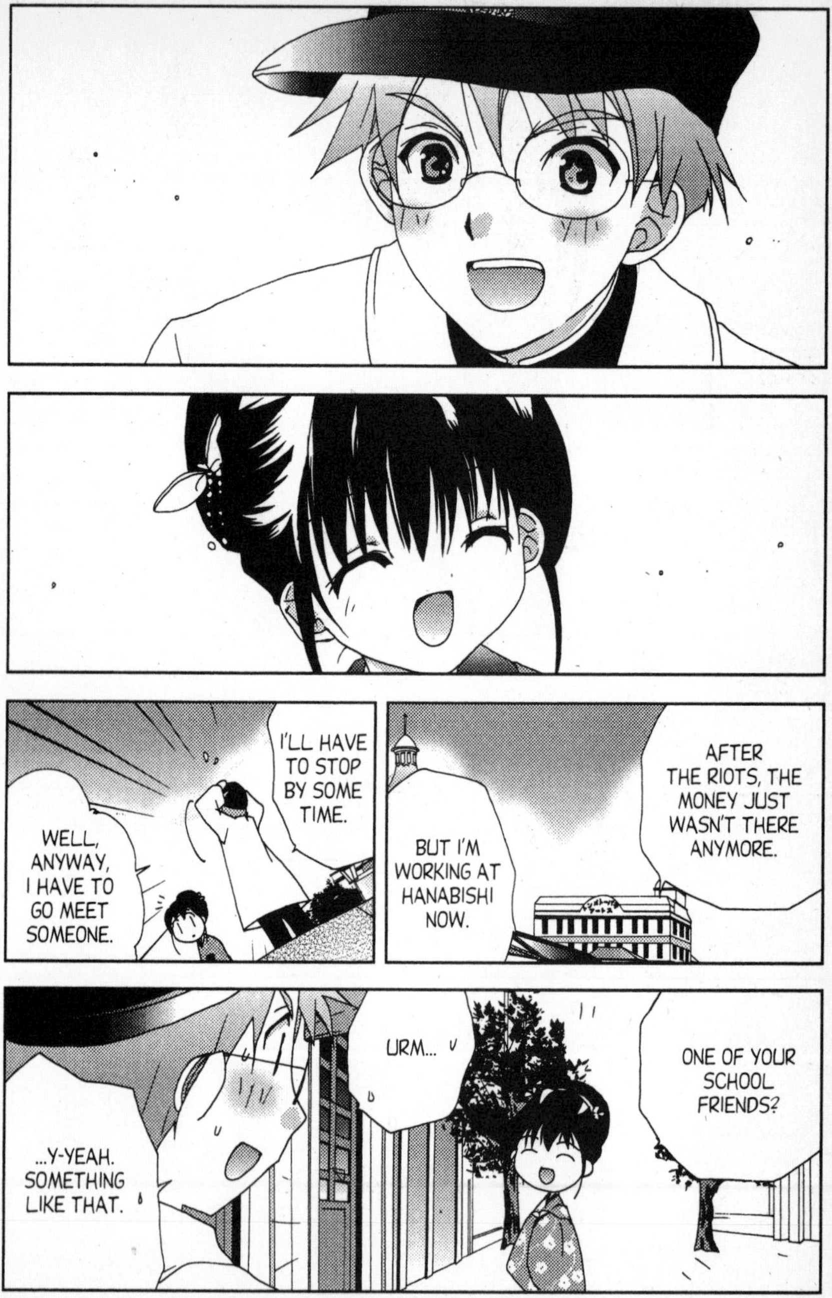
AFTER THE RIOTS, THE MONEY JUST WASN'T THERE ANYMORE.
BUT I'M WORKING AT HANABISHI NOW.
I'LL HAVE TO STOP BY SOME TIME.
WELL, ANYWAY, I HAVE TO GO MEET SOMEONE.
ONE OF YOUR SCHOOL FRIENDS?
URM...
...Y-YEAH. SOMETHING LIKE THAT.

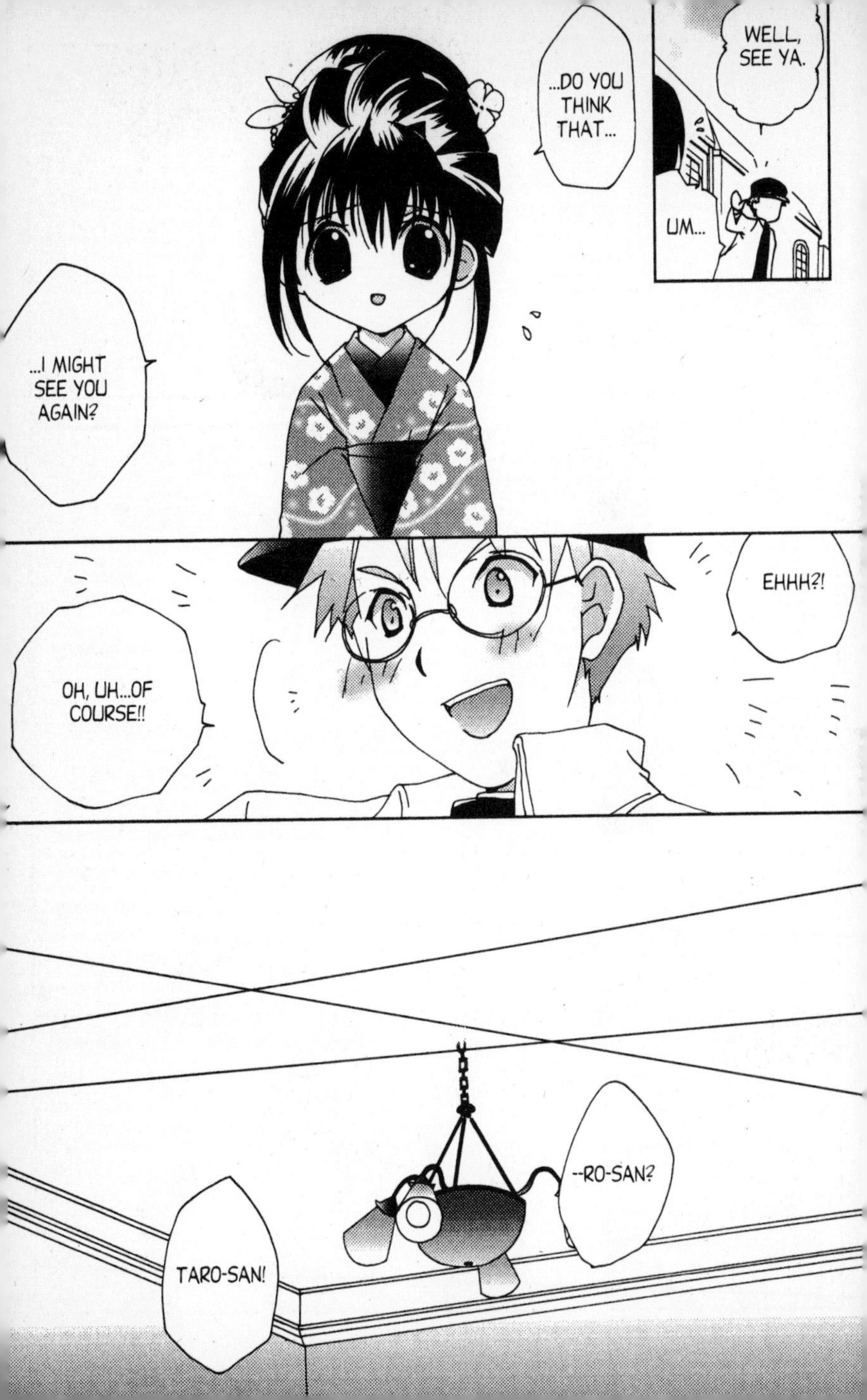
WELL, SEE YA.
UM...
...DO YOU THINK THAT...
...I MIGHT SEE YOU AGAIN?
EHHH?!
OH, UH...OF COURSE!!
--RO-SAN?
TARO-SAN!

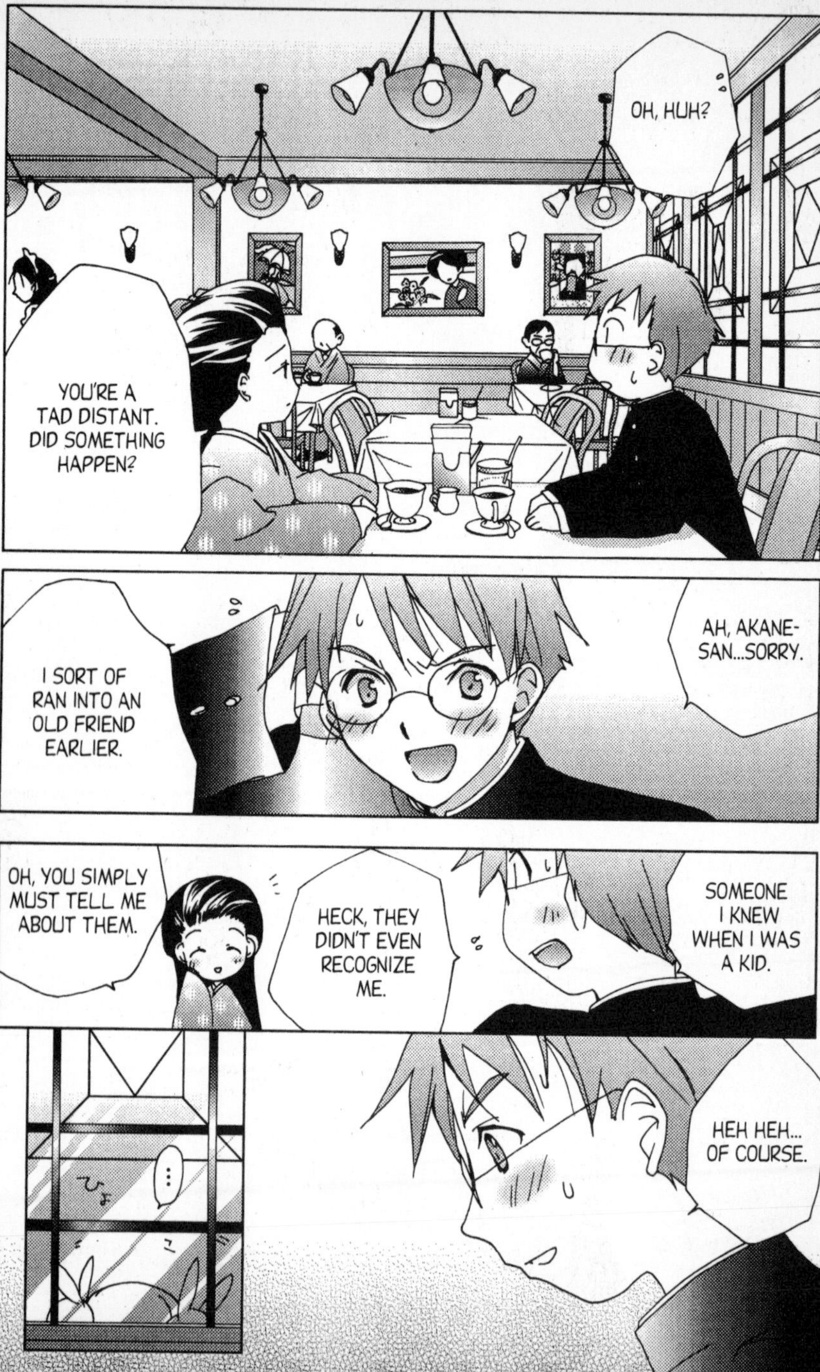
OH, HUH?
YOU'RE A TAD DISTANT. DID SOMETHING HAPPEN?
AH, AKANE-SAN...SORRY.
I SORT OF RAN INTO AN OLD FRIEND EARLIER.
SOMEONE I KNEW WHEN I WAS A KID.
HECK, THEY DIDN'T EVEN RECOGNIZE ME.
OH, YOU SIMPLY MUST TELL ME ABOUT THEM.
HEH HEH... OF COURSE.
...

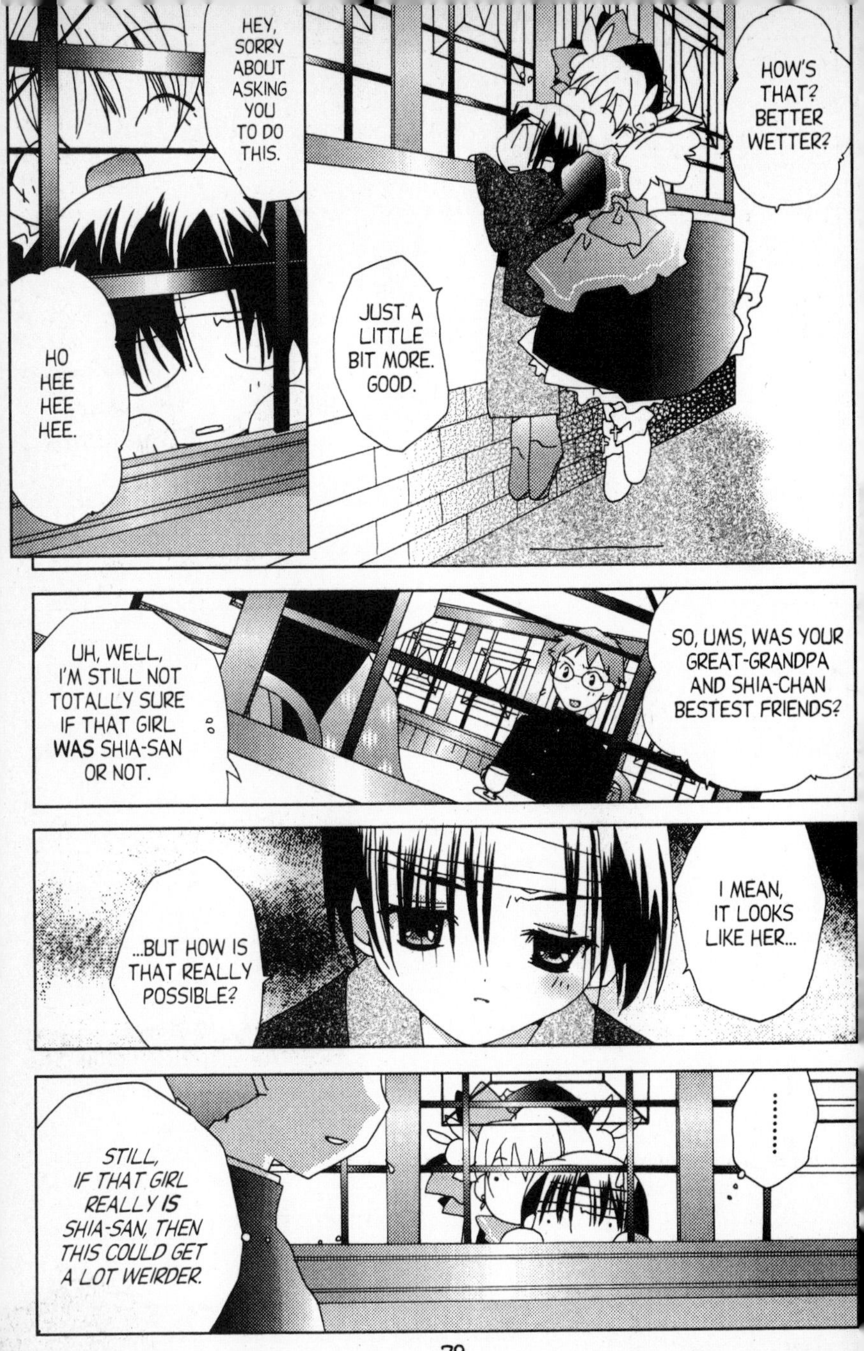
HOW'S THAT? BETTER WETTER?
HEY, SORRY ABOUT ASKING YOU TO DO THIS.
JUST A LITTLE BIT MORE. GOOD.
HO HEE HEE HEE.
SO, UMS, WAS YOUR GREAT-GRANDPA AND SHIA-CHAN BESTEST FRIENDS?
UH, WELL, I'M STILL NOT TOTALLY SURE IF THAT GIRL WAS SHIA-SAN OR NOT.
I MEAN, IT LOOKS LIKE HER...
...BUT HOW IS THAT REALLY POSSIBLE?
......
STILL, IF THAT GIRL REALLY IS SHIA-SAN, THEN THIS COULD GET A LOT WEIRDER.

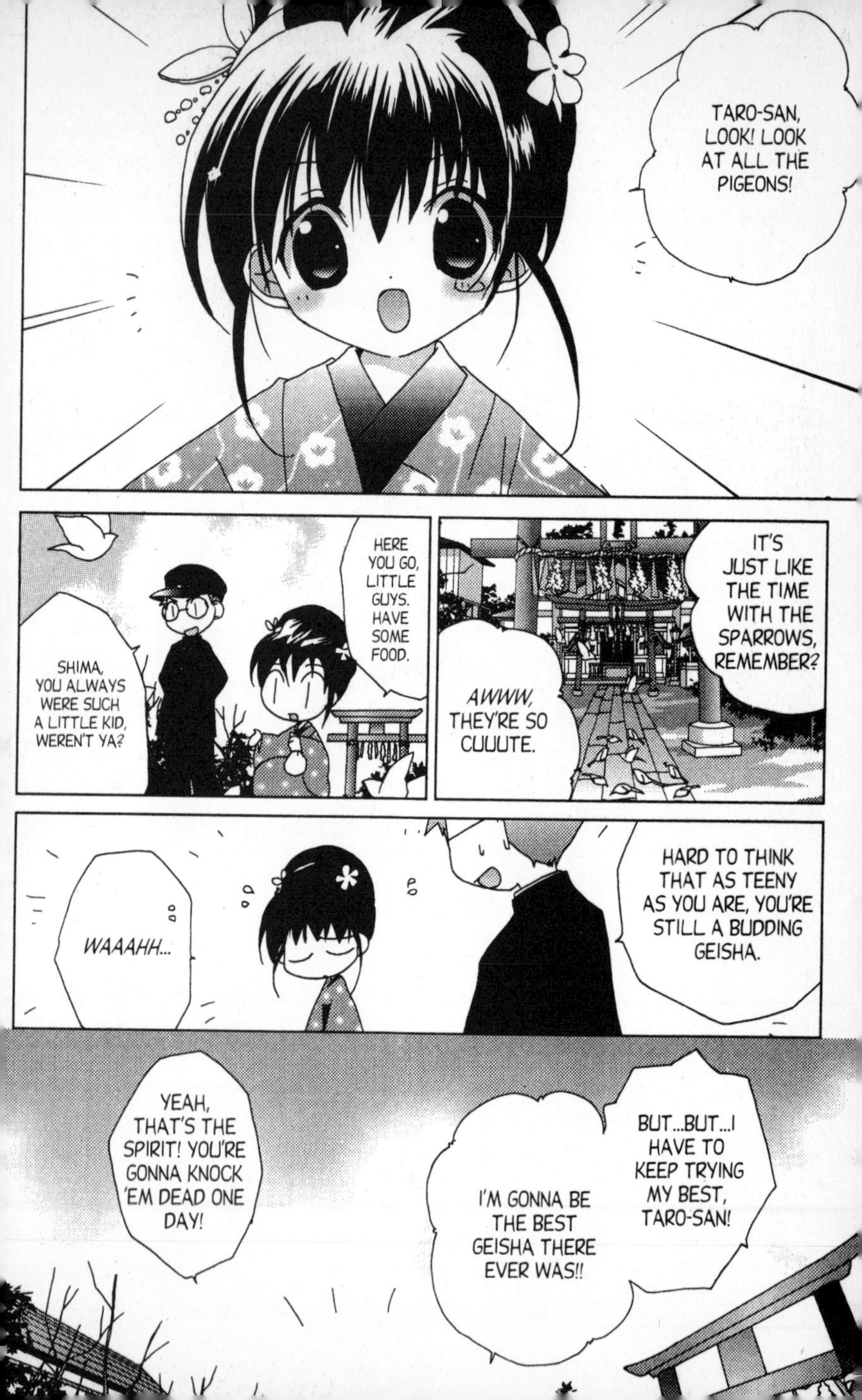
TARO-SAN, LOOK! LOOK AT ALL THE PIGEONS!
IT'S JUST LIKE THE TIME WITH THE SPARROWS, REMEMBER?
AWWW, THEY'RE SO CUUUTE.
HERE YOU GO, LITTLE GUYS. HAVE SOME FOOD.
SHIMA, YOU ALWAYS WERE SUCH A LITTLE KID, WEREN'T YA?
HARD TO THINK THAT AS TEENY AS YOU ARE, YOU'RE STILL A BUDDING GEISHA.
WAAAHH...
BUT...BUT...I HAVE TO KEEP TRYING MY BEST, TARO-SAN!
I'M GONNA BE THE BEST GEISHA THERE EVER WAS!!
YEAH, THAT'S THE SPIRIT! YOU'RE GONNA KNOCK 'EM DEAD ONE DAY!

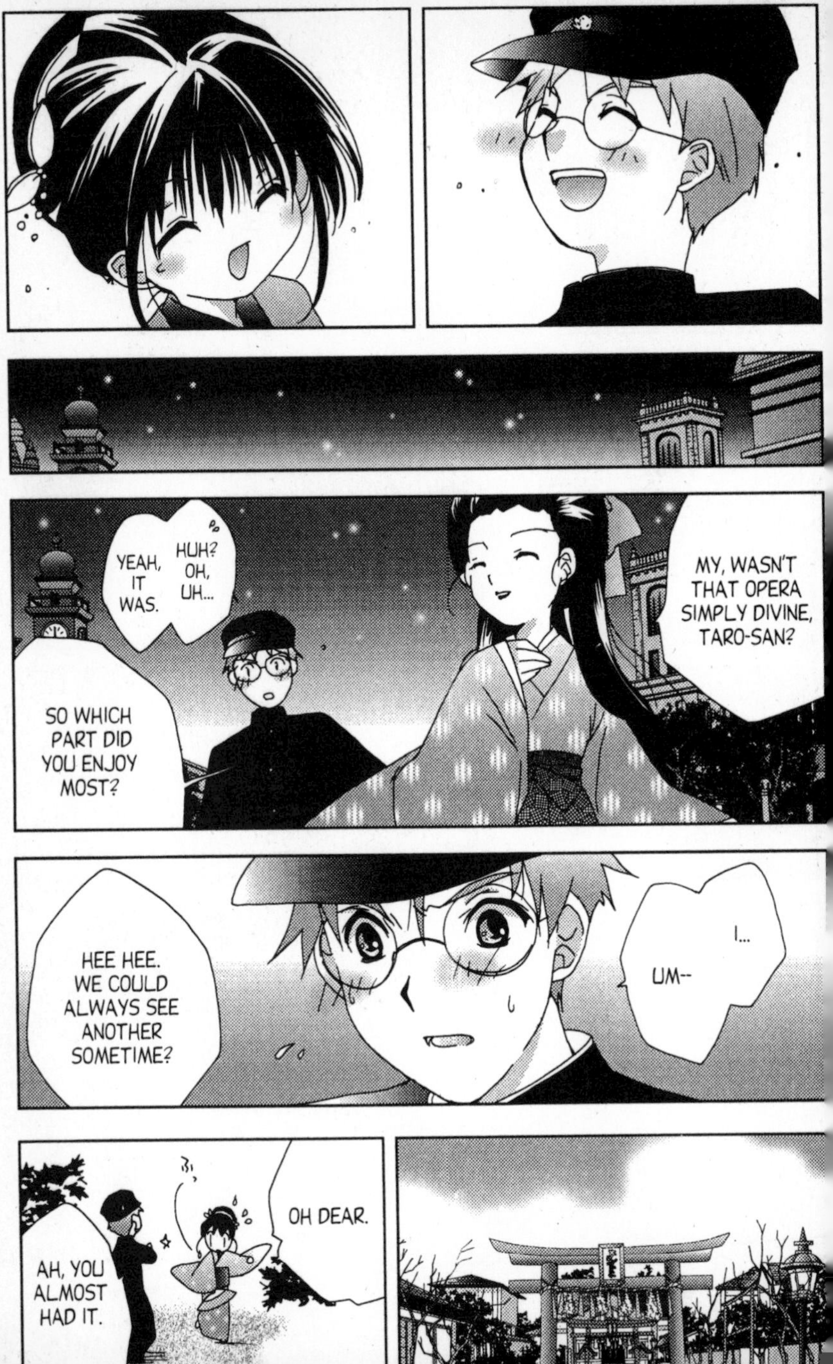
MY, WASN'T THAT OPERA SIMPLY DIVINE, TARO-SAN?
HUH? OH, UH...
YEAH, IT WAS.
SO WHICH PART DID YOU ENJOY MOST?
I... UM--
HEE HEE. WE COULD ALWAYS SEE ANOTHER SOMETIME?
OH DEAR.
AH, YOU ALMOST HAD IT.

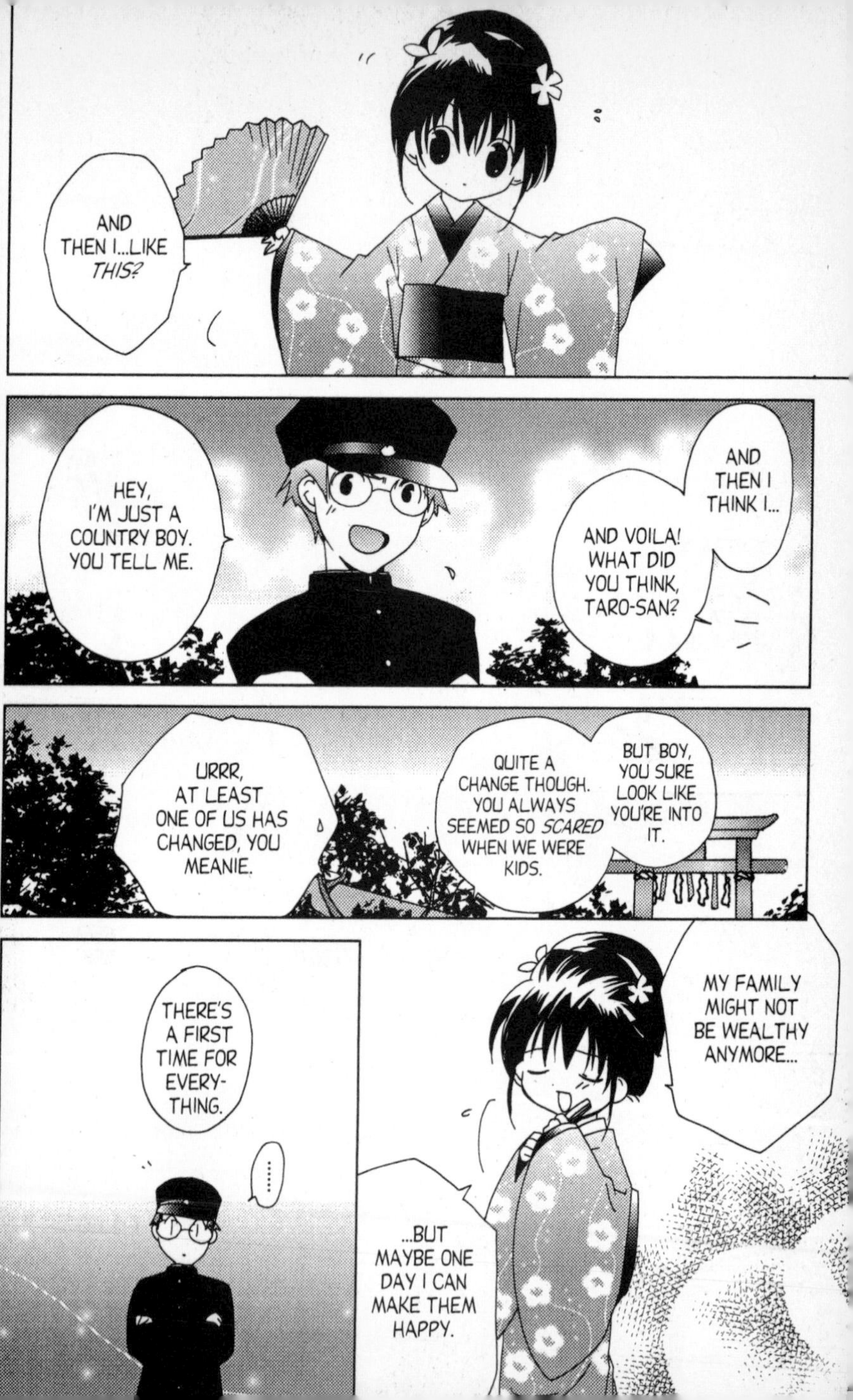
AND THEN I...LIKE *THIS?*
AND THEN I THINK I...
AND VOILA! WHAT DID YOU THINK, TARO-SAN?
HEY, I'M JUST A COUNTRY BOY. YOU TELL ME.
BUT BOY, YOU SURE LOOK LIKE YOU'RE INTO IT.
QUITE A CHANGE THOUGH. YOU ALWAYS SEEMED SO *SCARED* WHEN WE WERE KIDS.
URRR, AT LEAST ONE OF US HAS CHANGED, YOU MEANIE.
MY FAMILY MIGHT NOT BE WEALTHY ANYMORE...
...BUT MAYBE ONE DAY I CAN MAKE THEM HAPPY.
THERE'S A FIRST TIME FOR EVERY-THING.
......

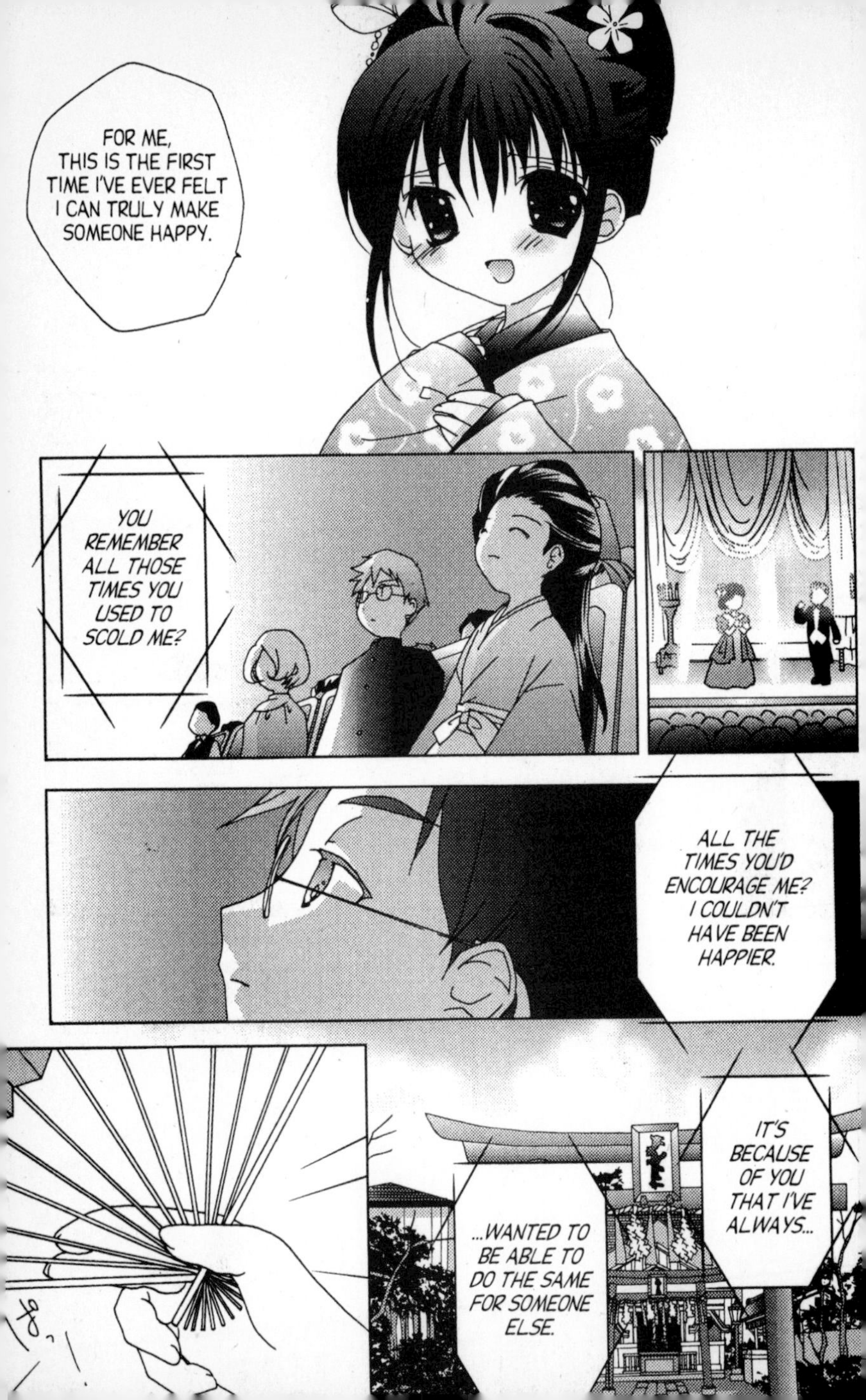
FOR ME, THIS IS THE FIRST TIME I'VE EVER FELT I CAN TRULY MAKE SOMEONE HAPPY.
YOU REMEMBER ALL THOSE TIMES YOU USED TO SCOLD ME?
ALL THE TIMES YOU'D ENCOURAGE ME? I COULDN'T HAVE BEEN HAPPIER.
IT'S BECAUSE OF YOU THAT I'VE ALWAYS...
...WANTED TO BE ABLE TO DO THE SAME FOR SOMEONE ELSE.

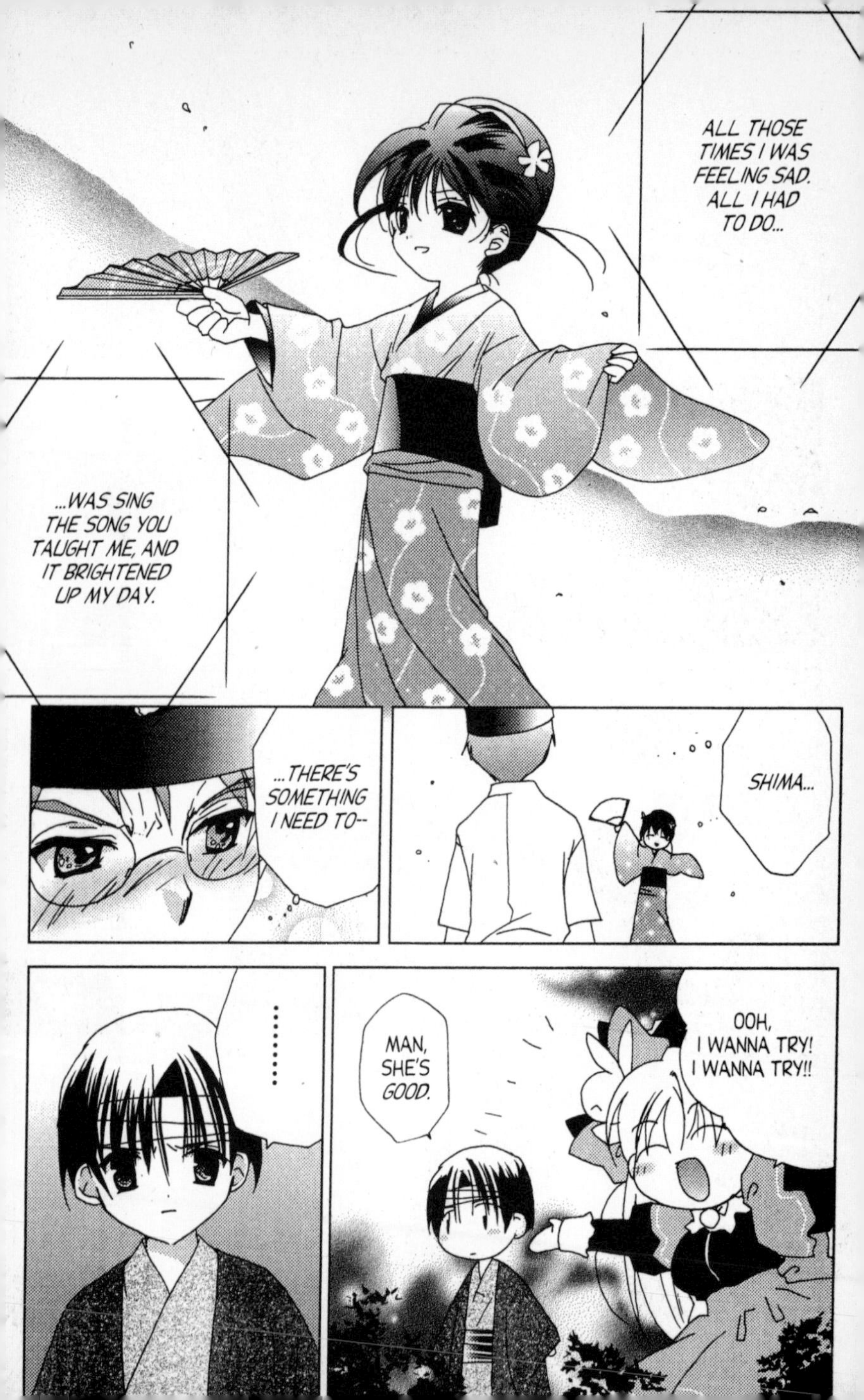
ALL THOSE TIMES I WAS FEELING SAD. ALL I HAD TO DO...
...WAS SING THE SONG YOU TAUGHT ME, AND IT BRIGHTENED UP MY DAY.
SHIMA...
...THERE'S SOMETHING I NEED TO--
OOH, I WANNA TRY! I WANNA TRY!!
MAN, SHE'S *GOOD.*
....

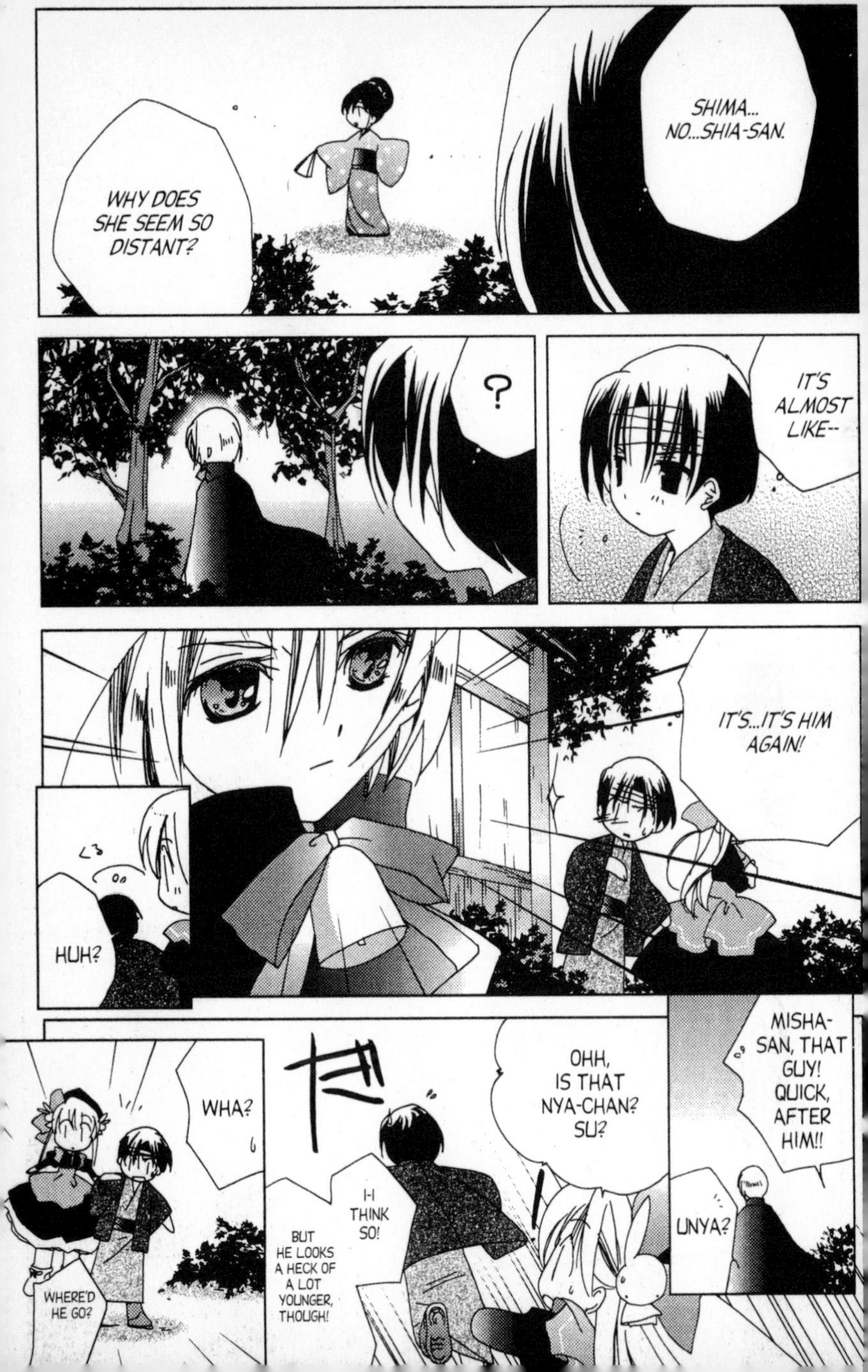
SHIMA...
NO...SHIA-SAN.
WHY DOES SHE SEEM SO DISTANT?
IT'S ALMOST LIKE--
?
IT'S...IT'S HIM AGAIN!
HUH?
MISHA-SAN, THAT GUY! QUICK, AFTER HIM!!
UNYA?
OHH, IS THAT NYA-CHAN? SU?
I-I THINK SO!
BUT HE LOOKS A HECK OF A LOT YOUNGER, THOUGH!
WHA?
WHERE'D HE GO?

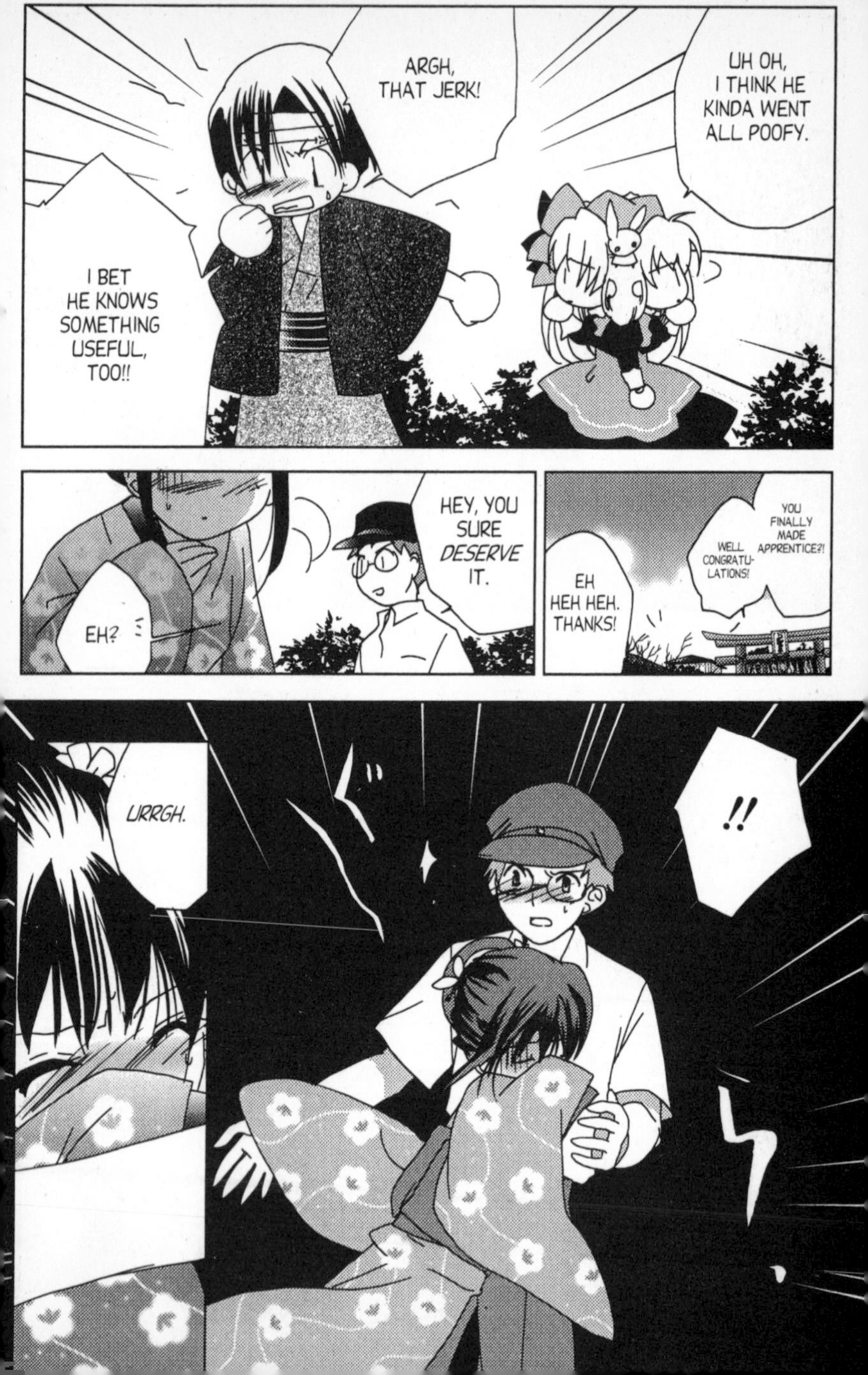
UH OH, I THINK HE KINDA WENT ALL POOFY.
ARGH, THAT JERK!
I BET HE KNOWS SOMETHING USEFUL, TOO!!
YOU FINALLY MADE APPRENTICE?!
WELL CONGRATU-LATIONS!
EH HEH HEH. THANKS!
HEY, YOU SURE *DESERVE* IT.
EH?
!!
URRGH.

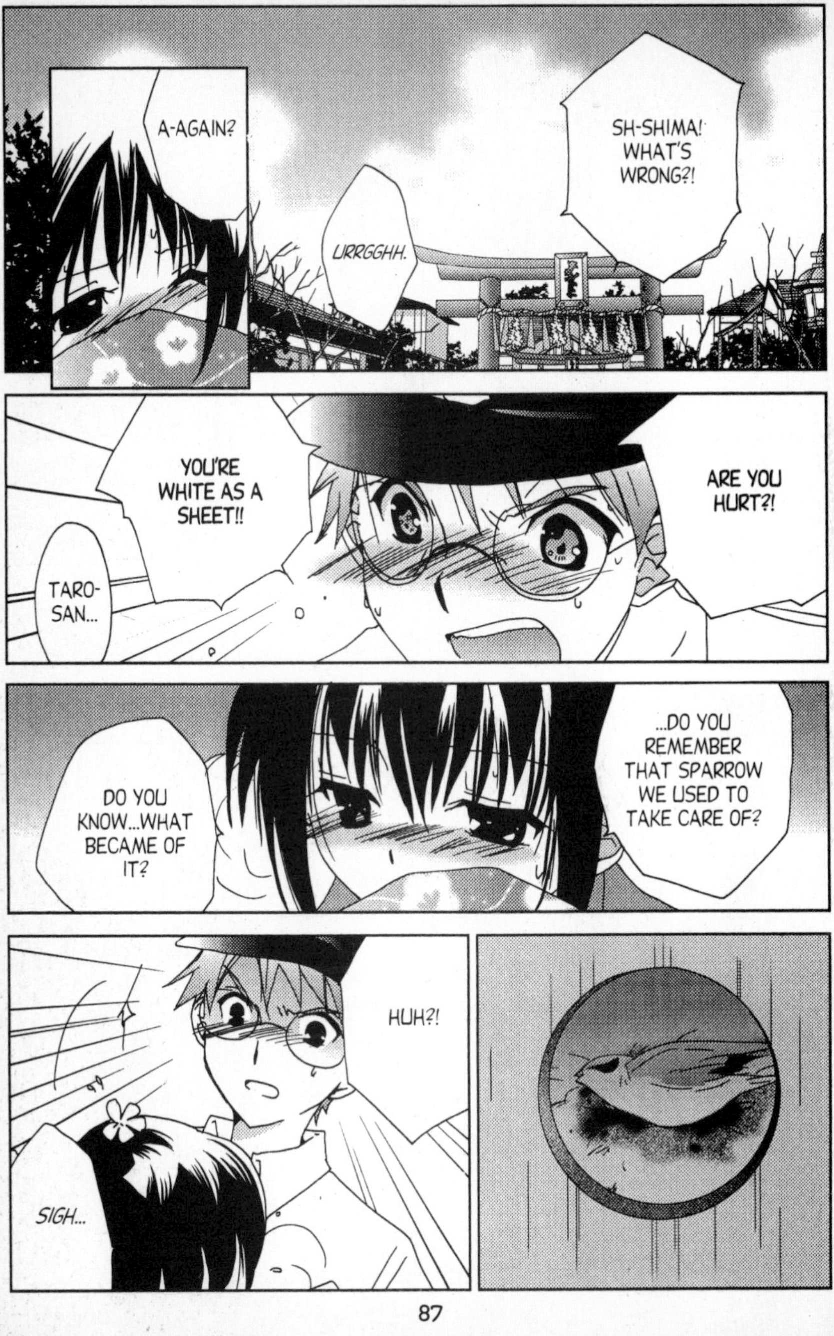
SH-SHIMA! WHAT'S WRONG?!
URRGGHH.
A-AGAIN?
ARE YOU HURT?!
YOU'RE WHITE AS A SHEET!!
TARO-SAN...
...DO YOU REMEMBER THAT SPARROW WE USED TO TAKE CARE OF?
DO YOU KNOW...WHAT BECAME OF IT?
HUH?!
SIGH...

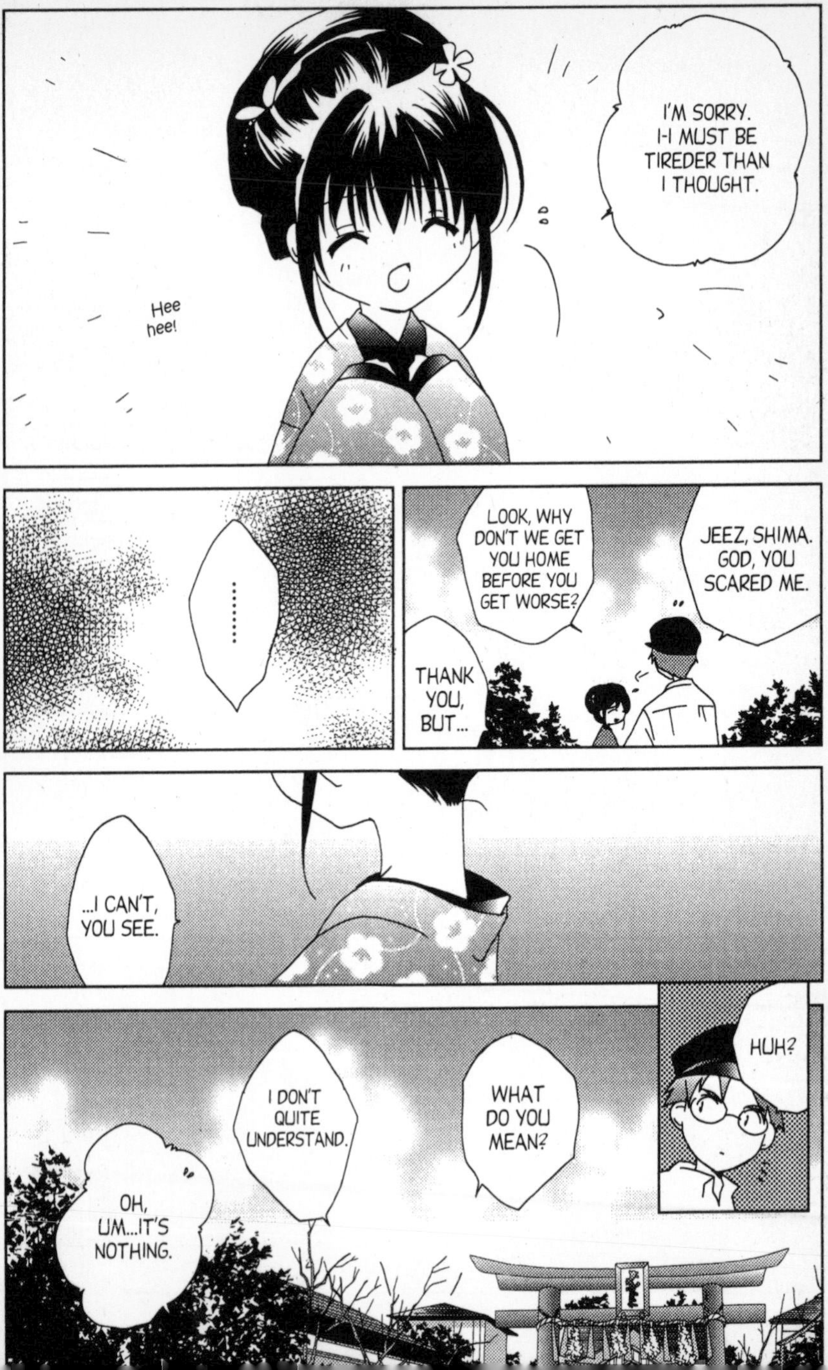
I'M SORRY. I-I MUST BE TIREDER THAN I THOUGHT.
Hee hee!
JEEZ, SHIMA. GOD, YOU SCARED ME.
LOOK, WHY DON'T WE GET YOU HOME BEFORE YOU GET WORSE?
THANK YOU, BUT...
....
...I CAN'T, YOU SEE.
HUH?
WHAT DO YOU MEAN?
I DON'T QUITE UNDERSTAND.
OH, UM...IT'S NOTHING.

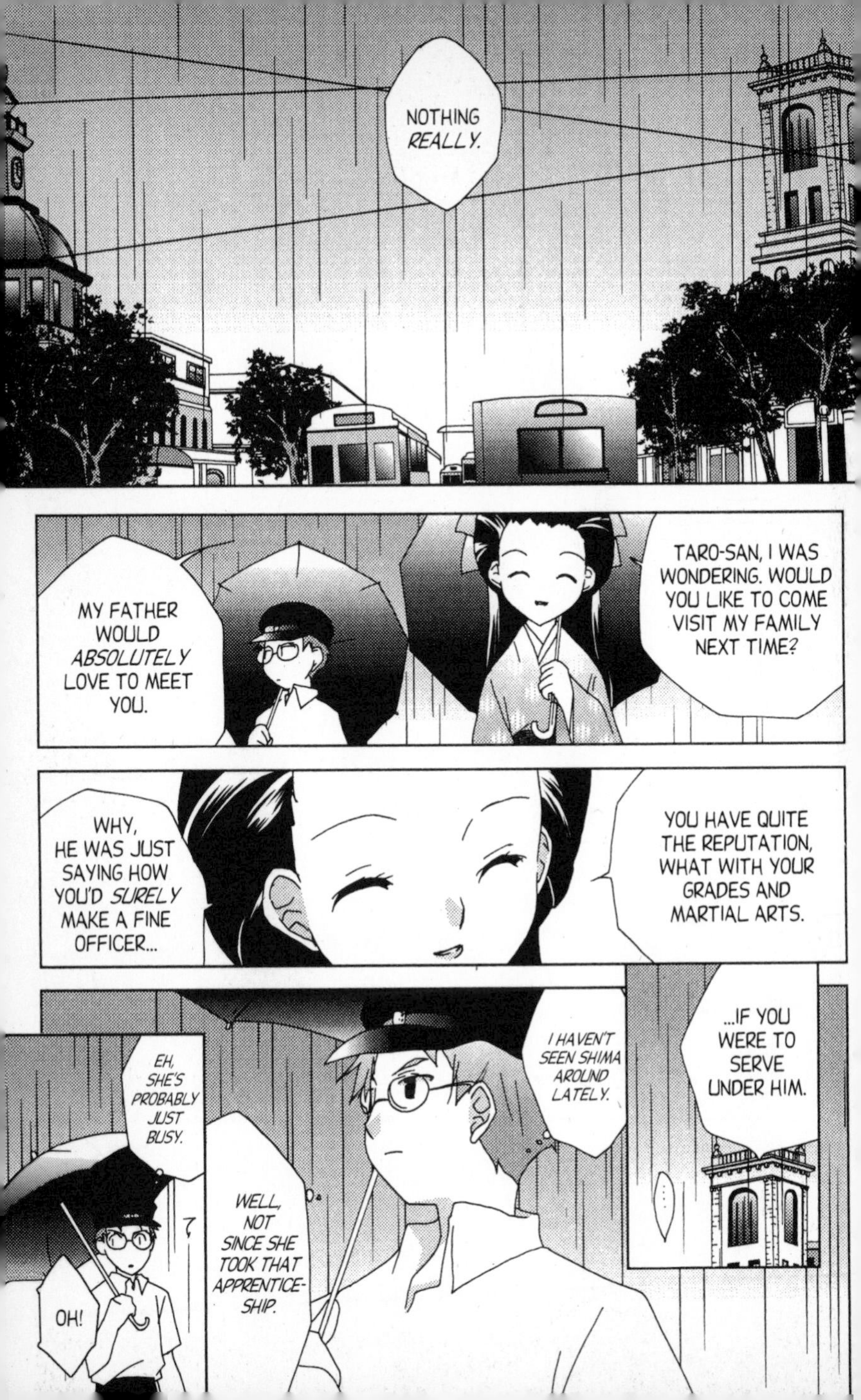

NOTHING REALLY.
TARO-SAN, I WAS WONDERING. WOULD YOU LIKE TO COME VISIT MY FAMILY NEXT TIME?
MY FATHER WOULD ABSOLUTELY LOVE TO MEET YOU.
YOU HAVE QUITE THE REPUTATION, WHAT WITH YOUR GRADES AND MARTIAL ARTS.
WHY, HE WAS JUST SAYING HOW YOU'D SURELY MAKE A FINE OFFICER...
...IF YOU WERE TO SERVE UNDER HIM.
...
I HAVEN'T SEEN SHIMA AROUND LATELY.
EH, SHE'S PROBABLY JUST BUSY.
WELL, NOT SINCE SHE TOOK THAT APPRENTICE-SHIP.
OH!

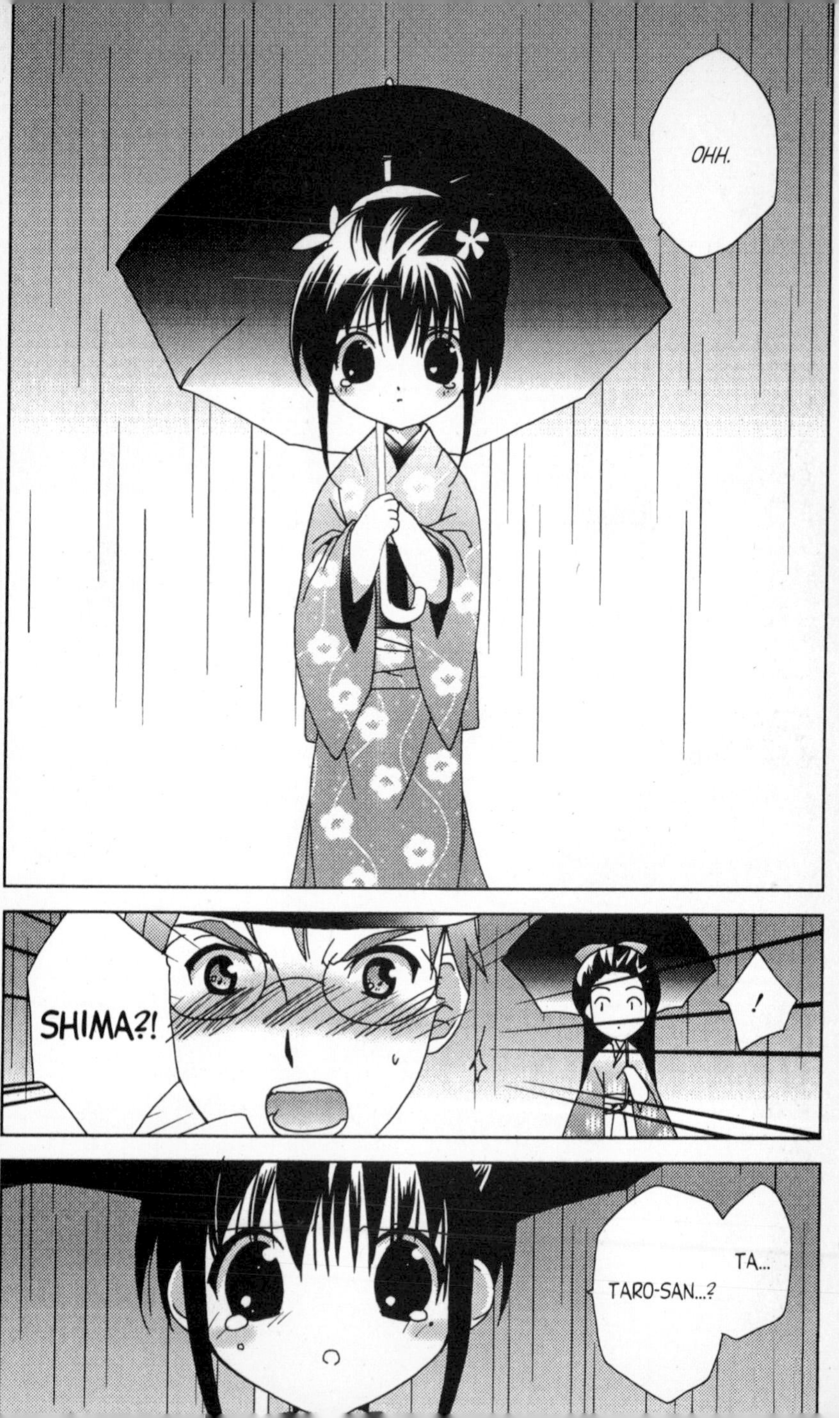
OHH.
!
SHIMA?!
TA... TARO-SAN...?

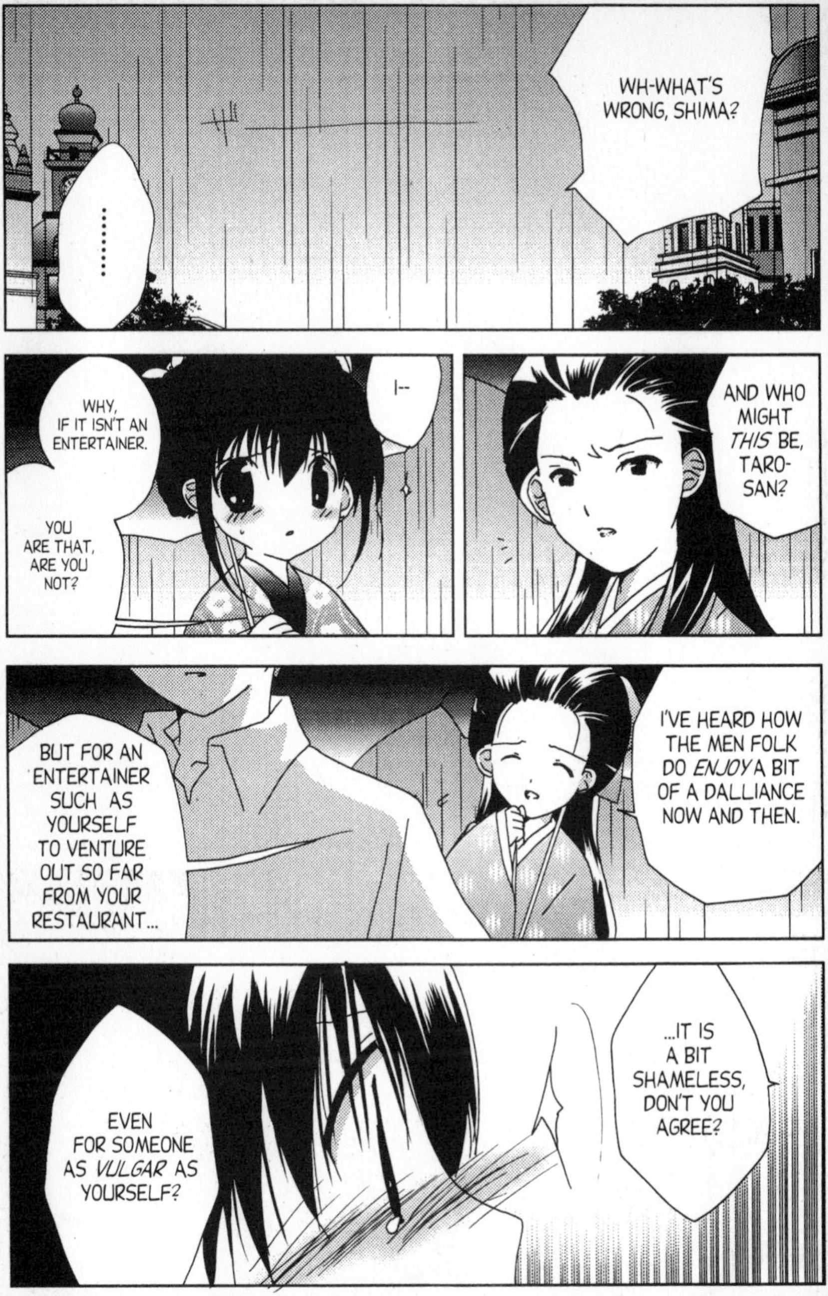
WH-WHAT'S WRONG, SHIMA?
......
AND WHO MIGHT *THIS* BE, TARO-SAN?
I--
WHY, IF IT ISN'T AN ENTERTAINER.
YOU ARE THAT, ARE YOU NOT?
I'VE HEARD HOW THE MEN FOLK DO *ENJOY* A BIT OF A DALLIANCE NOW AND THEN.
BUT FOR AN ENTERTAINER SUCH AS YOURSELF TO VENTURE OUT SO FAR FROM YOUR RESTAURANT...
...IT IS A BIT SHAMELESS, DON'T YOU AGREE?
EVEN FOR SOMEONE AS *VULGAR* AS YOURSELF?

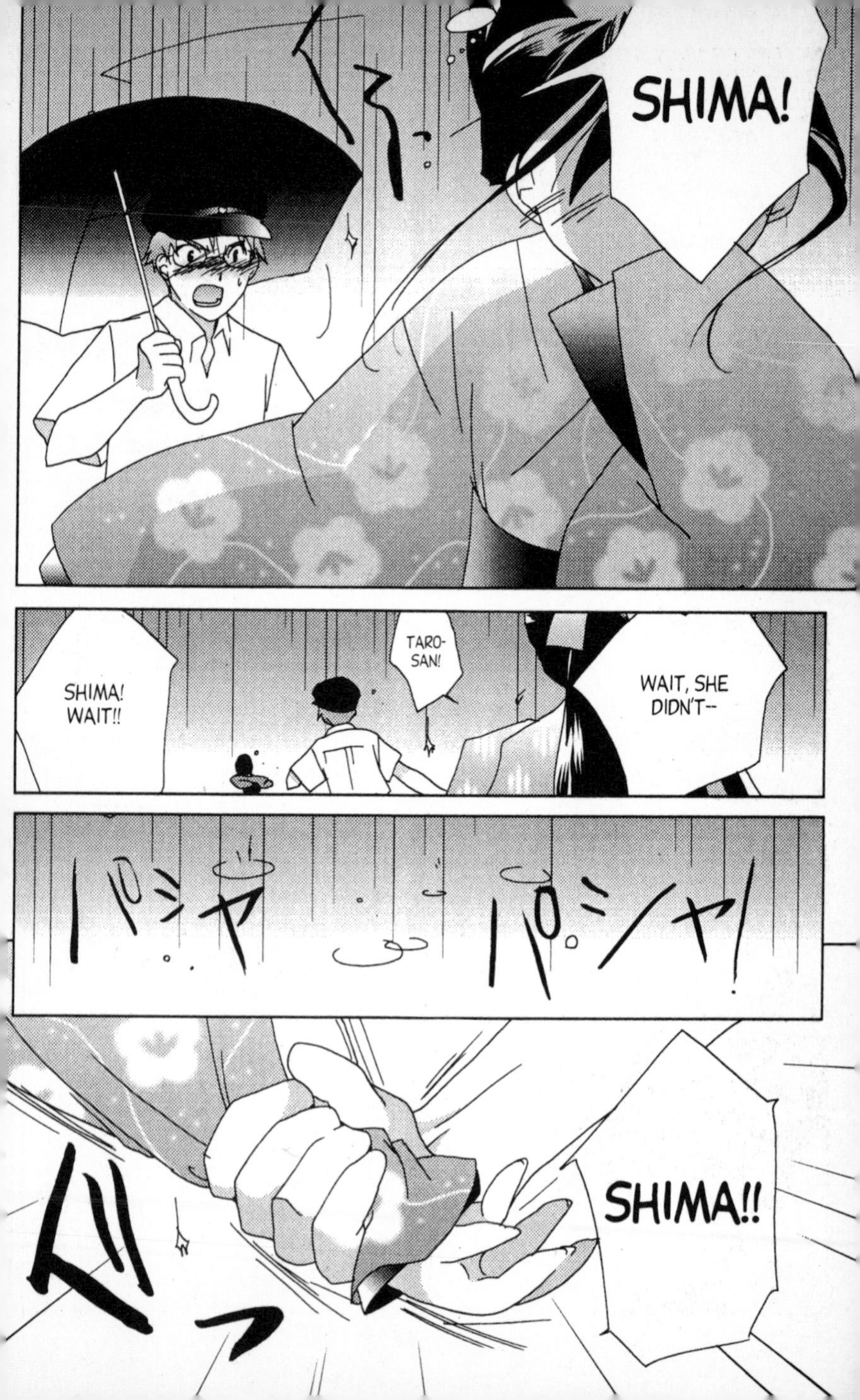
SHIMA!
WAIT, SHE DIDN'T--
TARO-SAN!
SHIMA! WAIT!!
SHIMA!!

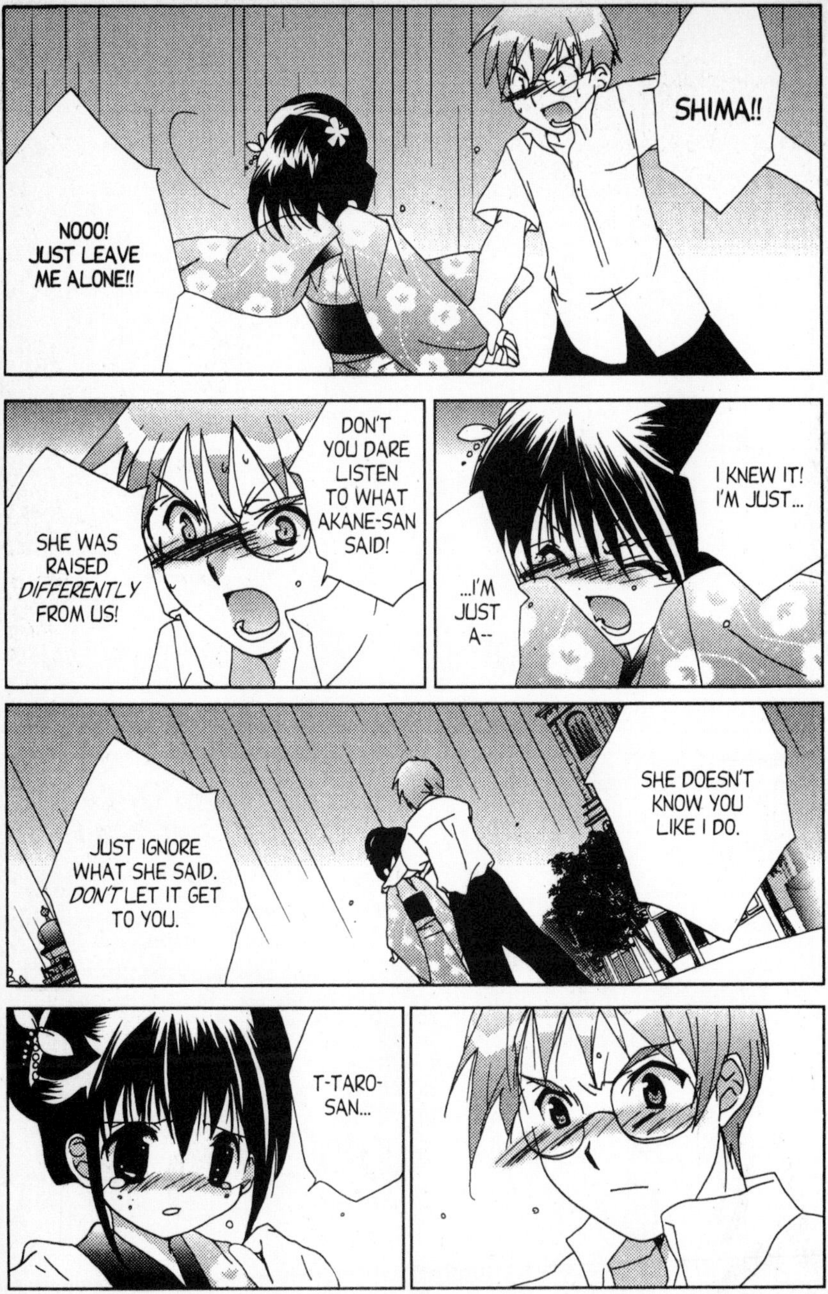
SHIMA!!
NOOO! JUST LEAVE ME ALONE!!
I KNEW IT! I'M JUST...
...I'M JUST A--
DON'T YOU DARE LISTEN TO WHAT AKANE-SAN SAID!
SHE WAS RAISED *DIFFERENTLY* FROM US!
SHE DOESN'T KNOW YOU LIKE I DO.
JUST IGNORE WHAT SHE SAID. *DON'T* LET IT GET TO YOU.
T-TARO-SAN...

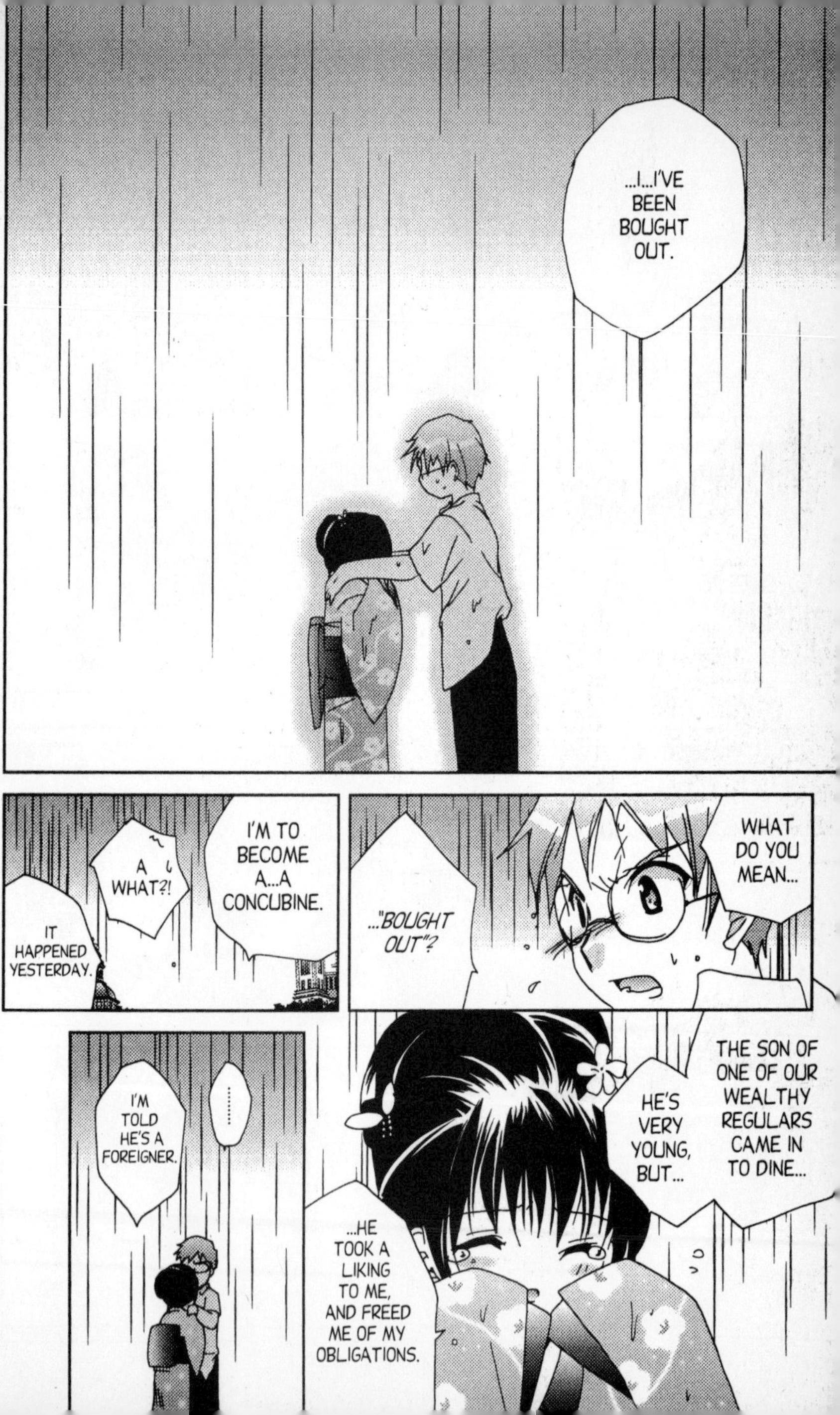
...I...I'VE BEEN BOUGHT OUT.
WHAT DO YOU MEAN...
..."BOUGHT OUT"?
I'M TO BECOME A...A CONCUBINE.
A WHAT?!
IT HAPPENED YESTERDAY.
THE SON OF ONE OF OUR WEALTHY REGULARS CAME IN TO DINE...
HE'S VERY YOUNG, BUT...
...HE TOOK A LIKING TO ME, AND FREED ME OF MY OBLIGATIONS.
......
I'M TOLD HE'S A FOREIGNER.

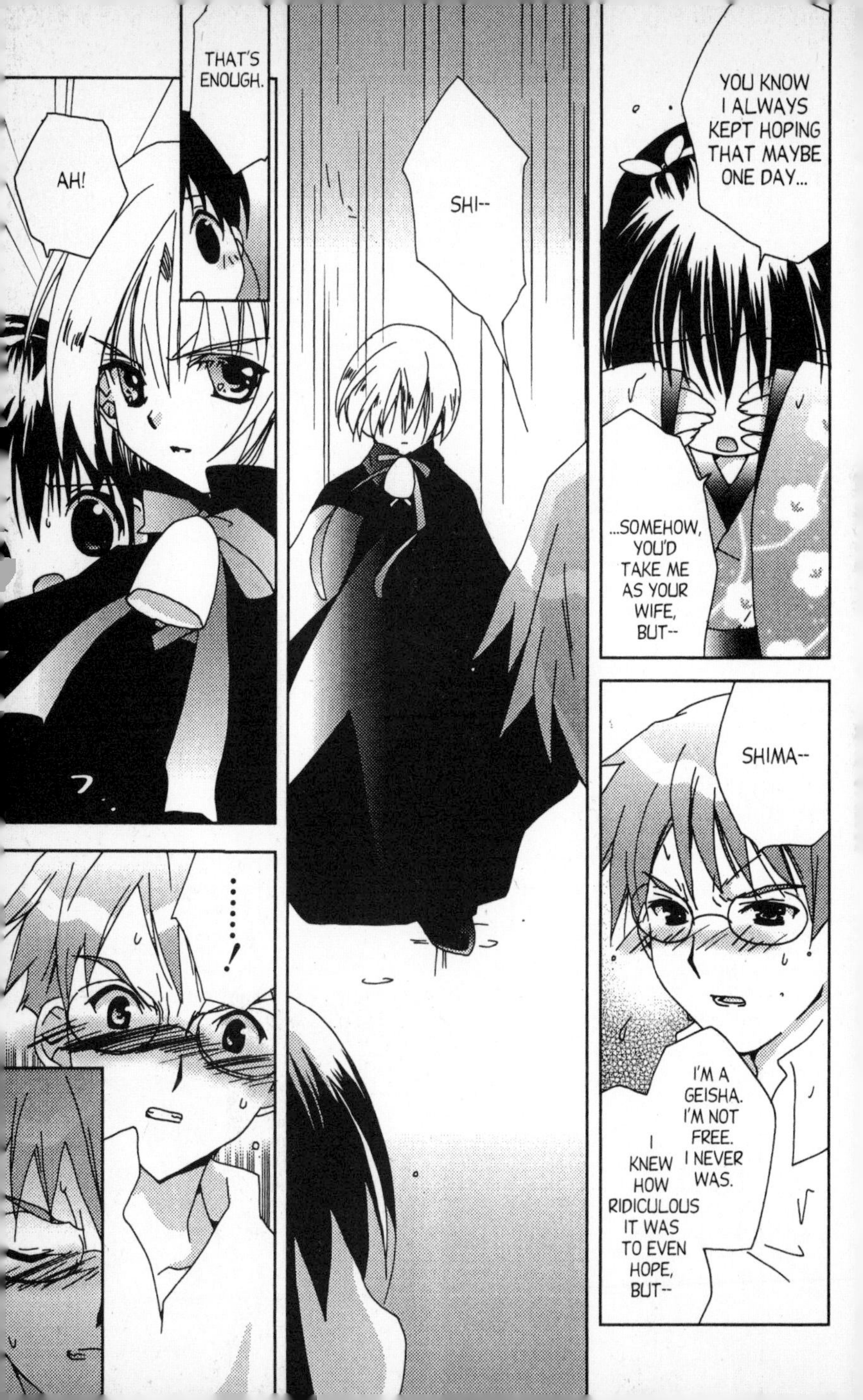
YOU KNOW I ALWAYS KEPT HOPING THAT MAYBE ONE DAY...
...SOMEHOW, YOU'D TAKE ME AS YOUR WIFE, BUT--
SHIMA--
I'M A GEISHA. I'M NOT FREE. I NEVER WAS.
I KNEW HOW RIDICULOUS IT WAS TO EVEN HOPE, BUT--
SHI--
THAT'S ENOUGH.
AH!
......!

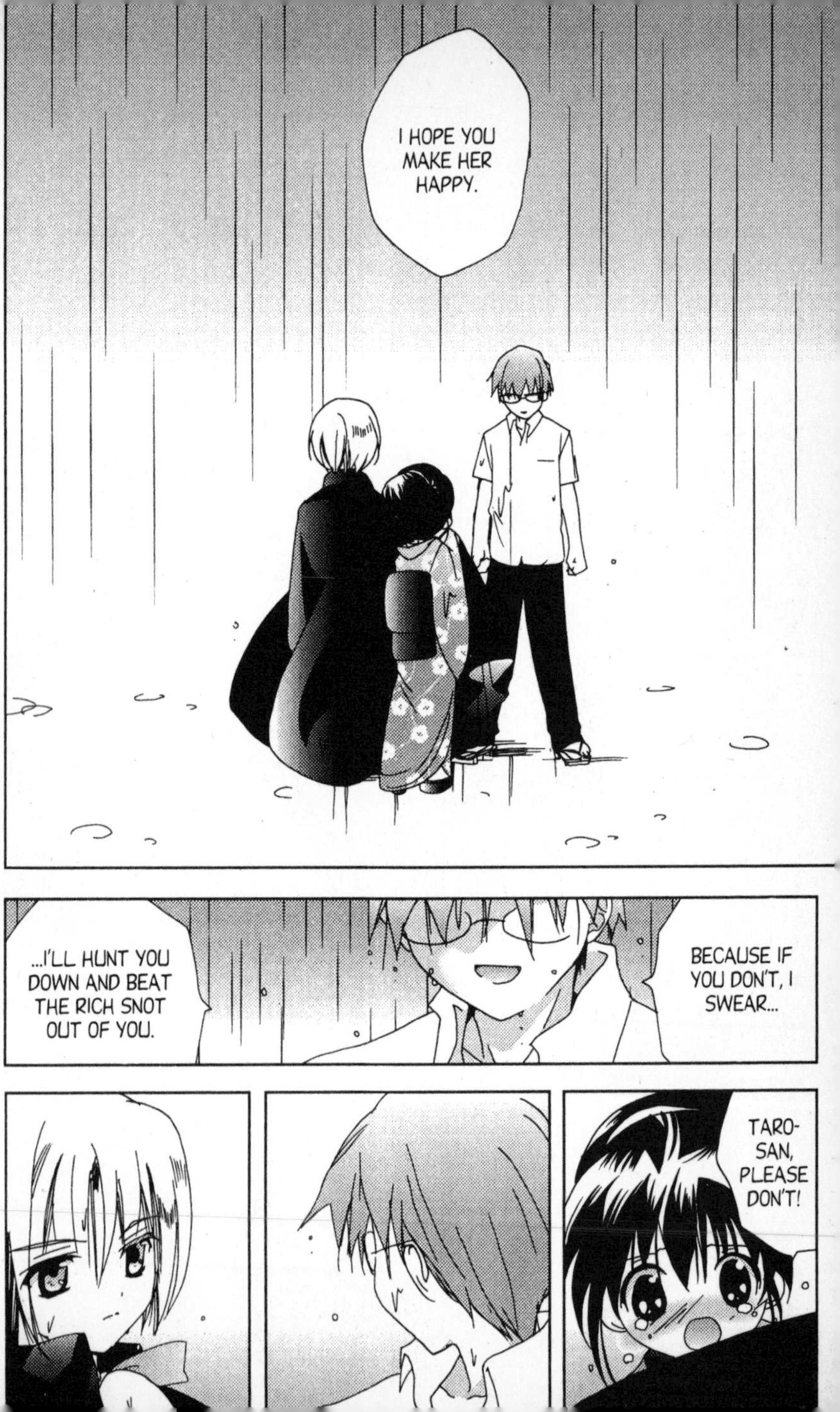
I HOPE YOU MAKE HER HAPPY.
BECAUSE IF YOU DON'T, I SWEAR...
...I'LL HUNT YOU DOWN AND BEAT THE RICH SNOT OUT OF YOU.
TARO-SAN, PLEASE DON'T!

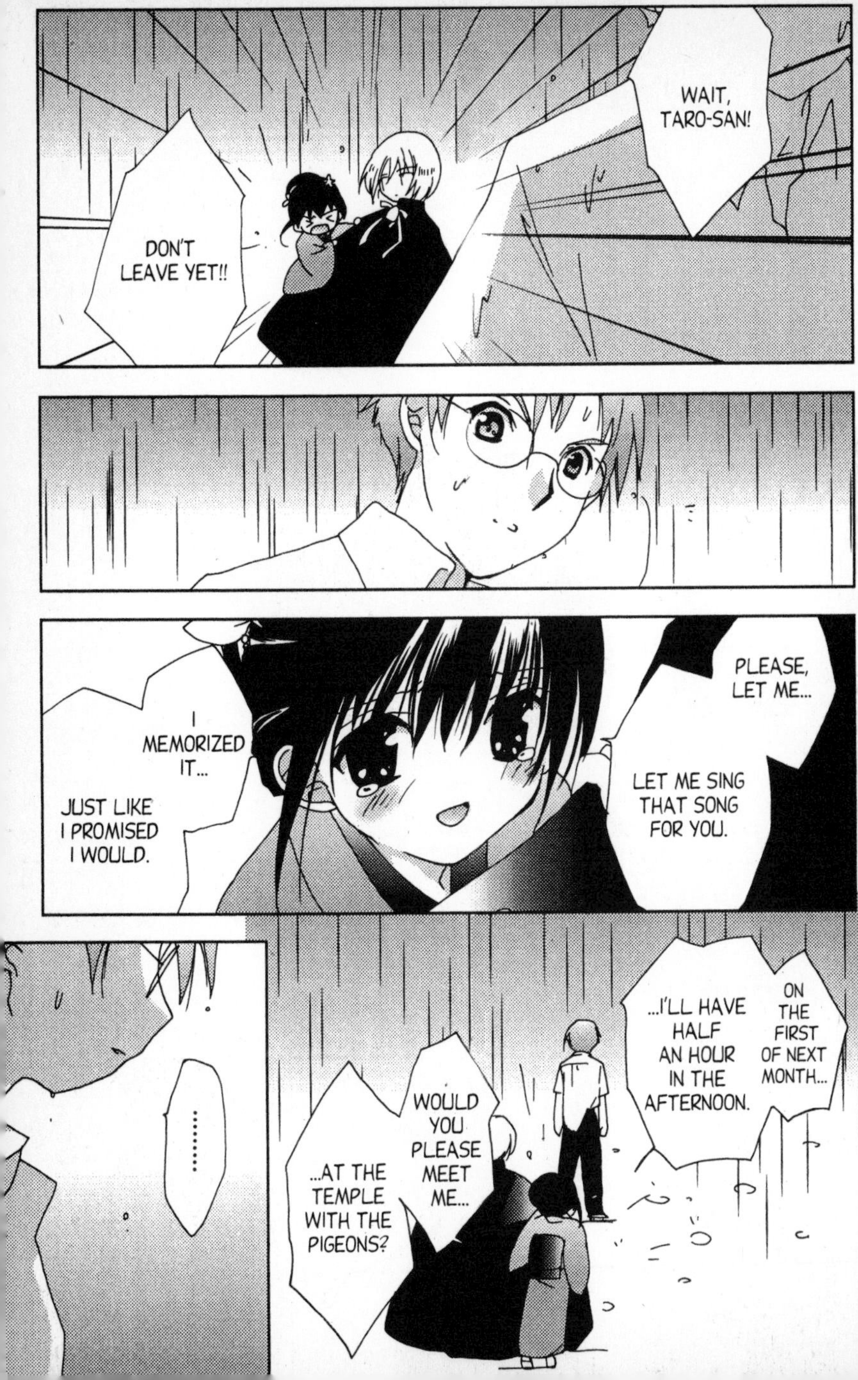
WAIT, TARO-SAN!
DON'T LEAVE YET!!
PLEASE, LET ME...
LET ME SING THAT SONG FOR YOU.
I MEMORIZED IT...
JUST LIKE I PROMISED I WOULD.
ON THE FIRST OF NEXT MONTH...
...I'LL HAVE HALF AN HOUR IN THE AFTERNOON.
WOULD YOU PLEASE MEET ME...
...AT THE TEMPLE WITH THE PIGEONS?
....

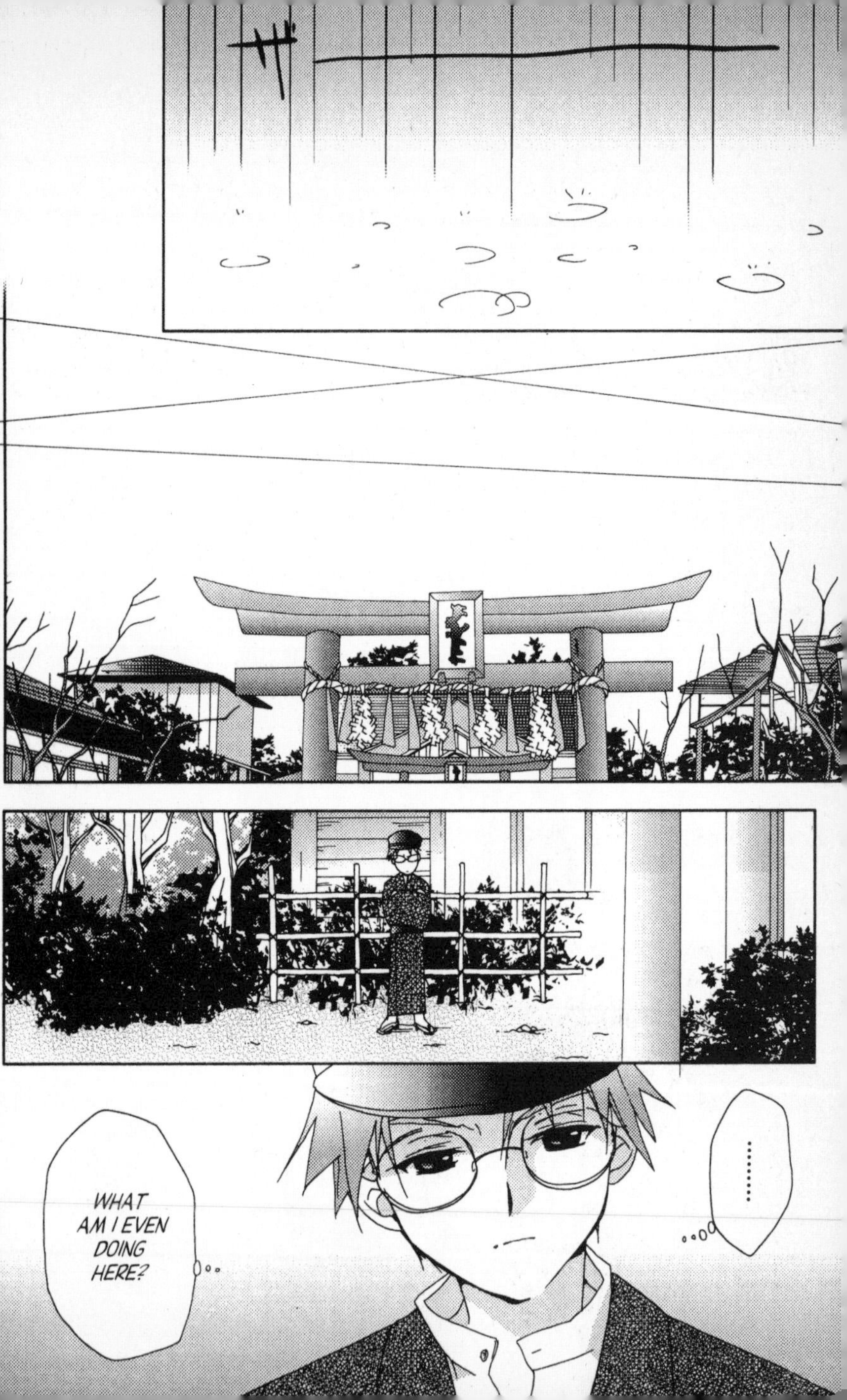
ザー
......
WHAT AM I EVEN DOING HERE?

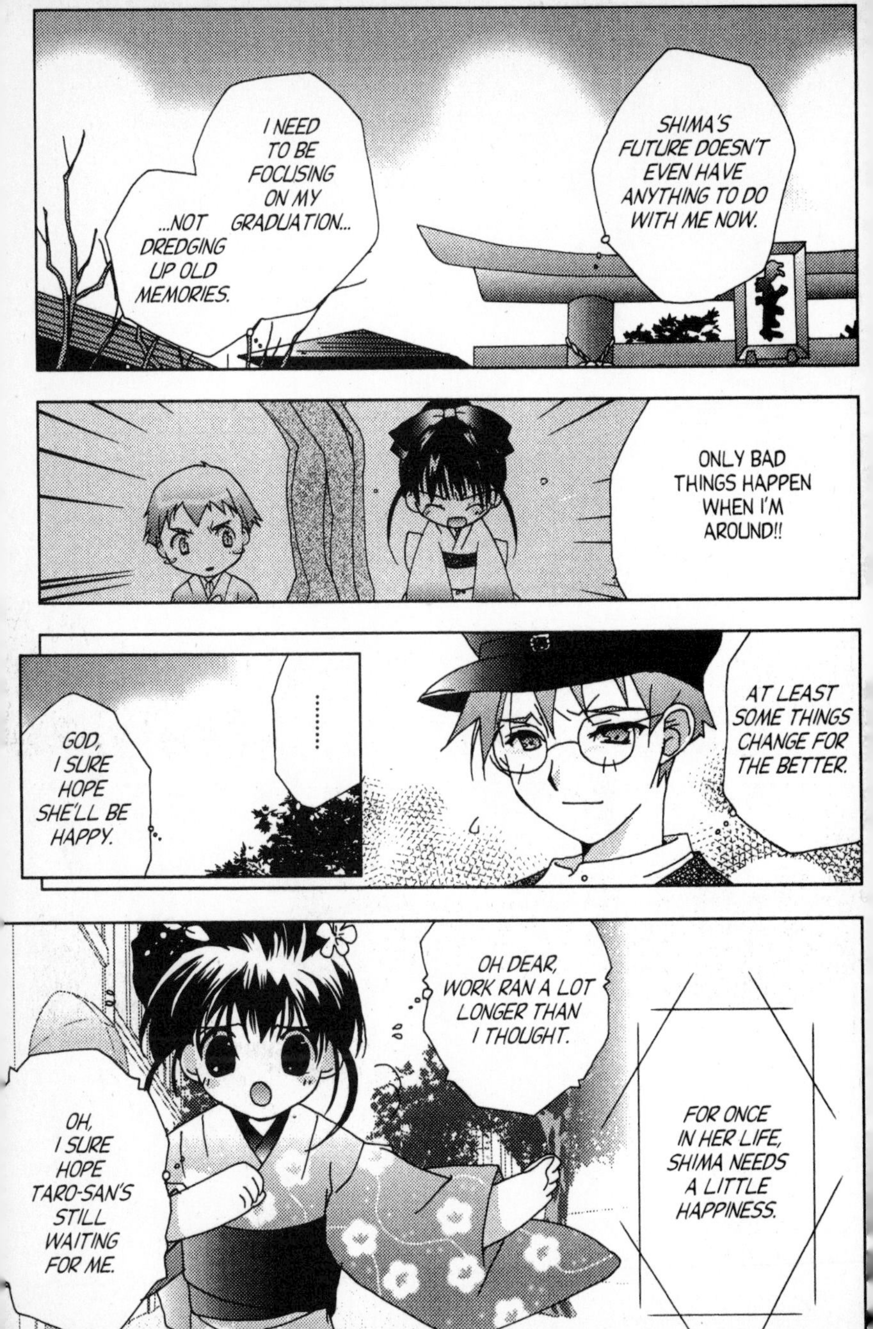
SHIMA'S FUTURE DOESN'T EVEN HAVE ANYTHING TO DO WITH ME NOW.
I NEED TO BE FOCUSING ON MY GRADUATION...
...NOT DREDGING UP OLD MEMORIES.
ONLY BAD THINGS HAPPEN WHEN I'M AROUND!!
AT LEAST SOME THINGS CHANGE FOR THE BETTER.
....
GOD, I SURE HOPE SHE'LL BE HAPPY.
FOR ONCE IN HER LIFE, SHIMA NEEDS A LITTLE HAPPINESS.
OH DEAR, WORK RAN A LOT LONGER THAN I THOUGHT.
OH, I SURE HOPE TARO-SAN'S STILL WAITING FOR ME.

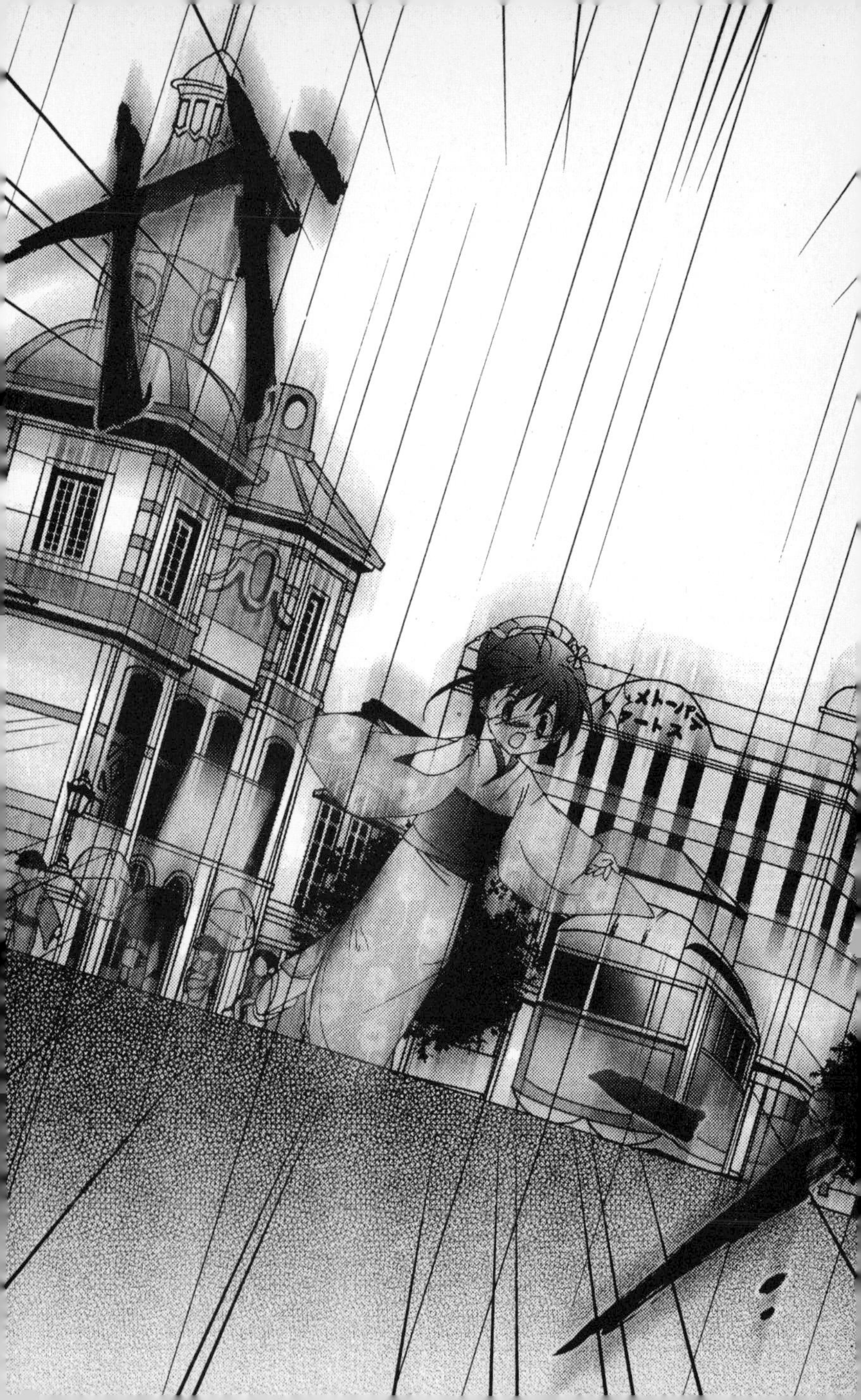

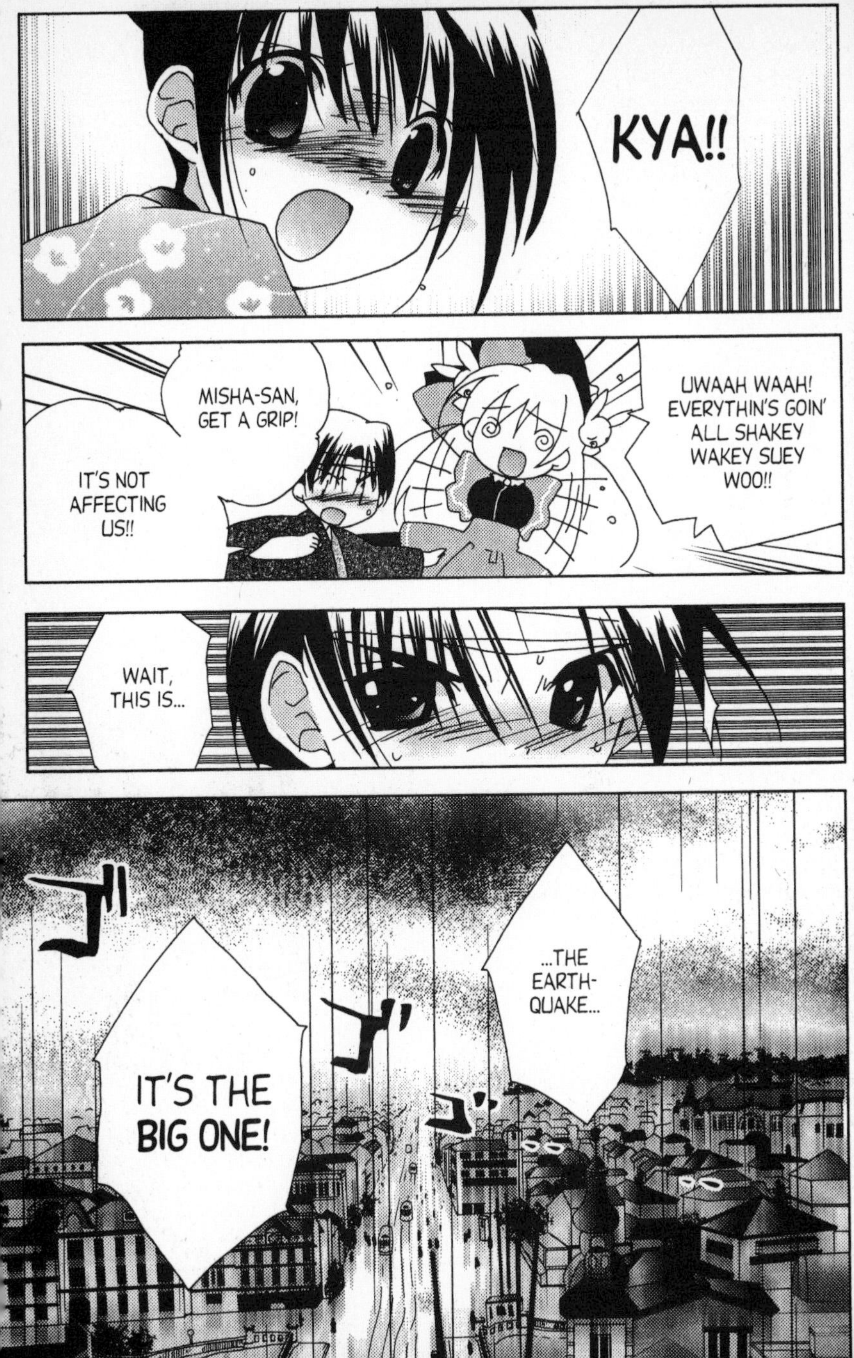
KYA!!
UWAAH WAAH! EVERYTHIN'S GOIN' ALL SHAKEY WAKEY SUEY WOO!!
MISHA-SAN, GET A GRIP!
IT'S NOT AFFECTING US!!
WAIT, THIS IS...
...THE EARTH-QUAKE...
IT'S THE BIG ONE!

Lesson 35
How to Find What You're Looking For: Part 3

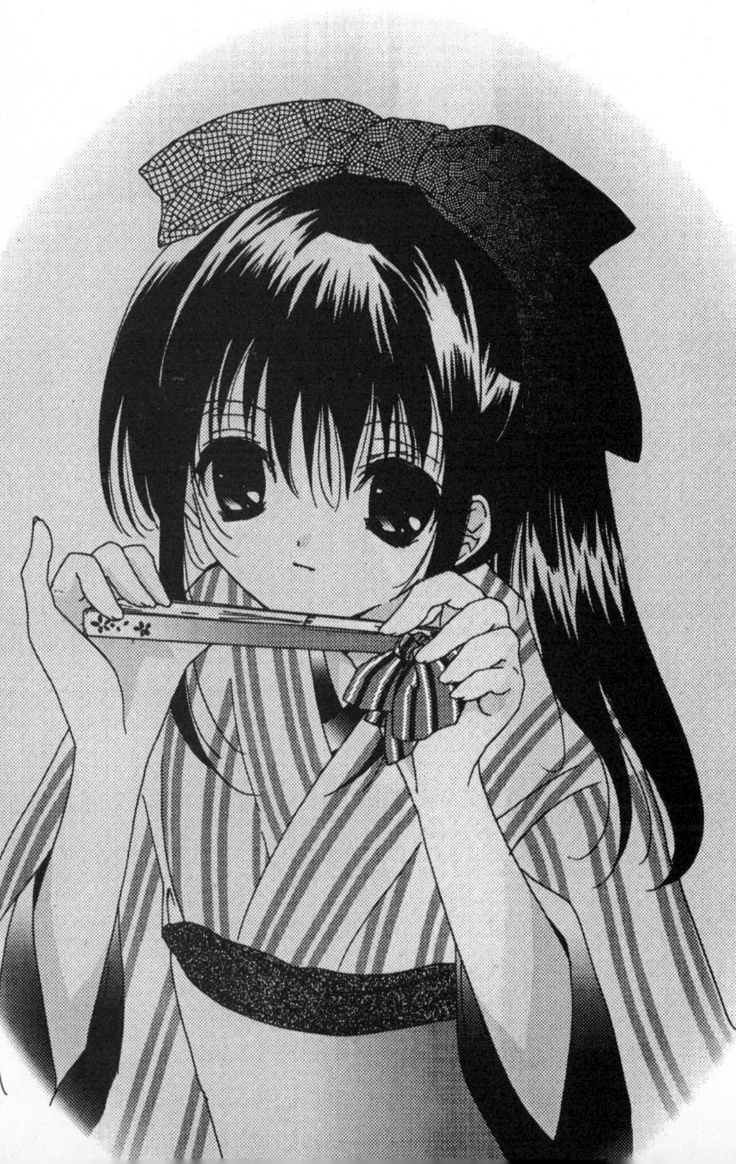

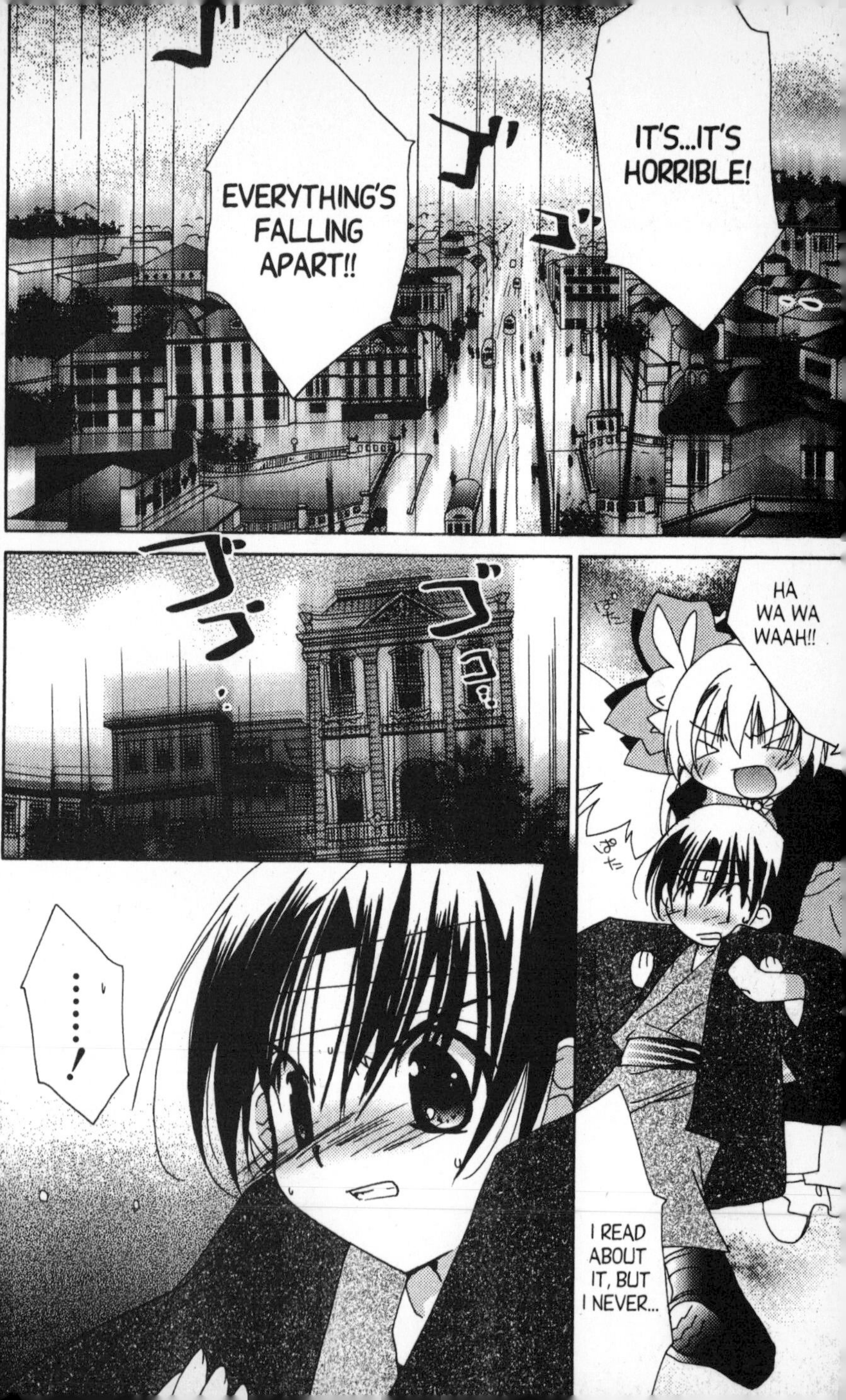
IT'S...IT'S HORRIBLE!
EVERYTHING'S FALLING APART!!
HA WA WA WAAH!!
I READ ABOUT IT, BUT I NEVER...
......!

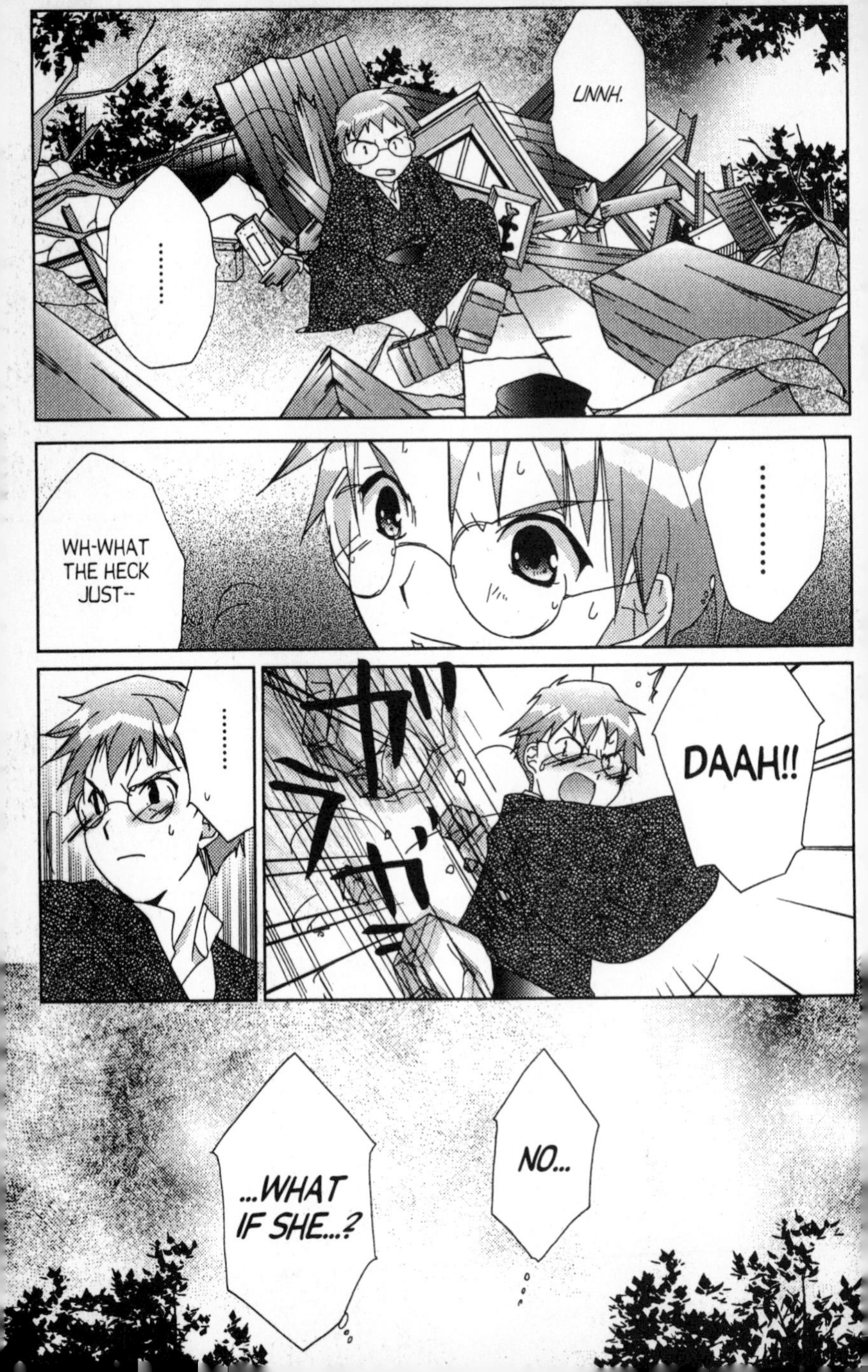
UNNH.
......
......
WH-WHAT THE HECK JUST--
DAAH!!
......
NO...
...WHAT IF SHE...?

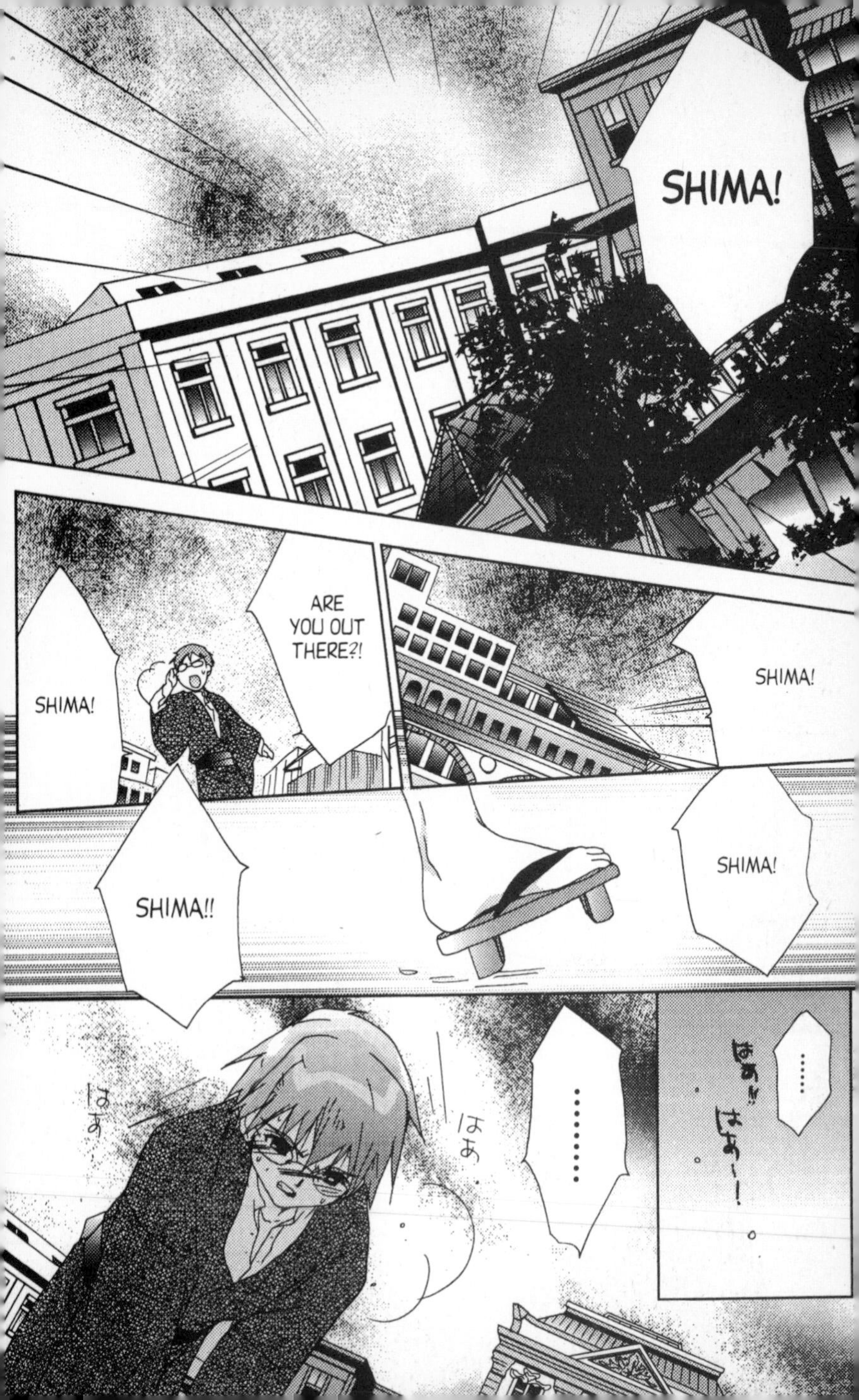

SHIMA!
SHIMA!
ARE YOU OUT THERE?!
SHIMA!
SHIMA!
SHIMA!!
……
………
はあ
はあ

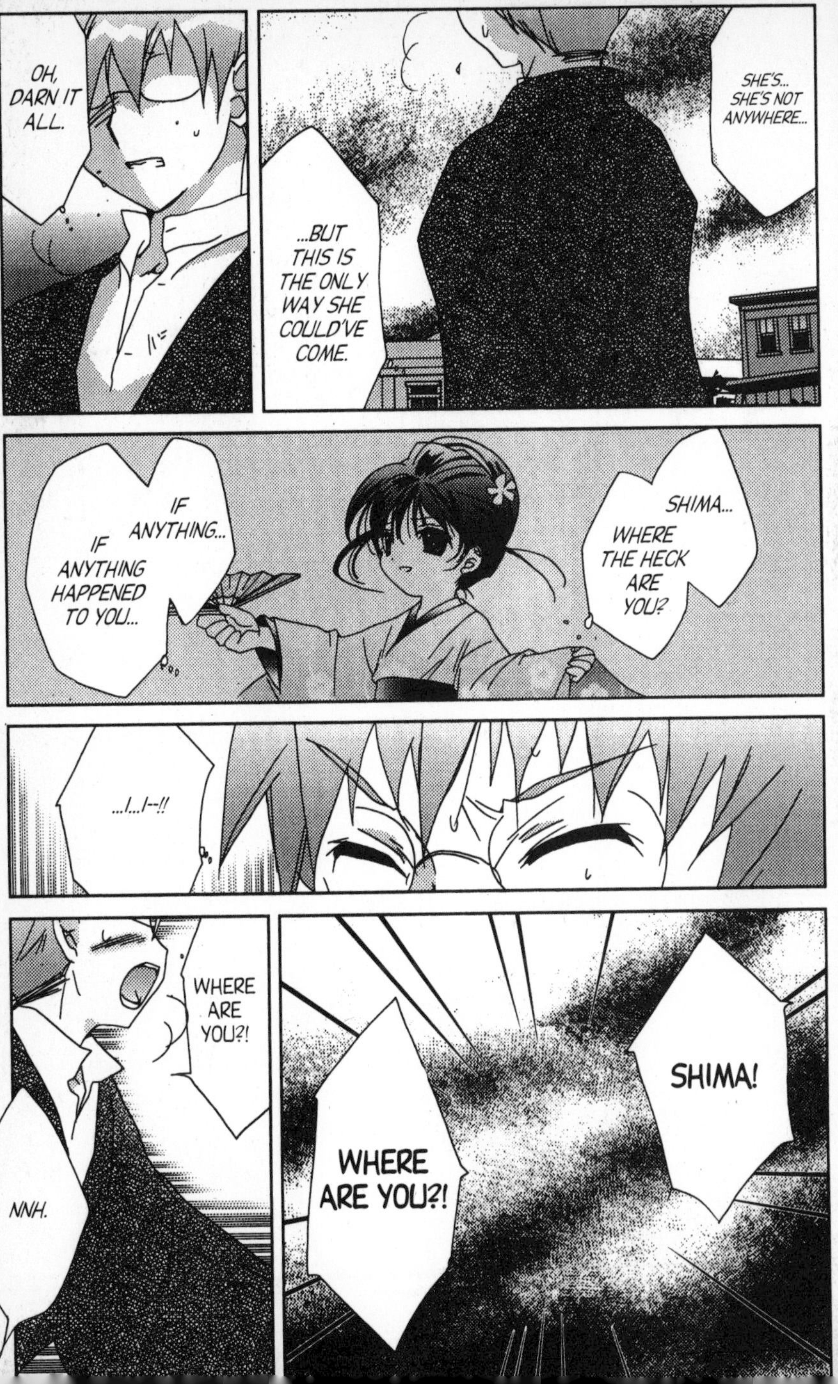
SHE'S... SHE'S NOT ANYWHERE...
...BUT THIS IS THE ONLY WAY SHE COULD'VE COME.
OH, DARN IT ALL.
SHIMA... WHERE THE HECK ARE YOU?
IF ANYTHING... IF ANYTHING HAPPENED TO YOU...
...I...I--!!
SHIMA!
WHERE ARE YOU?!
WHERE ARE YOU?!
NNH.

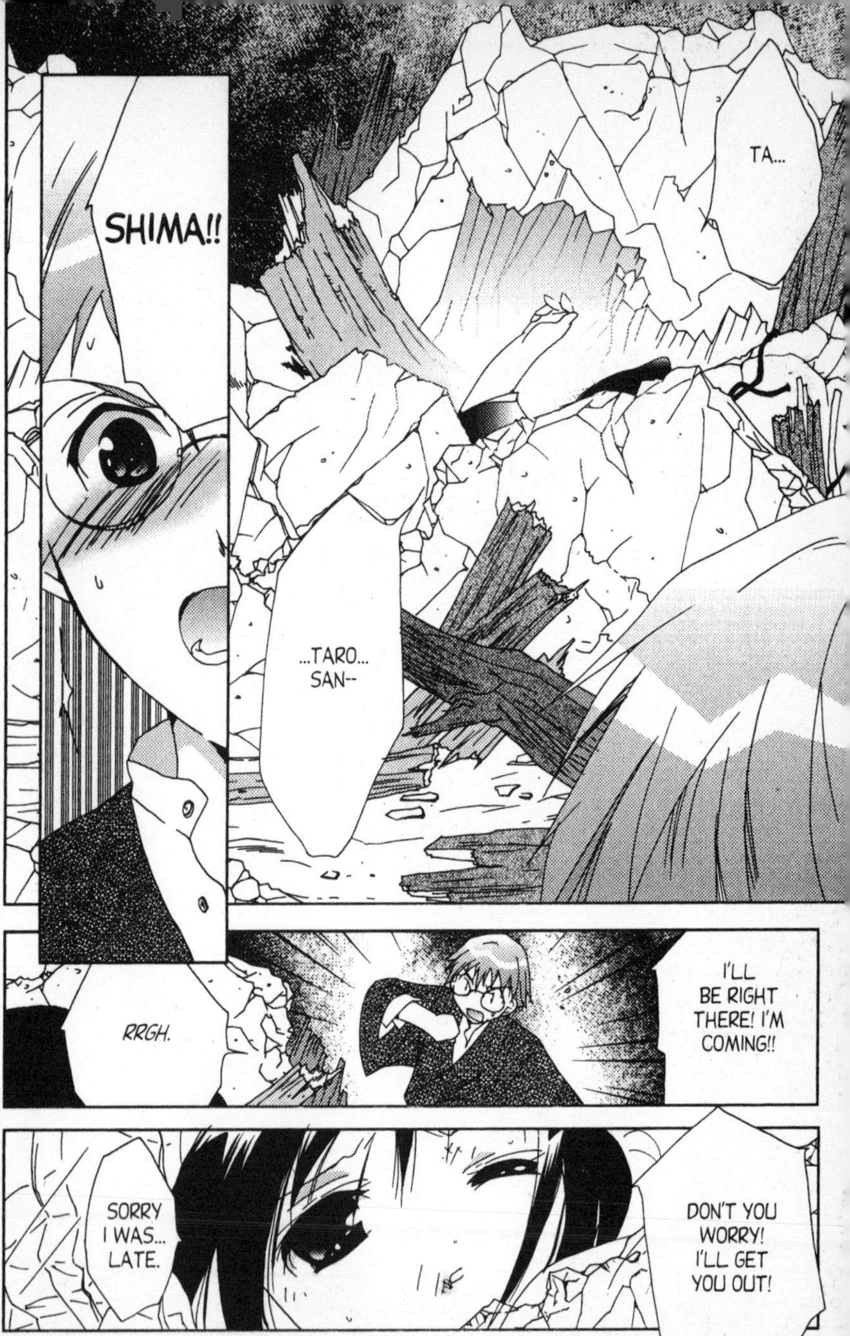
TA...
...TARO... SAN--
SHIMA!!
I'LL BE RIGHT THERE! I'M COMING!!
RRGH.
DON'T YOU WORRY! I'LL GET YOU OUT!
SORRY I WAS... LATE.

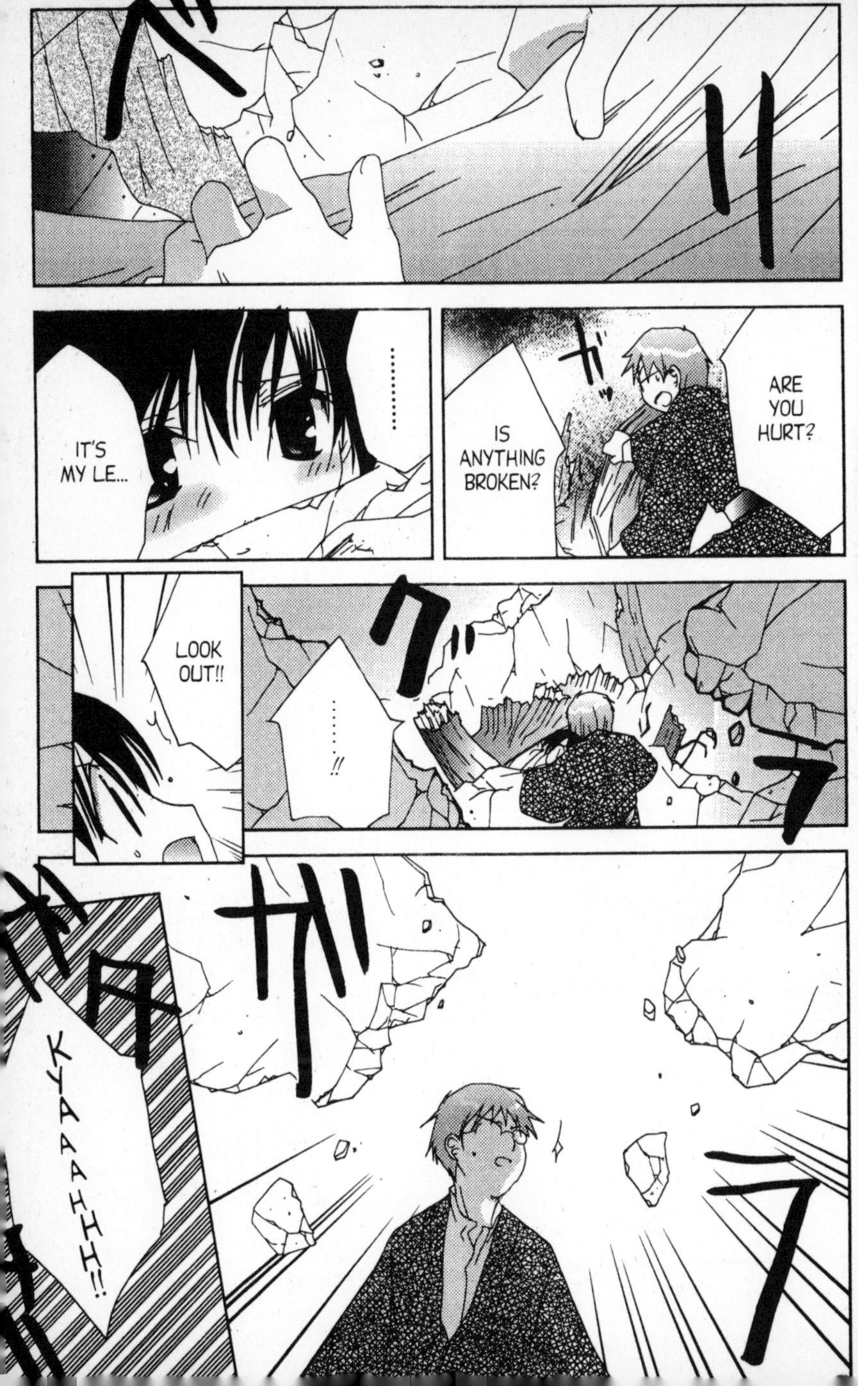
ARE YOU HURT?
IS ANYTHING BROKEN?
....
IT'S MY LE...
......!!
LOOK OUT!!
KYAAAAHHH!!

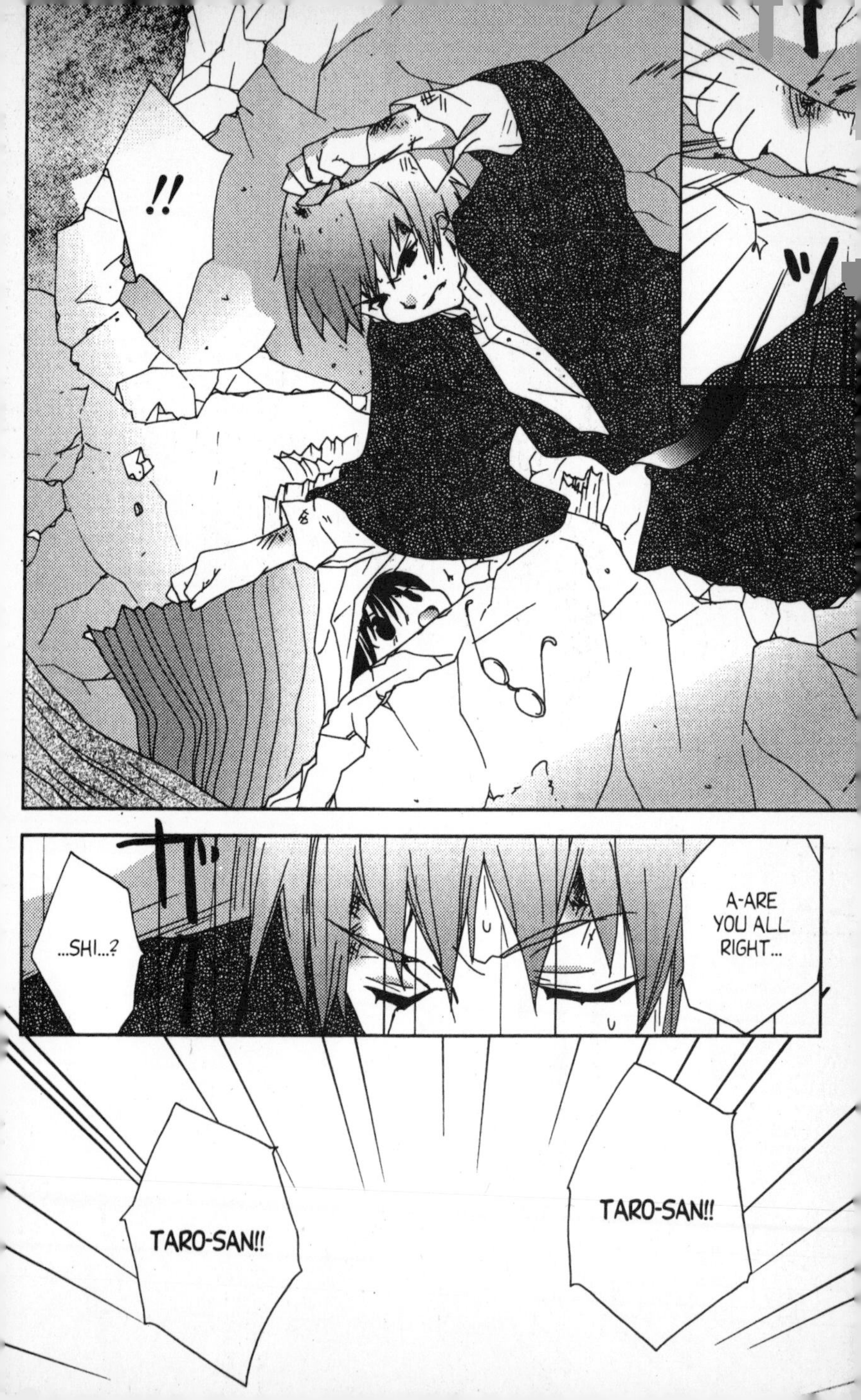
!!
A-ARE YOU ALL RIGHT...
...SHI...?
TARO-SAN!!
TARO-SAN!!

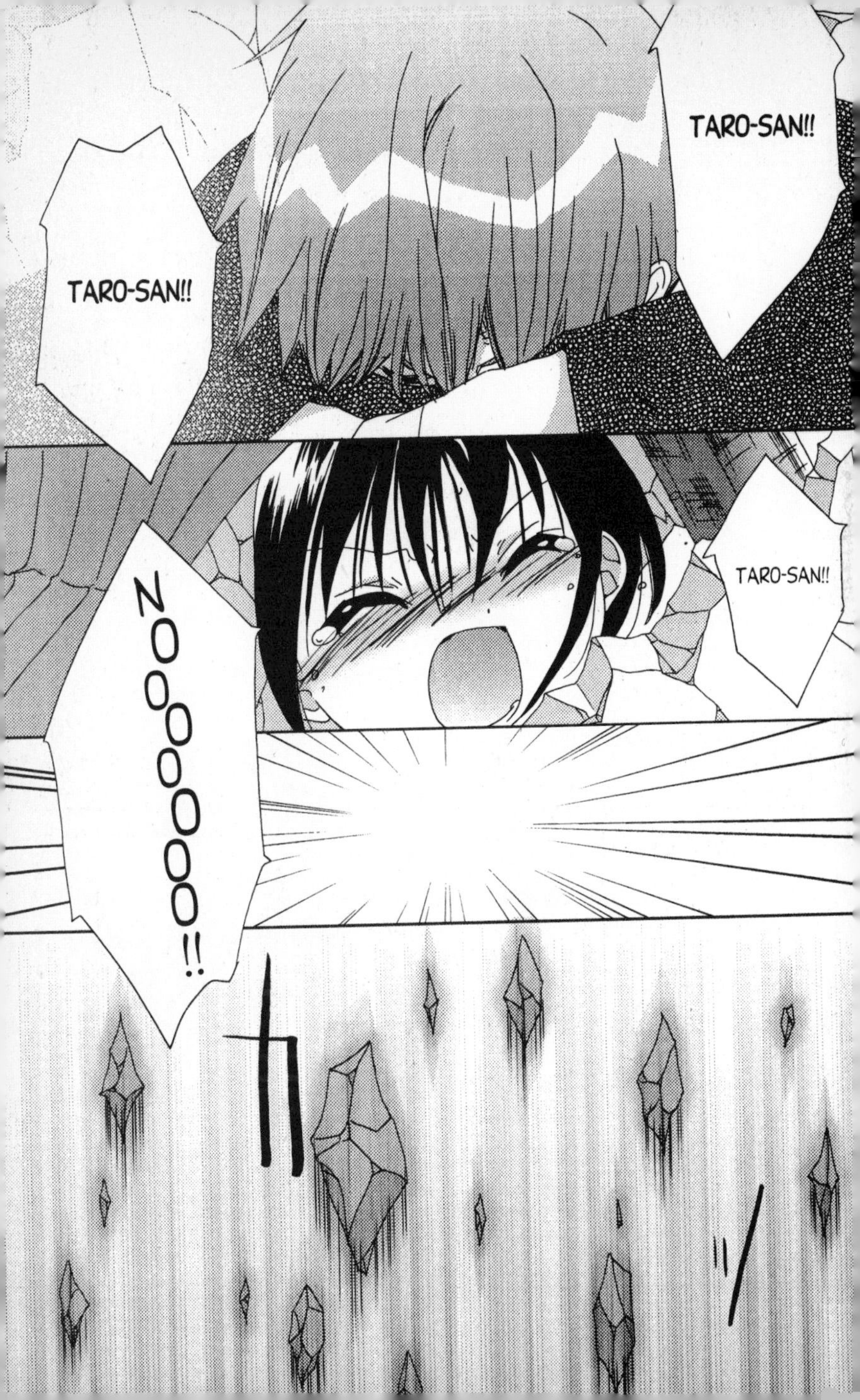
TARO-SAN!!
TARO-SAN!!
TARO-SAN!!
NOOOOOOO!!

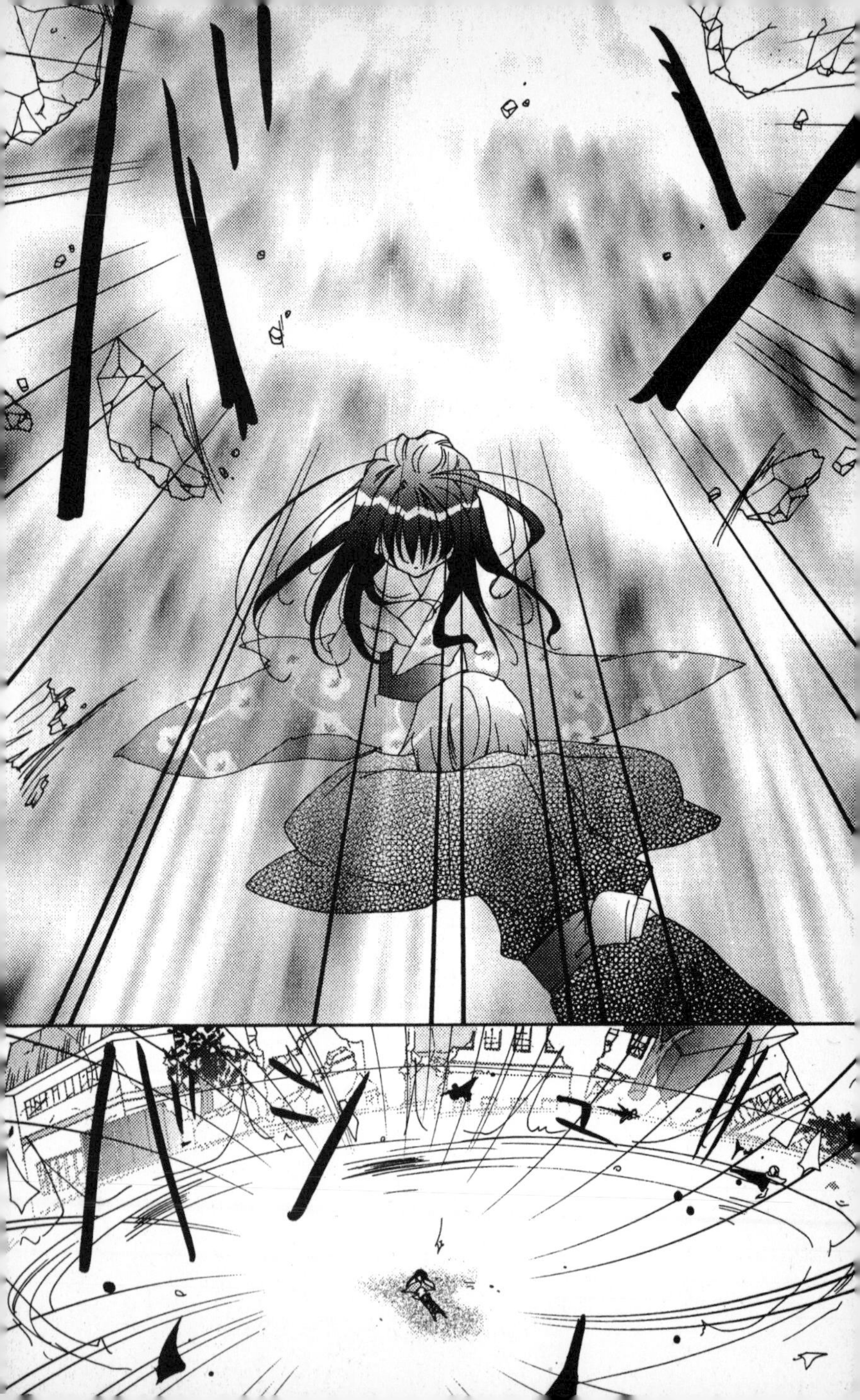

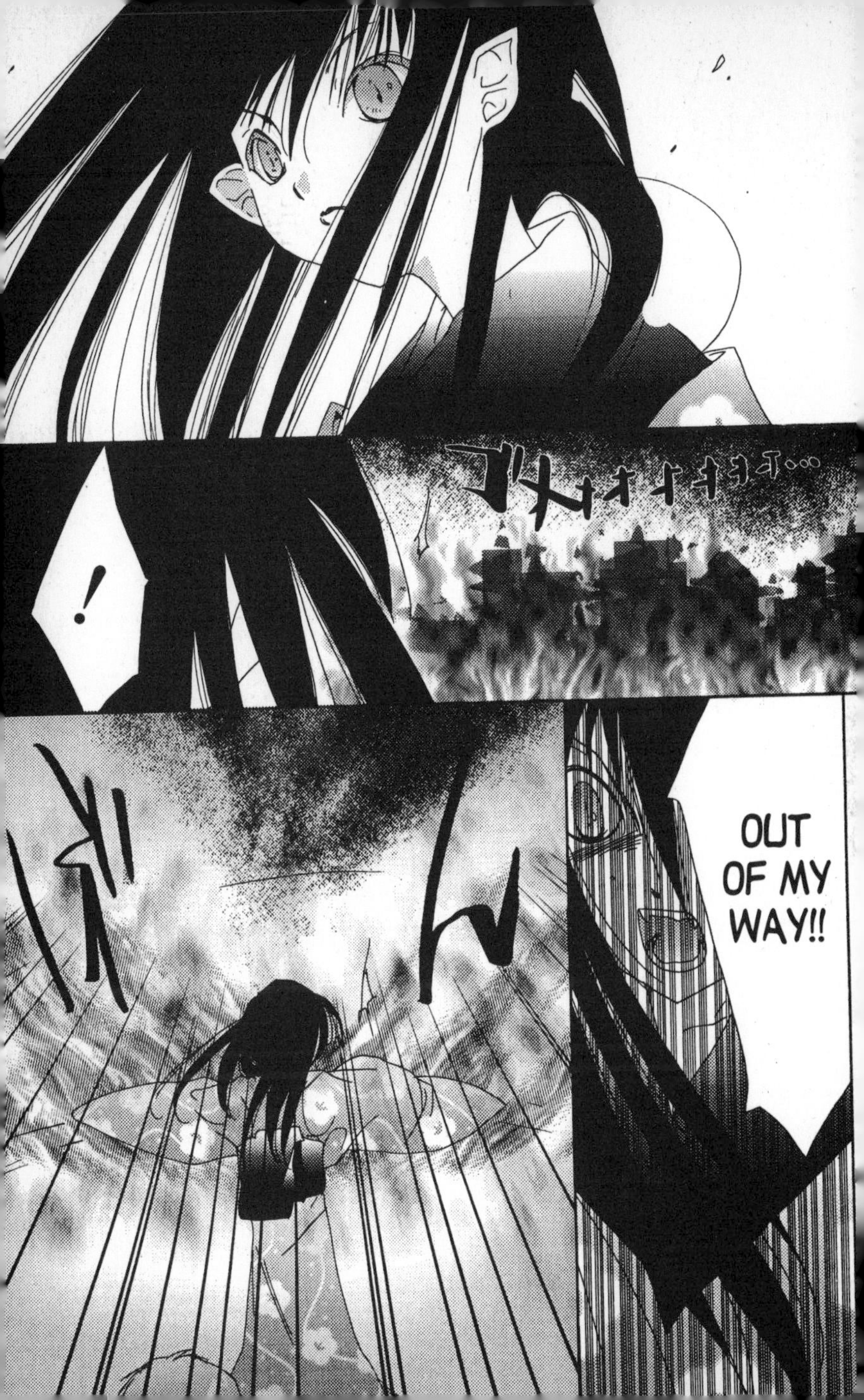
!
OUT OF MY WAY!!

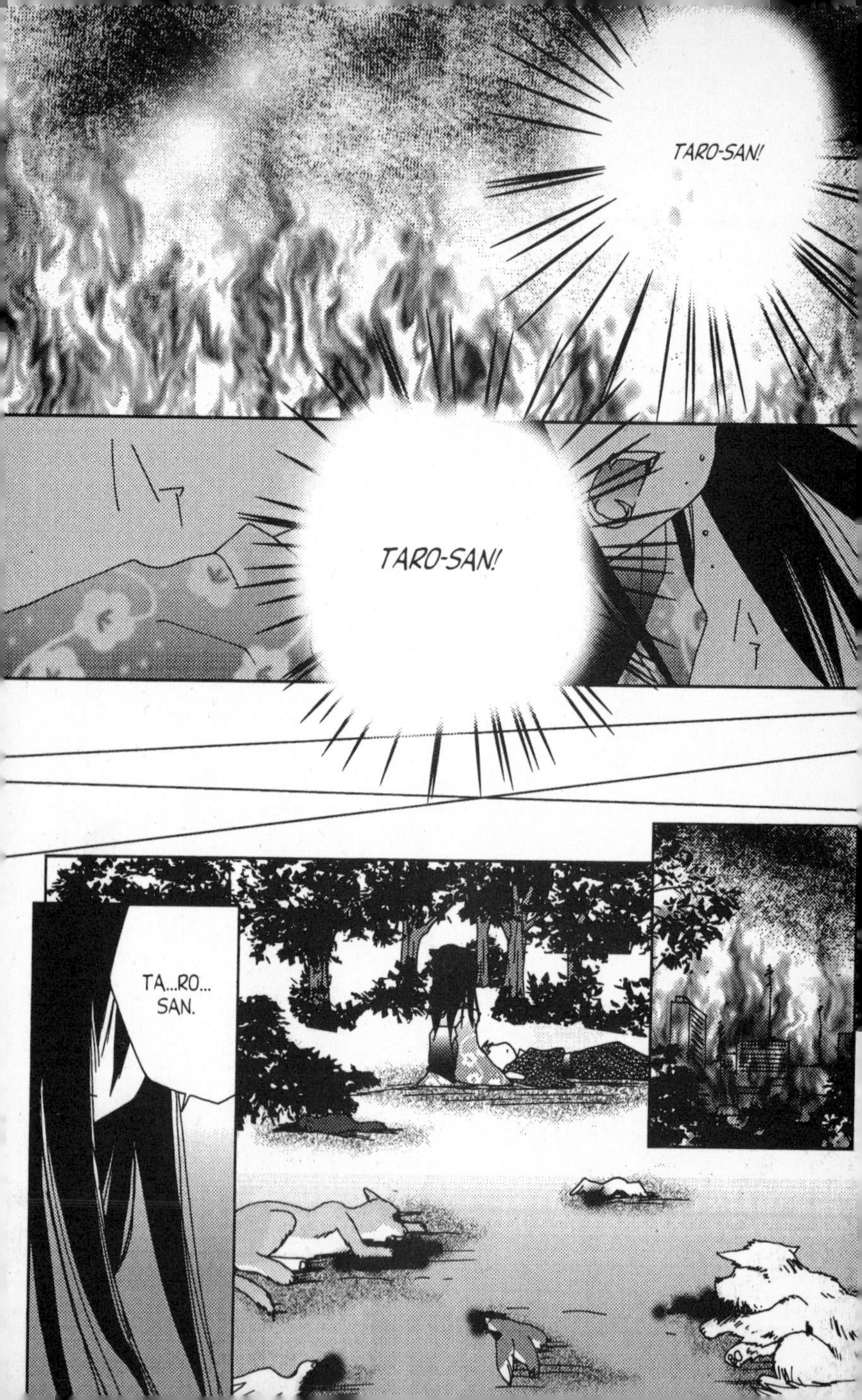
TARO-SAN!
TARO-SAN!
TA...RO... SAN.

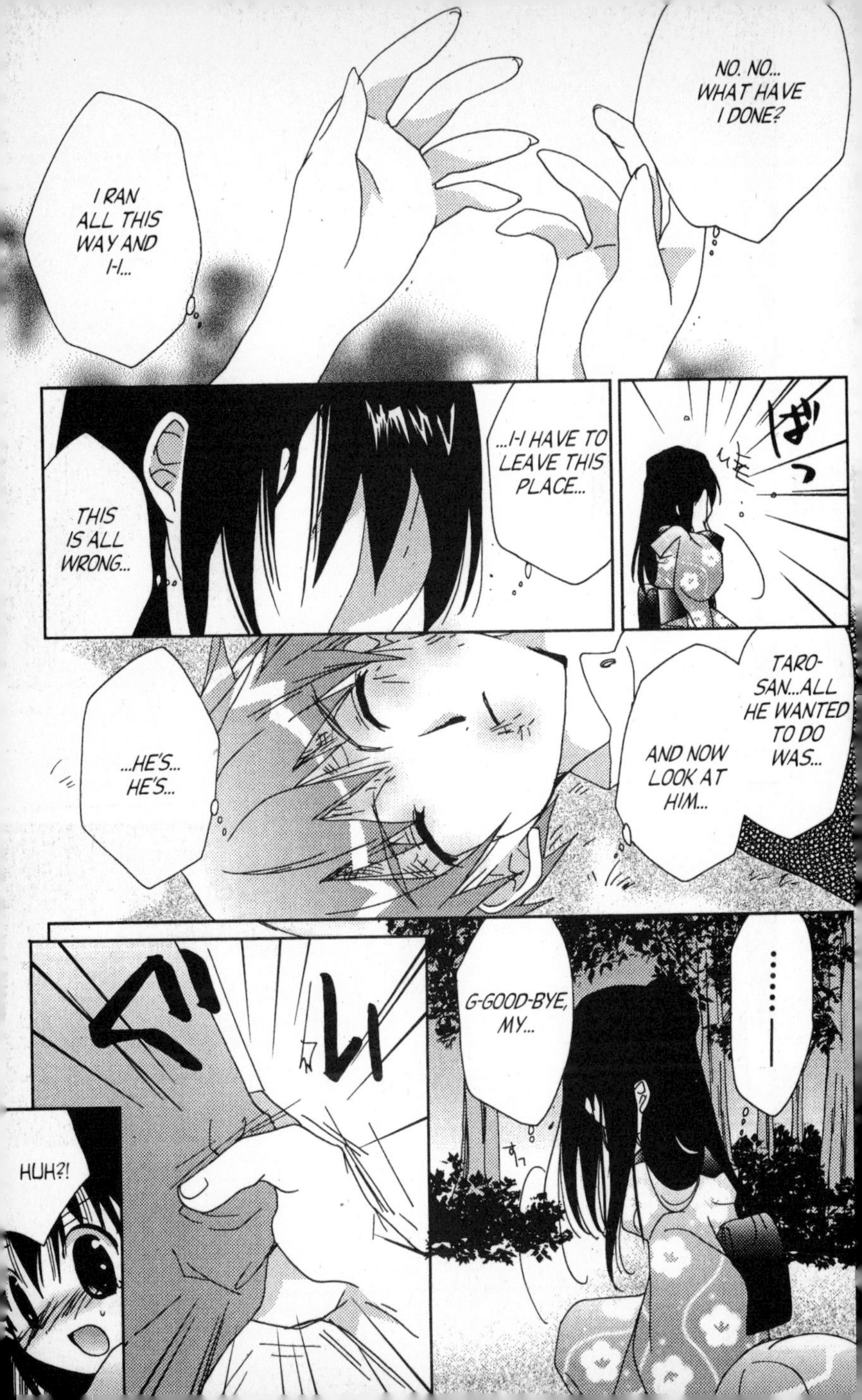
NO. NO... WHAT HAVE I DONE?
I RAN ALL THIS WAY AND I-I...
ばっ
...I-I HAVE TO LEAVE THIS PLACE...
THIS IS ALL WRONG...
TARO-SAN...ALL HE WANTED TO DO WAS...
AND NOW LOOK AT HIM...
...HE'S... HE'S...
......—
G-GOOD-BYE, MY...
ぐい
HUH?!

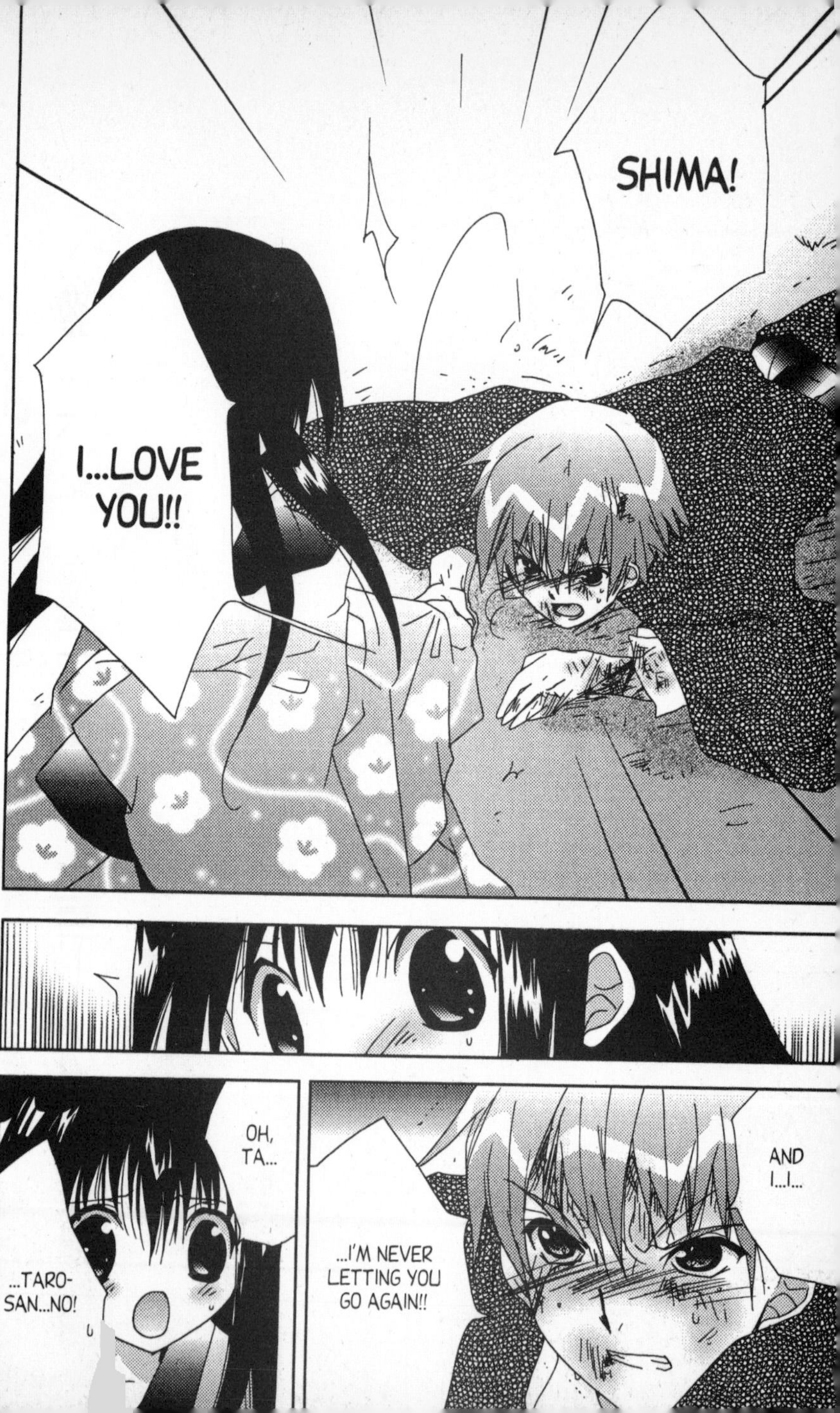
SHIMA!
I...LOVE YOU!!
AND I...I...
...I'M NEVER LETTING YOU GO AGAIN!!
OH, TA...
...TARO-SAN...NO!

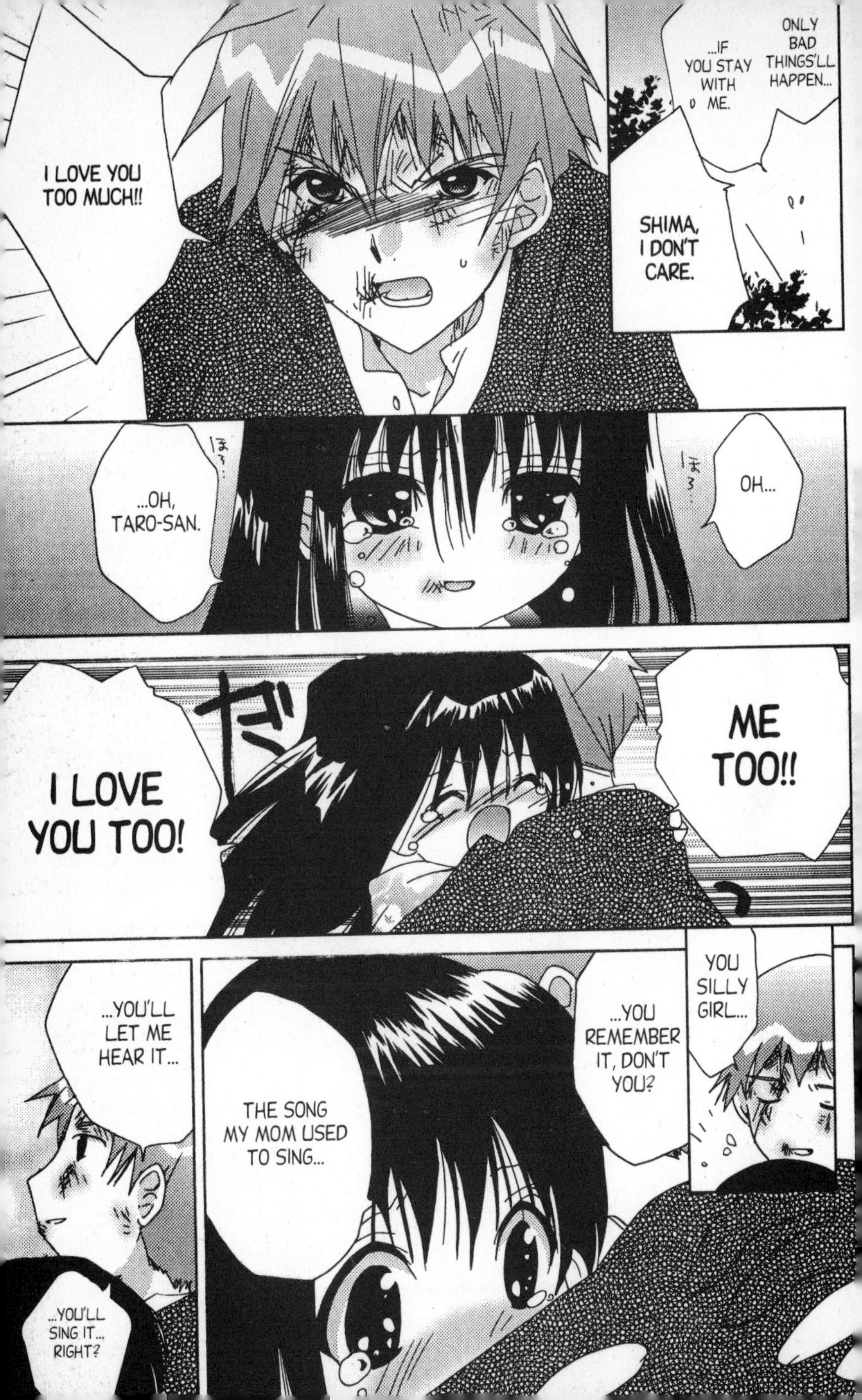
ONLY BAD THINGS'LL HAPPEN...
...IF YOU STAY WITH ME.
SHIMA, I DON'T CARE.
I LOVE YOU TOO MUCH!!
OH...
...OH, TARO-SAN.
ME TOO!!
I LOVE YOU TOO!
YOU SILLY GIRL...
...YOU REMEMBER IT, DON'T YOU?
THE SONG MY MOM USED TO SING...
...YOU'LL LET ME HEAR IT...
...YOU'LL SING IT... RIGHT?

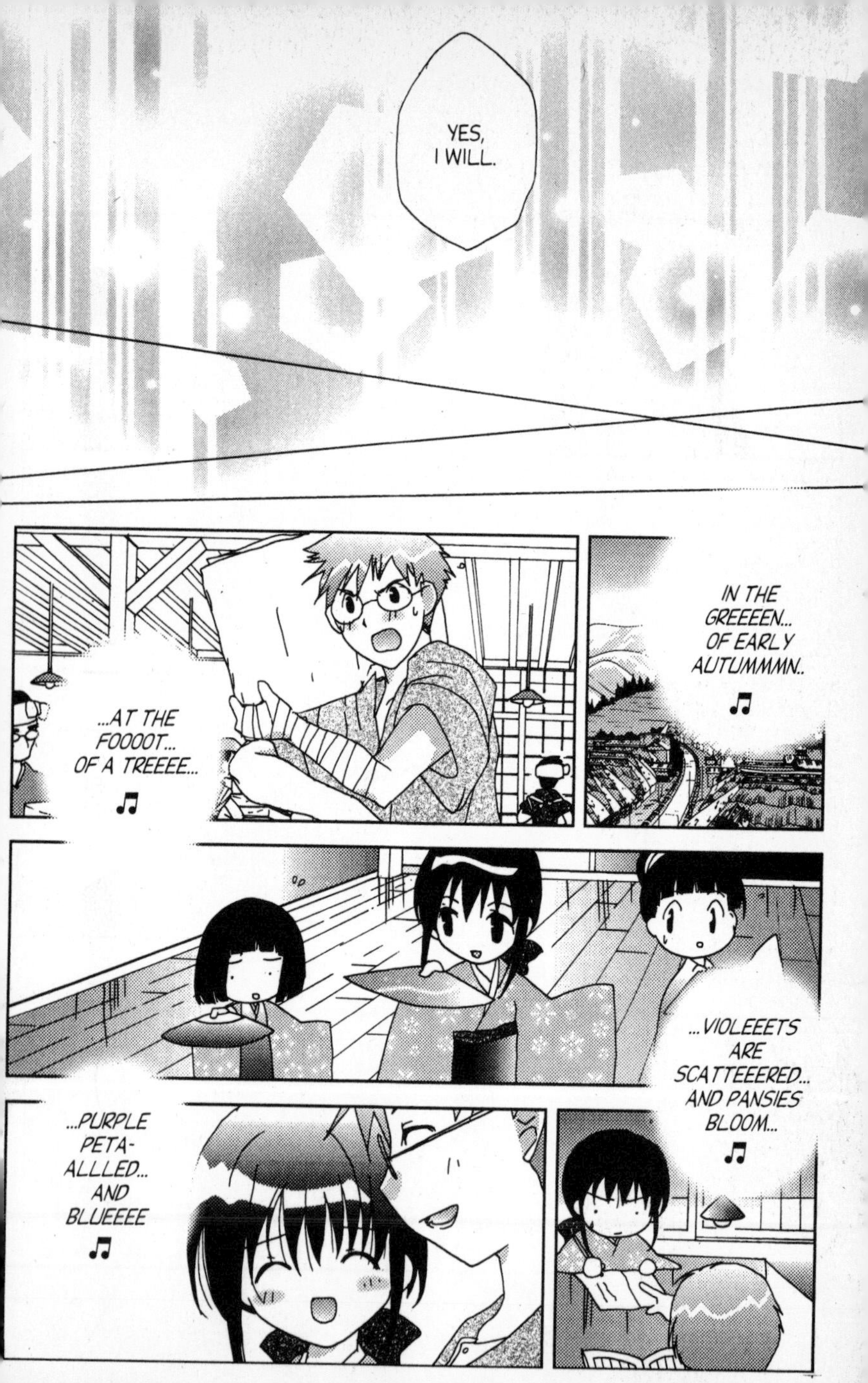
YES, I WILL.
IN THE GREEEEN... OF EARLY AUTUMMMN.. ♫
...AT THE FOOOOT... OF A TREEEE... ♫
...VIOLEEETS ARE SCATTEEERED... AND PANSIES BLOOM... ♫
...PURPLE PETA-ALLLED... AND BLUEEEE ♫

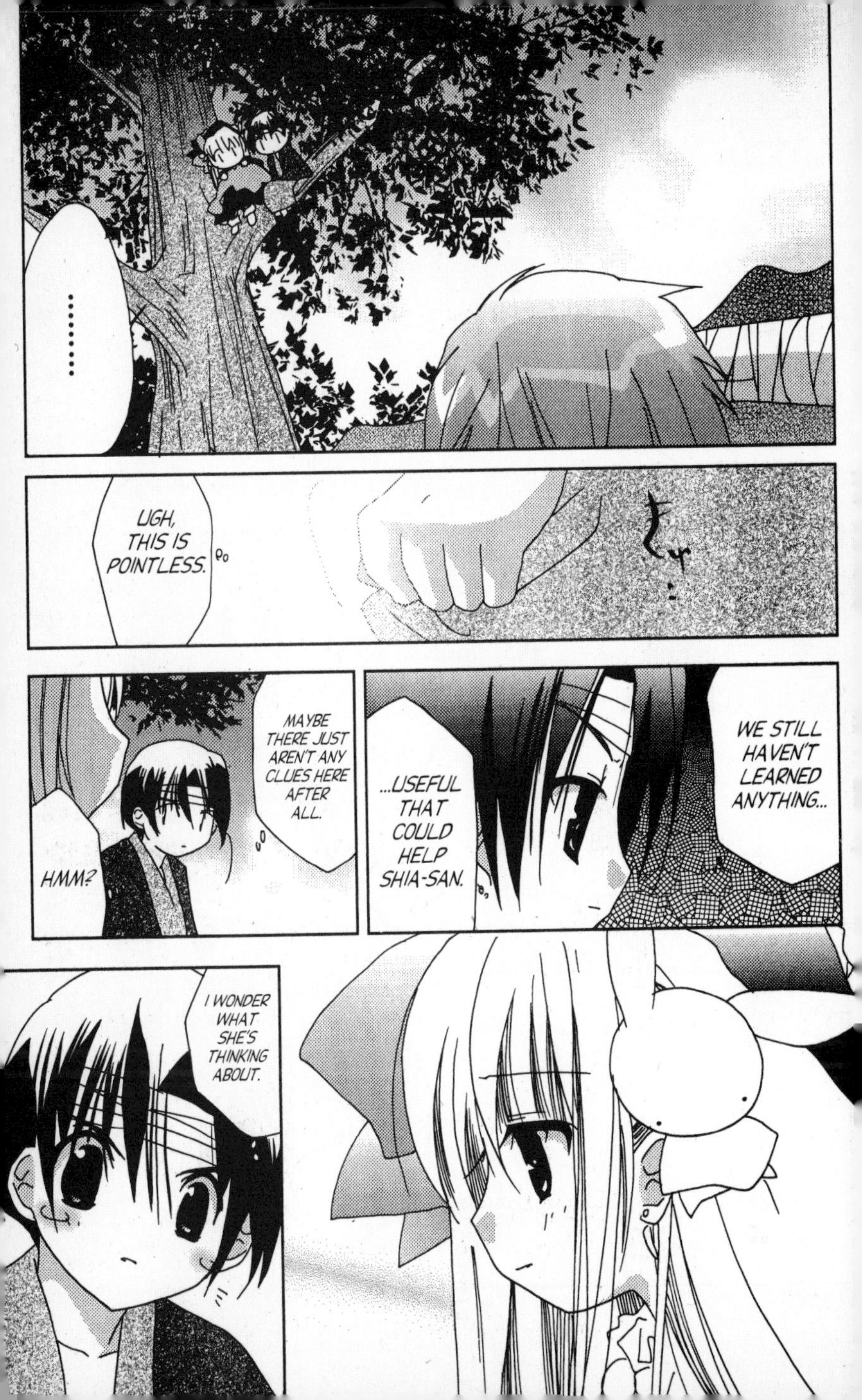

......
UGH, THIS IS POINTLESS.
WE STILL HAVEN'T LEARNED ANYTHING...
...USEFUL THAT COULD HELP SHIA-SAN.
MAYBE THERE JUST AREN'T ANY CLUES HERE AFTER ALL.
HMM?
I WONDER WHAT SHE'S THINKING ABOUT.

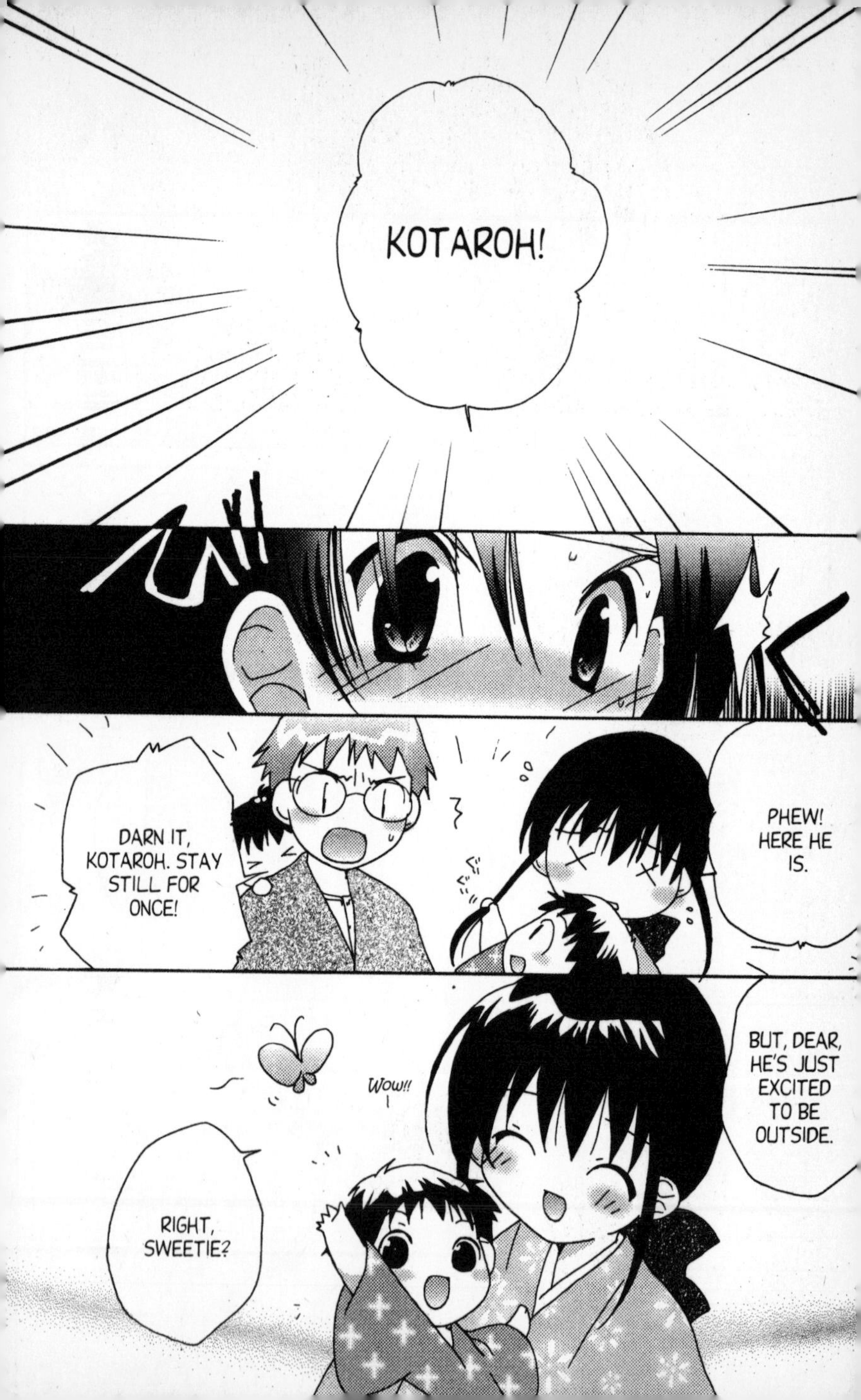
KOTAROH!
PHEW! HERE HE IS.
DARN IT, KOTAROH. STAY STILL FOR ONCE!
BUT, DEAR, HE'S JUST EXCITED TO BE OUTSIDE.
WOW!!
RIGHT, SWEETIE?

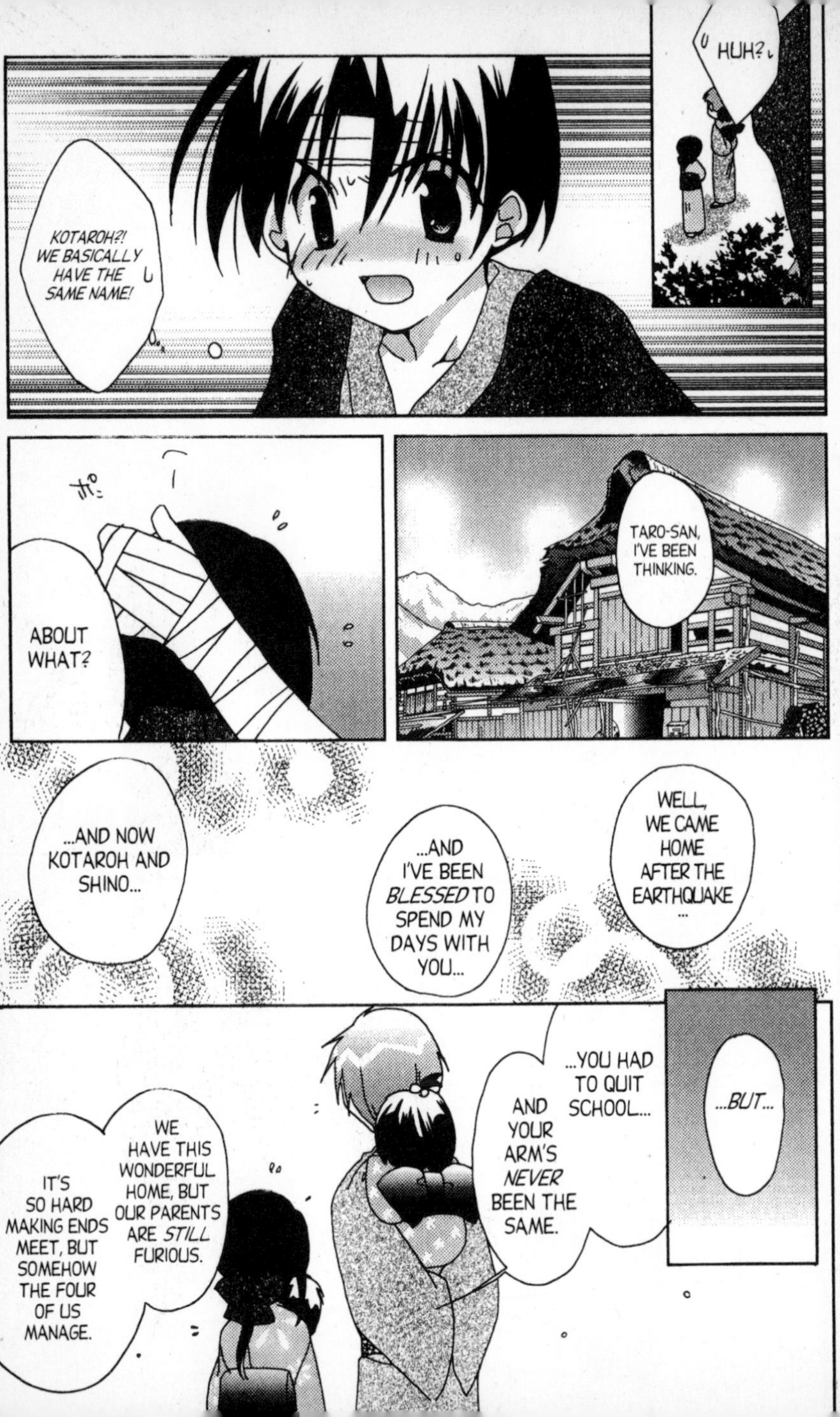
HUH?
KOTAROH?! WE BASICALLY HAVE THE SAME NAME!
TARO-SAN, I'VE BEEN THINKING.
ABOUT WHAT?
WELL, WE CAME HOME AFTER THE EARTHQUAKE...
...AND I'VE BEEN *BLESSED* TO SPEND MY DAYS WITH YOU...
...AND NOW KOTAROH AND SHINO...
...*BUT*...
...YOU HAD TO QUIT SCHOOL...
AND YOUR ARM'S *NEVER* BEEN THE SAME.
WE HAVE THIS WONDERFUL HOME, BUT OUR PARENTS ARE *STILL* FURIOUS.
IT'S SO HARD MAKING ENDS MEET, BUT SOMEHOW THE FOUR OF US MANAGE.

I'M HAPPY, SHIMA. THAT'S ALL THAT MATTERS.

I CAN'T HELP THINKING, WHAT IF YOU HADN'T--

SSSHHH.

WHAT ABOUT YOU?

That look!

...I'M HAPPY, TOO.

UH, I...

AHH!

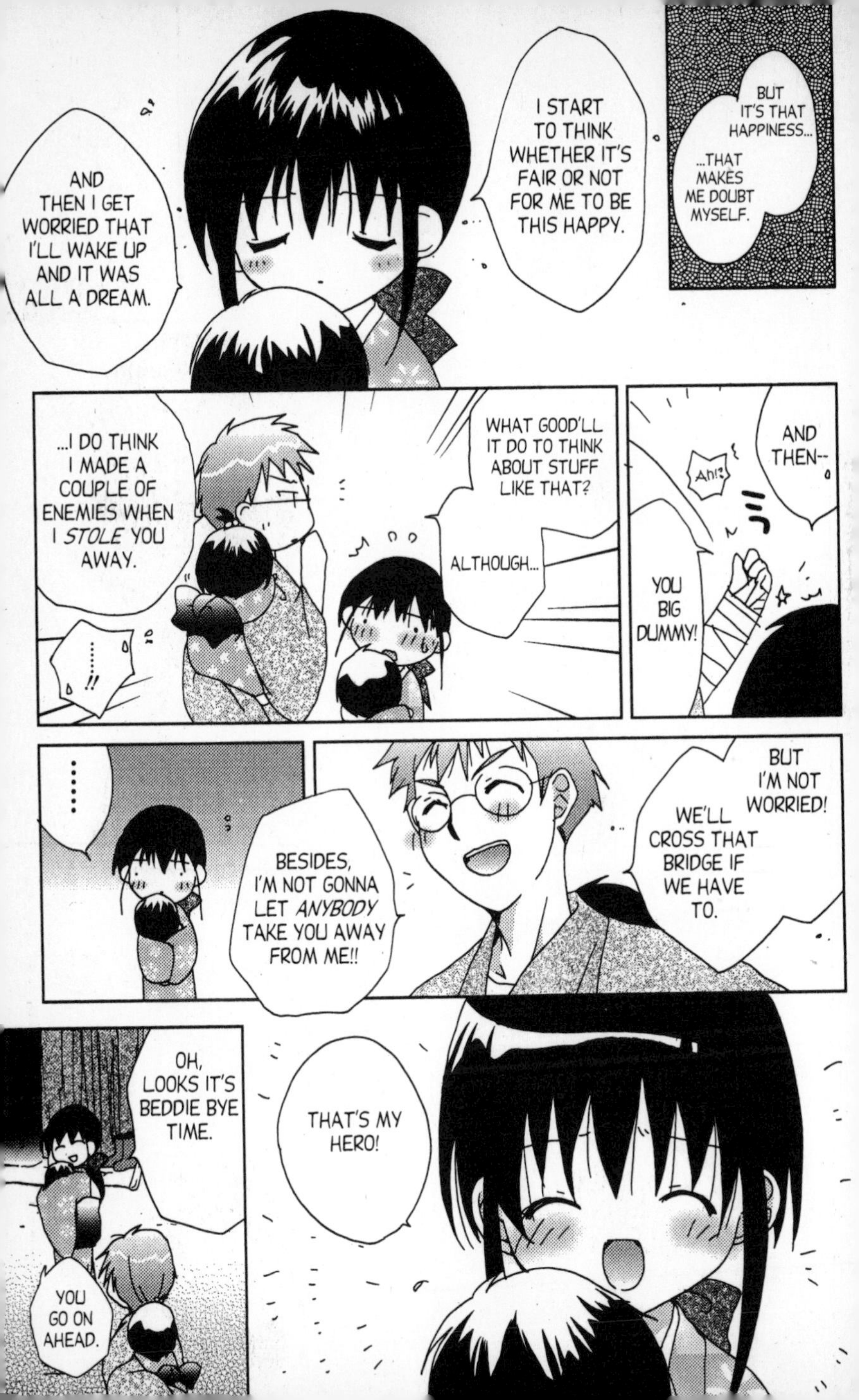
BUT IT'S THAT HAPPINESS...
...THAT MAKES ME DOUBT MYSELF.
I START TO THINK WHETHER IT'S FAIR OR NOT FOR ME TO BE THIS HAPPY.
AND THEN I GET WORRIED THAT I'LL WAKE UP AND IT WAS ALL A DREAM.
AND THEN--
Ah!?
YOU BIG DUMMY!
WHAT GOOD'LL IT DO TO THINK ABOUT STUFF LIKE THAT?
ALTHOUGH...
...I DO THINK I MADE A COUPLE OF ENEMIES WHEN I *STOLE* YOU AWAY.
......!!
BUT I'M NOT WORRIED!
WE'LL CROSS THAT BRIDGE IF WE HAVE TO.
BESIDES, I'M NOT GONNA LET *ANYBODY* TAKE YOU AWAY FROM ME!!
......
THAT'S MY HERO!
OH, LOOKS IT'S BEDDIE BYE TIME.
YOU GO ON AHEAD.

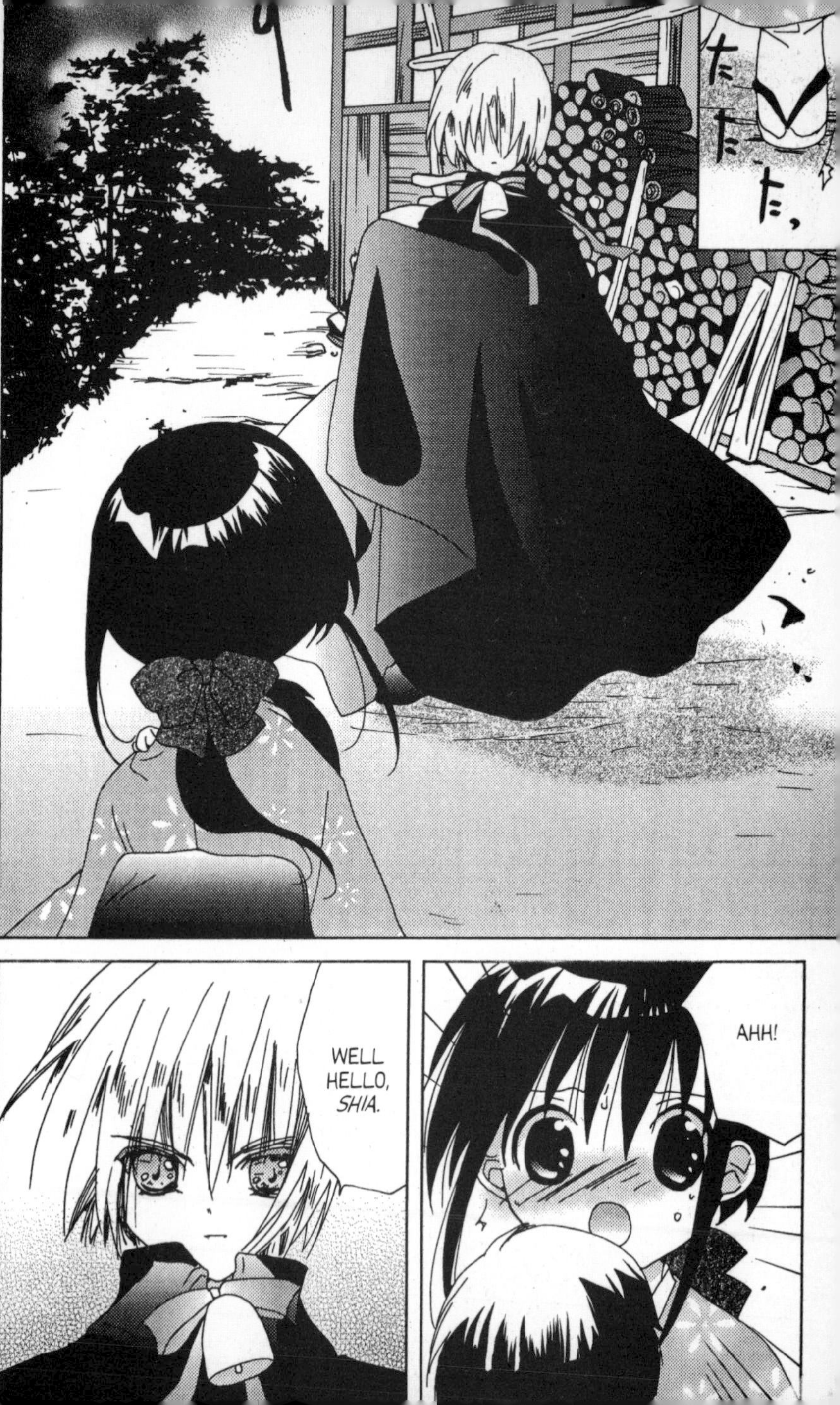
たたたっ
AHH!
WELL HELLO, *SHIA.*

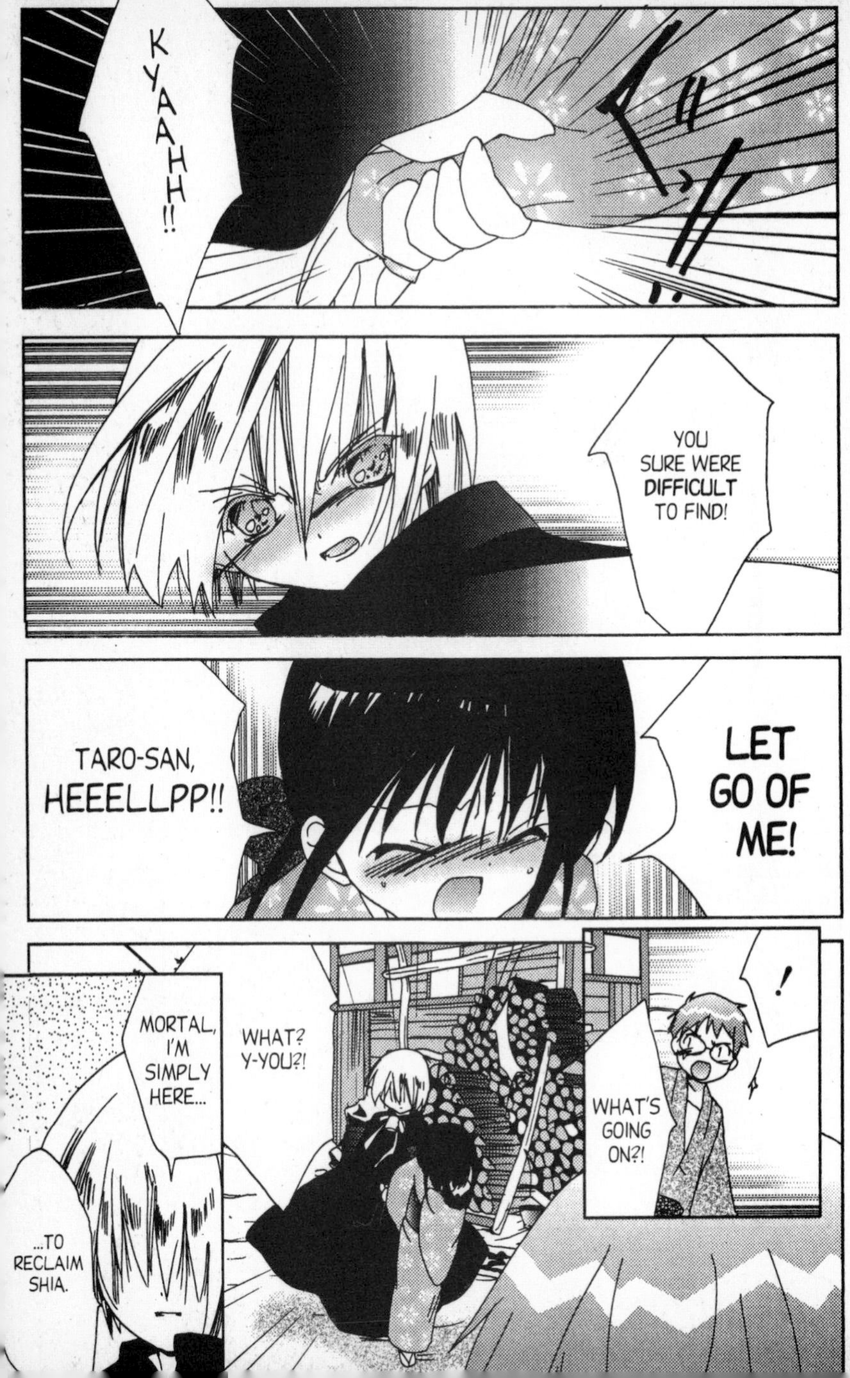
KYAAHH!!
YOU SURE WERE DIFFICULT TO FIND!
LET GO OF ME!
TARO-SAN, HEEELLPP!!
!
WHAT'S GOING ON?!
WHAT? Y-YOU?!
MORTAL, I'M SIMPLY HERE...
...TO RECLAIM SHIA.

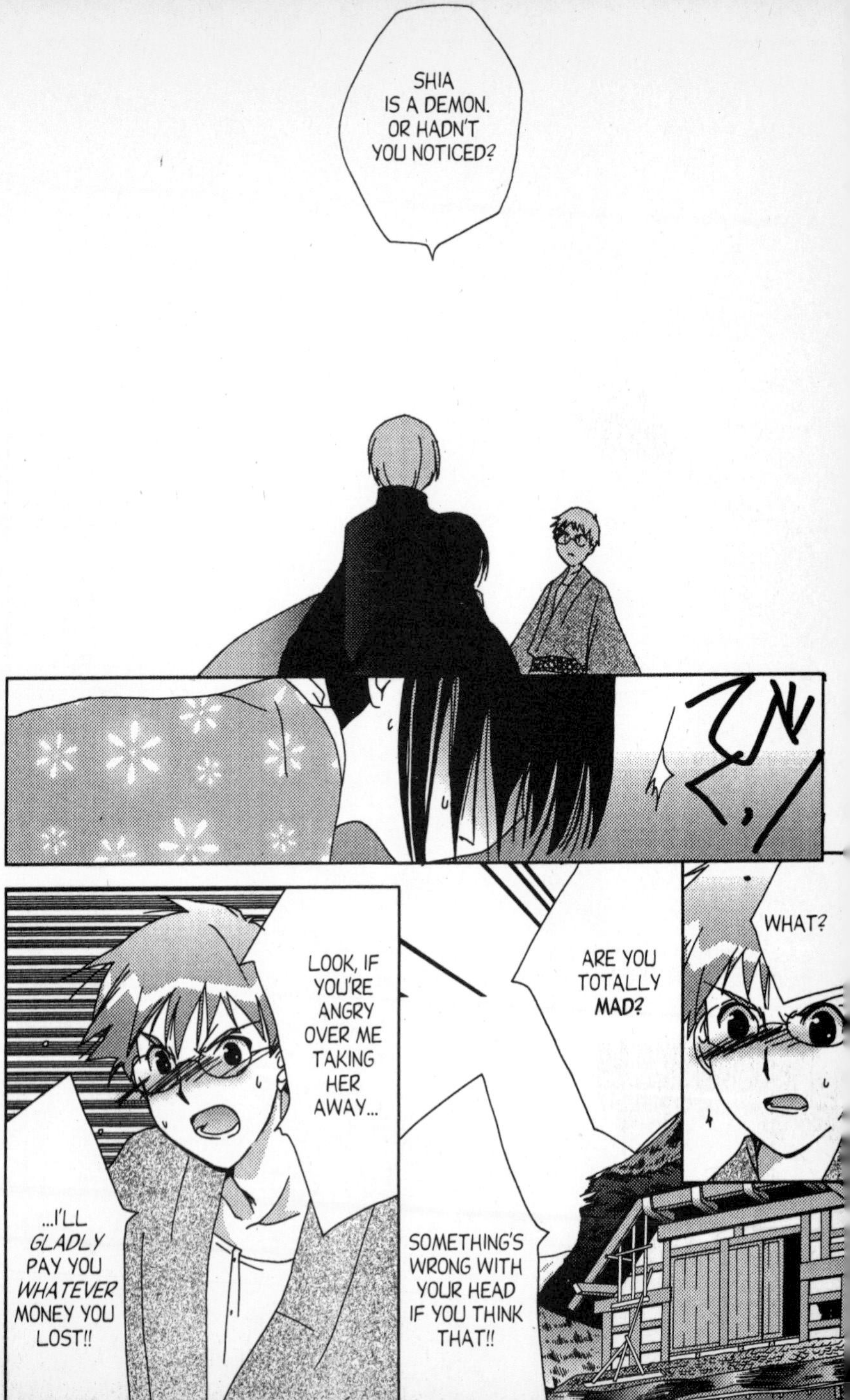
SHIA IS A DEMON. OR HADN'T YOU NOTICED?
WHAT?
ARE YOU TOTALLY *MAD?*
SOMETHING'S WRONG WITH YOUR HEAD IF YOU THINK THAT!!
LOOK, IF YOU'RE ANGRY OVER ME TAKING HER AWAY...
...I'LL *GLADLY* PAY YOU *WHATEVER* MONEY YOU LOST!!

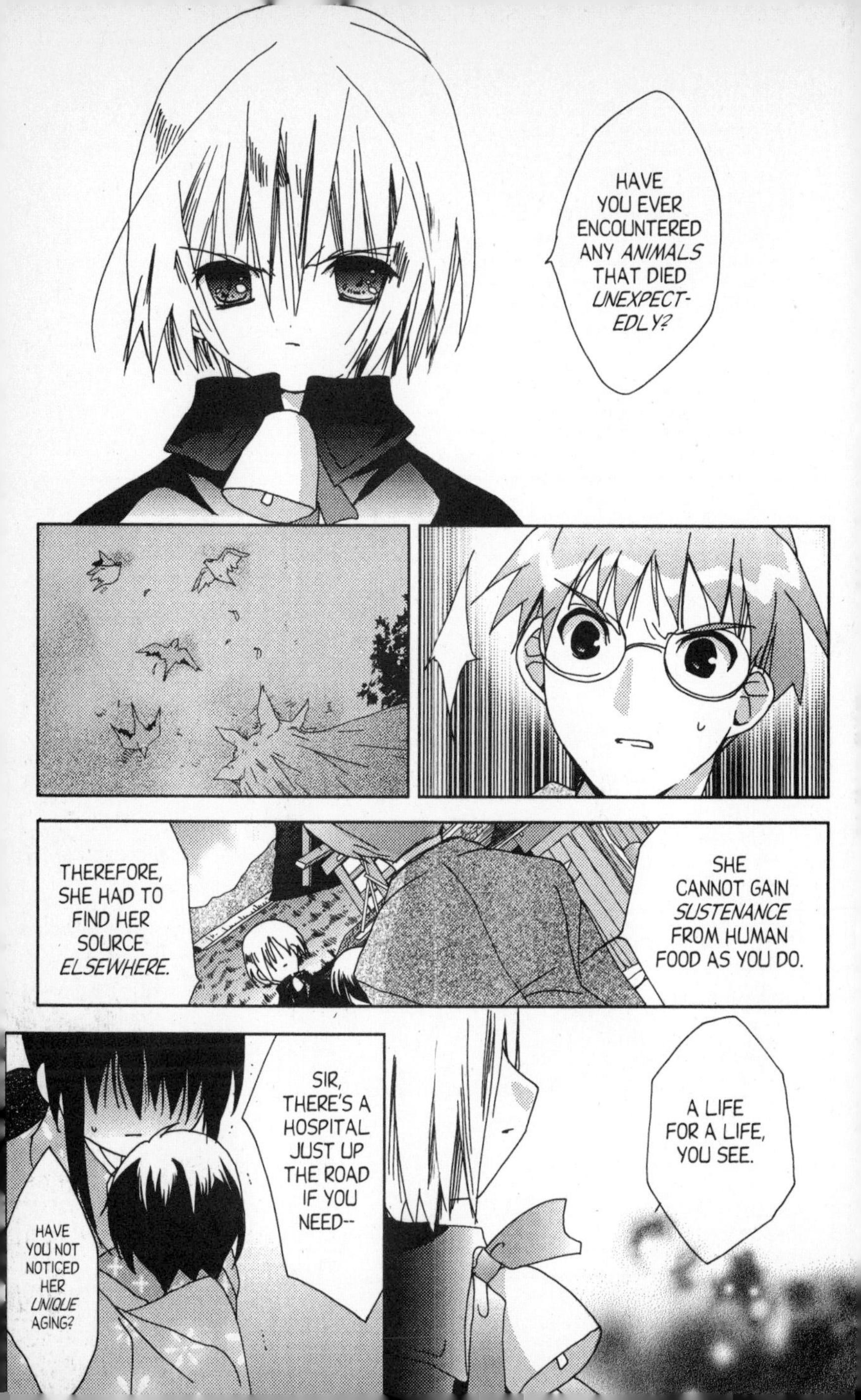
HAVE YOU EVER ENCOUNTERED ANY *ANIMALS* THAT DIED *UNEXPECT-EDLY?*
SHE CANNOT GAIN *SUSTENANCE* FROM HUMAN FOOD AS YOU DO.
THEREFORE, SHE HAD TO FIND HER SOURCE *ELSEWHERE.*
A LIFE FOR A LIFE, YOU SEE.
SIR, THERE'S A HOSPITAL JUST UP THE ROAD IF YOU NEED--
HAVE YOU NOT NOTICED HER *UNIQUE* AGING?

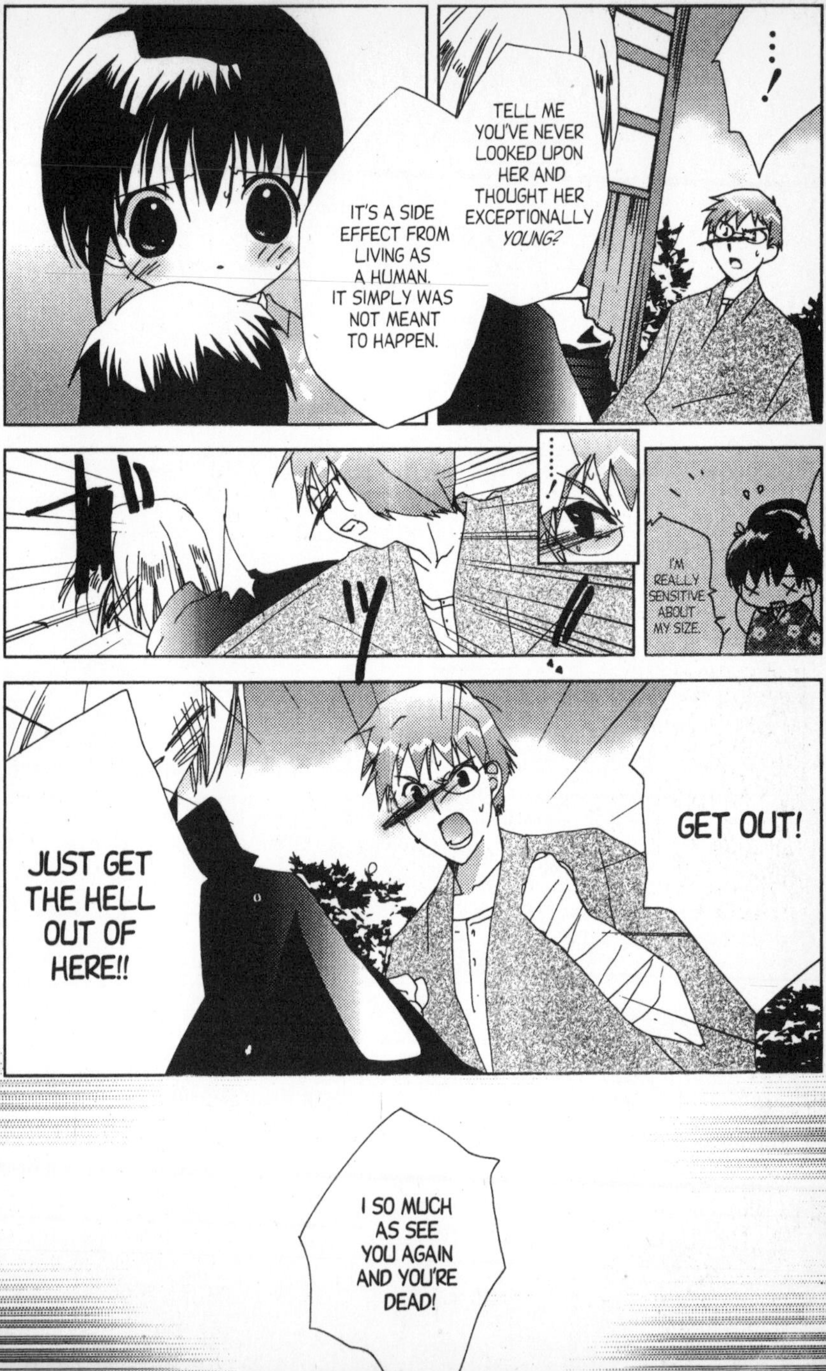
...!
TELL ME YOU'VE NEVER LOOKED UPON HER AND THOUGHT HER EXCEPTIONALLY *YOUNG?*
IT'S A SIDE EFFECT FROM LIVING AS A HUMAN. IT SIMPLY WAS NOT MEANT TO HAPPEN.
I'M REALLY SENSITIVE ABOUT MY SIZE.
......!
GET OUT!
JUST GET THE HELL OUT OF HERE!!
I SO MUCH AS SEE YOU AGAIN AND YOU'RE DEAD!

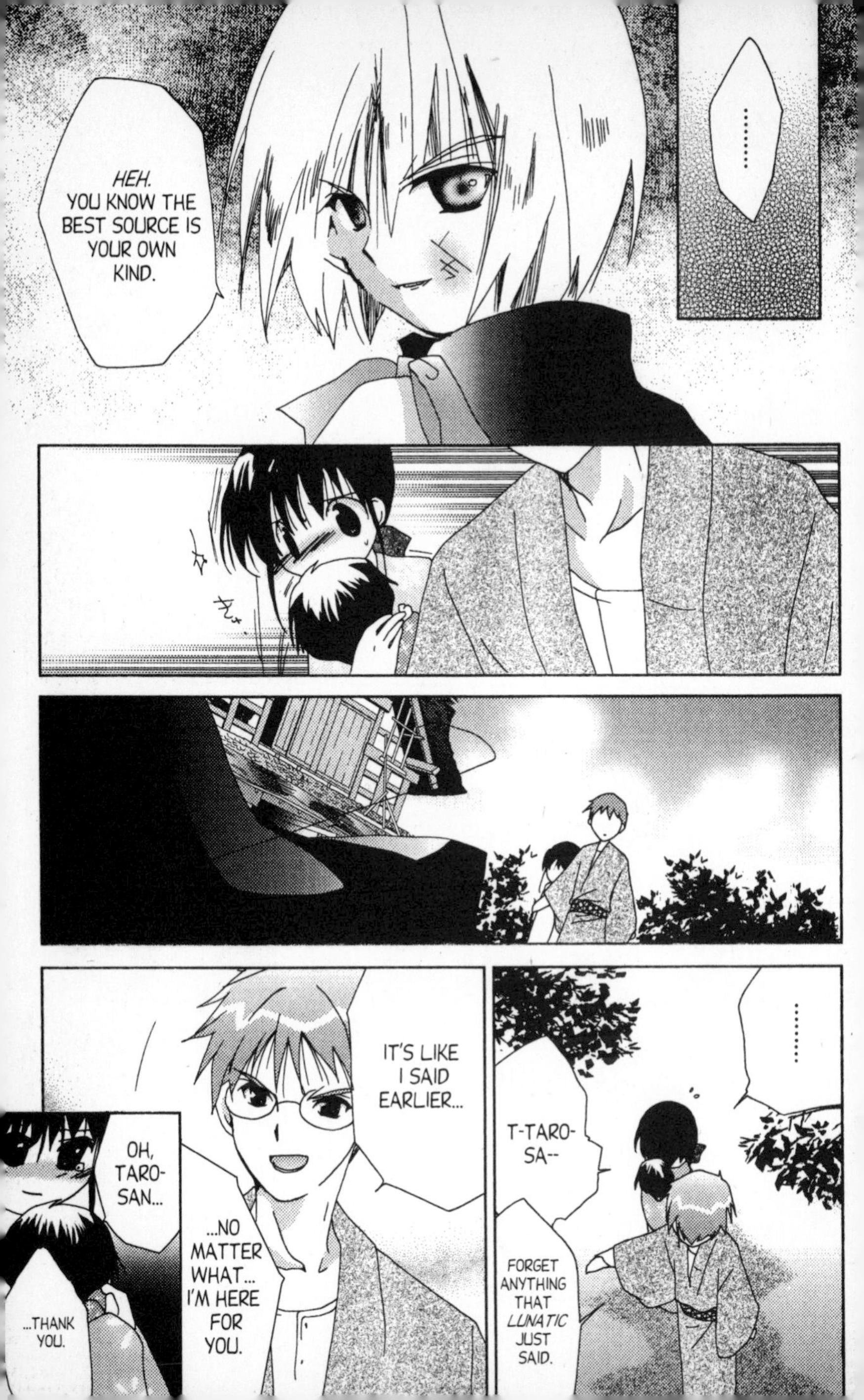
......
HEH. YOU KNOW THE BEST SOURCE IS YOUR OWN KIND.
......
T-TARO-SA--
FORGET ANYTHING THAT *LUNATIC* JUST SAID.
IT'S LIKE I SAID EARLIER...
...NO MATTER WHAT... I'M HERE FOR YOU.
OH, TARO-SAN...
...THANK YOU.

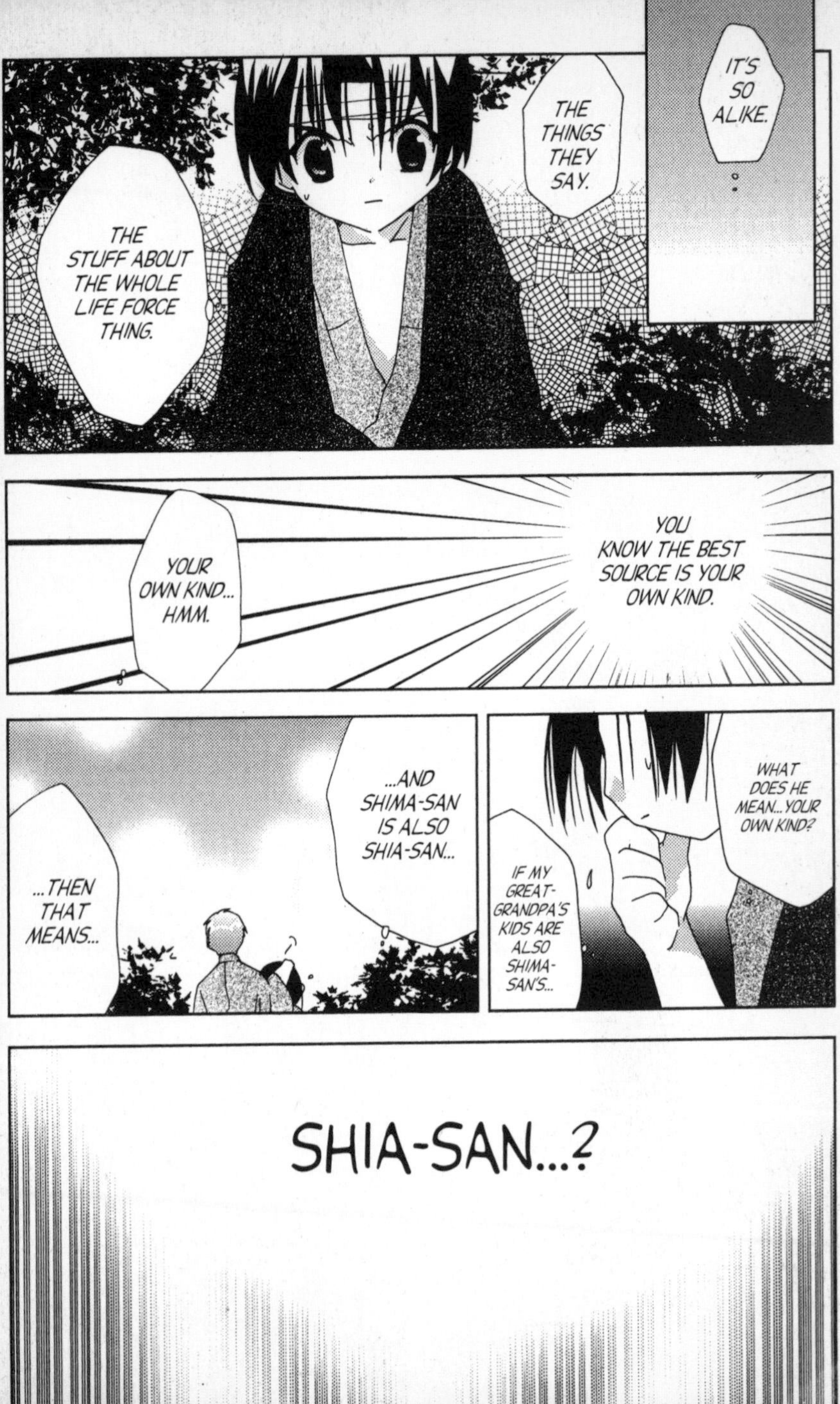
IT'S SO ALIKE.
THE THINGS THEY SAY.
THE STUFF ABOUT THE WHOLE LIFE FORCE THING.
YOU KNOW THE BEST SOURCE IS YOUR OWN KIND.
YOUR OWN KIND... HMM.
WHAT DOES HE MEAN...YOUR OWN KIND?
IF MY GREAT-GRANDPA'S KIDS ARE ALSO SHIMA-SAN'S...
...AND SHIMA-SAN IS ALSO SHIA-SAN...
...THEN THAT MEANS...
SHIA-SAN...?

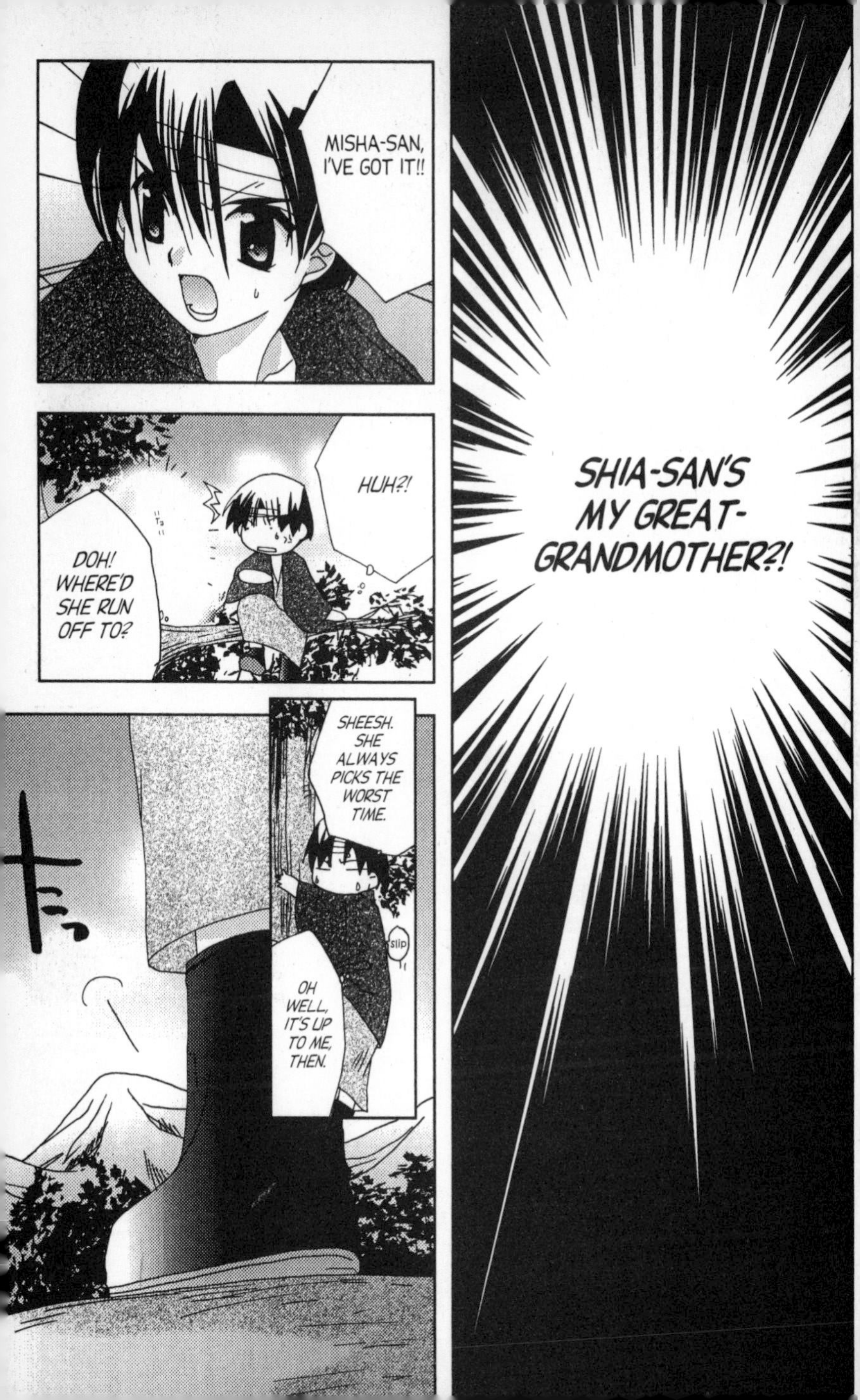
SHIA-SAN'S MY GREAT-GRANDMOTHER?!
MISHA-SAN, I'VE GOT IT!!
HUH?!
DOH! WHERE'D SHE RUN OFF TO?
SHEESH. SHE ALWAYS PICKS THE WORST TIME.
slip
OH WELL, IT'S UP TO ME, THEN.

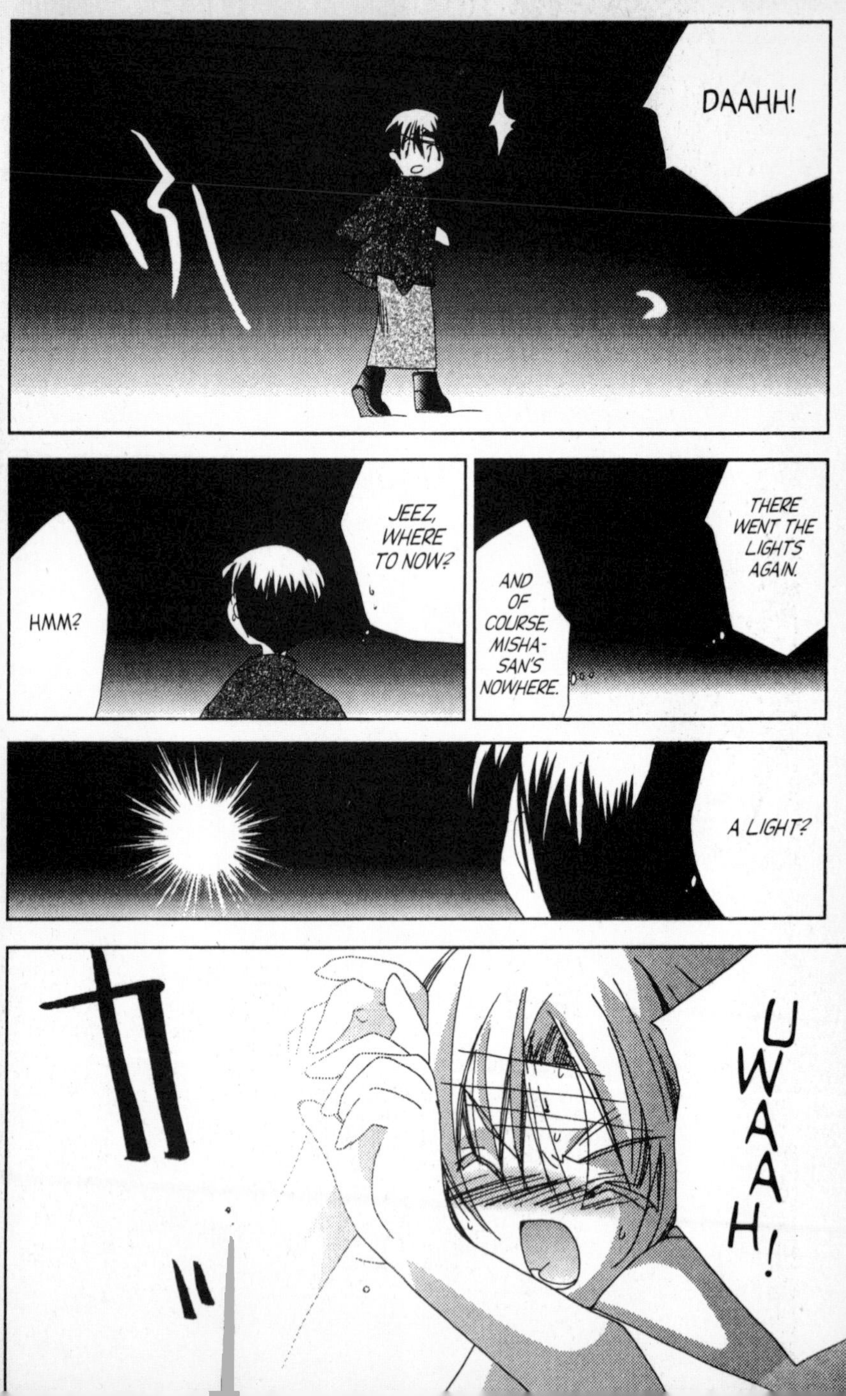
DAAHH!
THERE WENT THE LIGHTS AGAIN.
AND OF COURSE, MISHA-SAN'S NOWHERE.
JEEZ, WHERE TO NOW?
HMM?
A LIGHT?
UWAAH!

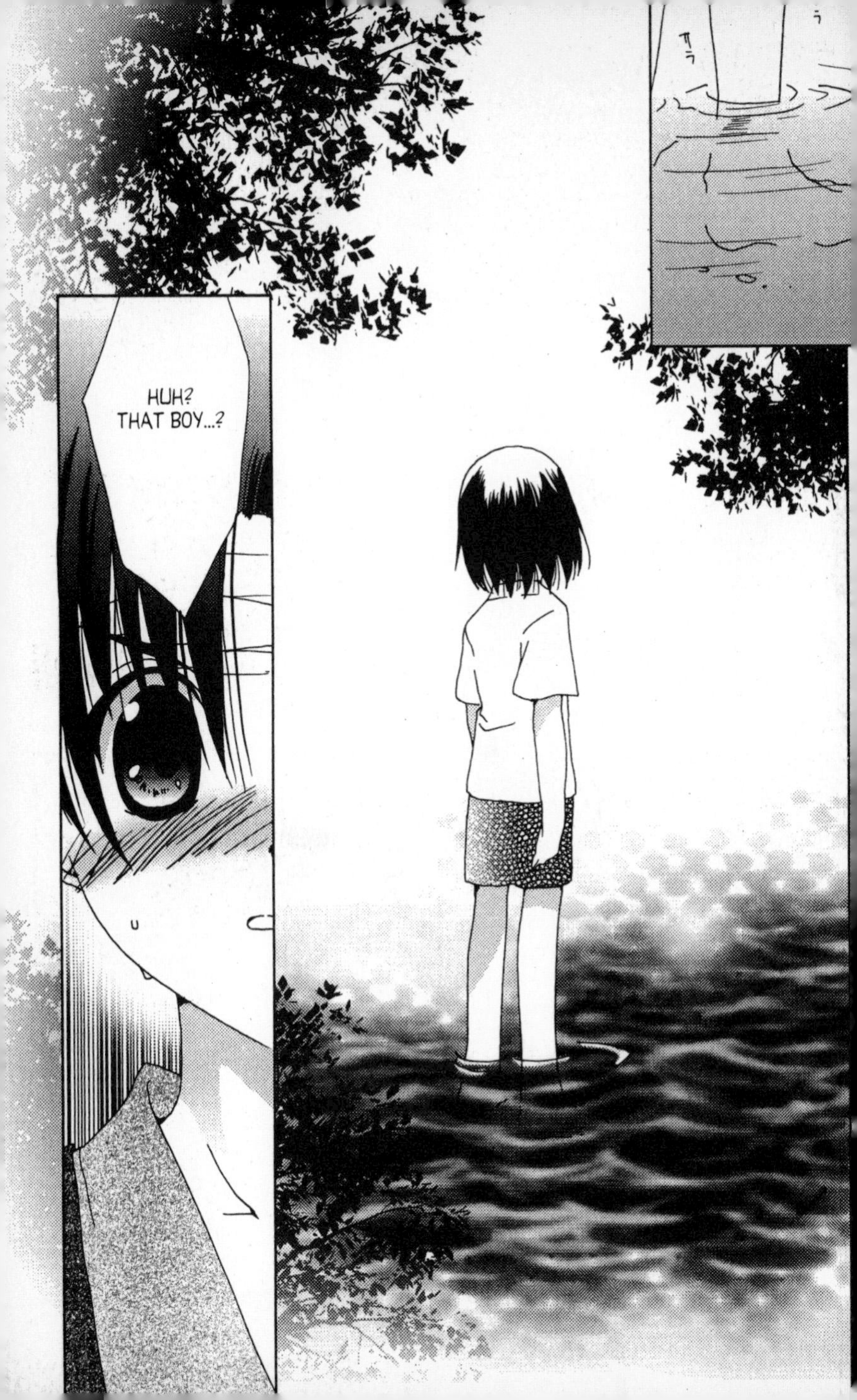
HUH?
THAT BOY...?

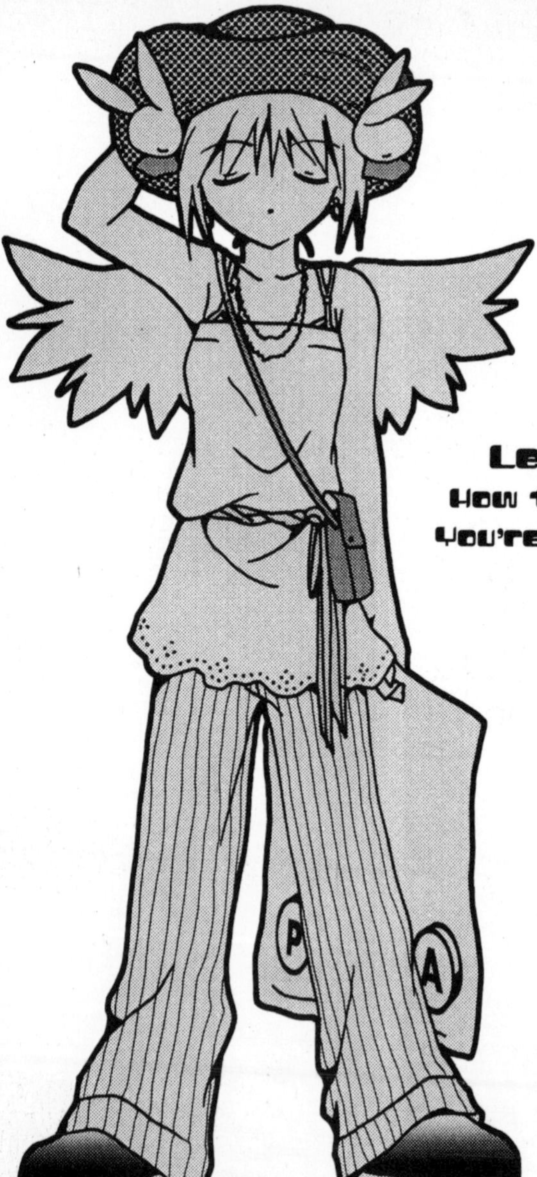
P
A

Lesson 36
How to Find What You're Looking For: Part 4

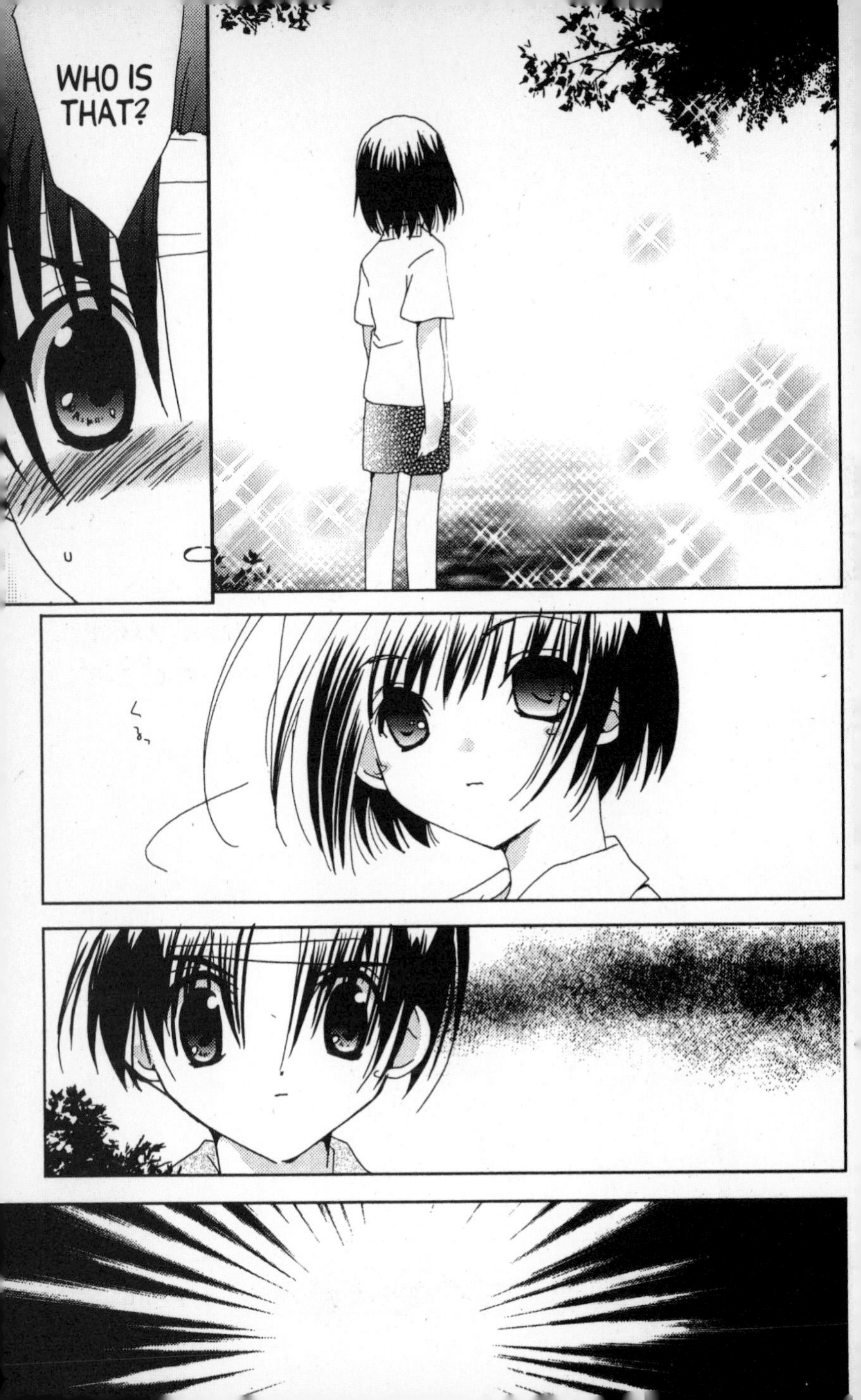
WHO IS THAT?

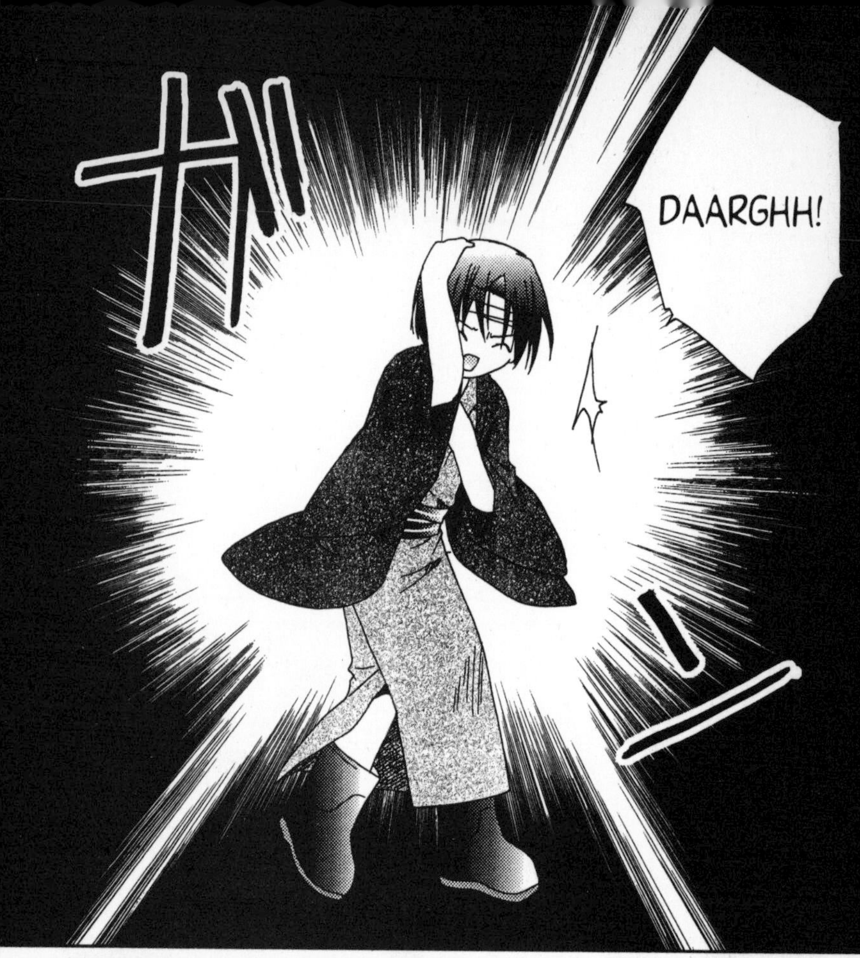
DAARGHH!

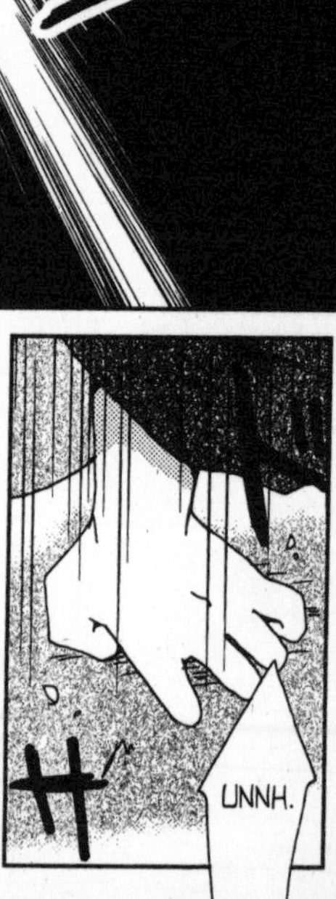
UNNH.

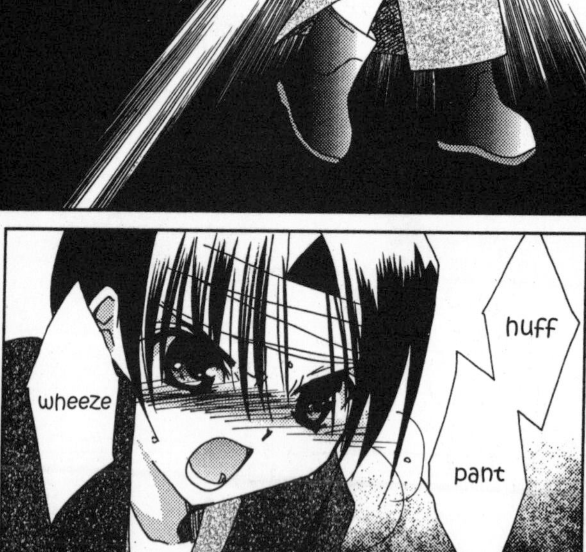
huff
pant
wheeze

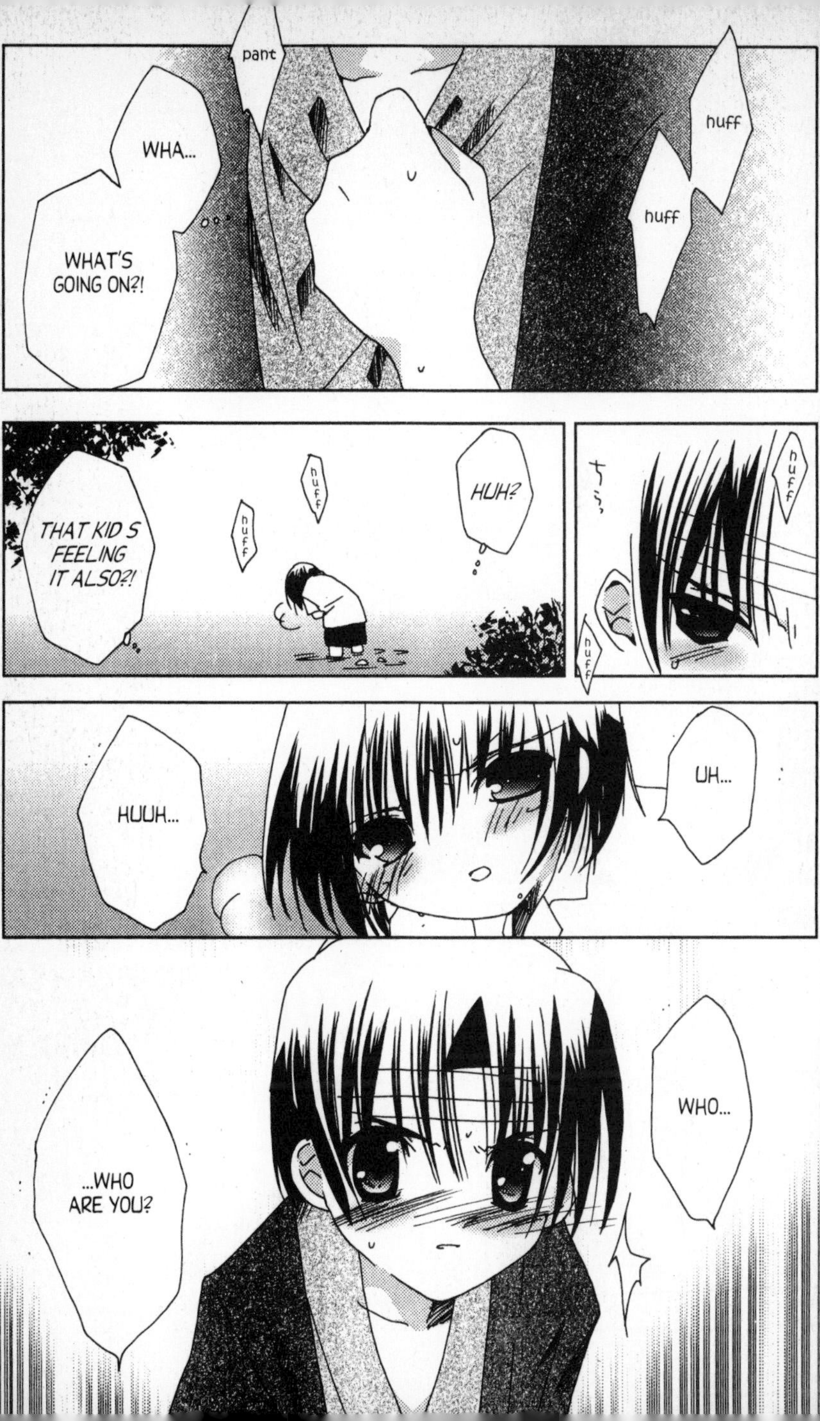
huff
pant
huff
WHA...
WHAT'S GOING ON?!
huff
huff
HUH?
huff
huff
THAT KID S FEELING IT ALSO?!
UH...
HUUH...
WHO...
...WHO ARE YOU?

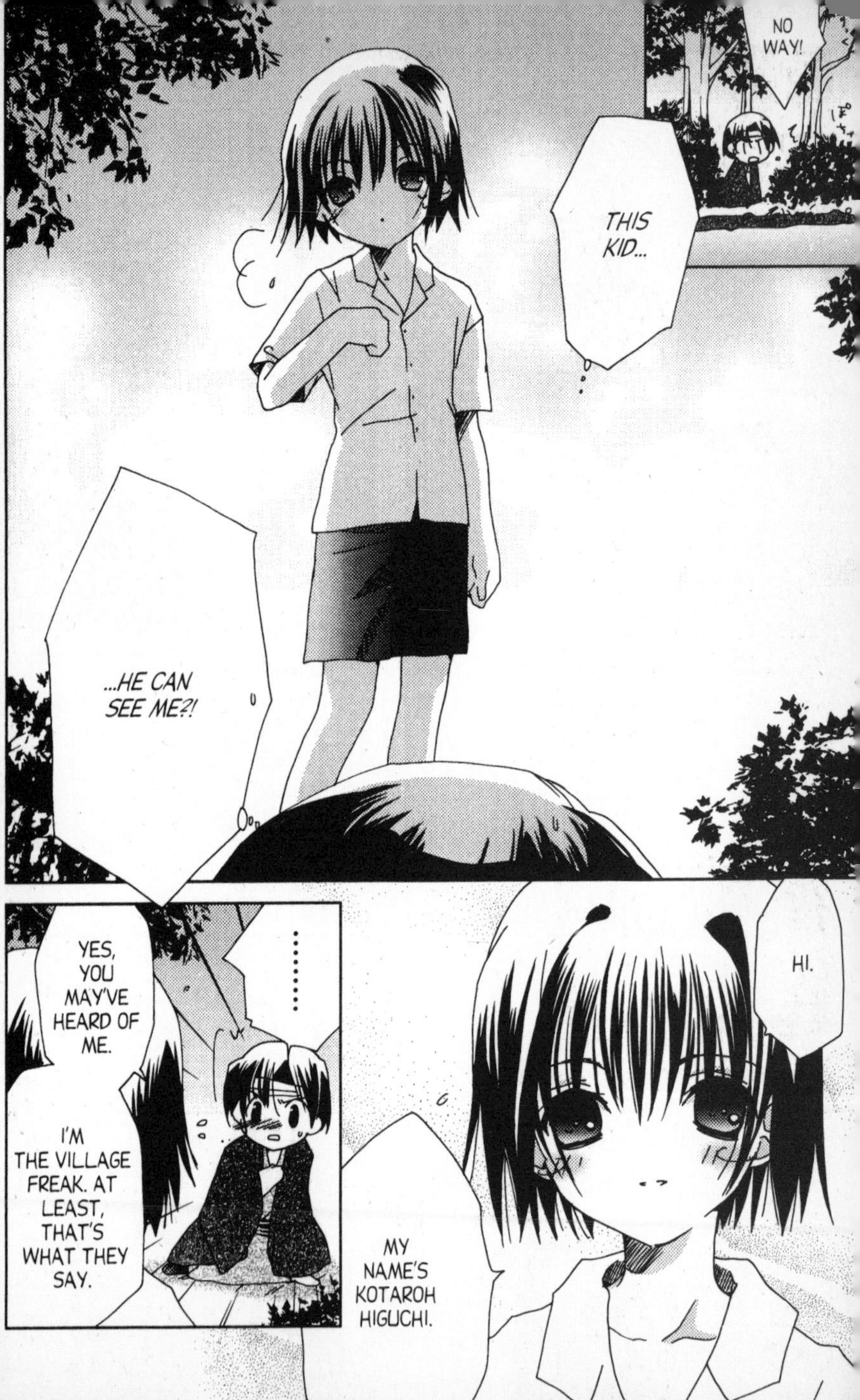
NO WAY!
THIS KID...
...HE CAN SEE ME?!
HI.
MY NAME'S KOTAROH HIGUCHI.
....
YES, YOU MAY'VE HEARD OF ME.
I'M THE VILLAGE FREAK. AT LEAST, THAT'S WHAT THEY SAY.

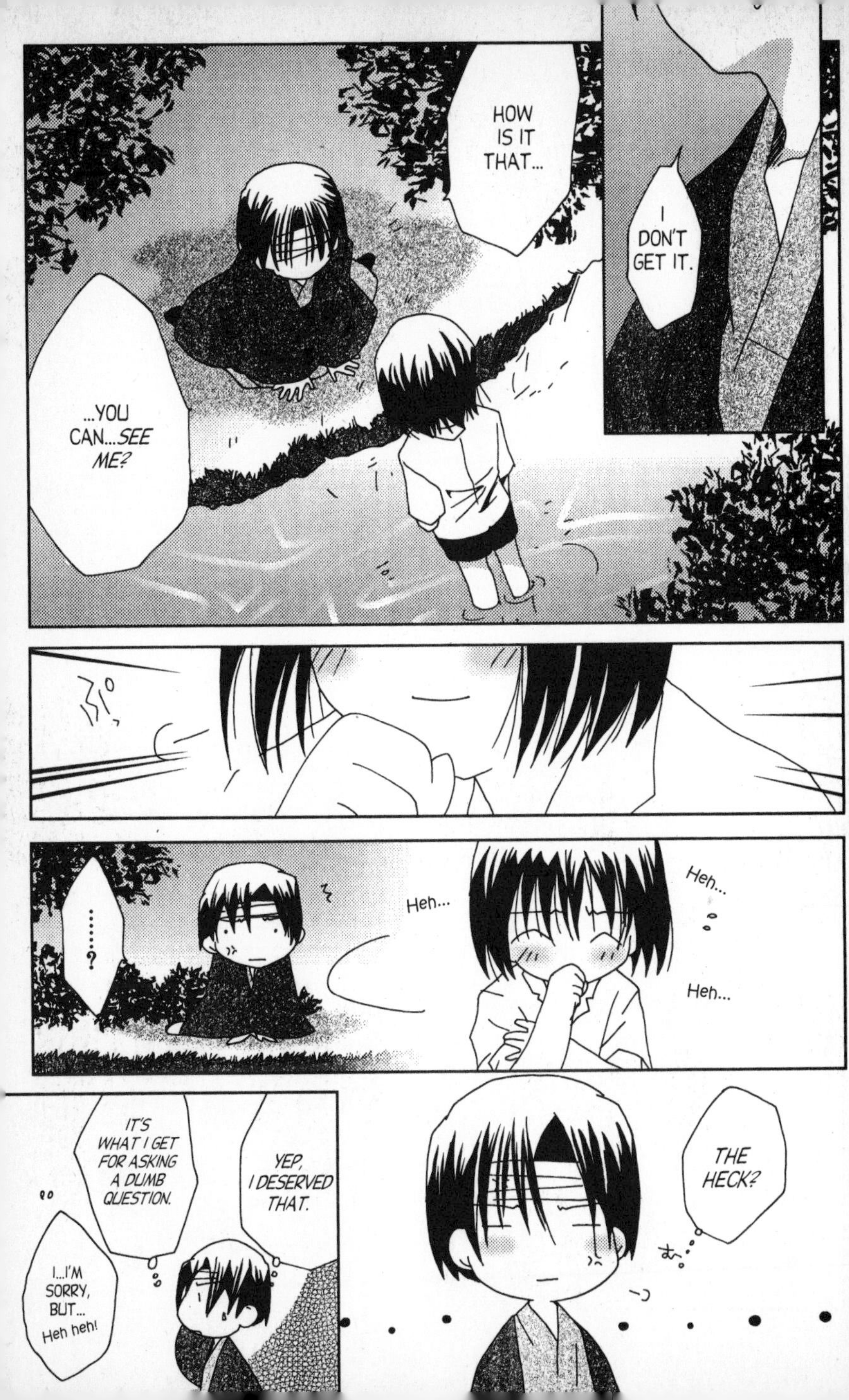
I DON'T GET IT.
HOW IS IT THAT...
...YOU CAN...*SEE* ME?
Heh...
Heh...
Heh...
......?
THE HECK?
YEP, I DESERVED THAT.
IT'S WHAT I GET FOR ASKING A DUMB QUESTION.
I...I'M SORRY, BUT... Heh heh!

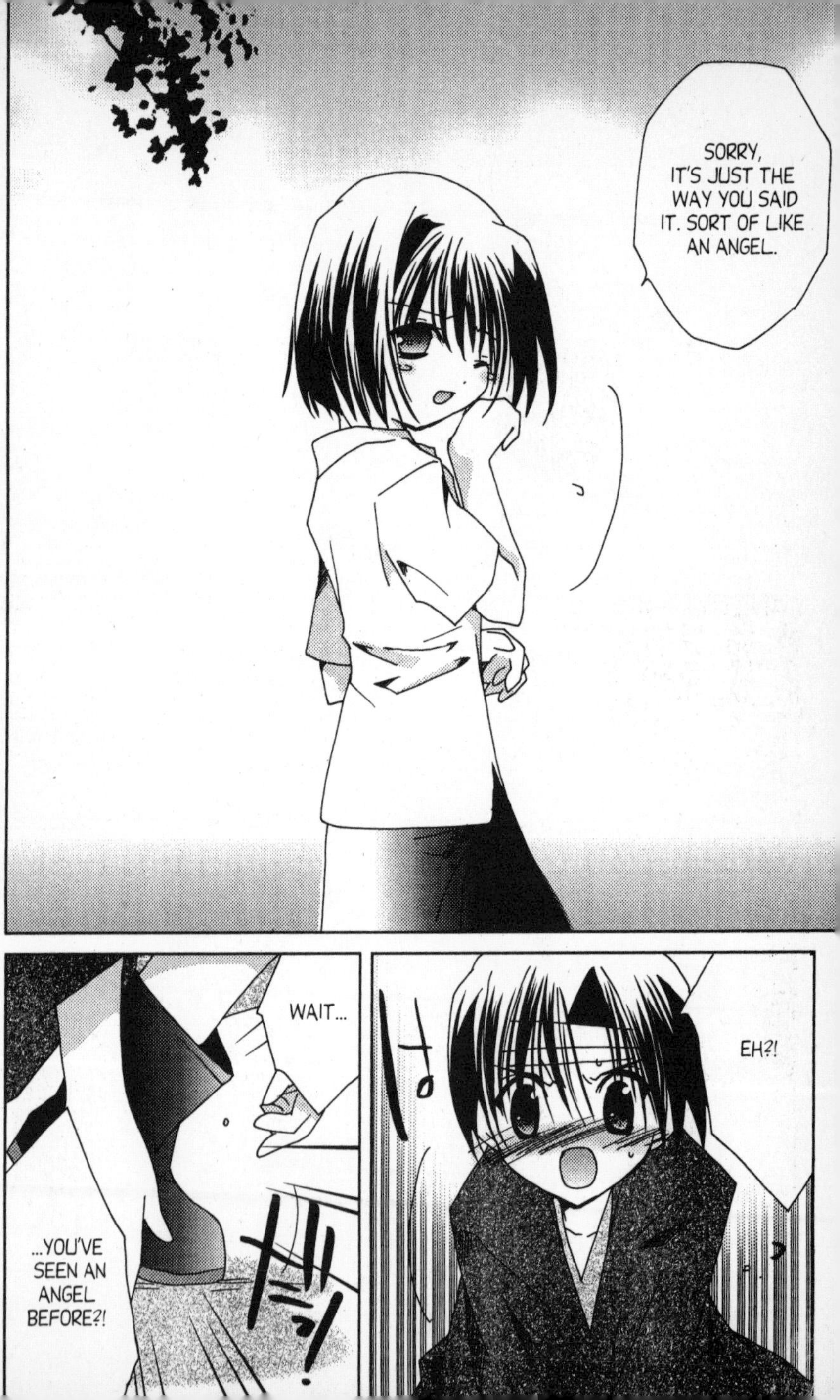
SORRY, IT'S JUST THE WAY YOU SAID IT. SORT OF LIKE AN ANGEL.
EH?!
WAIT...
...YOU'VE SEEN AN ANGEL BEFORE?!

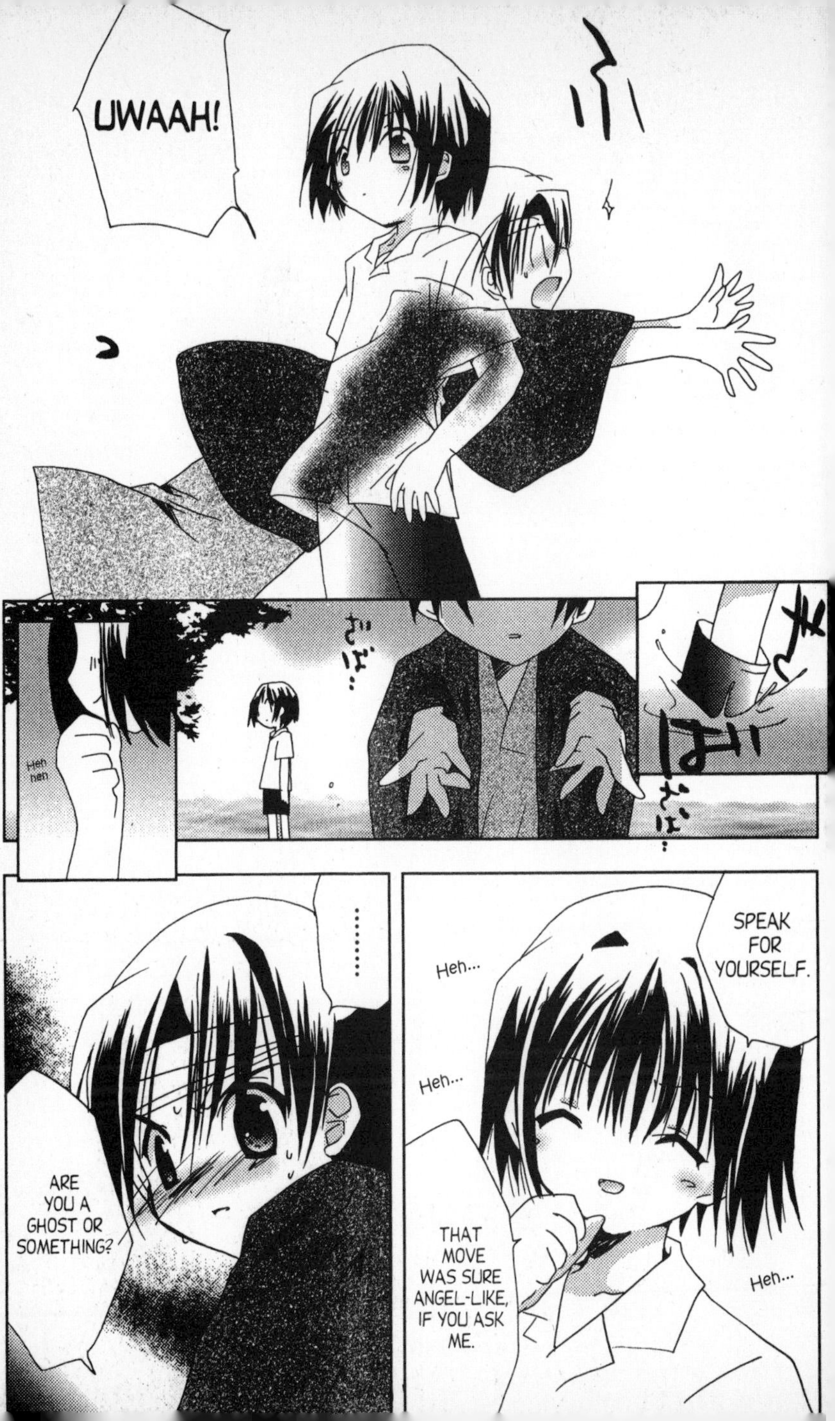
UWAAH!
Heh heh
SPEAK FOR YOURSELF.
Heh...
Heh...
THAT MOVE WAS SURE ANGEL-LIKE, IF YOU ASK ME.
Heh...
......
ARE YOU A GHOST OR SOMETHING?

ばしっ!!
huff
pant
puff
wheeze
pant
pant
...
huff
cough
けほっけほっ
cough

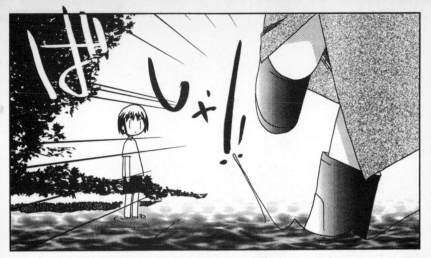

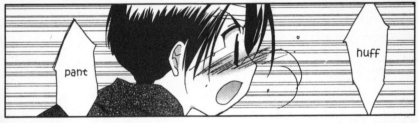

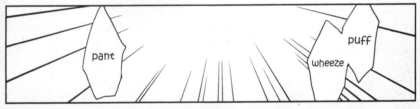

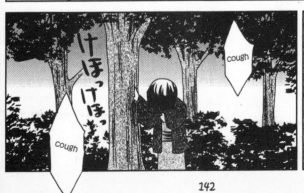

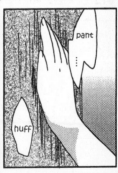

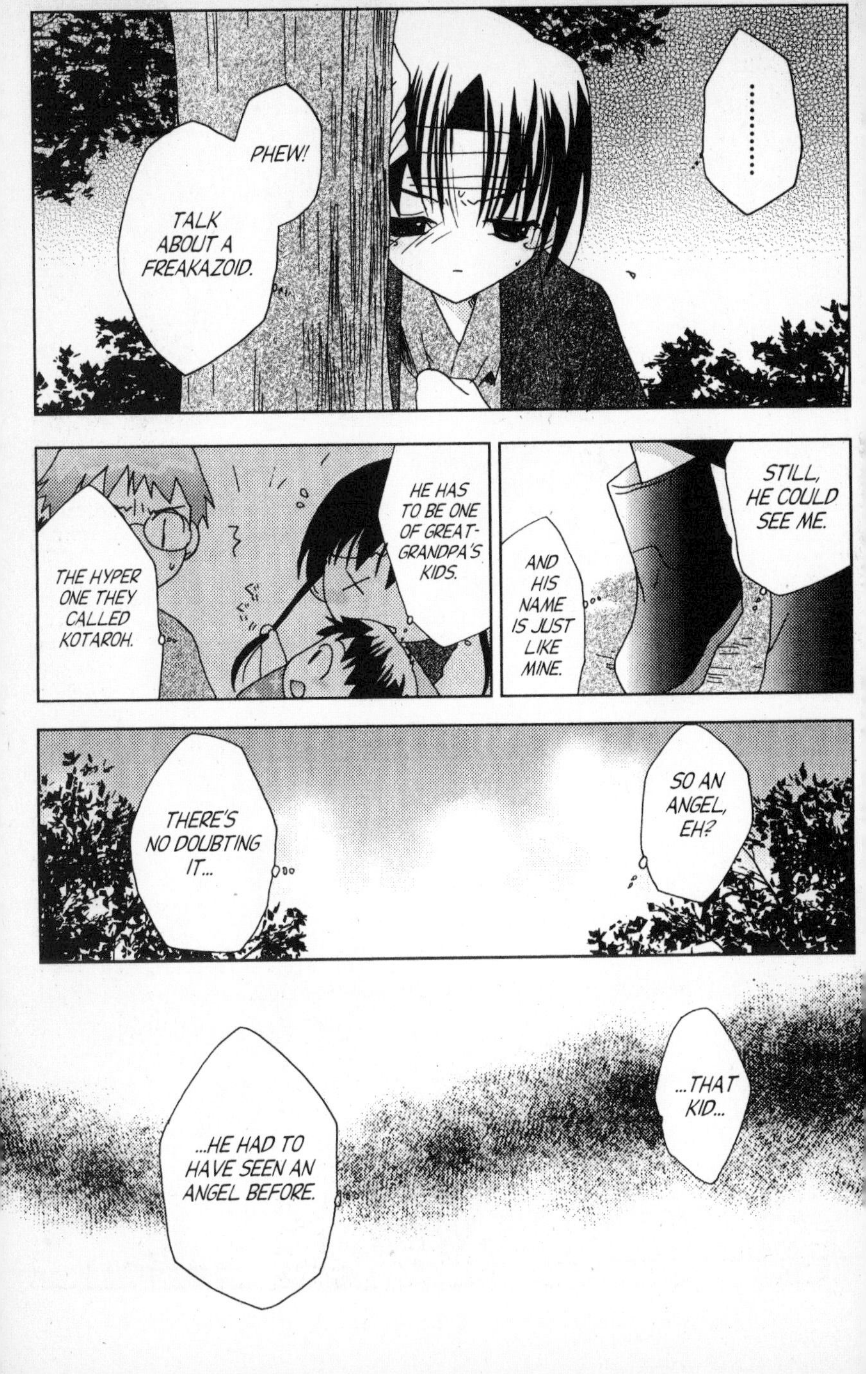
......
PHEW! TALK ABOUT A FREAKAZOID.
STILL, HE COULD SEE ME.
AND HIS NAME IS JUST LIKE MINE.
HE HAS TO BE ONE OF GREAT-GRANDPA'S KIDS.
THE HYPER ONE THEY CALLED KOTAROH.
SO AN ANGEL, EH?
THERE'S NO DOUBTING IT...
...THAT KID...
...HE HAD TO HAVE SEEN AN ANGEL BEFORE.

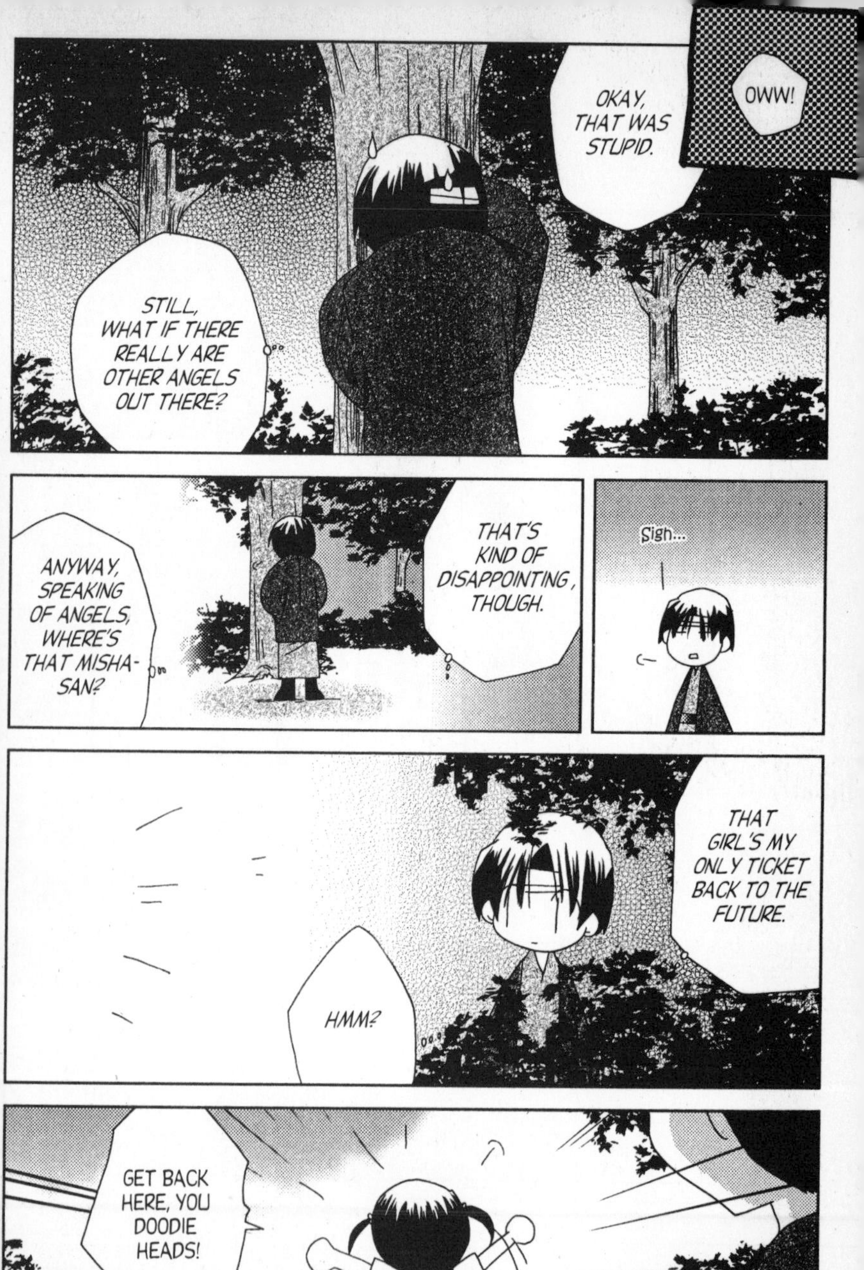
OWW!
OKAY, THAT WAS STUPID.
STILL, WHAT IF THERE REALLY ARE OTHER ANGELS OUT THERE?
Sigh...
THAT'S KIND OF DISAPPOINTING, THOUGH.
ANYWAY, SPEAKING OF ANGELS, WHERE'S THAT MISHA-SAN?
THAT GIRL'S MY ONLY TICKET BACK TO THE FUTURE.
HMM?
GET BACK HERE, YOU DOODIE HEADS!

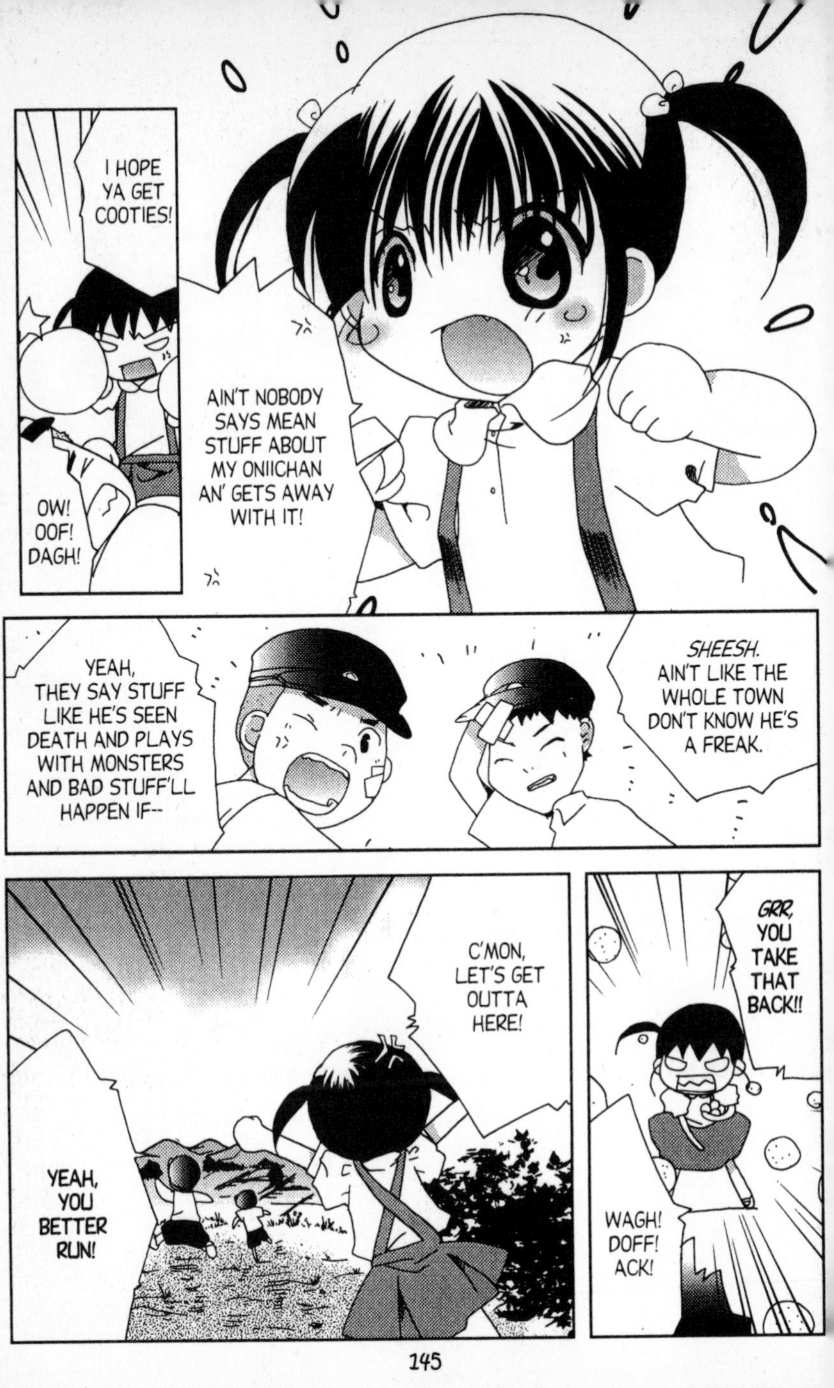
AIN'T NOBODY SAYS MEAN STUFF ABOUT MY ONIICHAN AN' GETS AWAY WITH IT!
I HOPE YA GET COOTIES!
OW! OOF! DAGH!
SHEESH. AIN'T LIKE THE WHOLE TOWN DON'T KNOW HE'S A FREAK.
YEAH, THEY SAY STUFF LIKE HE'S SEEN DEATH AND PLAYS WITH MONSTERS AND BAD STUFF'LL HAPPEN IF--
GRR, YOU TAKE THAT BACK!!
WAGH! DOFF! ACK!
C'MON, LET'S GET OUTTA HERE!
YEAH, YOU BETTER RUN!

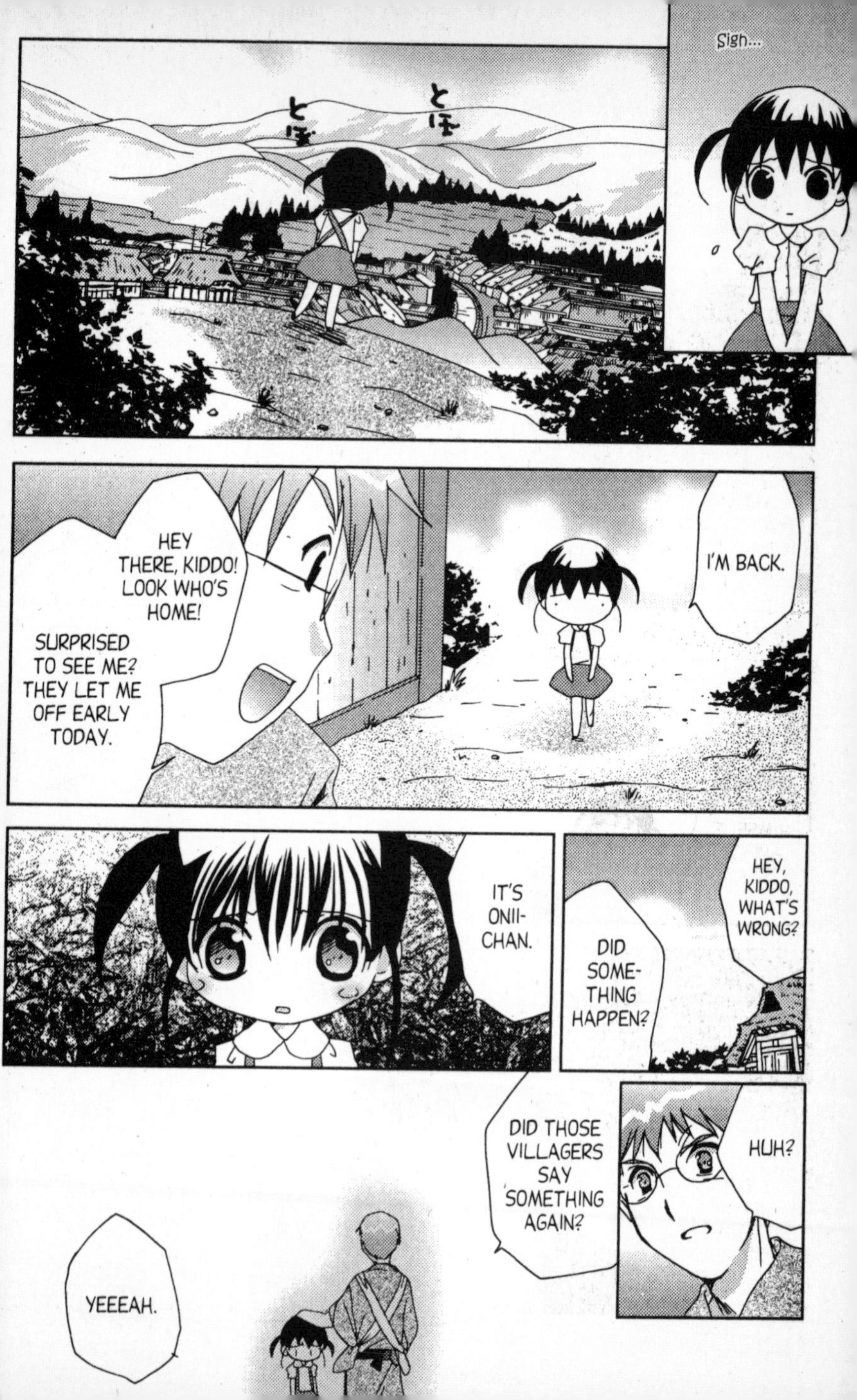
Sigh...
とぼとぼ
I'M BACK.
HEY THERE, KIDDO! LOOK WHO'S HOME!
SURPRISED TO SEE ME? THEY LET ME OFF EARLY TODAY.
HEY, KIDDO, WHAT'S WRONG?
DID SOME-THING HAPPEN?
IT'S ONII-CHAN.
HUH?
DID THOSE VILLAGERS SAY SOMETHING AGAIN?
YEEEAH.

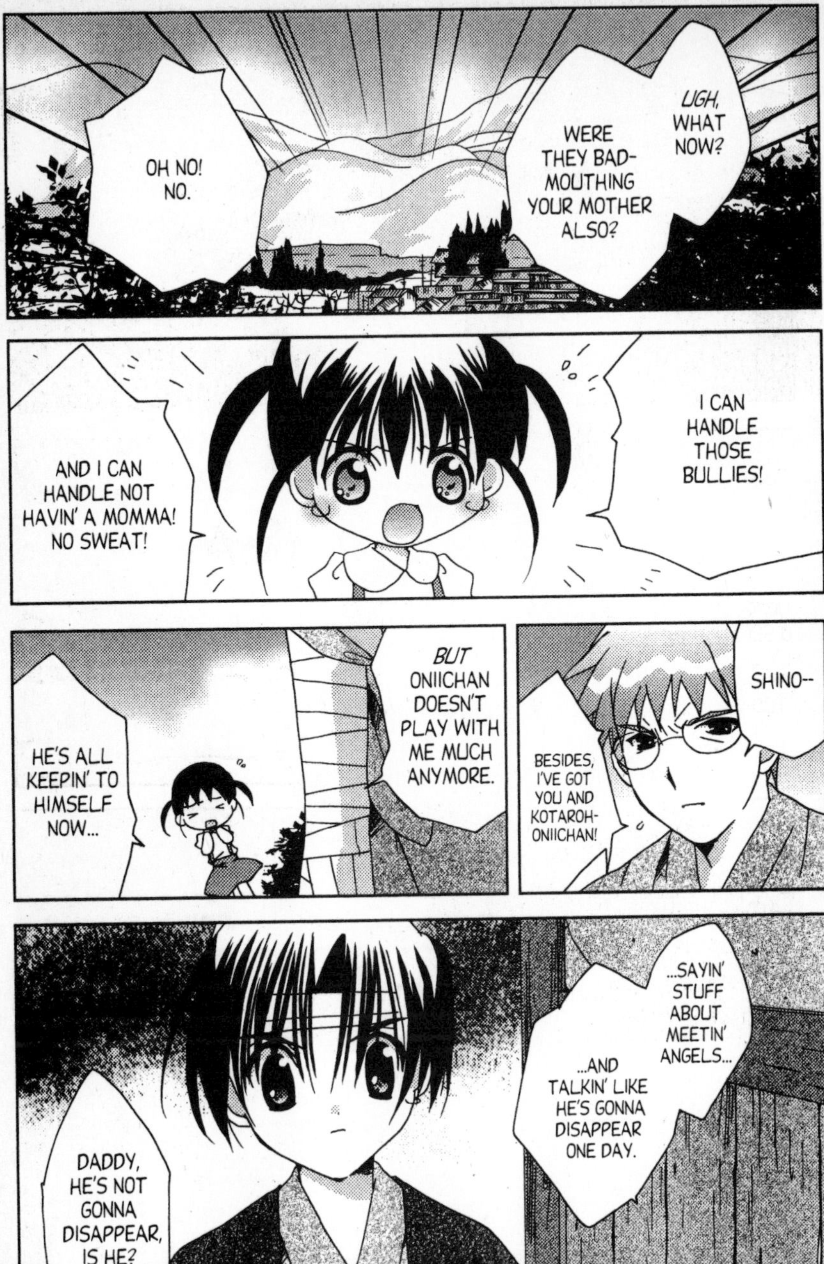
UGH, WHAT NOW?
WERE THEY BAD-MOUTHING YOUR MOTHER ALSO?
OH NO! NO.
I CAN HANDLE THOSE BULLIES!
AND I CAN HANDLE NOT HAVIN' A MOMMA! NO SWEAT!
SHINO--
BESIDES, I'VE GOT YOU AND KOTAROH-ONIICHAN!
BUT ONIICHAN DOESN'T PLAY WITH ME MUCH ANYMORE.
HE'S ALL KEEPIN' TO HIMSELF NOW...
...SAYIN' STUFF ABOUT MEETIN' ANGELS...
...AND TALKIN' LIKE HE'S GONNA DISAPPEAR ONE DAY.
DADDY, HE'S NOT GONNA DISAPPEAR, IS HE?

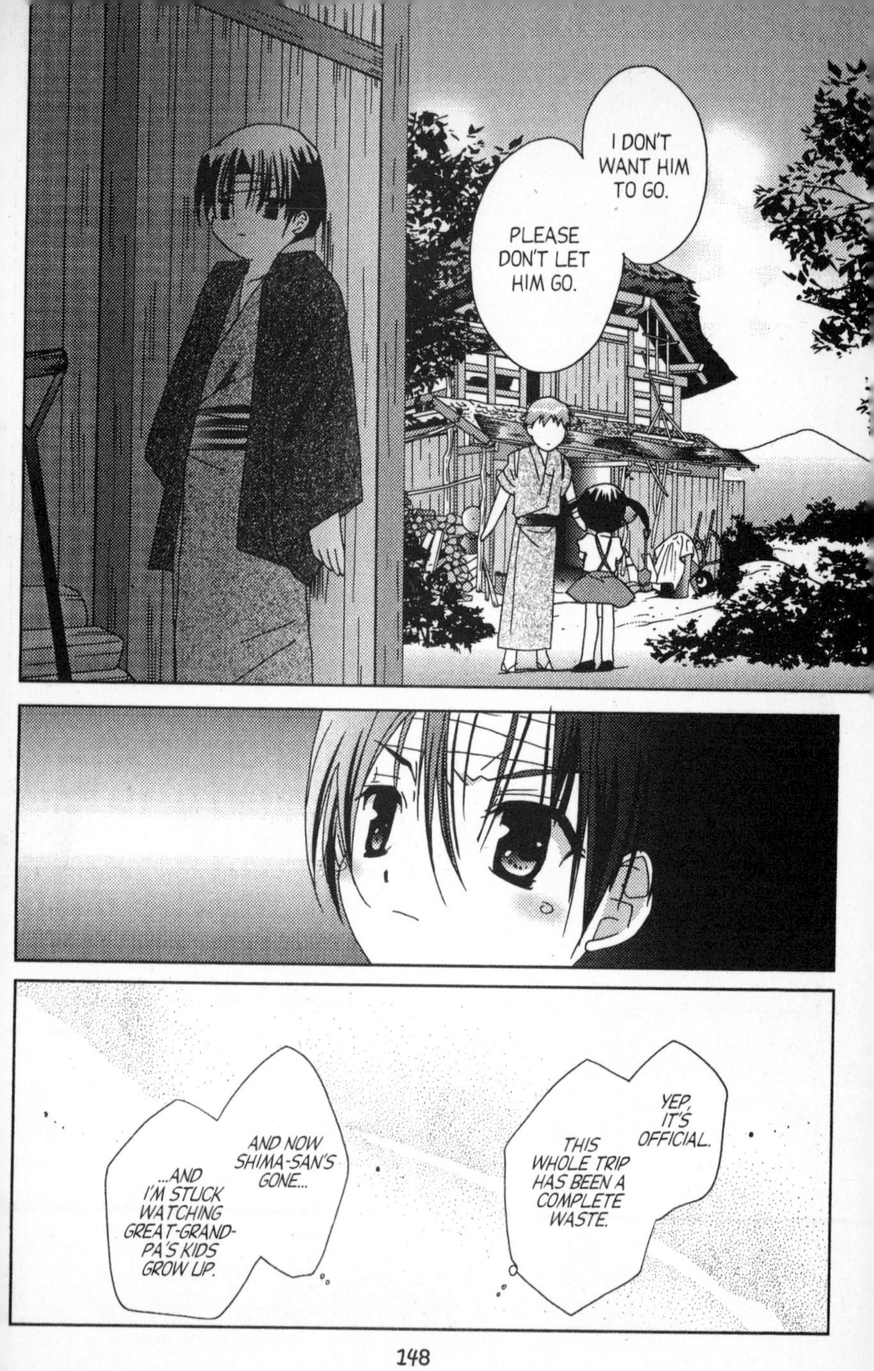
I DON'T WANT HIM TO GO.
PLEASE DON'T LET HIM GO.
YEP, IT'S OFFICIAL.
THIS WHOLE TRIP HAS BEEN A COMPLETE WASTE.
AND NOW SHIMA-SAN'S GONE...
...AND I'M STUCK WATCHING GREAT-GRAND-PA'S KIDS GROW UP.

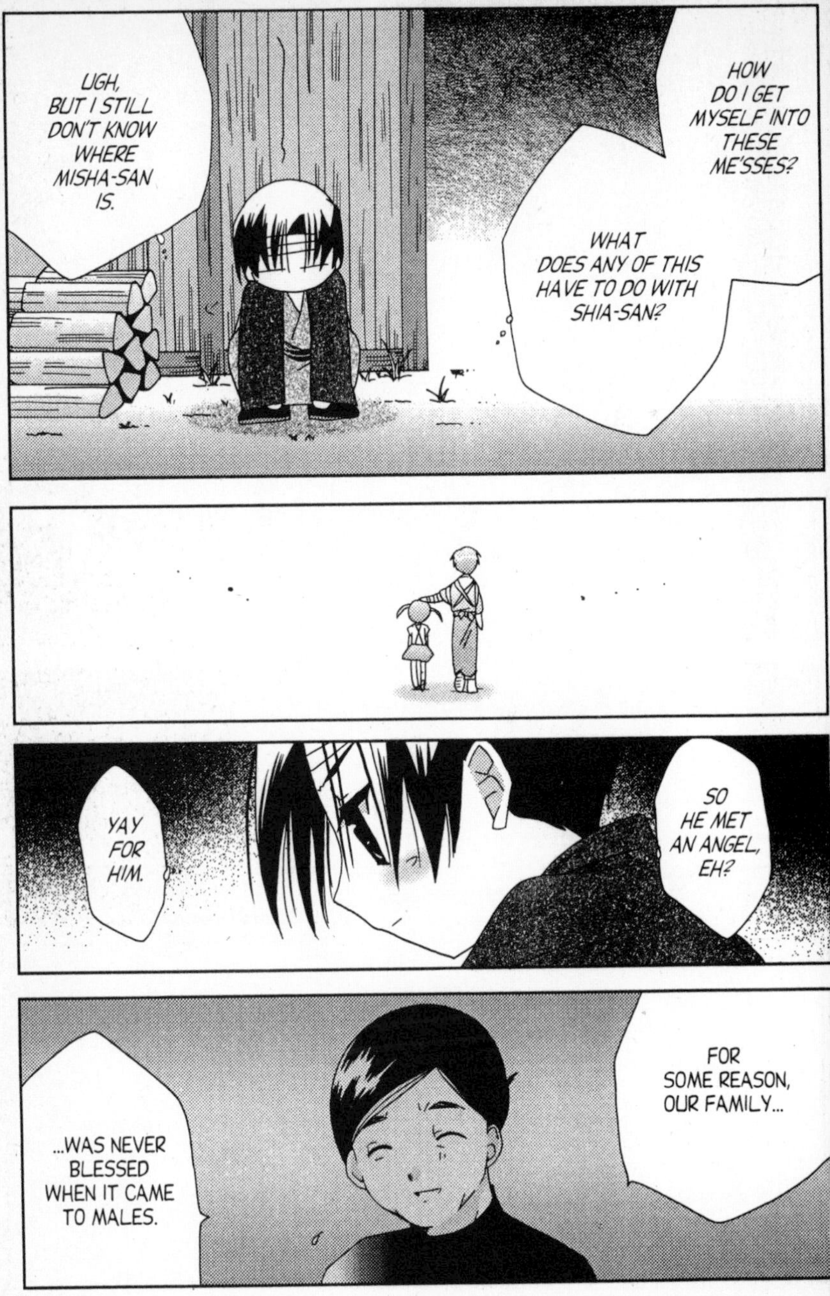
HOW DO I GET MYSELF INTO THESE ME'SSES?
WHAT DOES ANY OF THIS HAVE TO DO WITH SHIA-SAN?
UGH, BUT I STILL DON'T KNOW WHERE MISHA-SAN IS.
SO HE MET AN ANGEL, EH?
YAY FOR HIM.
FOR SOME REASON, OUR FAMILY...
...WAS NEVER BLESSED WHEN IT CAME TO MALES.

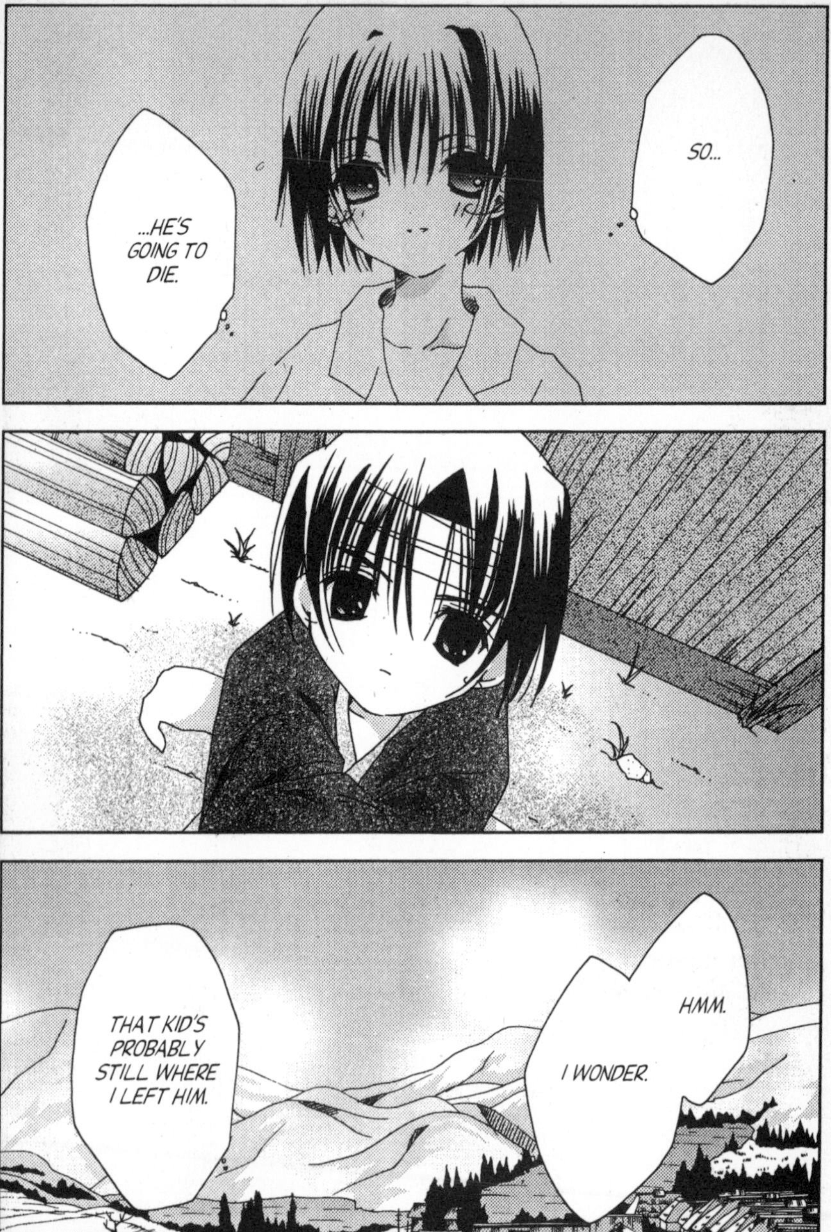
SO...
...HE'S GOING TO DIE.
HMM.
I WONDER.
THAT KID'S PROBABLY STILL WHERE I LEFT HIM.

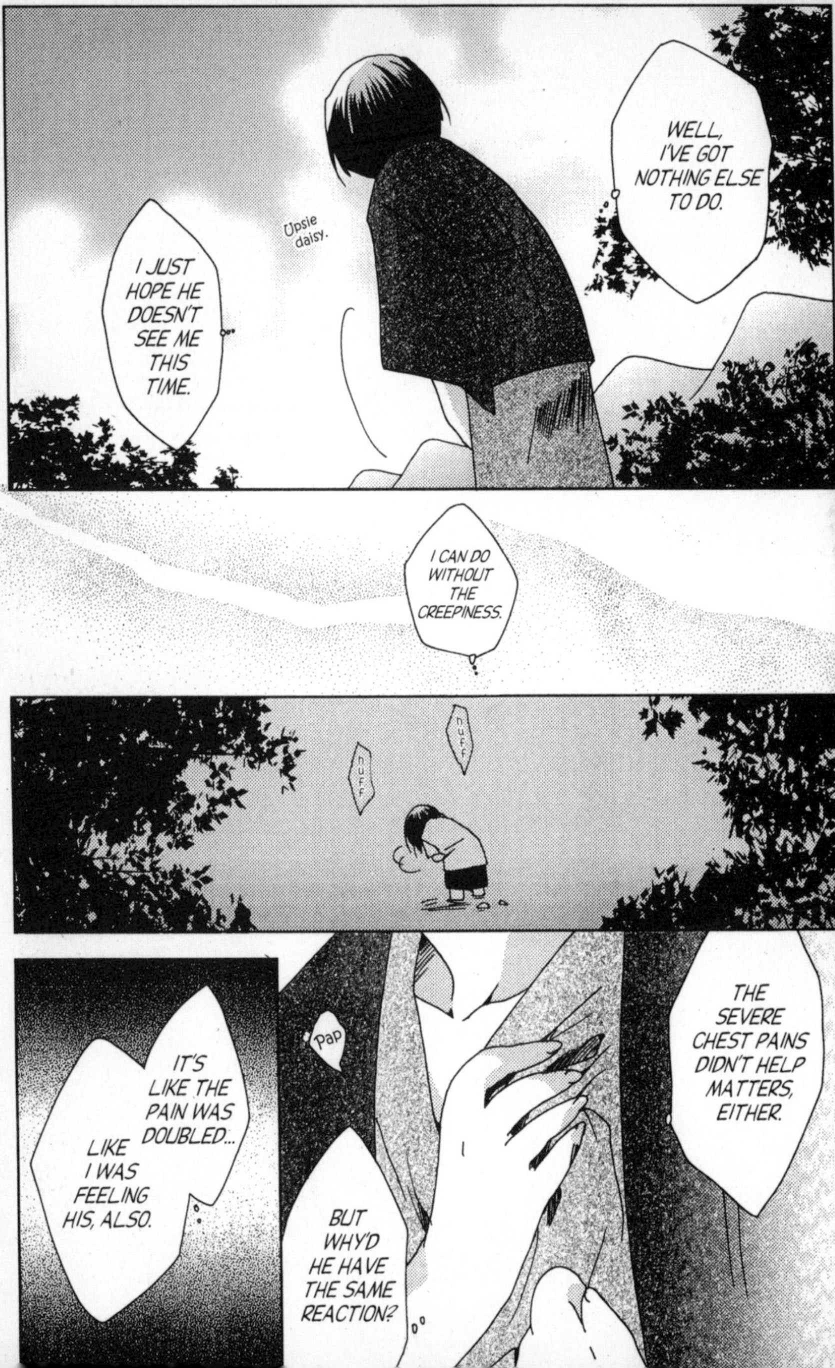
WELL, I'VE GOT NOTHING ELSE TO DO.
Upsie daisy.
I JUST HOPE HE DOESN'T SEE ME THIS TIME.
I CAN DO WITHOUT THE CREEPINESS.
huff
huff
THE SEVERE CHEST PAINS DIDN'T HELP MATTERS, EITHER.
Pap
IT'S LIKE THE PAIN WAS DOUBLED...
LIKE I WAS FEELING HIS, ALSO.
BUT WHY'D HE HAVE THE SAME REACTION?

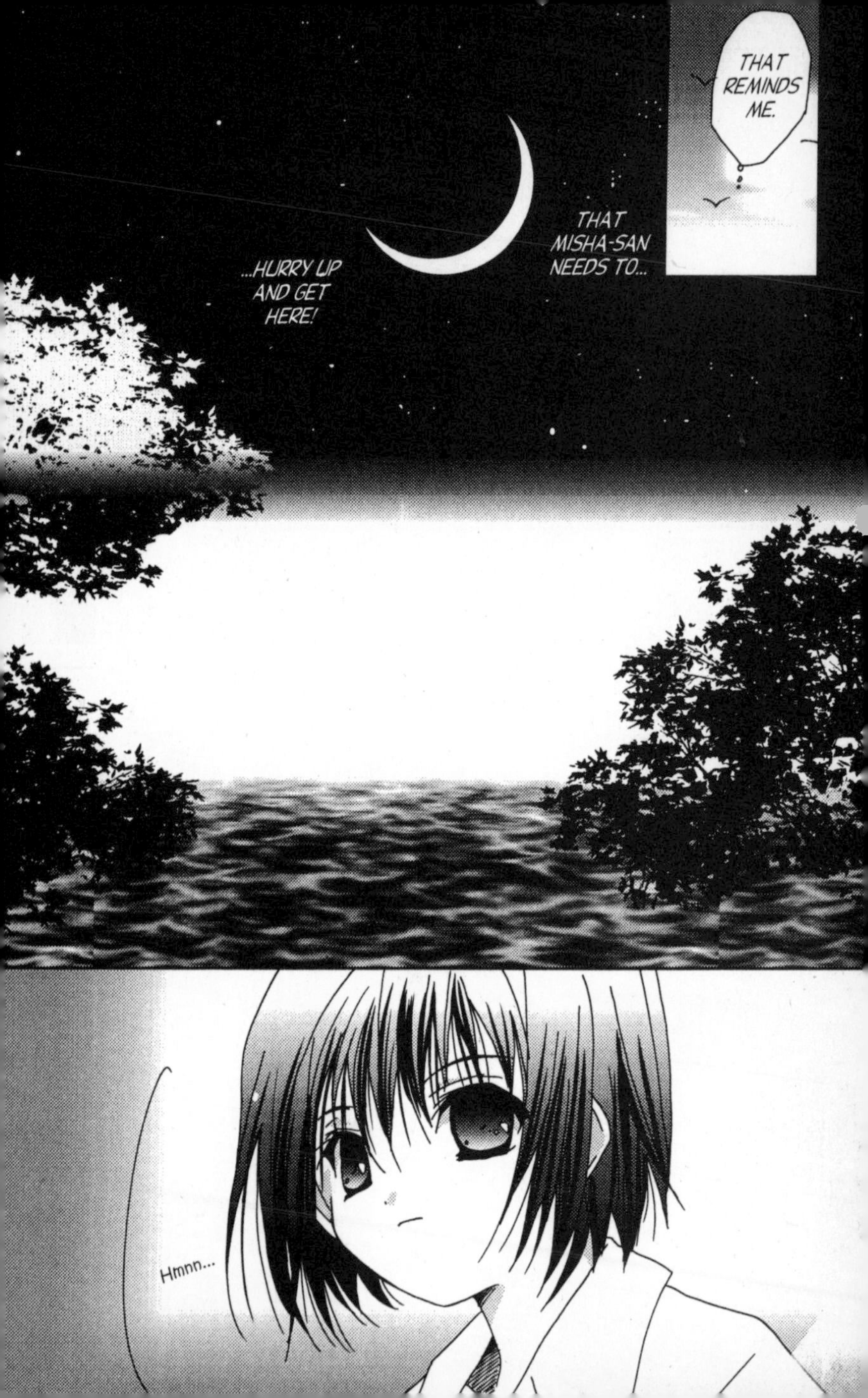
THAT REMINDS ME.
THAT MISHA-SAN NEEDS TO...
...HURRY UP AND GET HERE!
Hmnn...

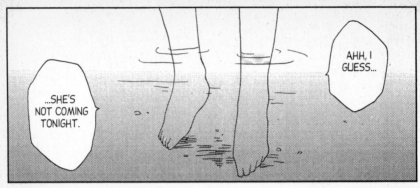

...SHE'S NOT COMING TONIGHT.

AHH, I GUESS...

HOPE THIS ISN'T TOO CONSPICUOUS.

sneaky sneak

OH!

THERE HE IS!!

OHH!!

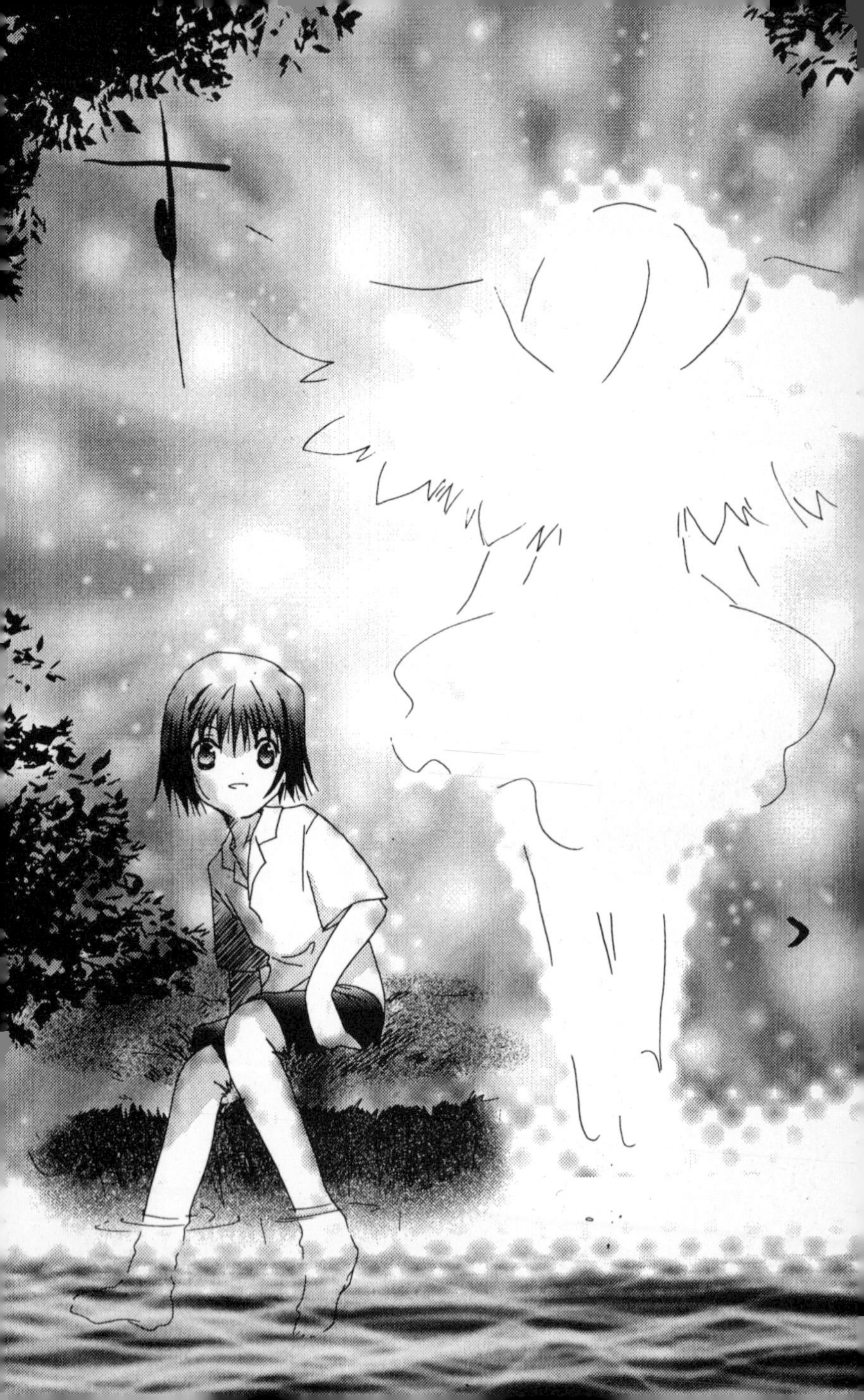

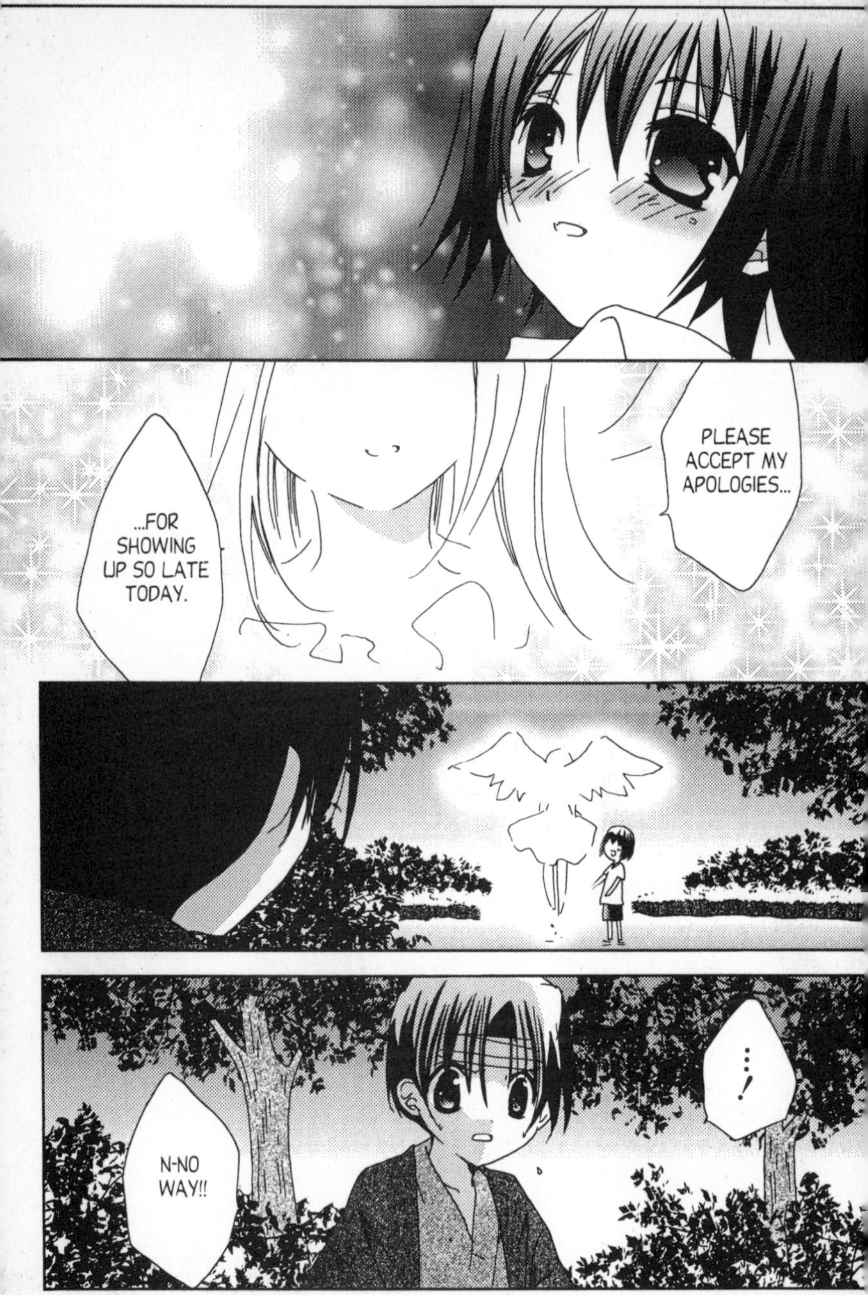
PLEASE ACCEPT MY APOLOGIES...
...FOR SHOWING UP SO LATE TODAY.
...!
N-NO WAY!!

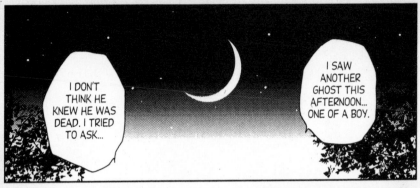

I SAW ANOTHER GHOST THIS AFTERNOON... ONE OF A BOY.
I DON'T THINK HE KNEW HE WAS DEAD. I TRIED TO ASK...
...BUT HE JUST RAN AWAY.
JUST LIKE EVERYONE ELSE OUT THERE.
BUT NOT YOU. YOU'RE DIFFERENT.
AND I LOVE HOW THIS BODY LETS ME SEE YOU.
I'M VERY HAPPY TO SEE YOU TOO.
IT'S SO EXCITING TO ACTUALLY BE ABLE TO SPEAK TO A HUMAN.

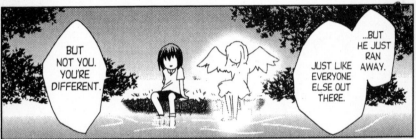

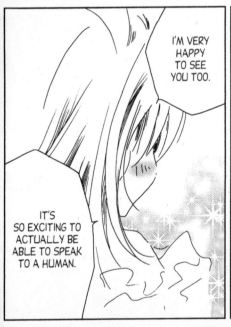

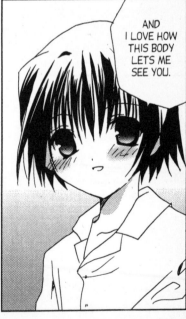

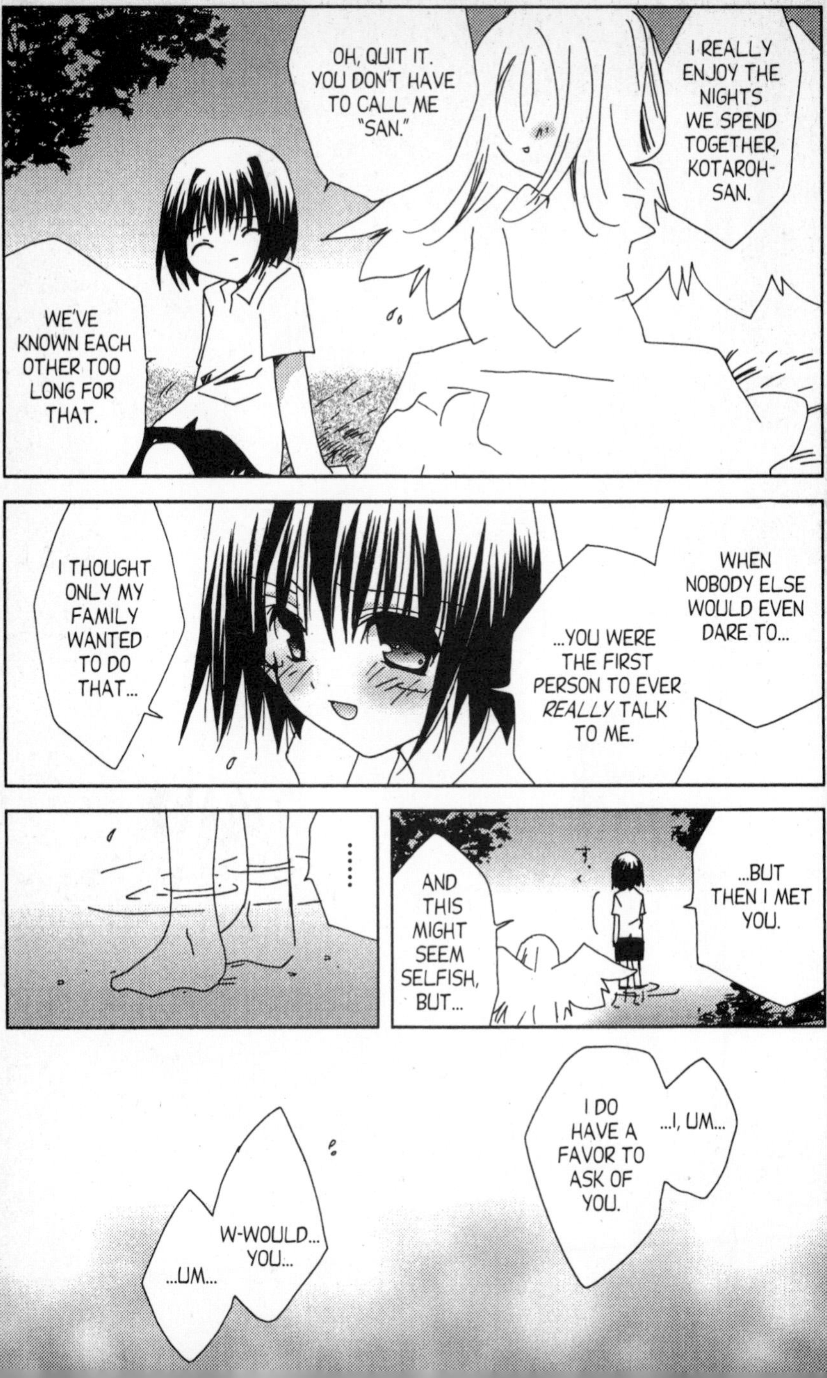

I REALLY ENJOY THE NIGHTS WE SPEND TOGETHER, KOTAROH-SAN.
OH, QUIT IT. YOU DON'T HAVE TO CALL ME "SAN."
WE'VE KNOWN EACH OTHER TOO LONG FOR THAT.
WHEN NOBODY ELSE WOULD EVEN DARE TO...
...YOU WERE THE FIRST PERSON TO EVER *REALLY* TALK TO ME.
I THOUGHT ONLY MY FAMILY WANTED TO DO THAT...
...BUT THEN I MET YOU.
AND THIS MIGHT SEEM SELFISH, BUT...
......
...I, UM...
I DO HAVE A FAVOR TO ASK OF YOU.
W-WOULD... YOU...
...UM...

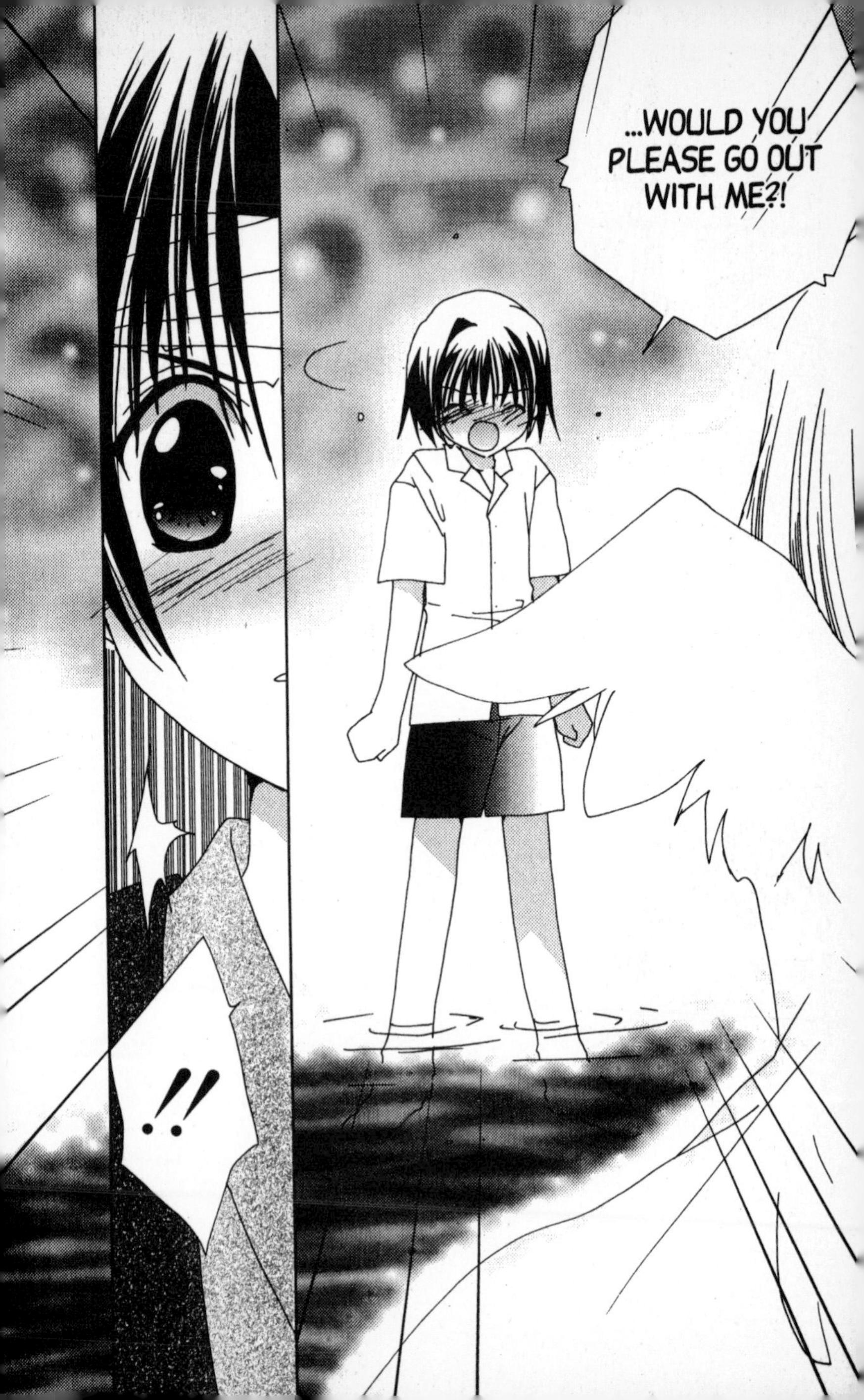
...WOULD YOU PLEASE GO OUT WITH ME?!
!!

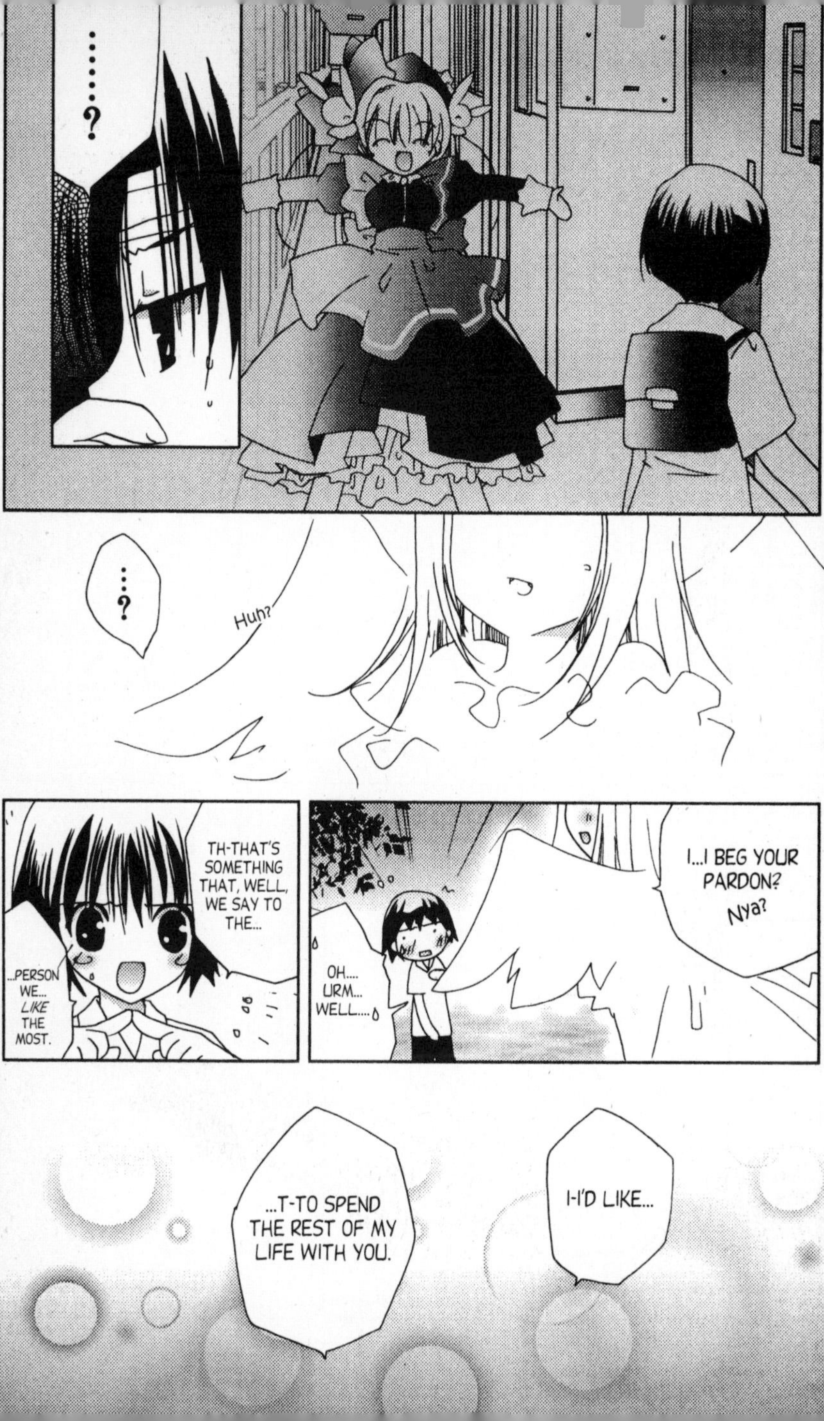
...?
Huh?
...?
I...I BEG YOUR PARDON? Nya?
OH.... URM... WELL....
TH-THAT'S SOMETHING THAT, WELL, WE SAY TO THE...
...PERSON WE... *LIKE* THE MOST.
I-I'D LIKE...
...T-TO SPEND THE REST OF MY LIFE WITH YOU.

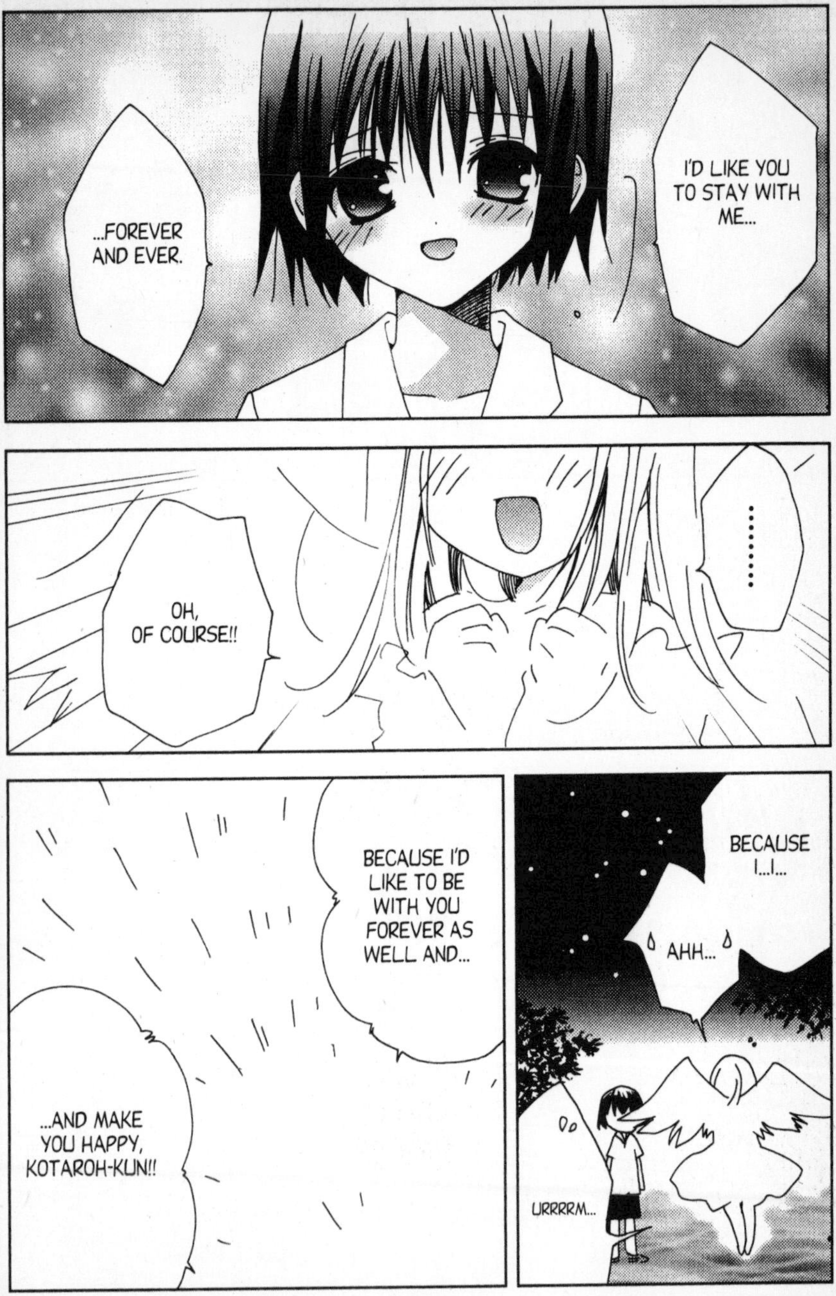
I'D LIKE YOU TO STAY WITH ME...
...FOREVER AND EVER.
....
OH, OF COURSE!!
BECAUSE I...I...
AHH...
URRRRM...
BECAUSE I'D LIKE TO BE WITH YOU FOREVER AS WELL AND...
...AND MAKE YOU HAPPY, KOTAROH-KUN!!

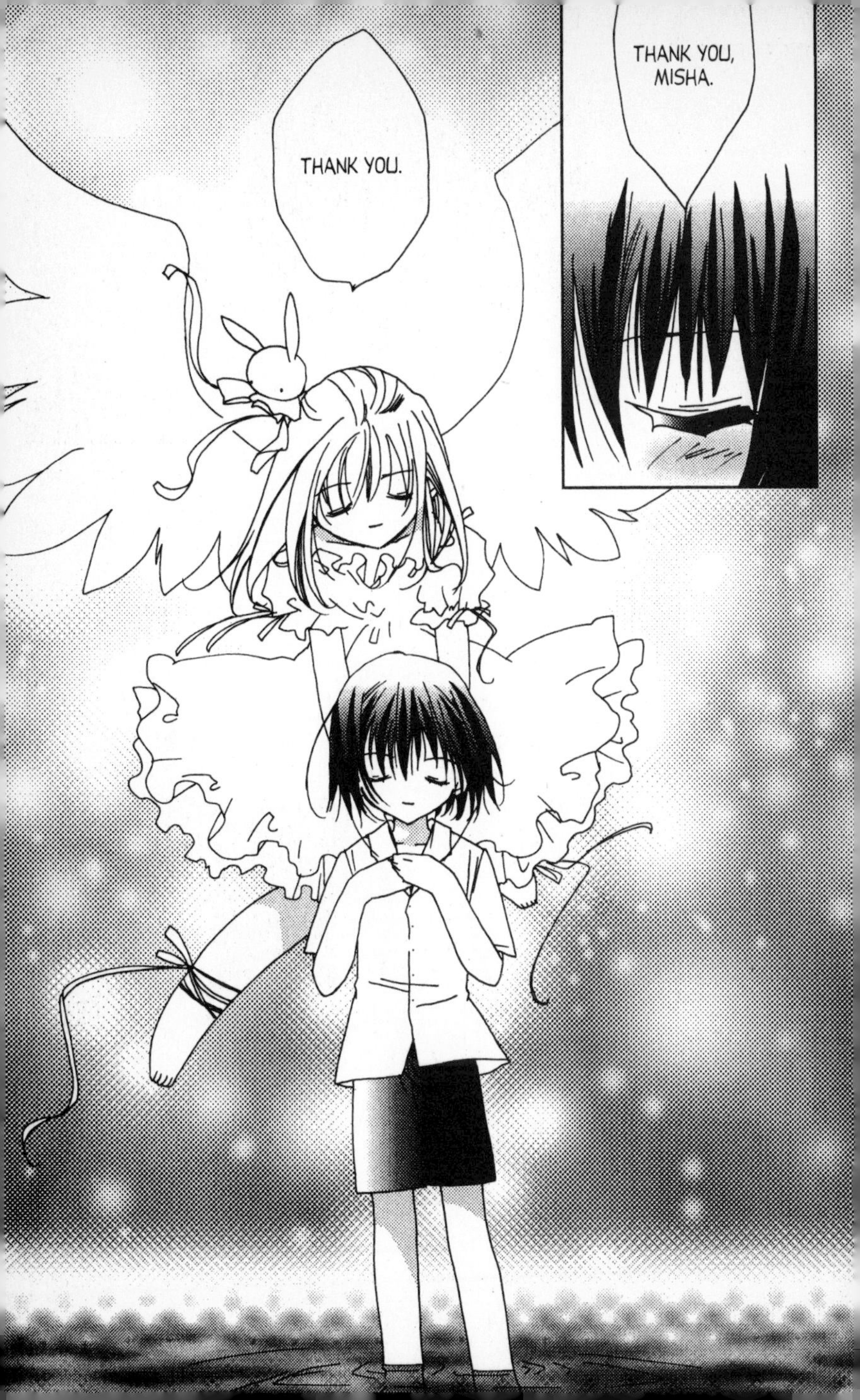
THANK YOU, MISHA.
THANK YOU.

WHOOOOOOAAI

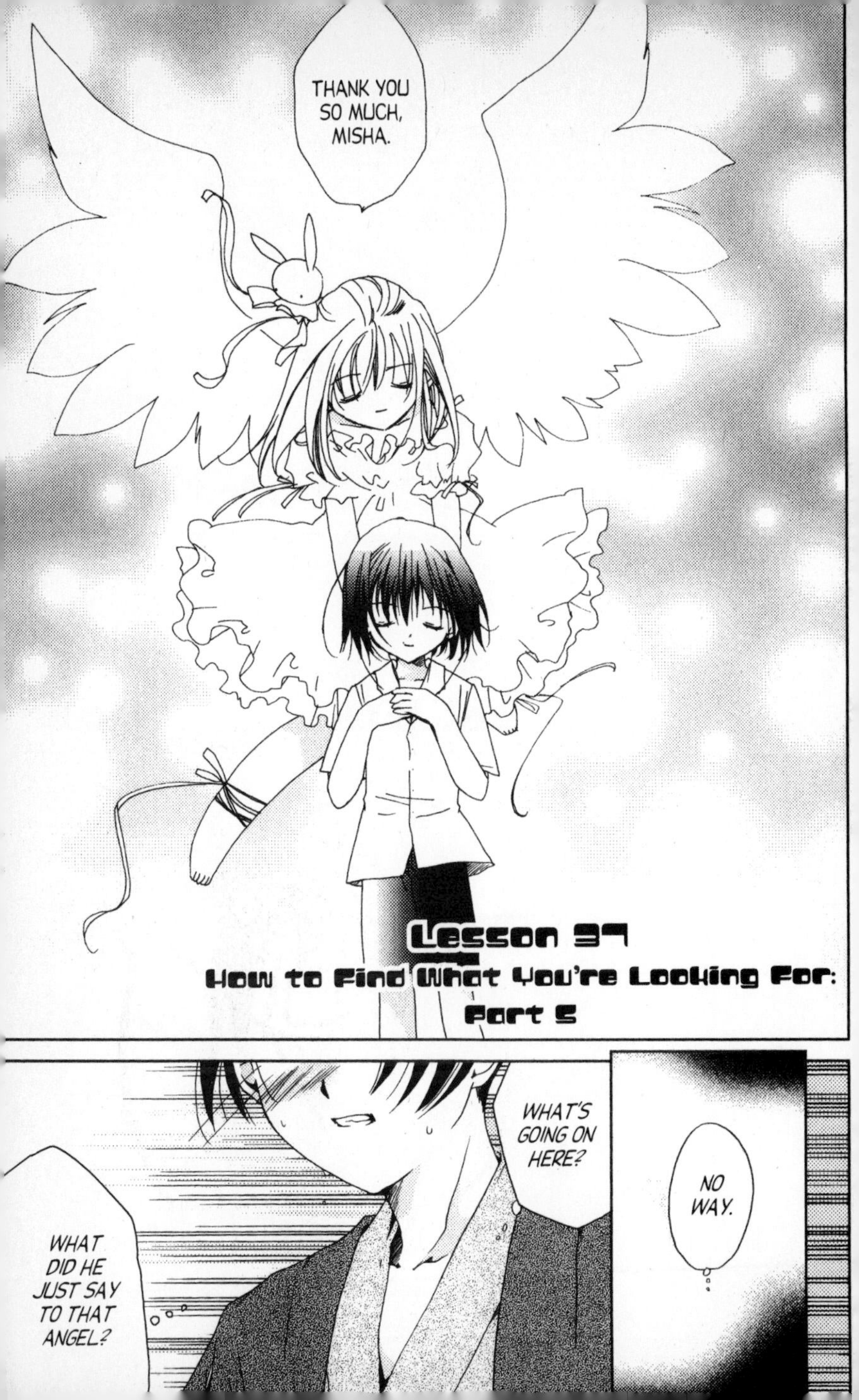
THANK YOU SO MUCH, MISHA.
Lesson 37
How to Find What You're Looking For: Part 5
NO WAY.
WHAT'S GOING ON HERE?
WHAT DID HE JUST SAY TO THAT ANGEL?

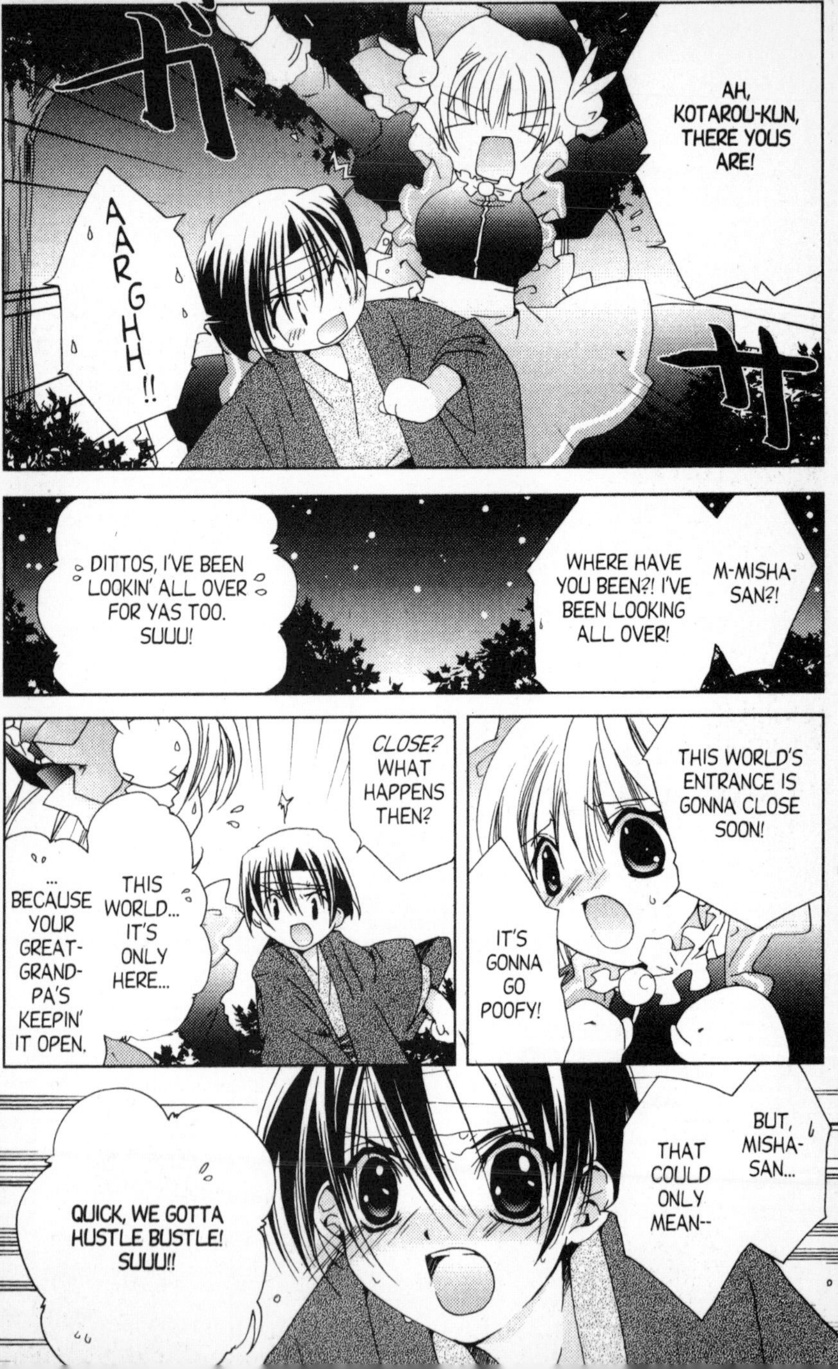
AH, KOTAROU-KUN, THERE YOUS ARE!
AARGHH!!
M-MISHA-SAN?!
WHERE HAVE YOU BEEN?! I'VE BEEN LOOKING ALL OVER!
DITTOS, I'VE BEEN LOOKIN' ALL OVER FOR YAS TOO. SUUU!
THIS WORLD'S ENTRANCE IS GONNA CLOSE SOON!
IT'S GONNA GO POOFY!
CLOSE? WHAT HAPPENS THEN?
THIS WORLD... IT'S ONLY HERE...
...BECAUSE YOUR GREAT-GRANDPA'S KEEPIN' IT OPEN.
BUT, MISHA-SAN...
THAT COULD ONLY MEAN--
QUICK, WE GOTTA HUSTLE BUSTLE! SUUU!!

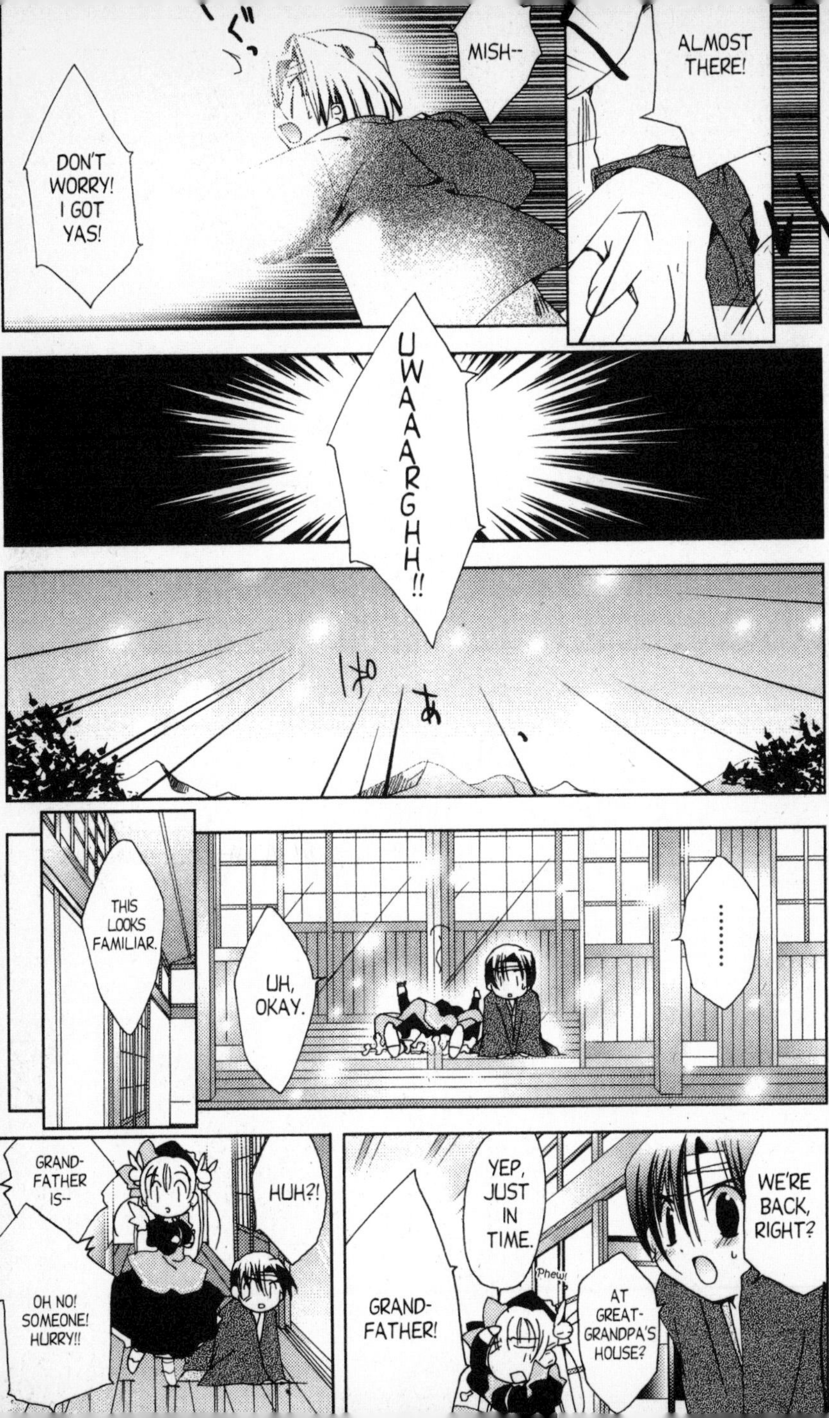
ALMOST THERE!
MISH--
DON'T WORRY! I GOT YAS!
UWAAAARGHH!!
......
UH, OKAY.
THIS LOOKS FAMILIAR.
WE'RE BACK, RIGHT?
AT GREAT-GRANDPA'S HOUSE?
YEP, JUST IN TIME.
Phew!
GRAND-FATHER!
HUH?!
GRAND-FATHER IS--
OH NO! SOMEONE! HURRY!!

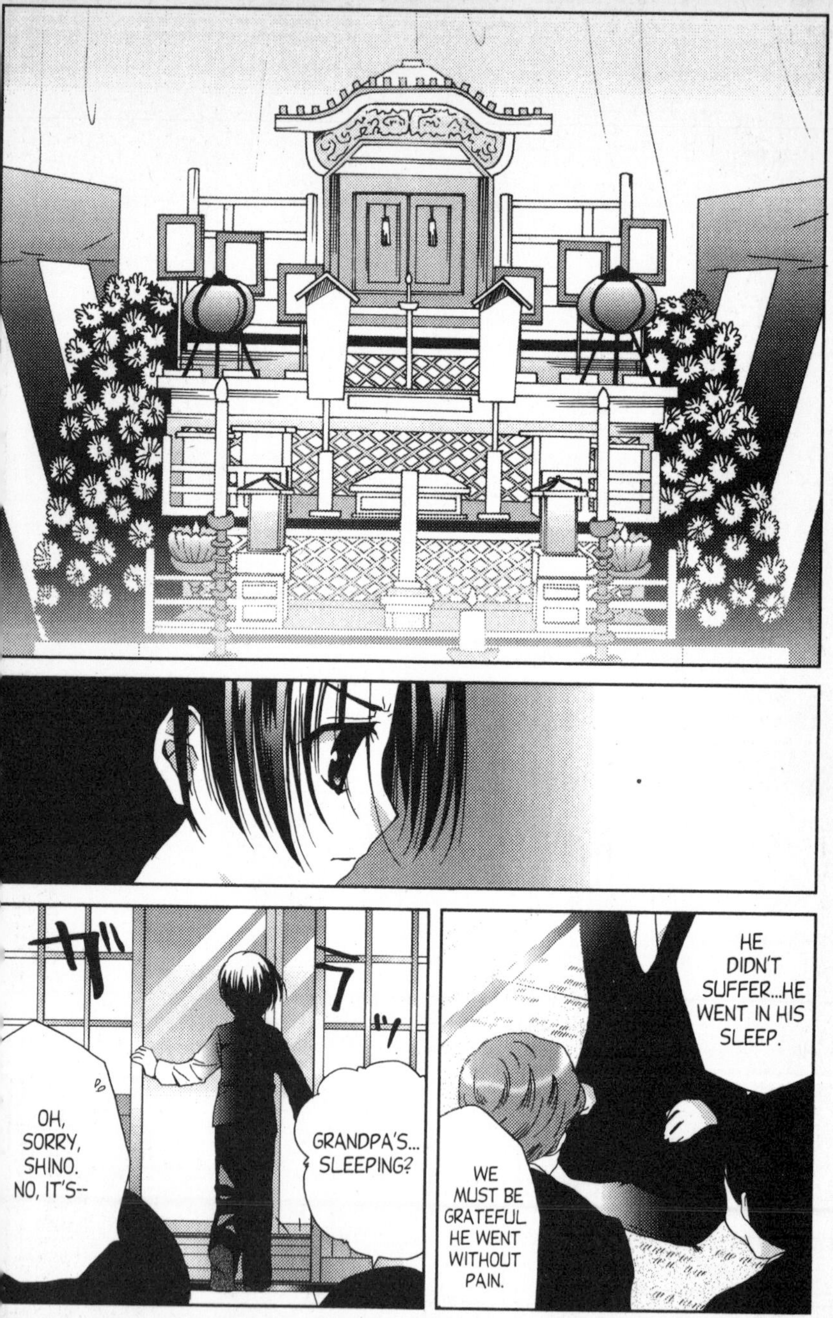
HE DIDN'T SUFFER...HE WENT IN HIS SLEEP.
WE MUST BE GRATEFUL HE WENT WITHOUT PAIN.
ガラッ
GRANDPA'S... SLEEPING?
OH, SORRY, SHINO. NO, IT'S--

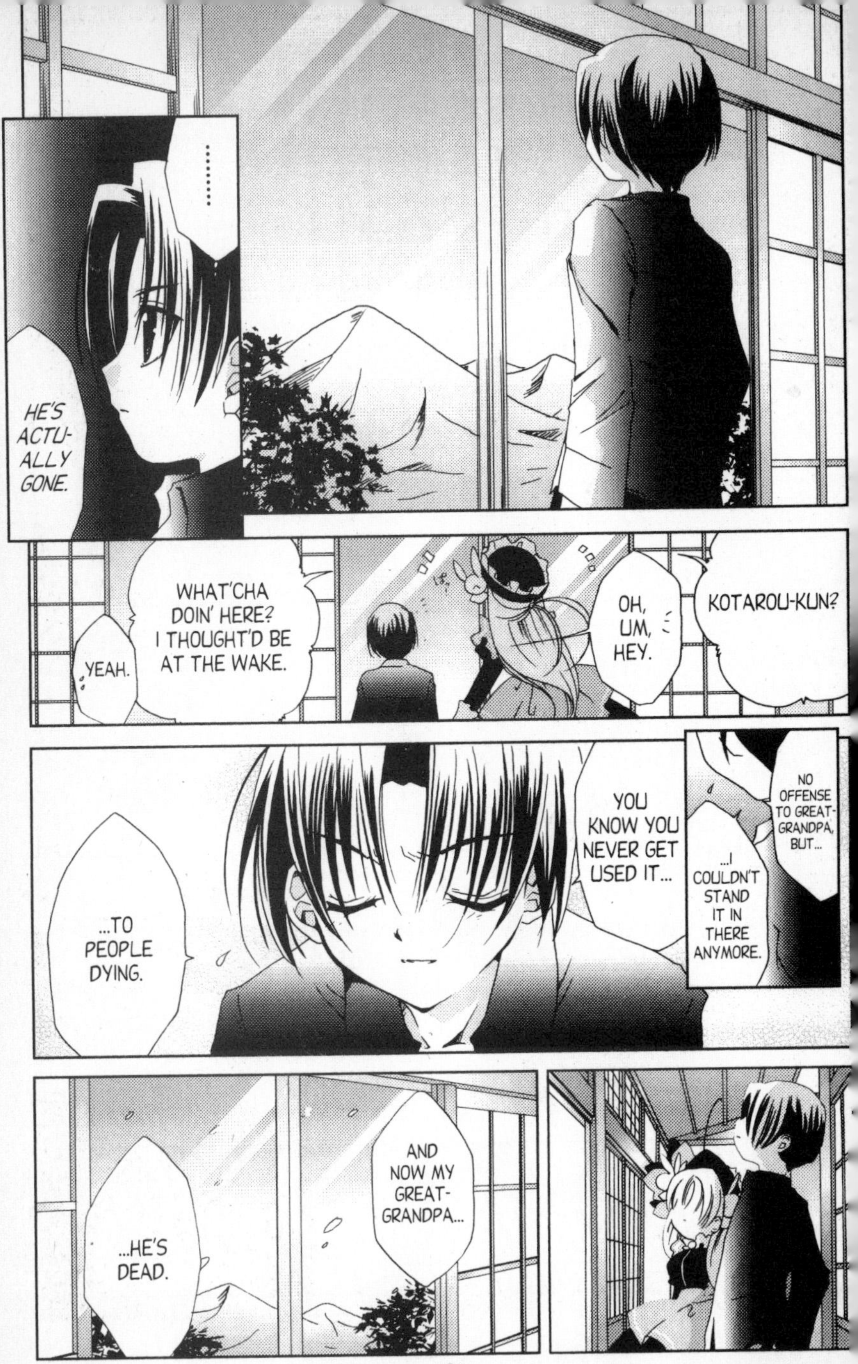
......
HE'S ACTU-ALLY GONE.
KOTAROU-KUN?
OH, UM, HEY.
WHAT'CHA DOIN' HERE? I THOUGHT'D BE AT THE WAKE.
YEAH.
NO OFFENSE TO GREAT-GRANDPA, BUT...
...I COULDN'T STAND IT IN THERE ANYMORE.
YOU KNOW YOU NEVER GET USED IT...
...TO PEOPLE DYING.
AND NOW MY GREAT-GRANDPA...
...HE'S DEAD.

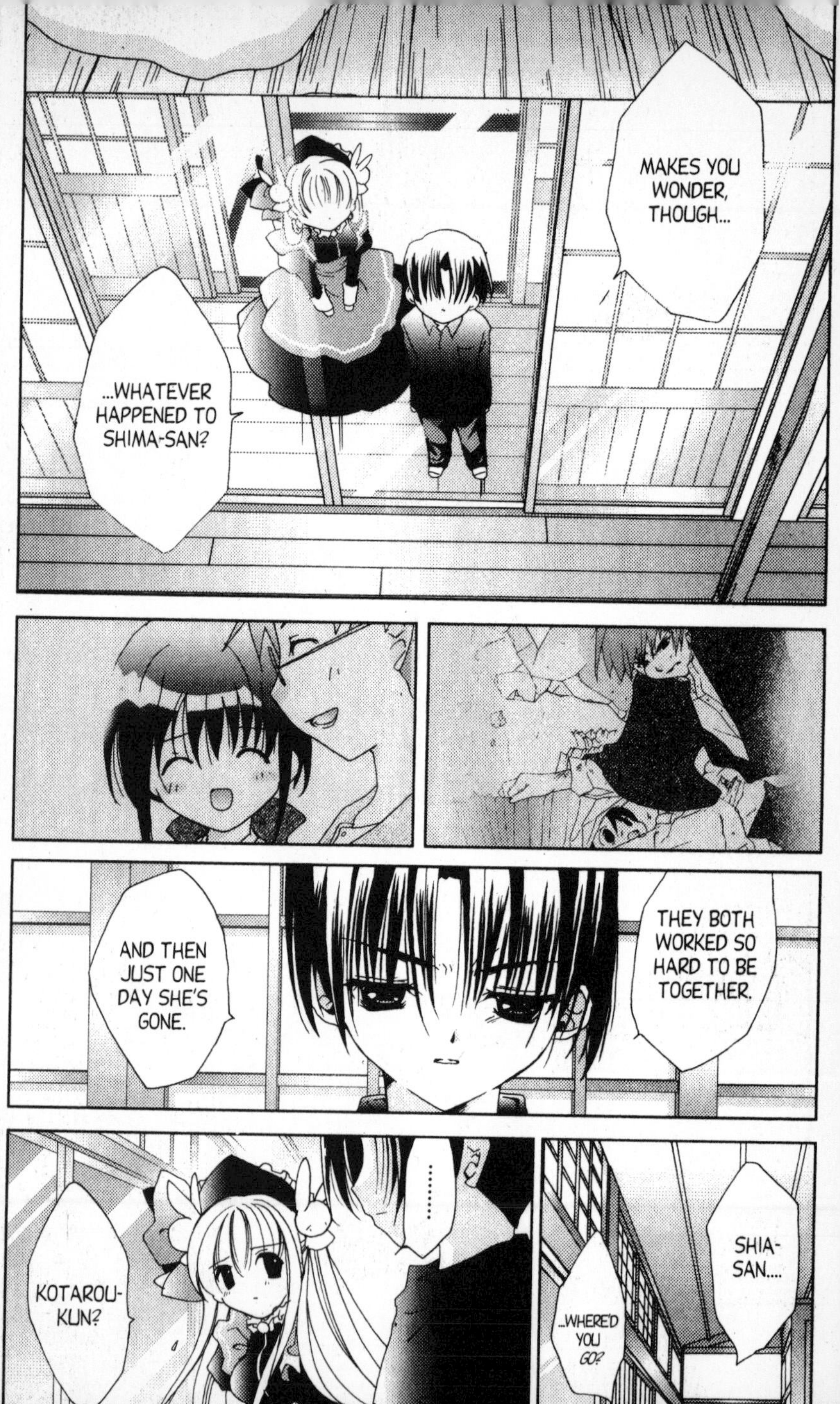
MAKES YOU WONDER, THOUGH...
...WHATEVER HAPPENED TO SHIMA-SAN?
THEY BOTH WORKED SO HARD TO BE TOGETHER.
AND THEN JUST ONE DAY SHE'S GONE.
SHIA-SAN....
...WHERE'D YOU GO?
......
KOTAROU-KUN?

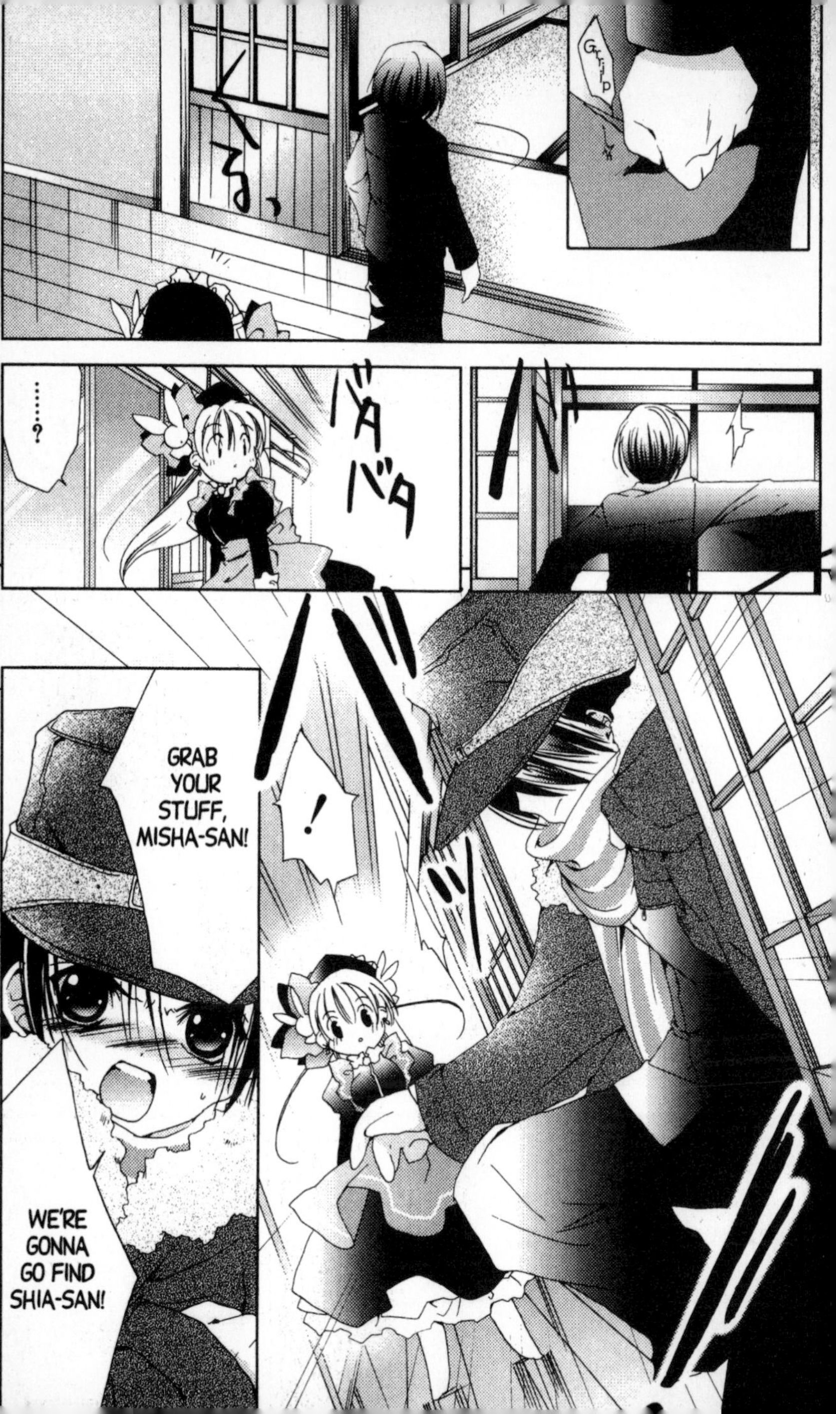

Grrip
バタ バタ
……?
!
GRAB YOUR STUFF, MISHA-SAN!
WE'RE GONNA GO FIND SHIA-SAN!

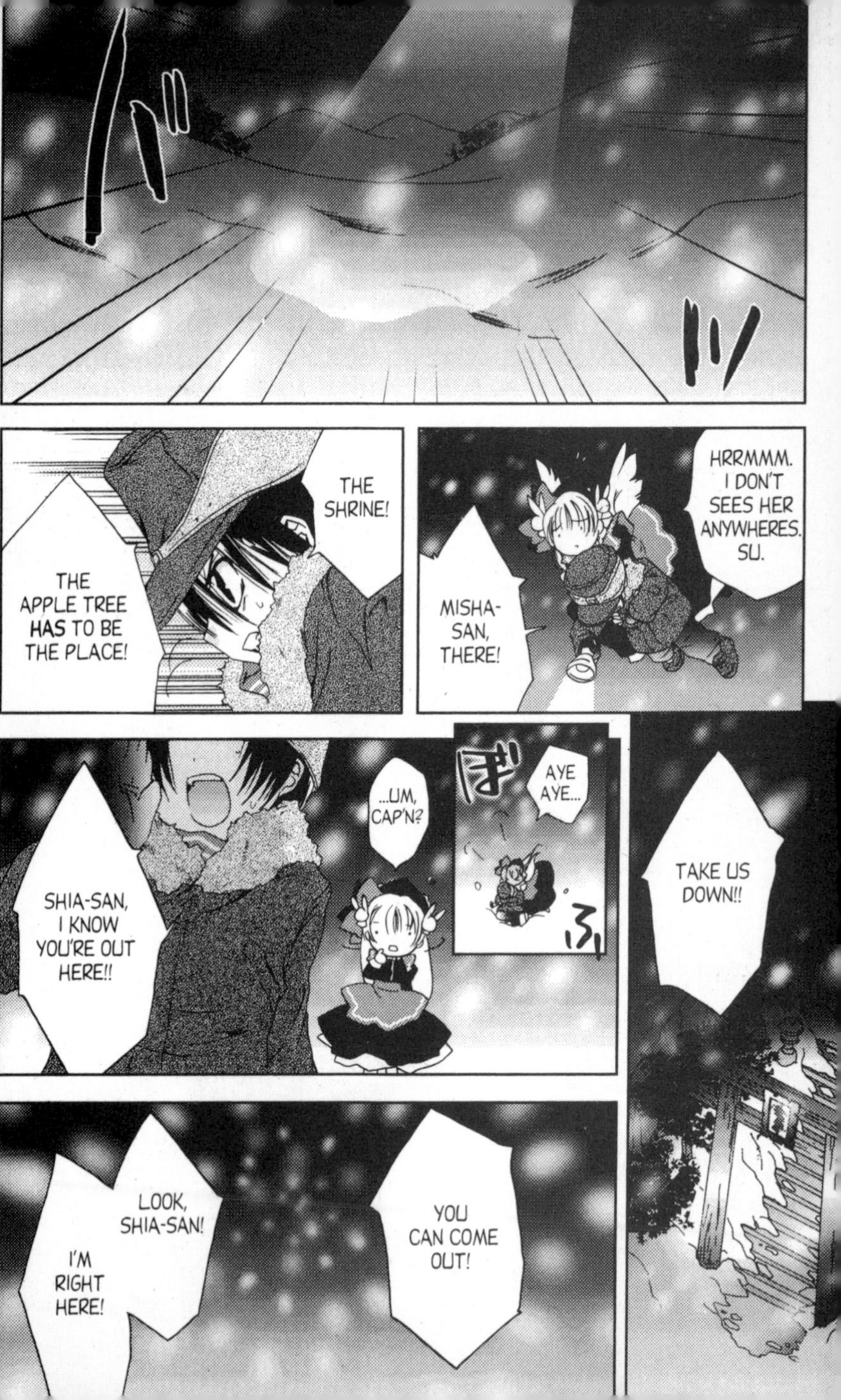
HRRMMM. I DON'T SEES HER ANYWHERES. SU.
MISHA-SAN, THERE!
THE SHRINE!
THE APPLE TREE HAS TO BE THE PLACE!
TAKE US DOWN!!
AYE AYE...
ぼ
ふ
...UM, CAP'N?
SHIA-SAN, I KNOW YOU'RE OUT HERE!!
YOU CAN COME OUT!
LOOK, SHIA-SAN!
I'M RIGHT HERE!

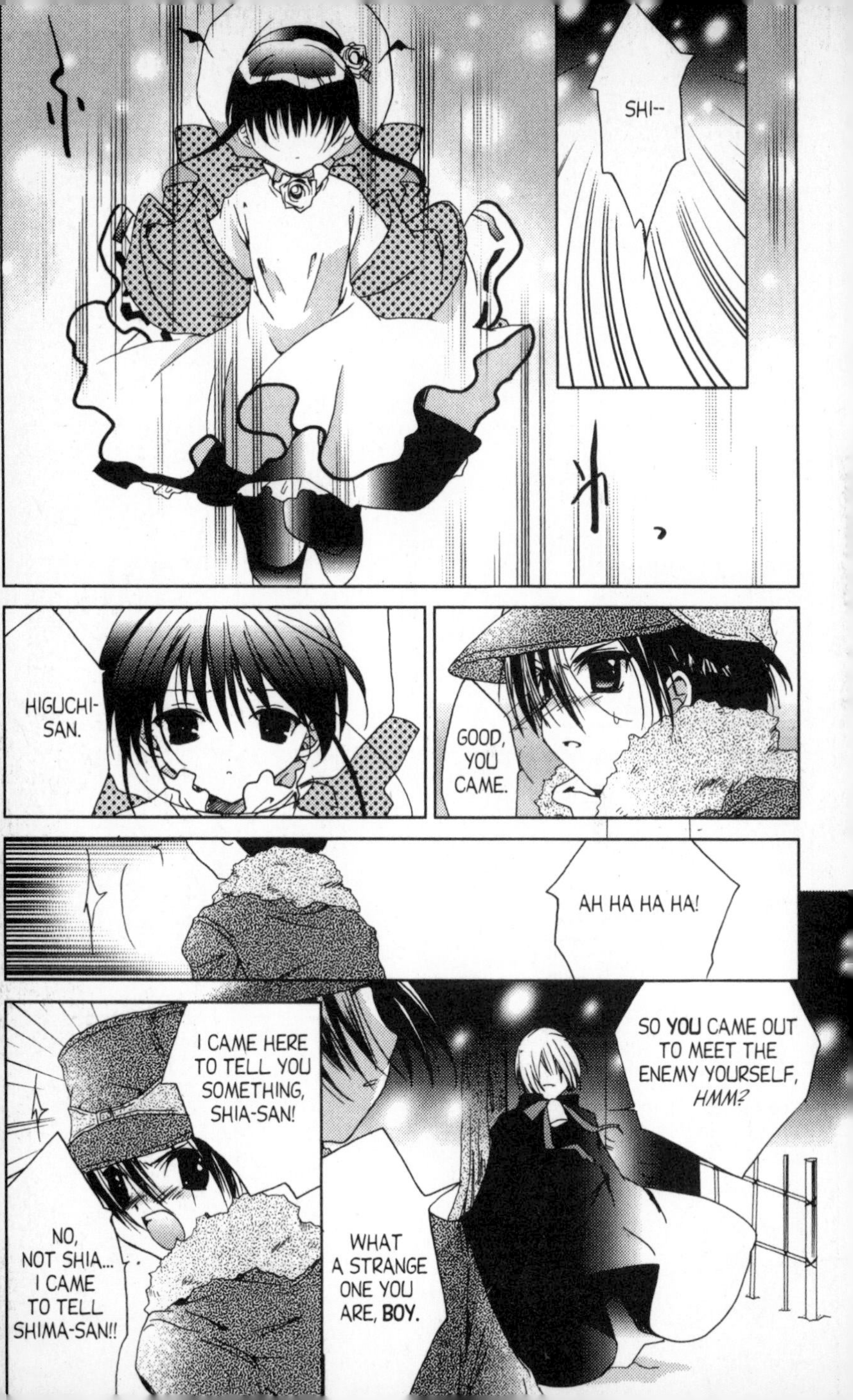
SHI--
GOOD, YOU CAME.
HIGUCHI-SAN.
AH HA HA HA!
SO **YOU** CAME OUT TO MEET THE ENEMY YOURSELF, *HMM?*
WHAT A STRANGE ONE YOU ARE, **BOY.**
I CAME HERE TO TELL YOU SOMETHING, SHIA-SAN!
NO, NOT SHIA... I CAME TO TELL SHIMA-SAN!!

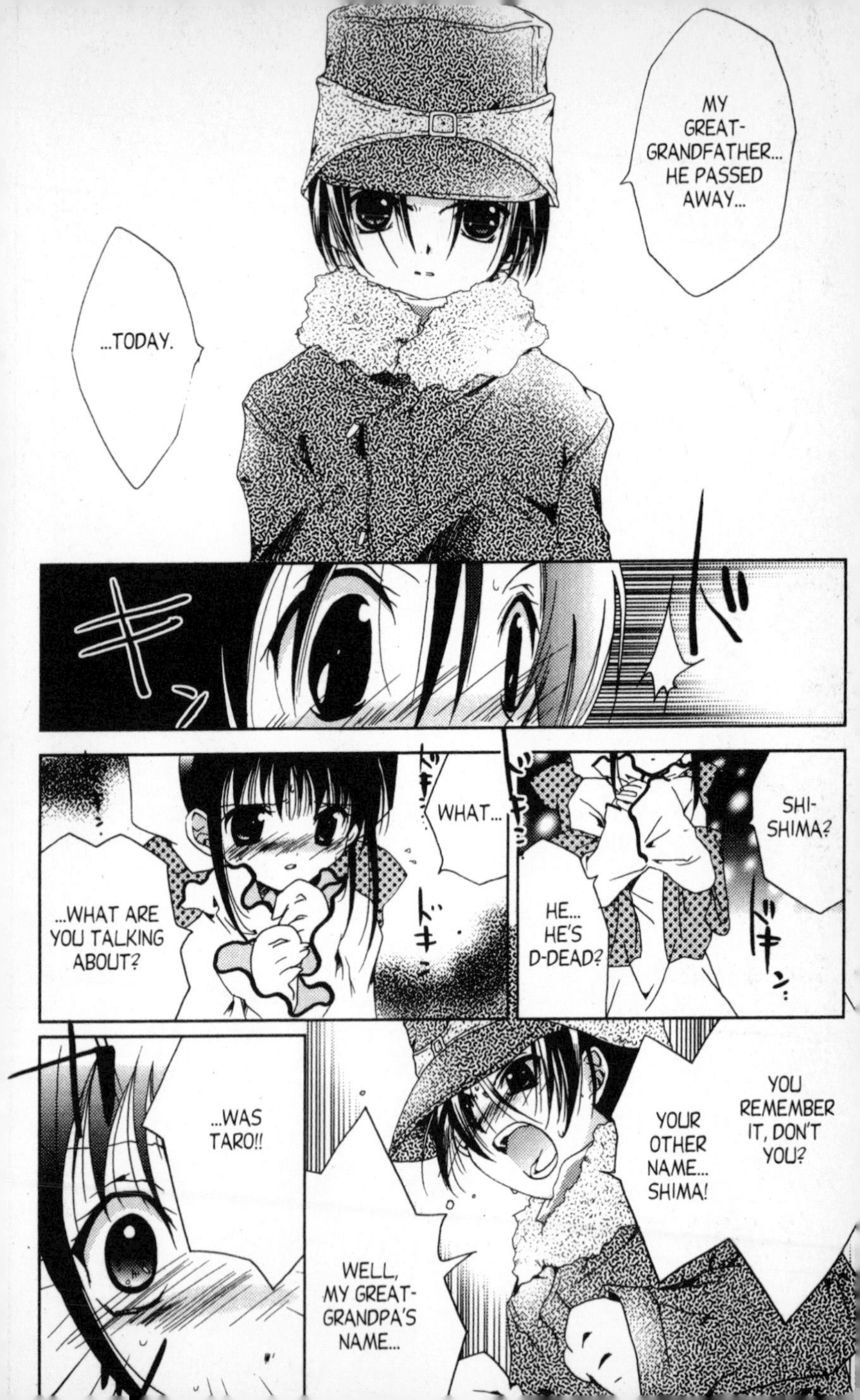
MY GREAT-GRANDFATHER... HE PASSED AWAY...
...TODAY.
キッ
SHI-SHIMA?
HE... HE'S D-DEAD?
WHAT...
...WHAT ARE YOU TALKING ABOUT?
YOU REMEMBER IT, DON'T YOU?
YOUR OTHER NAME... SHIMA!
WELL, MY GREAT-GRANDPA'S NAME...
...WAS TARO!!

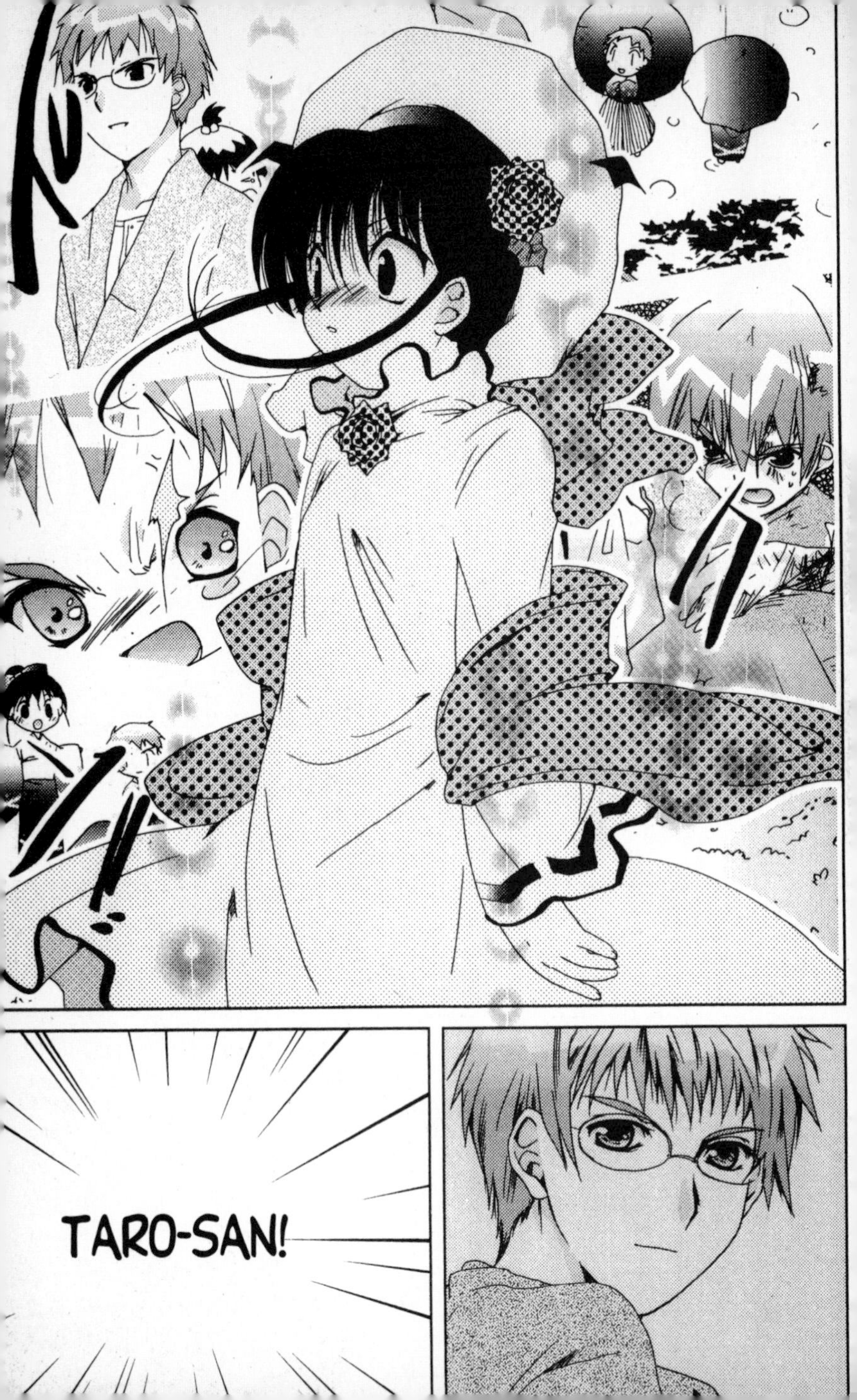
TARO-SAN!

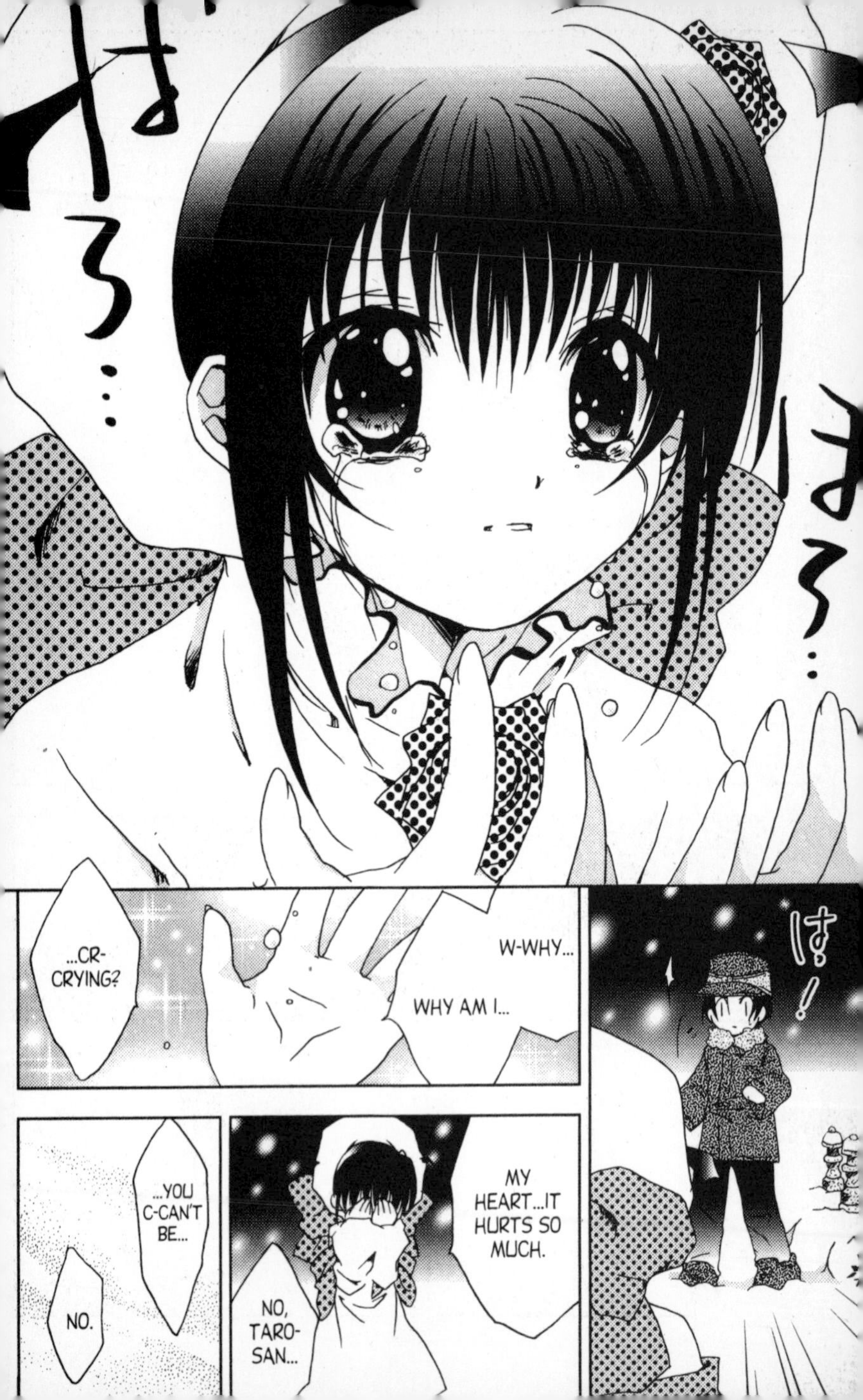

ほろ…
はろ…
は!
W-WHY...
WHY AM I...
...CR- CRYING?
MY HEART...IT HURTS SO MUCH.
NO, TARO-SAN...
...YOU C-CAN'T BE...
NO.

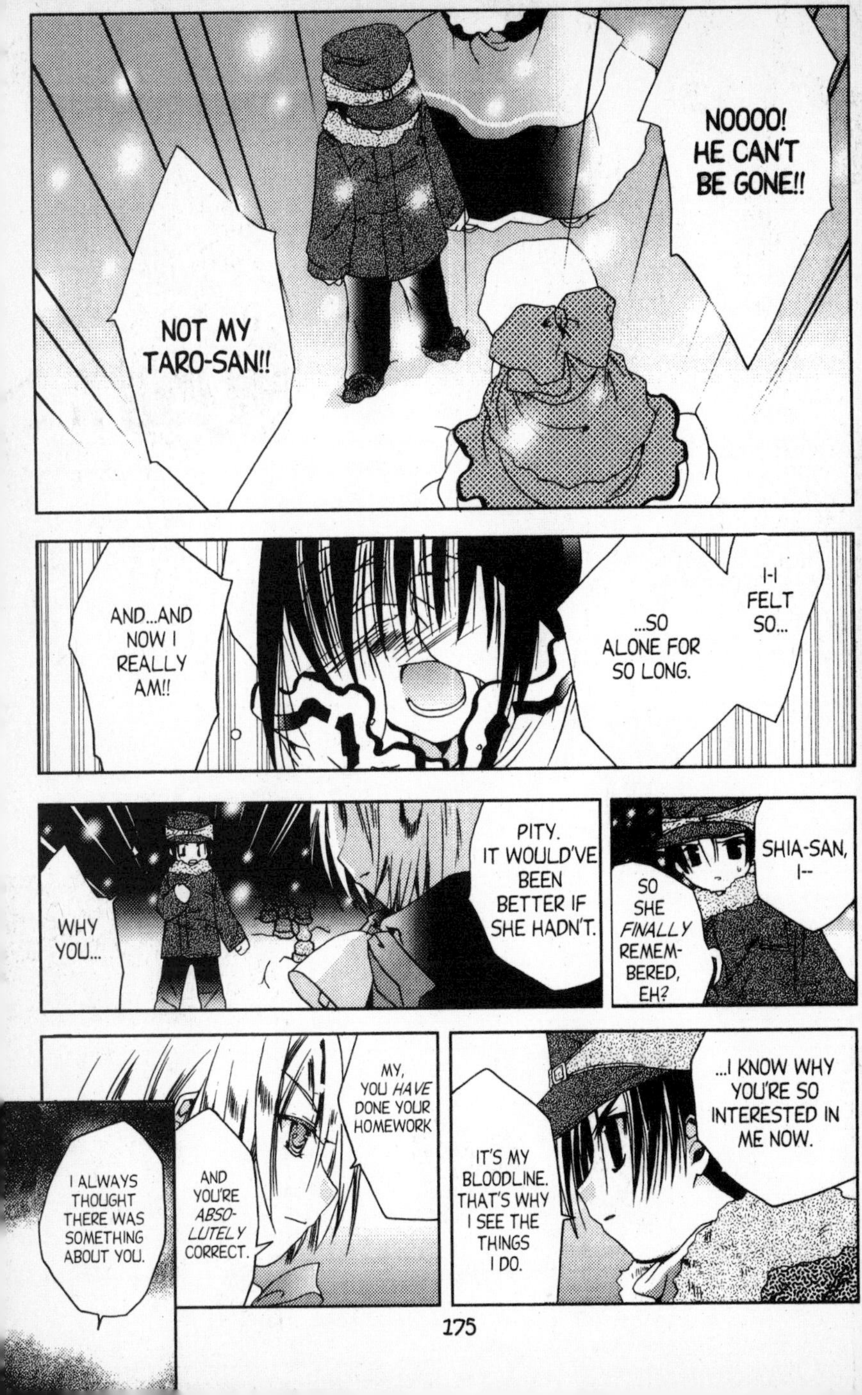
NOOOO! HE CAN'T BE GONE!!
NOT MY TARO-SAN!!
I-I FELT SO...
...SO ALONE FOR SO LONG.
AND...AND NOW I REALLY AM!!
SHIA-SAN, I--
SO SHE *FINALLY* REMEM-BERED, EH?
PITY. IT WOULD'VE BEEN BETTER IF SHE HADN'T.
WHY YOU...
...I KNOW WHY YOU'RE SO INTERESTED IN ME NOW.
IT'S MY BLOODLINE. THAT'S WHY I SEE THE THINGS I DO.
MY, YOU *HAVE* DONE YOUR HOMEWORK
AND YOU'RE *ABSO-LUTELY* CORRECT.
I ALWAYS THOUGHT THERE WAS SOMETHING ABOUT YOU.

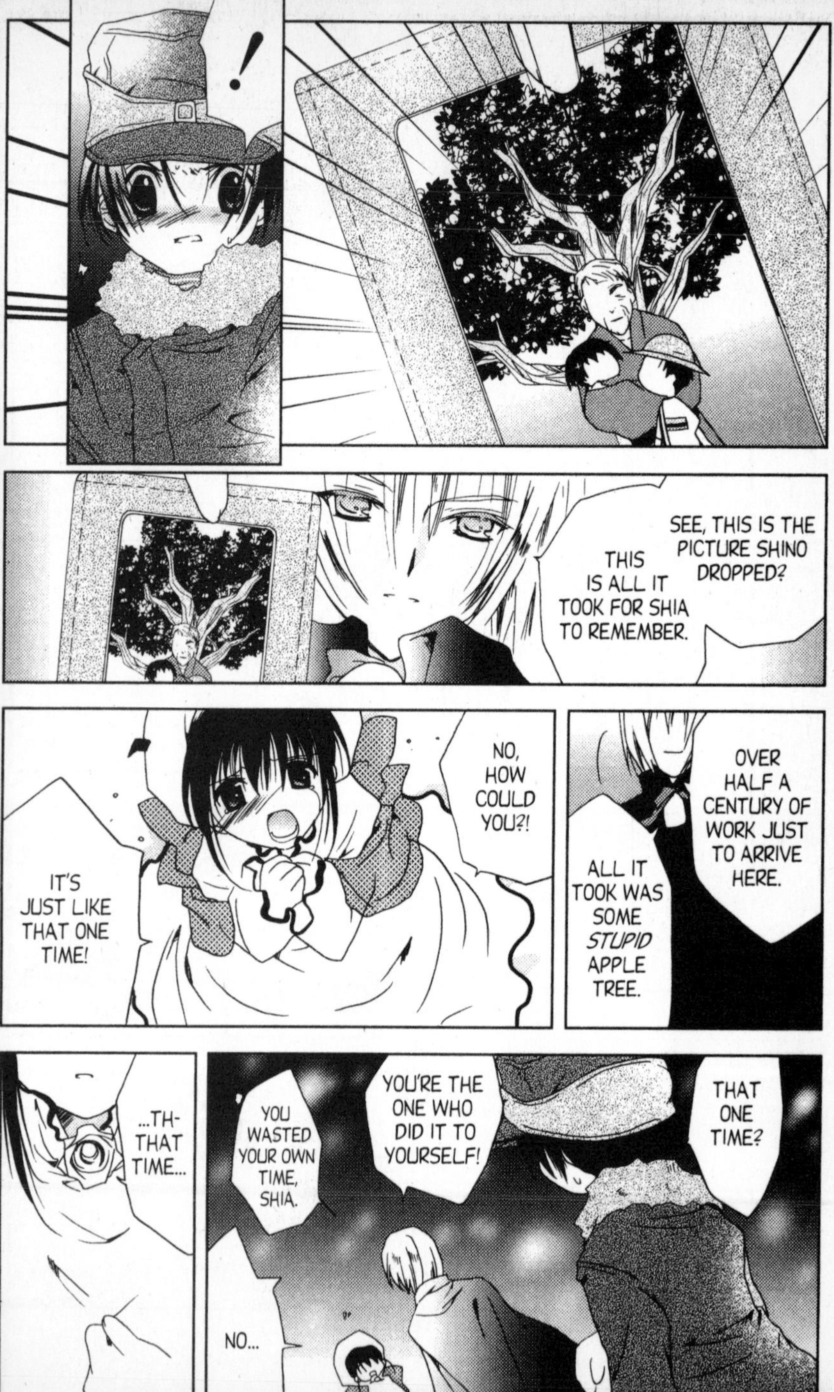
!
SEE, THIS IS THE PICTURE SHINO DROPPED?
THIS IS ALL IT TOOK FOR SHIA TO REMEMBER.
OVER HALF A CENTURY OF WORK JUST TO ARRIVE HERE.
ALL IT TOOK WAS SOME *STUPID* APPLE TREE.
NO, HOW COULD YOU?!
IT'S JUST LIKE THAT ONE TIME!
THAT ONE TIME?
YOU'RE THE ONE WHO DID IT TO YOURSELF!
YOU WASTED YOUR OWN TIME, SHIA.
NO...
...TH-THAT TIME...

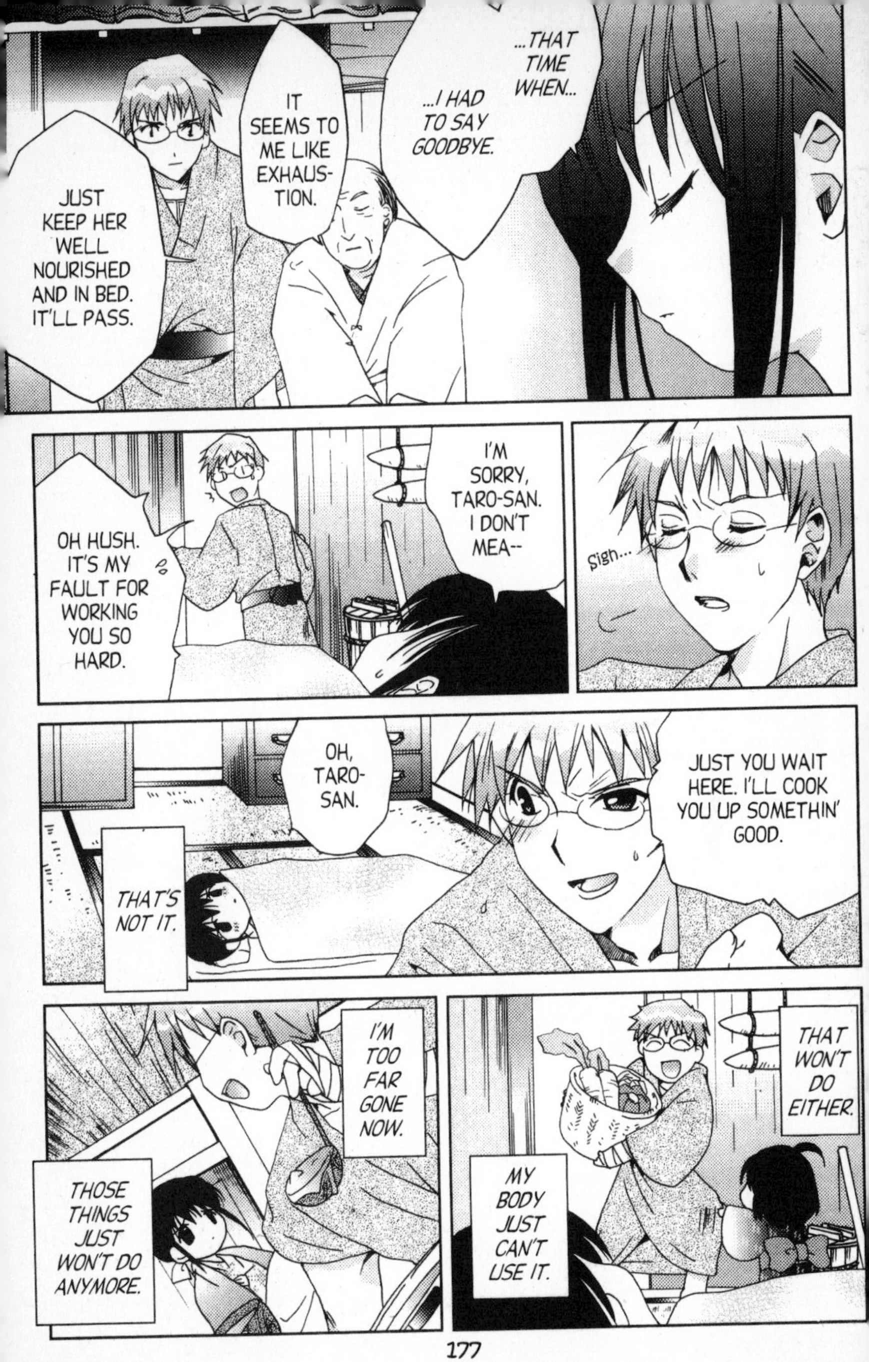
...THAT TIME WHEN...
...I HAD TO SAY GOODBYE.
IT SEEMS TO ME LIKE EXHAUSTION.
JUST KEEP HER WELL NOURISHED AND IN BED. IT'LL PASS.
Sigh...
I'M SORRY, TARO-SAN. I DON'T MEA--
OH HUSH. IT'S MY FAULT FOR WORKING YOU SO HARD.
JUST YOU WAIT HERE. I'LL COOK YOU UP SOMETHIN' GOOD.
OH, TARO-SAN.
THAT'S NOT IT.
THAT WON'T DO EITHER.
MY BODY JUST CAN'T USE IT.
I'M TOO FAR GONE NOW.
THOSE THINGS JUST WON'T DO ANYMORE.

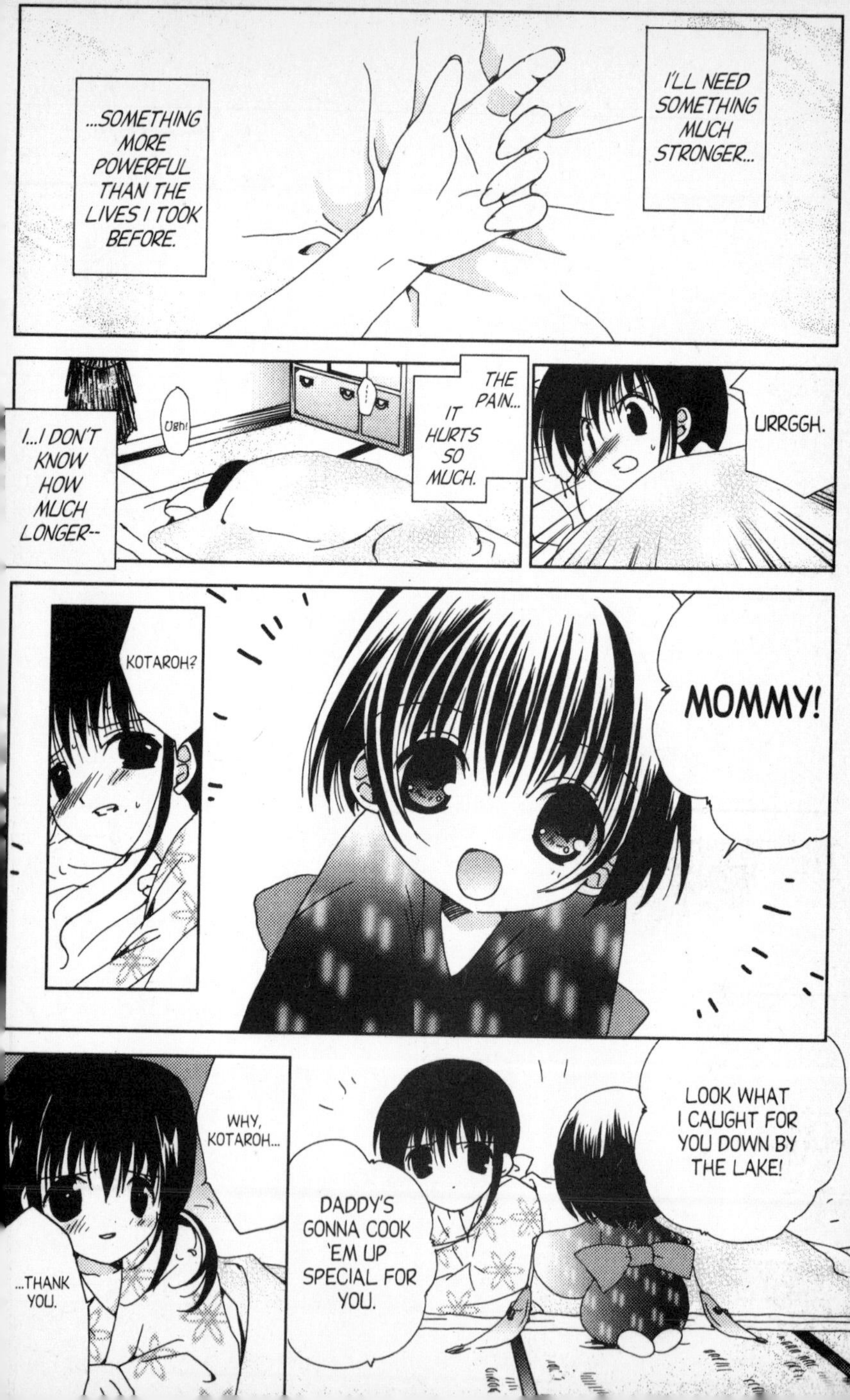
I'LL NEED SOMETHING MUCH STRONGER...
...SOMETHING MORE POWERFUL THAN THE LIVES I TOOK BEFORE.
URRGGH.
THE PAIN... IT HURTS SO MUCH.
...!
Ugh!
I...I DON'T KNOW HOW MUCH LONGER--
MOMMY!
KOTAROH?
LOOK WHAT I CAUGHT FOR YOU DOWN BY THE LAKE!
DADDY'S GONNA COOK 'EM UP SPECIAL FOR YOU.
WHY, KOTAROH...
...THANK YOU.

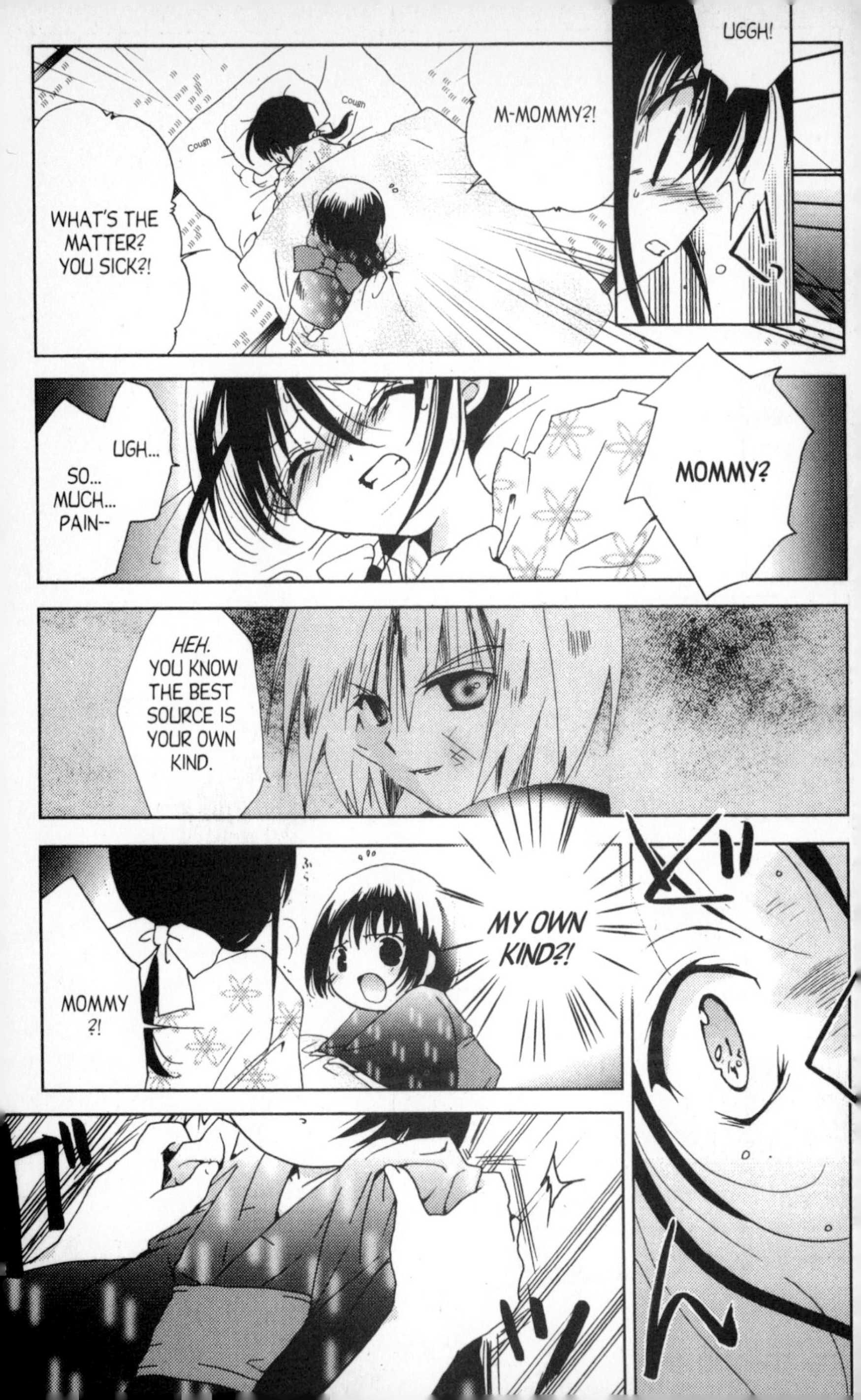
UGGH!
M-MOMMY?!
Cough
Cough
WHAT'S THE MATTER? YOU SICK?!
MOMMY?
UGH...
SO... MUCH... PAIN--
HEH. YOU KNOW THE BEST SOURCE IS YOUR OWN KIND.
MY OWN KIND?!
MOMMY ?!

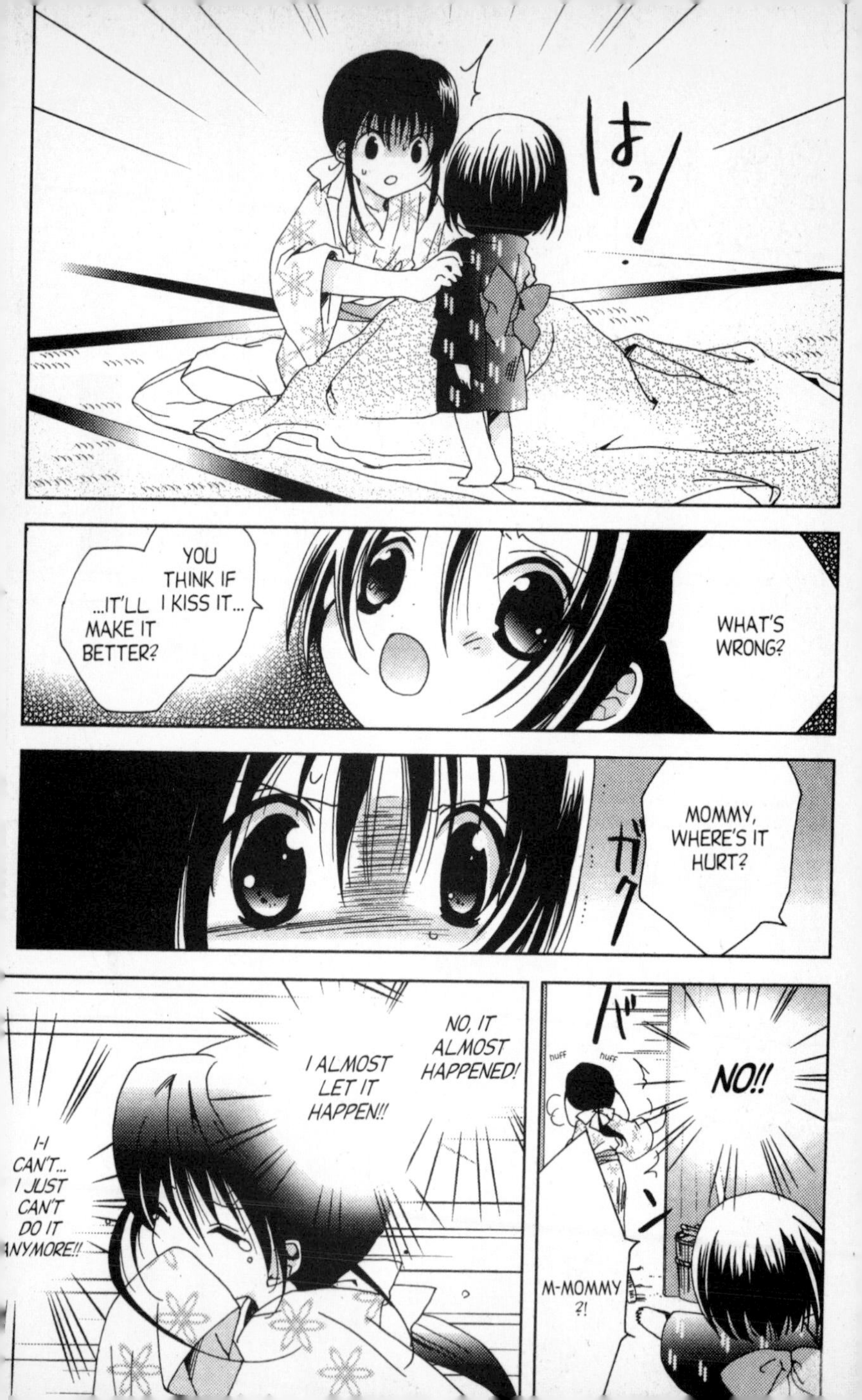
はっ
WHAT'S WRONG?
YOU THINK IF I KISS IT...
...IT'LL MAKE IT BETTER?
MOMMY, WHERE'S IT HURT?
ガク
バ
huff
huff
NO!!
ン
M-MOMMY ?!
NO, IT ALMOST HAPPENED!
I ALMOST LET IT HAPPEN!!
I-I CAN'T... I JUST CAN'T DO IT ANYMORE!!

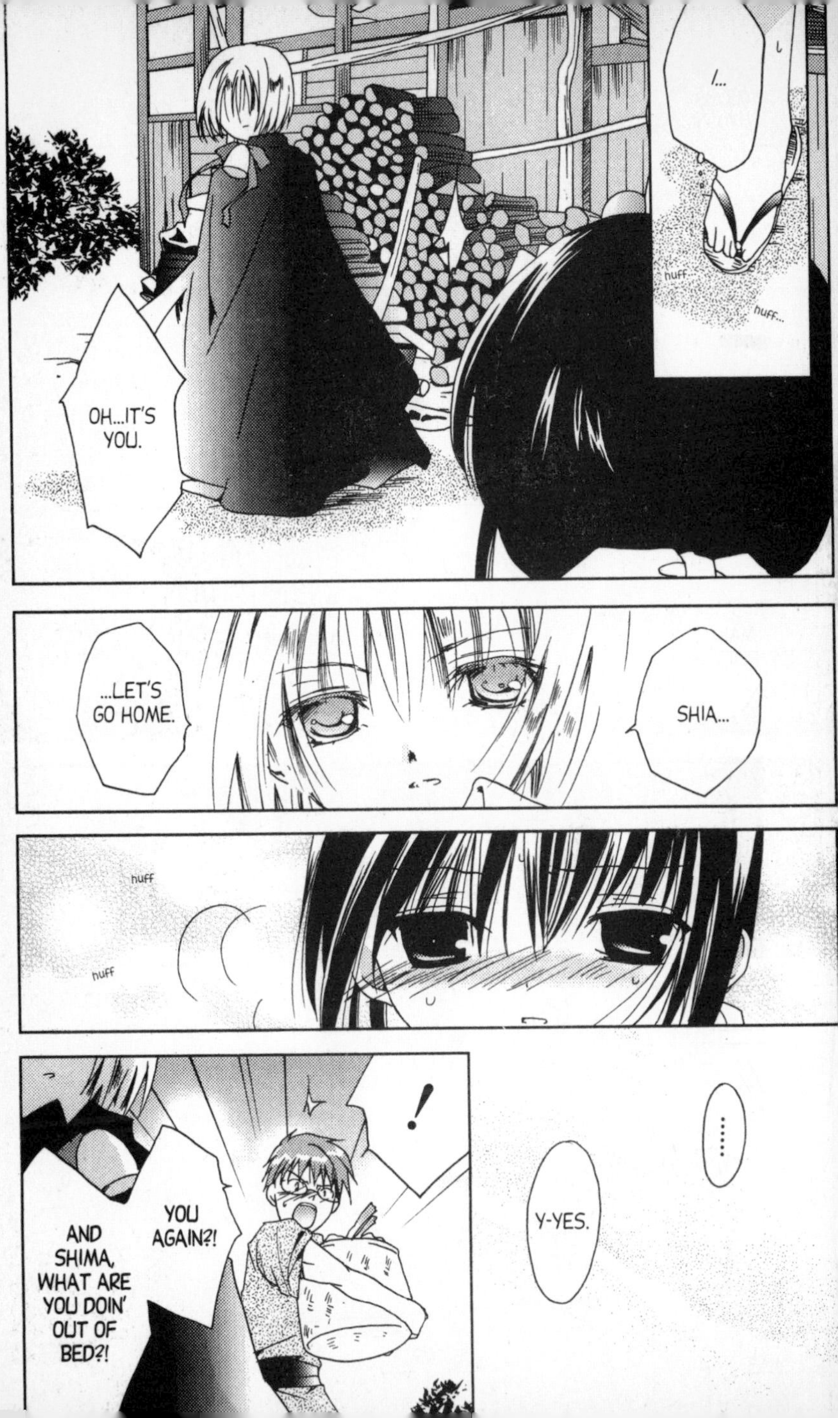
I...
huff
huff...
OH...IT'S YOU.
SHIA...
...LET'S GO HOME.
huff
huff
......
Y-YES.
!
YOU AGAIN?!
AND SHIMA, WHAT ARE YOU DOIN' OUT OF BED?!

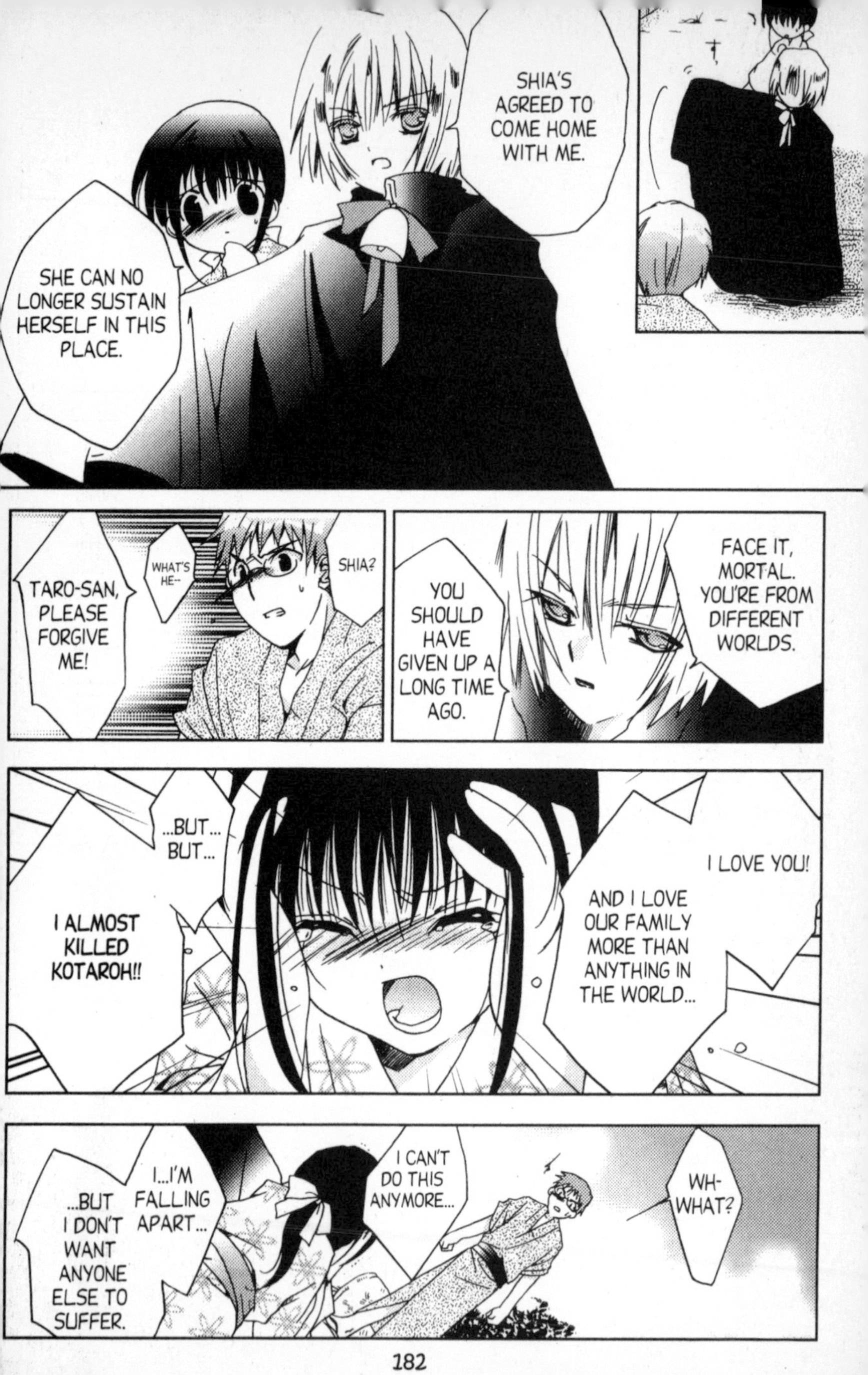
SHIA'S AGREED TO COME HOME WITH ME.
SHE CAN NO LONGER SUSTAIN HERSELF IN THIS PLACE.
FACE IT, MORTAL. YOU'RE FROM DIFFERENT WORLDS.
YOU SHOULD HAVE GIVEN UP A LONG TIME AGO.
SHIA?
WHAT'S HE--
TARO-SAN, PLEASE FORGIVE ME!
I LOVE YOU!
AND I LOVE OUR FAMILY MORE THAN ANYTHING IN THE WORLD...
...BUT... BUT...
I ALMOST KILLED KOTAROH!!
WH-WHAT?
I CAN'T DO THIS ANYMORE...
I...I'M FALLING APART...
...BUT I DON'T WANT ANYONE ELSE TO SUFFER.

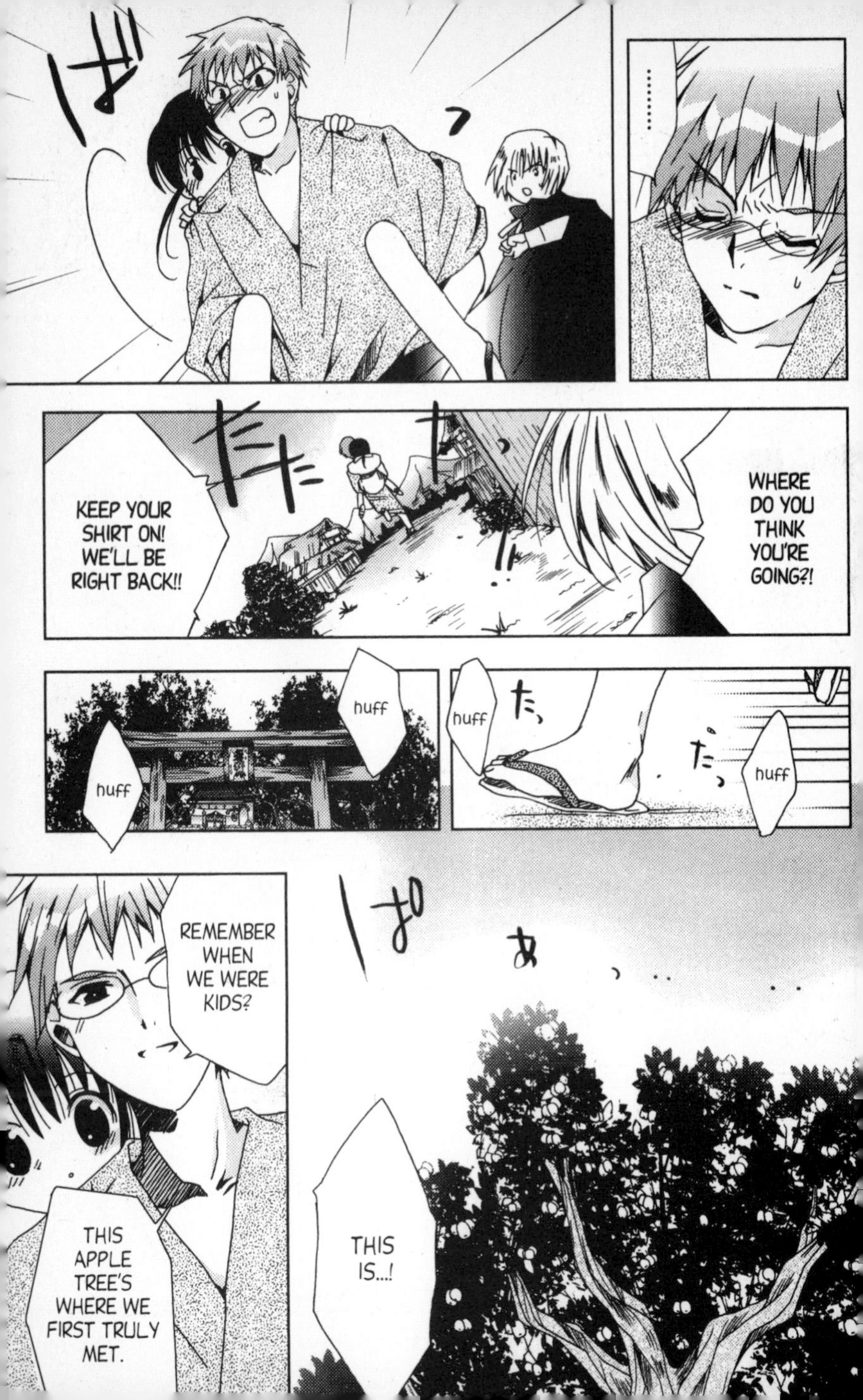
......
ばっ
WHERE DO YOU THINK YOU'RE GOING?!
KEEP YOUR SHIRT ON! WE'LL BE RIGHT BACK!!
huff
たっ
たっ
huff
huff
huff
ぱ
あっ...
THIS IS...!
REMEMBER WHEN WE WERE KIDS?
THIS APPLE TREE'S WHERE WE FIRST TRULY MET.

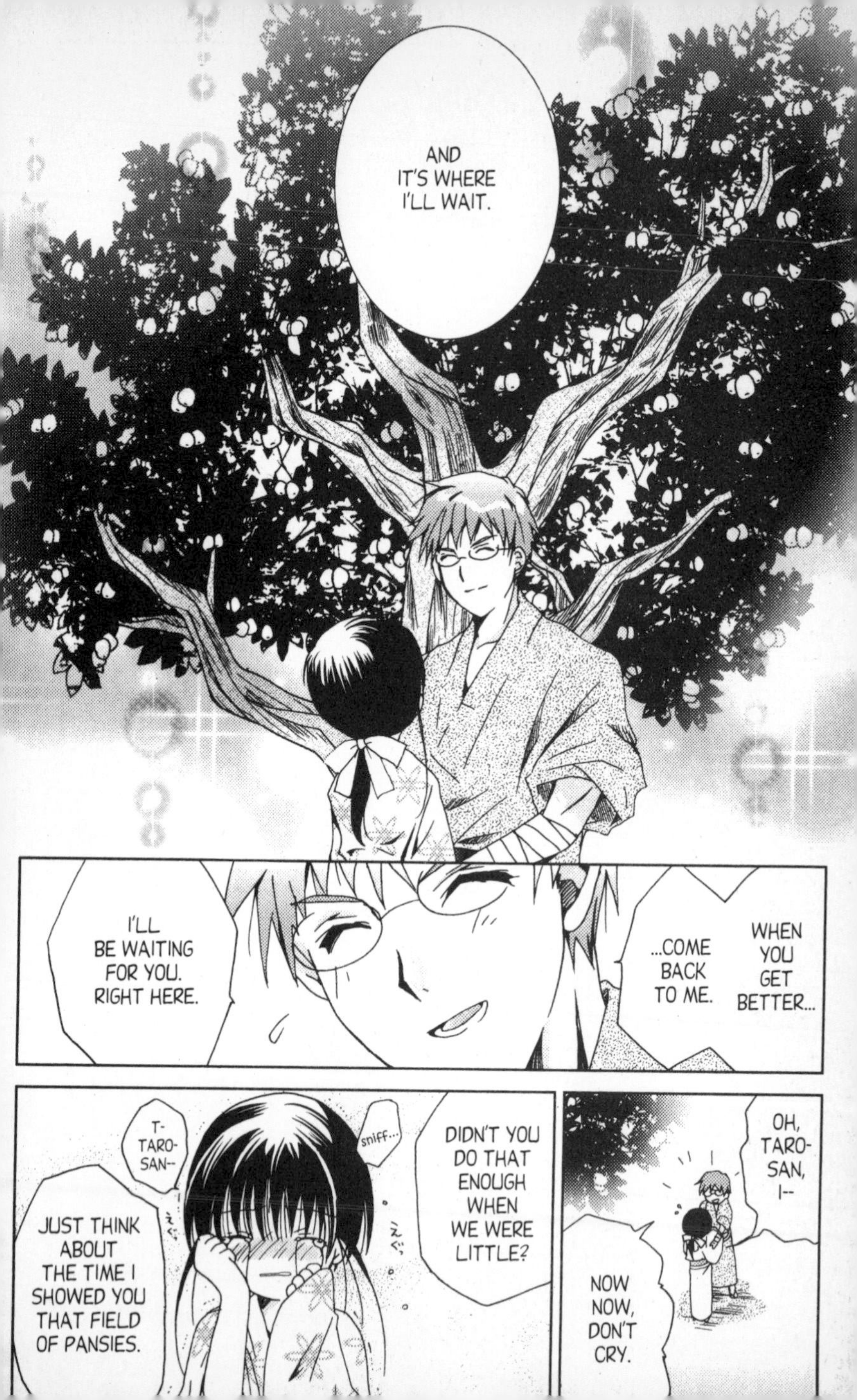
AND IT'S WHERE I'LL WAIT.
WHEN YOU GET BETTER...
...COME BACK TO ME.
I'LL BE WAITING FOR YOU. RIGHT HERE.
OH, TARO-SAN, I--
NOW NOW, DON'T CRY.
DIDN'T YOU DO THAT ENOUGH WHEN WE WERE LITTLE?
sniff...
T-TARO-SAN--
JUST THINK ABOUT THE TIME I SHOWED YOU THAT FIELD OF PANSIES.

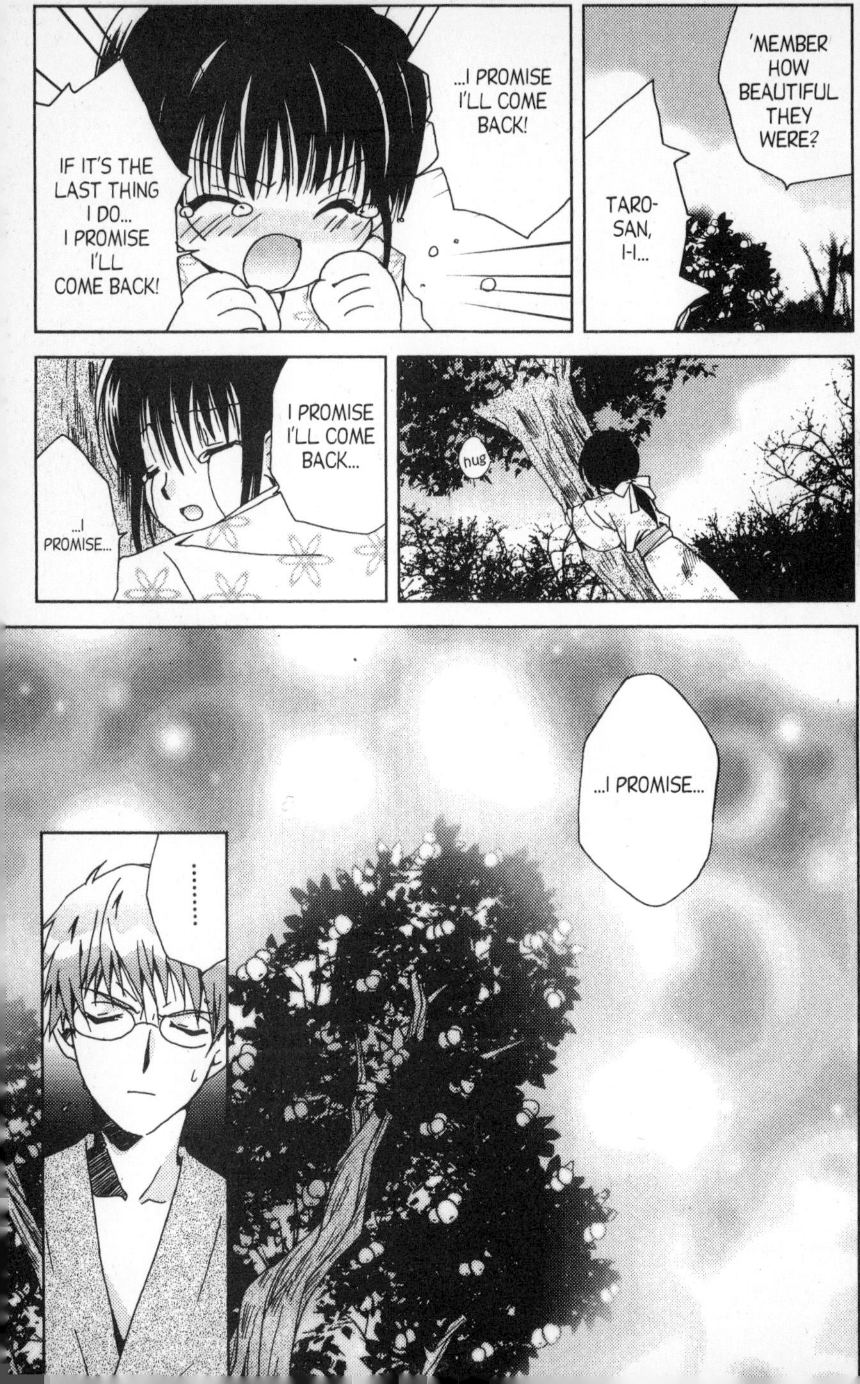
'MEMBER HOW BEAUTIFUL THEY WERE?
TARO-SAN, I-I...
...I PROMISE I'LL COME BACK!
IF IT'S THE LAST THING I DO... I PROMISE I'LL COME BACK!
hug
I PROMISE I'LL COME BACK...
...I PROMISE...
...I PROMISE...

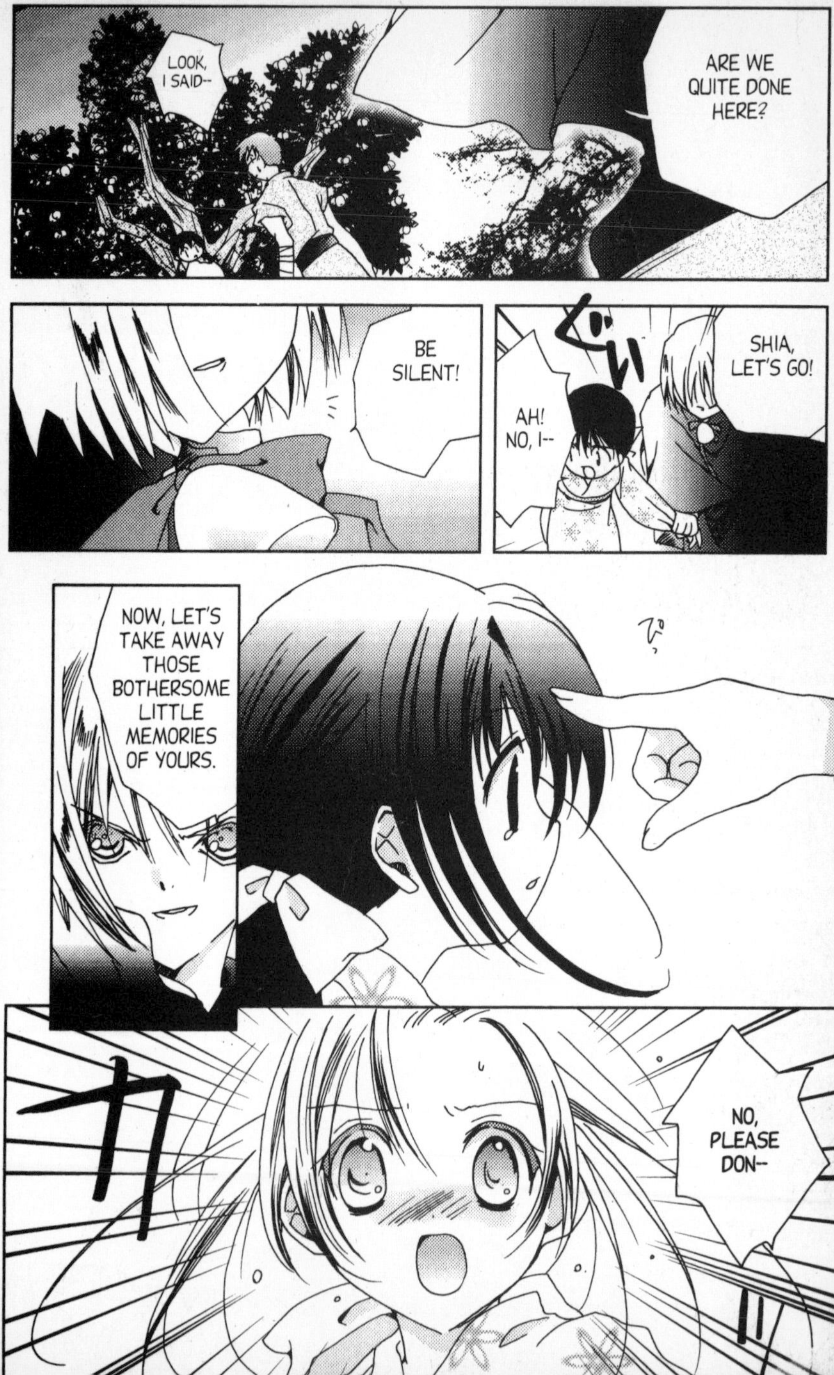
ARE WE QUITE DONE HERE?
LOOK, I SAID--
SHIA, LET'S GO!
AH! NO, I--
BE SILENT!
NOW, LET'S TAKE AWAY THOSE BOTHERSOME LITTLE MEMORIES OF YOURS.
NO, PLEASE DON--

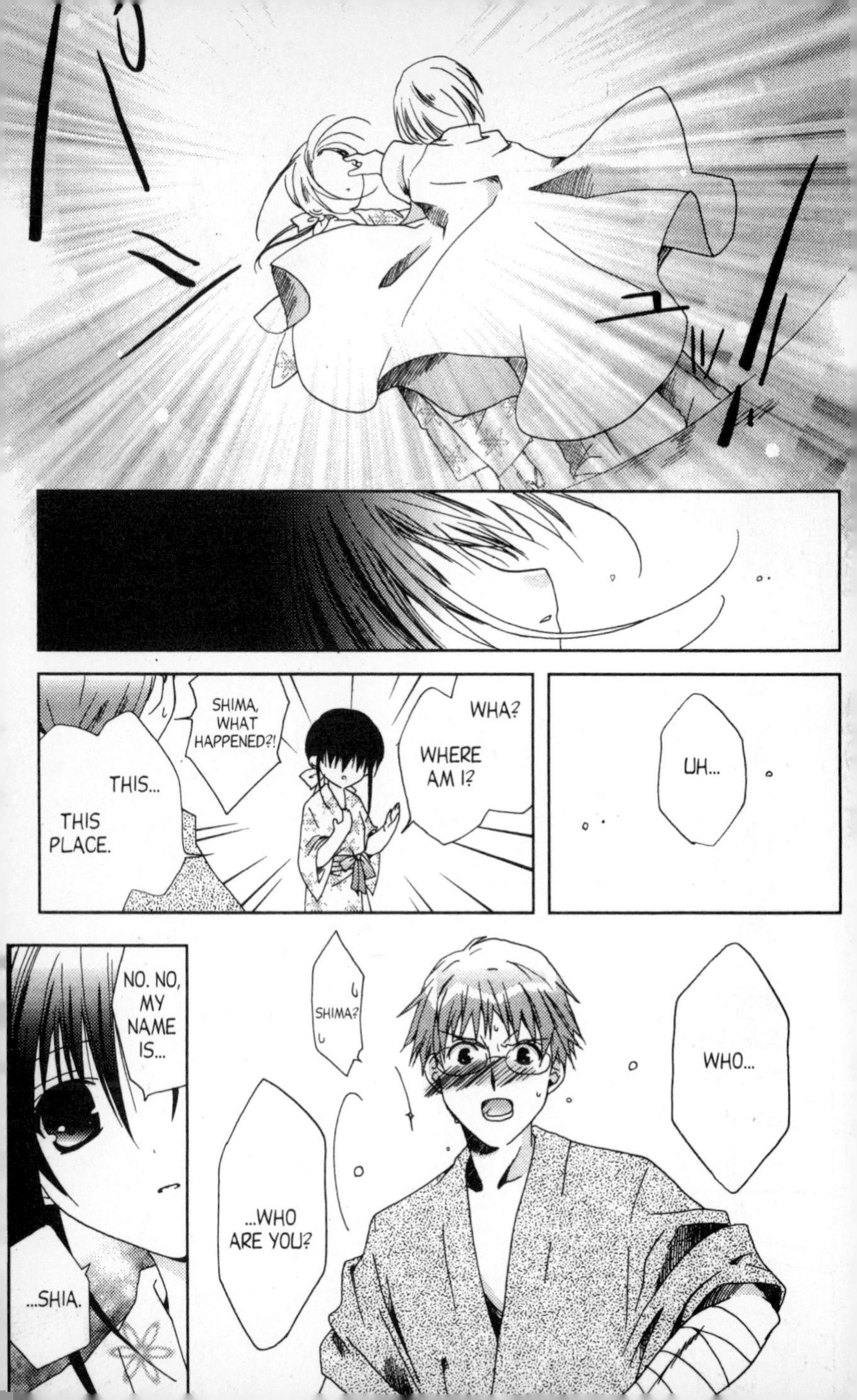
UH...
WHA?
WHERE AM I?
SHIMA, WHAT HAPPENED?!
THIS...
THIS PLACE.
WHO...
SHIMA?
...WHO ARE YOU?
NO. NO, MY NAME IS...
...SHIA.

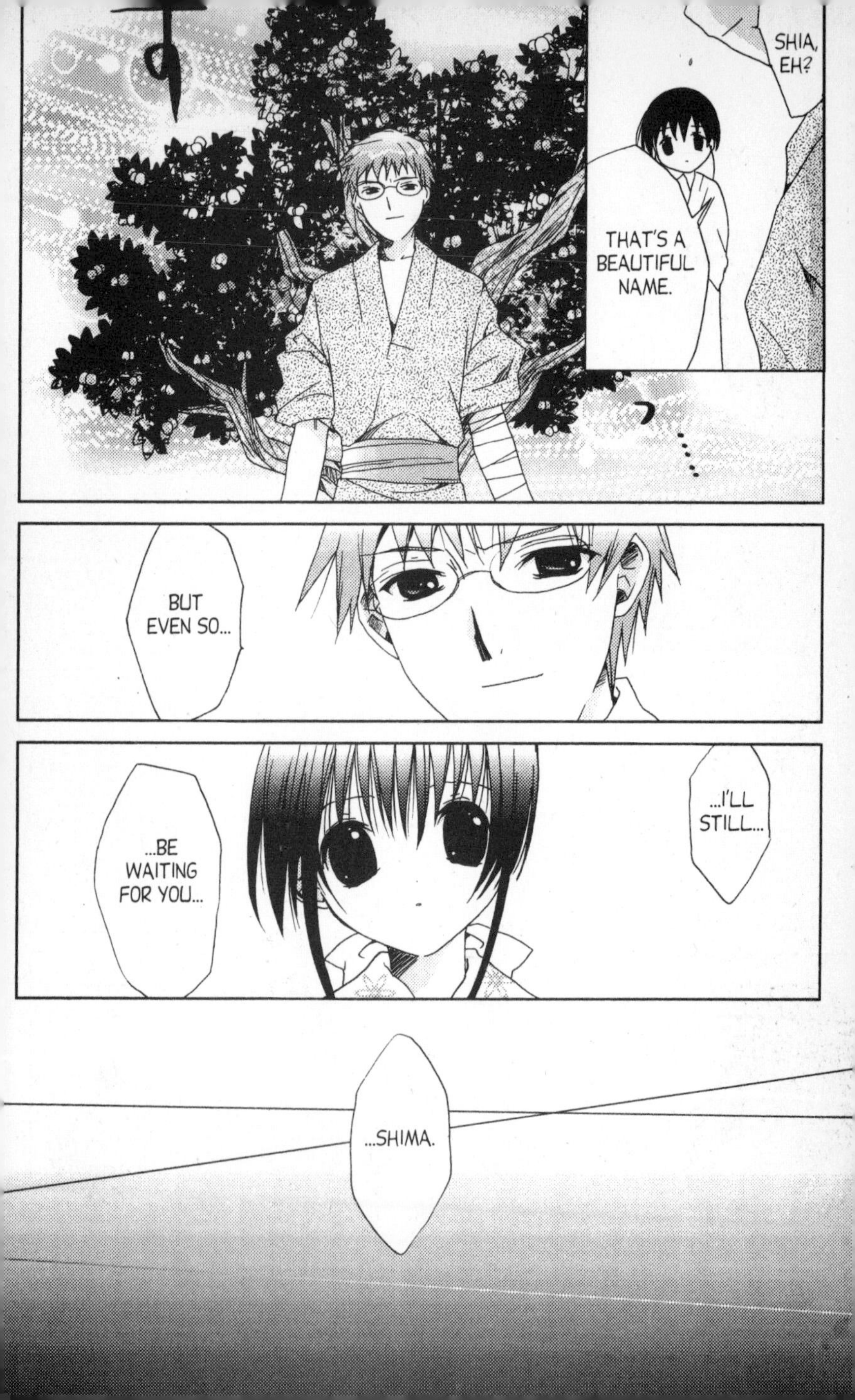
SHIA, EH?
THAT'S A BEAUTIFUL NAME.
BUT EVEN SO...
...I'LL STILL...
...BE WAITING FOR YOU...
...SHIMA.

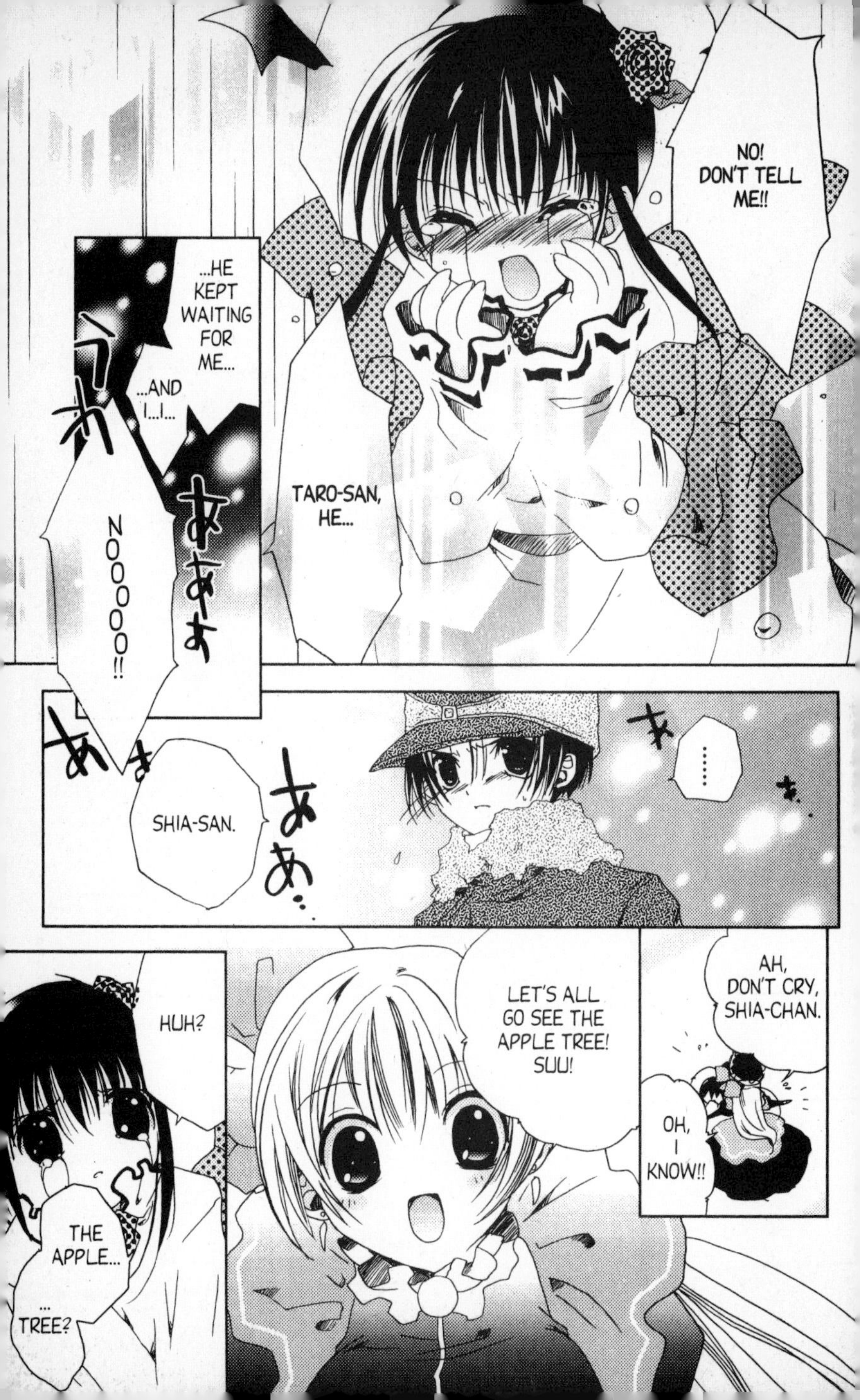
NO! DON'T TELL ME!!
TARO-SAN, HE...
...HE KEPT WAITING FOR ME...
...AND I...I...
NOOOOOO!!
......
SHIA-SAN.
AH, DON'T CRY, SHIA-CHAN.
OH, I KNOW!!
LET'S ALL GO SEE THE APPLE TREE! SUU!
HUH?
THE APPLE...
...TREE?

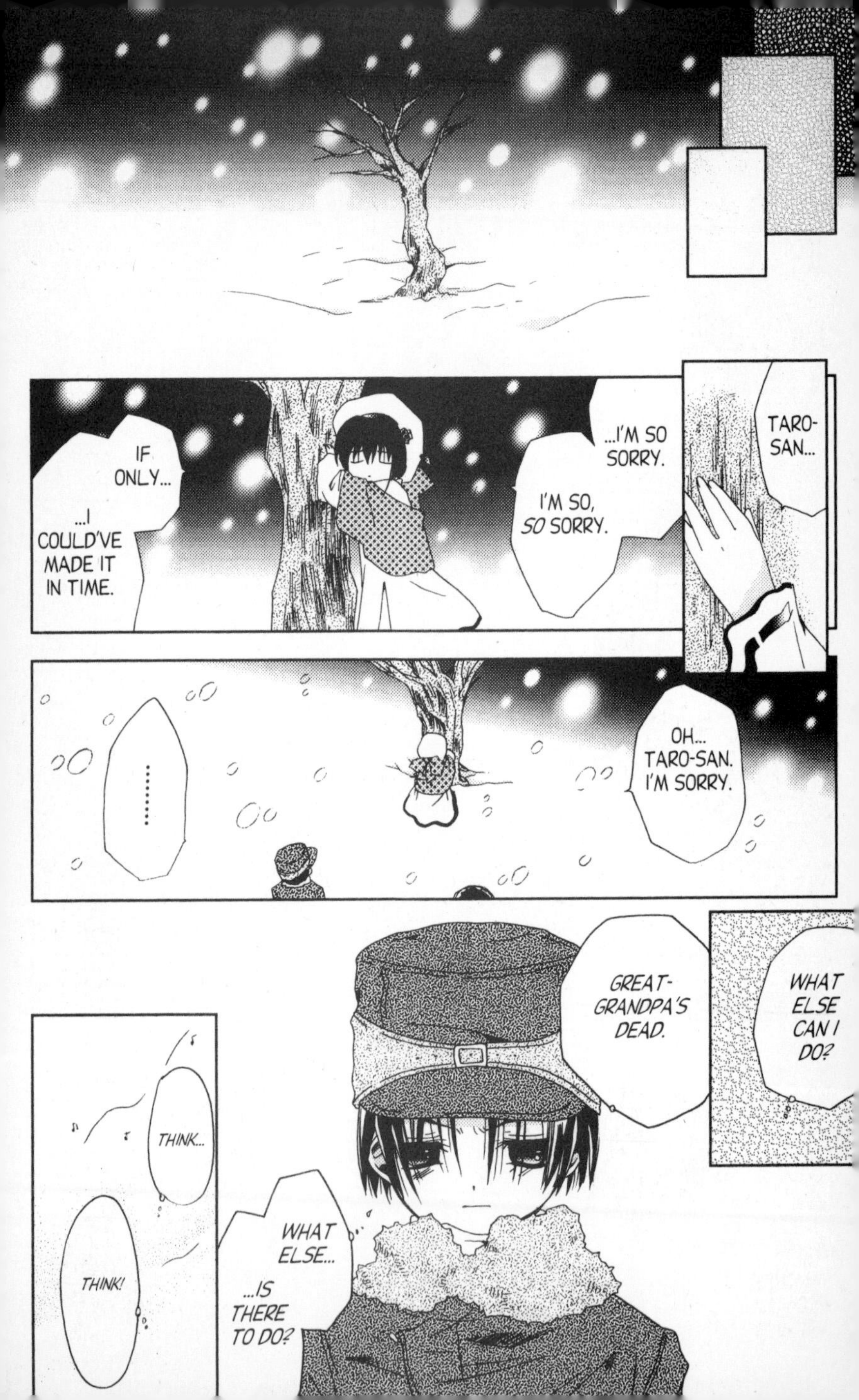
TARO-SAN...
...I'M SO SORRY.
I'M SO, *SO* SORRY.
IF ONLY...
...I COULD'VE MADE IT IN TIME.
OH... TARO-SAN. I'M SORRY.
....
WHAT ELSE CAN I DO?
GREAT-GRANDPA'S DEAD.
WHAT ELSE...
...IS THERE TO DO?
THINK...
THINK!

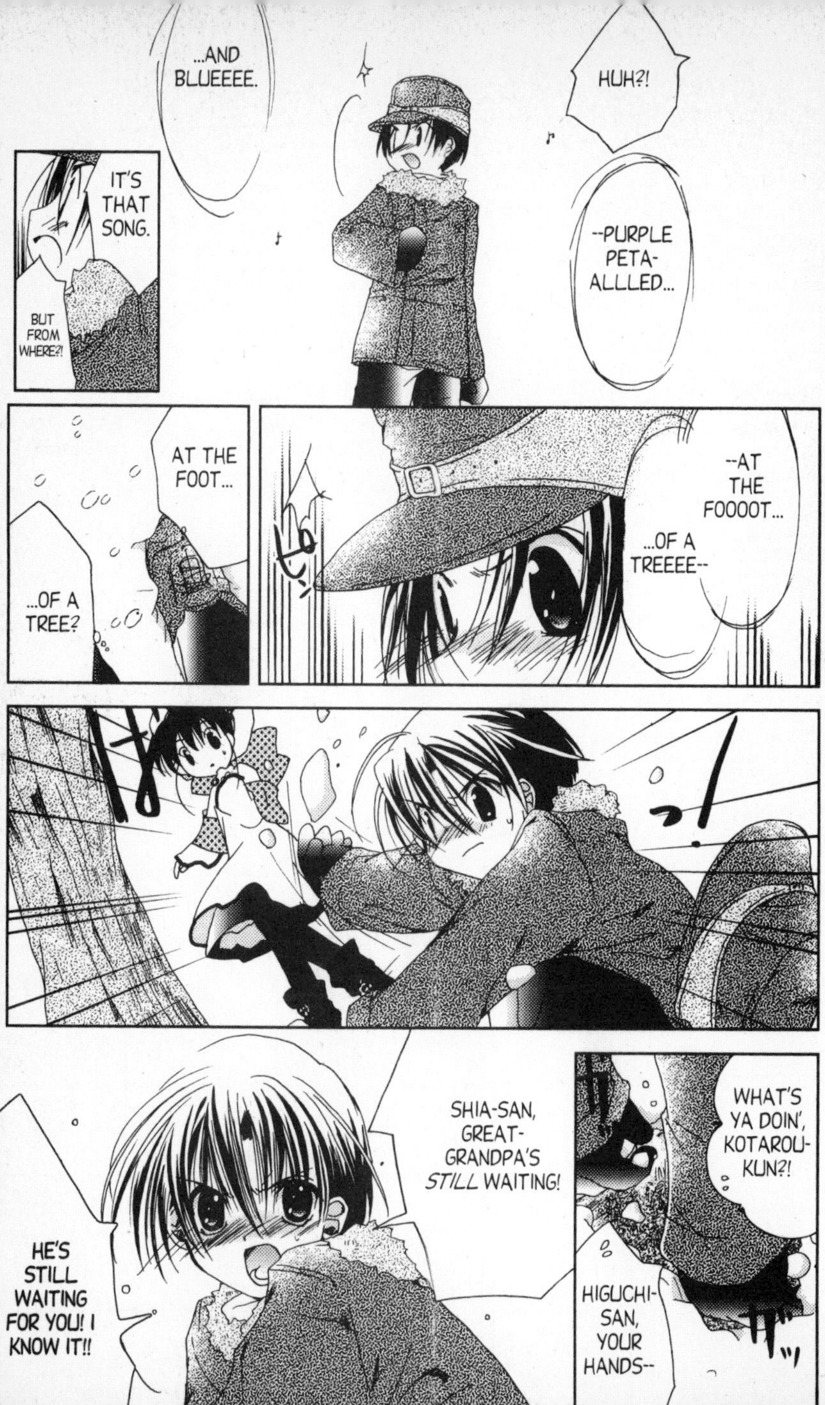
...AND BLUEEEE.
HUH?!
--PURPLE PETA-ALLLED...
IT'S THAT SONG.
BUT FROM WHERE?!
--AT THE FOOOOT...
...OF A TREEEE--
AT THE FOOT...
...OF A TREE?
WHAT'S YA DOIN', KOTAROU-KUN?!
HIGUCHI-SAN, YOUR HANDS--
SHIA-SAN, GREAT-GRANDPA'S *STILL* WAITING!
HE'S STILL WAITING FOR YOU! I KNOW IT!!

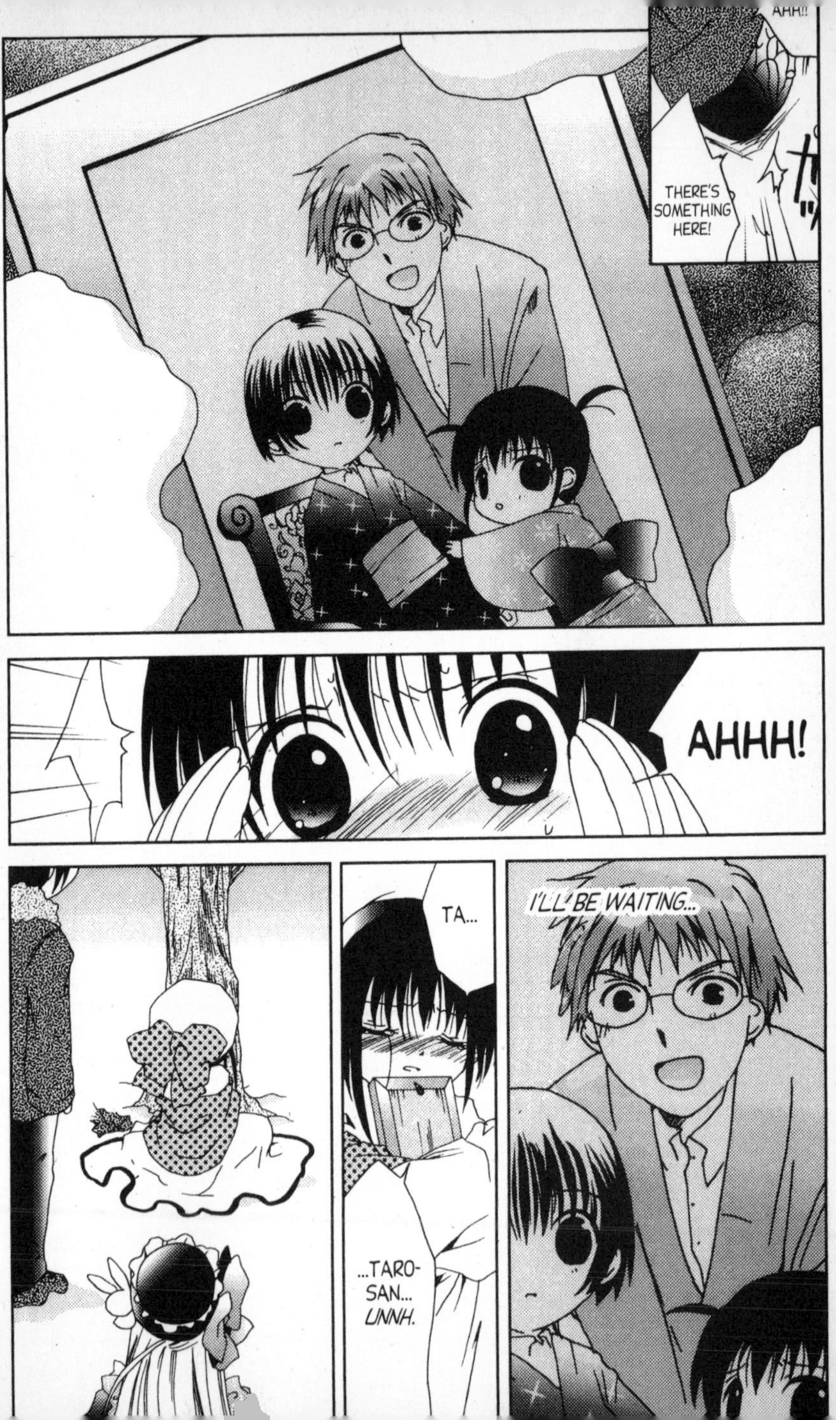
AHH!!
THERE'S SOMETHING HERE!
AHHH!
I'LL BE WAITING...
TA...
...TARO-SAN... UNNH.

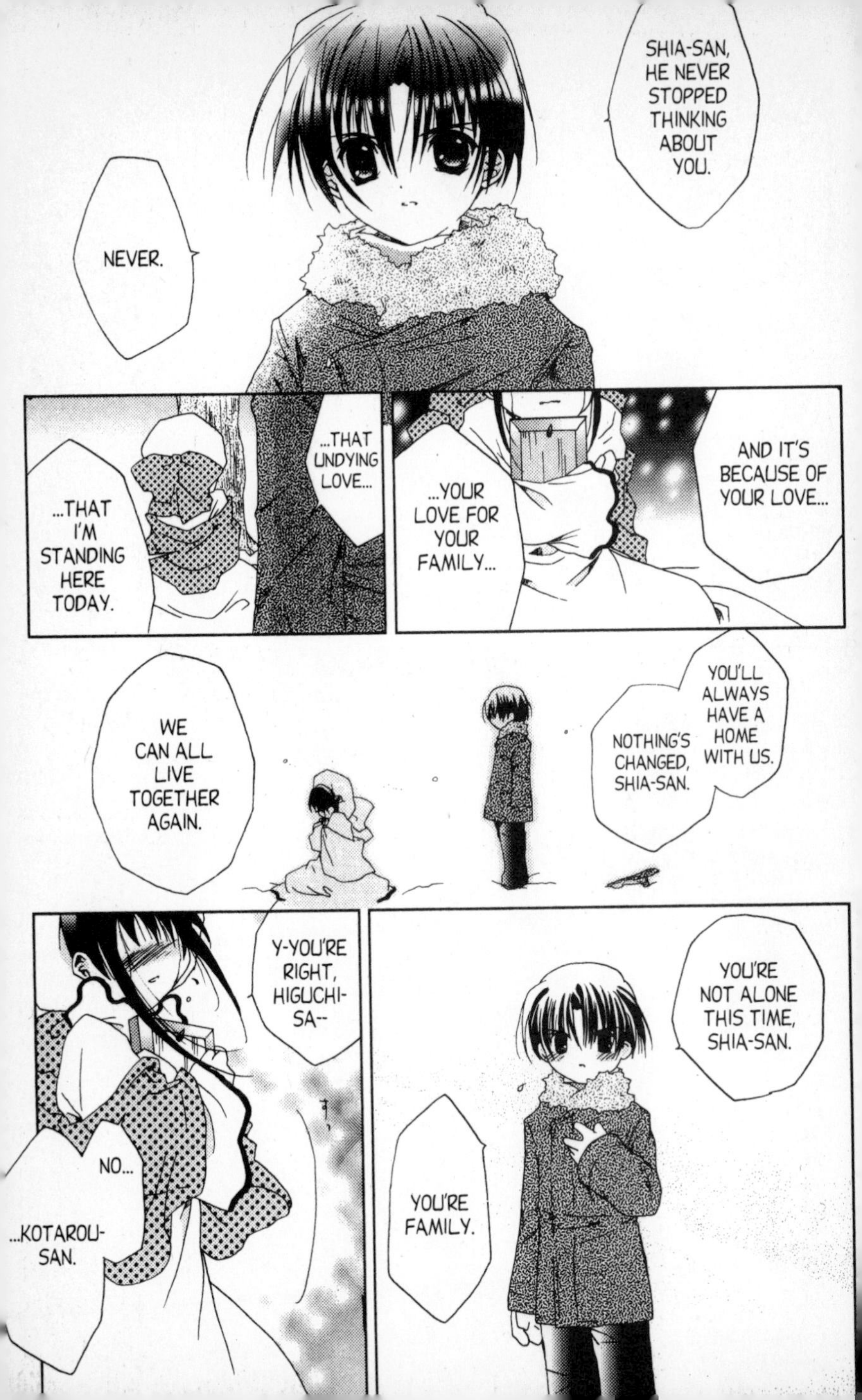
SHIA-SAN, HE NEVER STOPPED THINKING ABOUT YOU.
NEVER.
AND IT'S BECAUSE OF YOUR LOVE...
...YOUR LOVE FOR YOUR FAMILY...
...THAT UNDYING LOVE...
...THAT I'M STANDING HERE TODAY.
YOU'LL ALWAYS HAVE A HOME WITH US.
NOTHING'S CHANGED, SHIA-SAN.
WE CAN ALL LIVE TOGETHER AGAIN.
YOU'RE NOT ALONE THIS TIME, SHIA-SAN.
YOU'RE FAMILY.
Y-YOU'RE RIGHT, HIGUCHI-SA--
NO...
...KOTAROU-SAN.

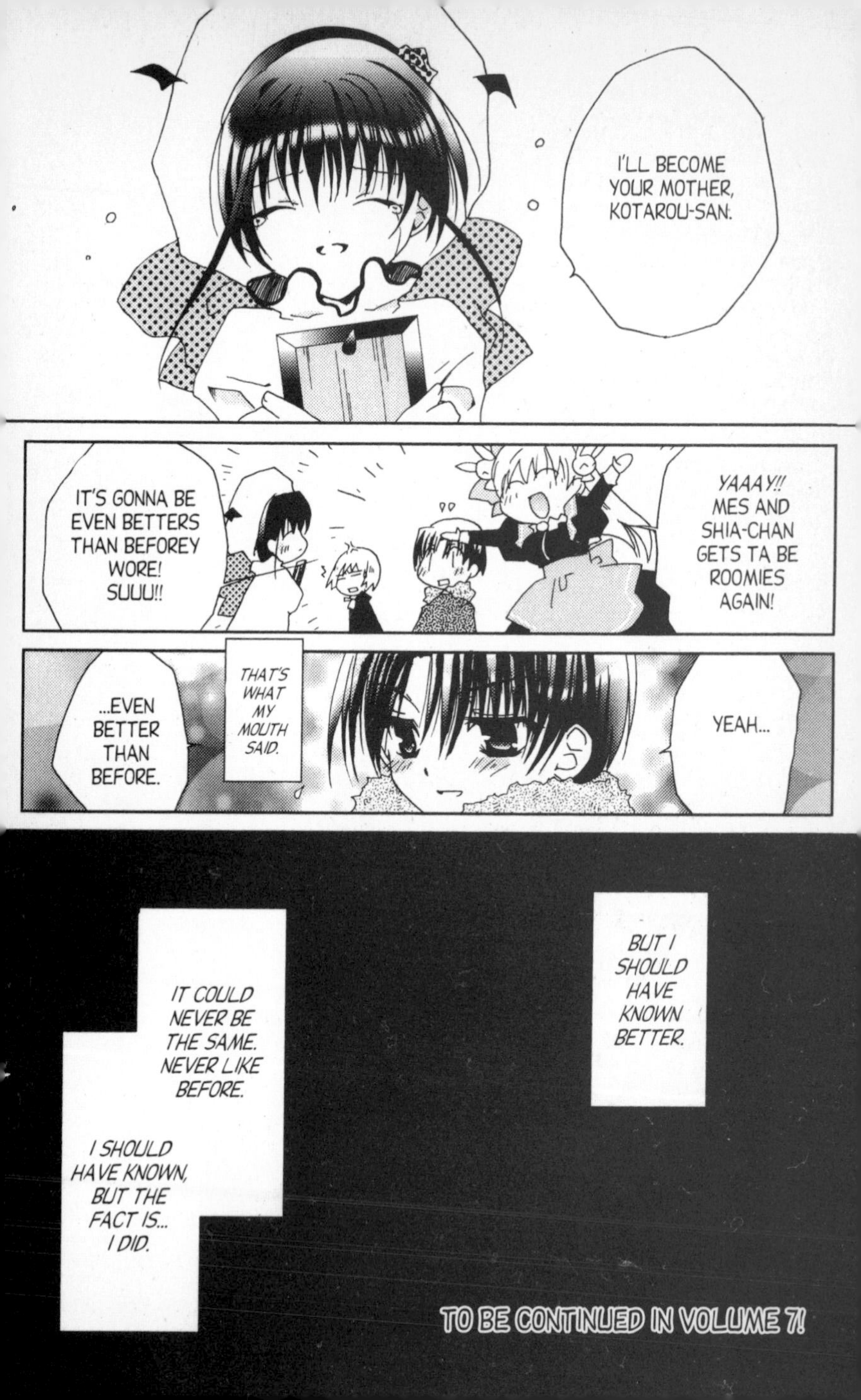
I'LL BECOME YOUR MOTHER, KOTAROU-SAN.
YAAAY!! MES AND SHIA-CHAN GETS TA BE ROOMIES AGAIN!
IT'S GONNA BE EVEN BETTERS THAN BEFOREY WORE! SUUU!!
YEAH...
THAT'S WHAT MY MOUTH SAID.
...EVEN BETTER THAN BEFORE.
BUT I SHOULD HAVE KNOWN BETTER.
IT COULD NEVER BE THE SAME. NEVER LIKE BEFORE.
I SHOULD HAVE KNOWN, BUT THE FACT IS... I DID.
TO BE CONTINUED IN VOLUME 7!

• AFTERWORD...

■ Hello there, and thank you very much for reading through Volume 6!! Koge-Donbo is in the house!

■ Well, as you can see, this is Volume 6. It's funny, whenever I'm drawing this manga, there are so many spots that I think I can make look really good, but for some reason, when I look back over the pages, I seem to forget everything I told myself during the original process. Doh! Maybe I just get nervous or something.

■ Anyhow, the biggest thing in this volume is probably getting to see Nya in action. You may be thinking, "Is this guy gonna go through the entire series just as 'Nya'?" Well, no worries there because his name is going to be revealed in the third book of the *Pita-Ten* novel series!! Hee hee, I guess it sort of happened while I had it shoved on the back burner. Thank you, Ochiai-san! (BTW: in the novel there were a ton of parts where I just kind of said, "Sorry, I didn't really think about it," and had to have Ochiai-san help me fill in all the gaps.) Hope you check it out anyway. *Ahhh*, I love thee, Nya. He's so much fun.

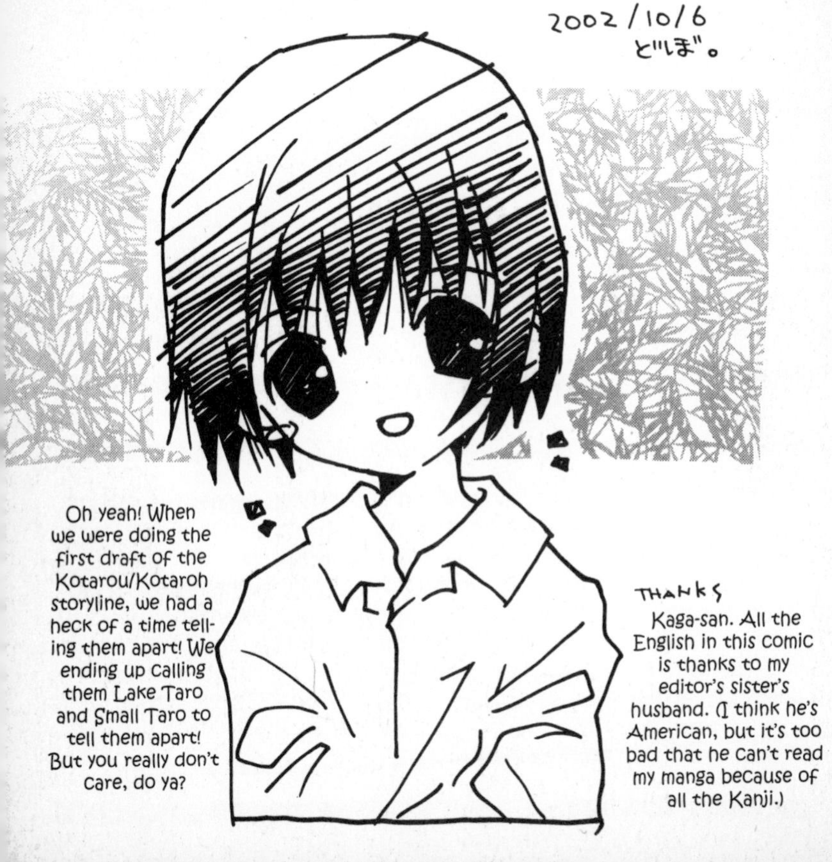
2002/10/6
どんぼ。
Oh yeah! When we were doing the first draft of the Kotarou/Kotaroh storyline, we had a heck of a time telling them apart! We ending up calling them Lake Taro and Small Taro to tell them apart! But you really don't care, do ya?
THANKS
Kaga-san. All the English in this comic is thanks to my editor's sister's husband. (I think he's American, but it's too bad that he can't read my manga because of all the Kanji.)

In the Next Volume of...

PITA-TEN

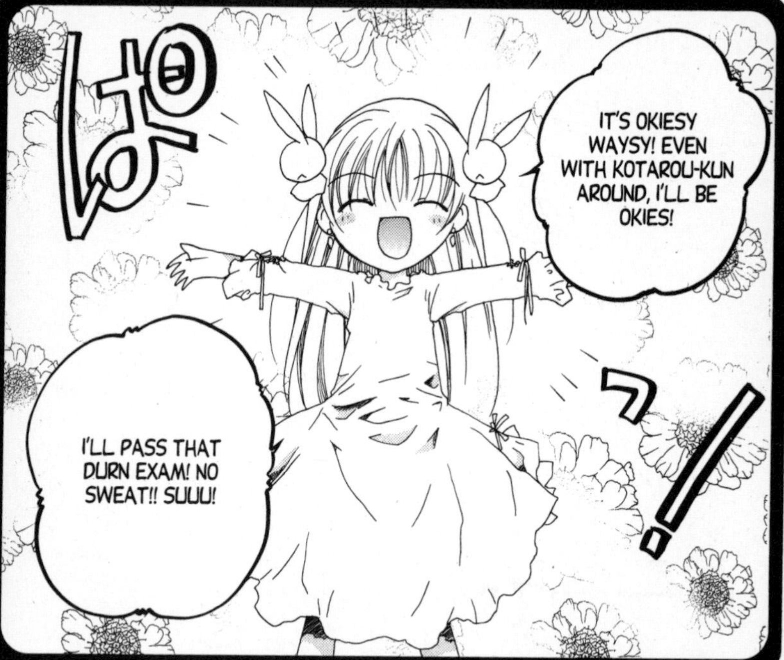
IT'S OKIESY WAYSY! EVEN WITH KOTAROU-KUN AROUND, I'LL BE OKIES!
I'LL PASS THAT DURN EXAM! NO SWEAT!! SUUU!

It is a time for mourning in the Higuchi household as last respects are paid to Kotarou's dearly departed great-grandfather. As Shia comes to grips with the life that she lost so long ago, Kotarou looks toward the New Year for inspiration. Even Misha is her usual, perky self. And yet, a smile is often the only thing that can truly disguise one's own fate. The dark secret that Misha has been harboring--the very reason for her coming to Earth--is finally revealed. Unfortunately, her friendship with Kotarou might not be strong enough to withstand the shocking truth in this, the penultimate volume of *Pita-Ten*!

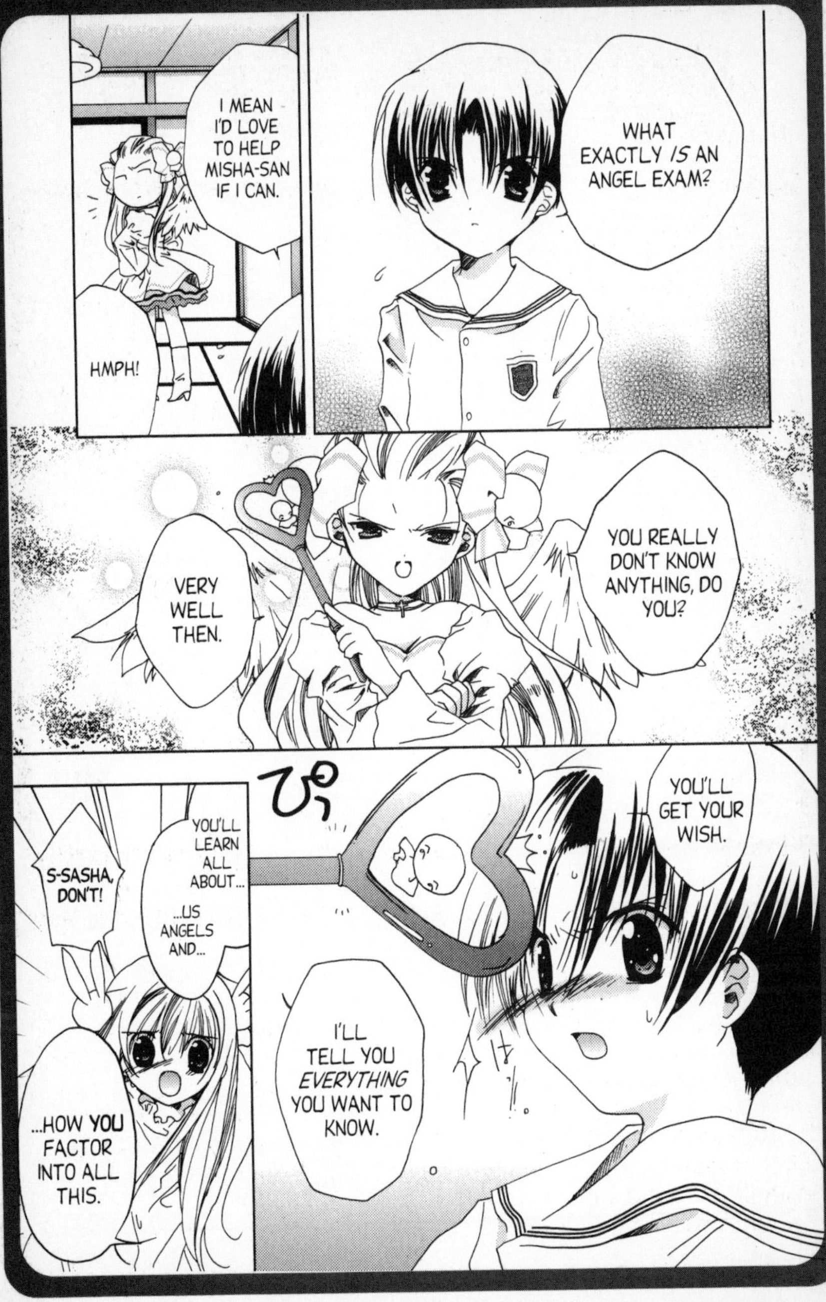

WHAT EXACTLY *IS* AN ANGEL EXAM?
I MEAN I'D LOVE TO HELP MISHA-SAN IF I CAN.
HMPH!
YOU REALLY DON'T KNOW ANYTHING, DO YOU?
VERY WELL THEN.
YOU'LL GET YOUR WISH.
ぴっ
I'LL TELL YOU *EVERYTHING* YOU WANT TO KNOW.
YOU'LL LEARN ALL ABOUT...
...US ANGELS AND...
...HOW **YOU** FACTOR INTO ALL THIS.
S-SASHA, DON'T!

ALSO AVAILABLE FROM TOKYOPOP®

PET SHOP OF HORRORS
PITA-TEN
PLANET LADDER
PLANETES
PRIEST
PRINCESS AI
PSYCHIC ACADEMY
QUEEN'S KNIGHT, THE
RAGNAROK
RAVE MASTER
REALITY CHECK
REBIRTH
REBOUND
REMOTE
RISING STARS OF MANGA
SABER MARIONETTE J
SAILOR MOON
SAINT TAIL
SAIYUKI
SAMURAI DEEPER KYO
SAMURAI GIRL REAL BOUT HIGH SCHOOL
SCRYED
SEIKAI TRILOGY, THE
SGT. FROG
SHAOLIN SISTERS
SHIRAHIME-SYO: SNOW GODDESS TALES
SHUTTERBOX
SKULL MAN, THE
SNOW DROP
SORCERER HUNTERS
STONE
SUIKODEN III
SUKI
THREADS OF TIME
TOKYO BABYLON
TOKYO MEW MEW
TOKYO TRIBES
TRAMPS LIKE US
UNDER THE GLASS MOON
VAMPIRE GAME
VISION OF ESCAFLOWNE, THE
WARRIORS OF TAO
WILD ACT
WISH
WORLD OF HARTZ
X-DAY
ZODIAC P.I.

NOVELS

CLAMP SCHOOL PARANORMAL INVESTIGATORS
KARMA CLUB
SAILOR MOON
SLAYERS

ART BOOKS

ART OF CARDCAPTOR SAKURA
ART OF MAGIC KNIGHT RAYEARTH, THE
PEACH: MIWA UEDA ILLUSTRATIONS

ANIME GUIDES

COWBOY BEBOP
GUNDAM TECHNICAL MANUALS
SAILOR MOON SCOUT GUIDES

TOKYOPOP KIDS

STRAY SHEEP

CINE-MANGA™

ALADDIN
CARDCAPTORS
DUEL MASTERS
FAIRLY ODDPARENTS, THE
FAMILY GUY
FINDING NEMO
G.I. JOE SPY TROOPS
GREATEST STARS OF THE NBA
JACKIE CHAN ADVENTURES
JIMMY NEUTRON: BOY GENIUS, THE ADVENTURES OF
KIM POSSIBLE
LILO & STITCH: THE SERIES
LIZZIE MCGUIRE
LIZZIE MCGUIRE MOVIE, THE
MALCOLM IN THE MIDDLE
POWER RANGERS: DINO THUNDER
POWER RANGERS: NINJA STORM
PRINCESS DIARIES 2
RAVE MASTER
SHREK 2
SIMPLE LIFE, THE
SPONGEBOB SQUAREPANTS
SPY KIDS 2
SPY KIDS 3-D: GAME OVER
THAT'S SO RAVEN
TOTALLY SPIES
TRANSFORMERS: ARMADA
TRANSFORMERS: ENERGON

You want it? We got it!
A full range of TOKYOPOP
products are available now at:
www.TOKYOPOP.com/shop

05.26.04T

ALSO AVAILABLE FROM 🐢 TOKYOPOP®

MANGA

.HACK//LEGEND OF THE TWILIGHT
@LARGE
ABENOBASHI: MAGICAL SHOPPING ARCADE
A.I. LOVE YOU
AI YORI AOSHI
ANGELIC LAYER
ARM OF KANNON
BABY BIRTH
BATTLE ROYALE
BATTLE VIXENS
BRAIN POWERED
BRIGADOON
B'TX
CANDIDATE FOR GODDESS, THE
CARDCAPTOR SAKURA
CARDCAPTOR SAKURA - MASTER OF THE CLOW
CHOBITS
CHRONICLES OF THE CURSED SWORD
CLAMP SCHOOL DETECTIVES
CLOVER
COMIC PARTY
CONFIDENTIAL CONFESSIONS
CORRECTOR YUI
COWBOY BEBOP
COWBOY BEBOP: SHOOTING STAR
CRAZY LOVE STORY
CRESCENT MOON
CROSS
CULDCEPT
CYBORG 009
D•N•ANGEL
DEMON DIARY
DEMON ORORON, THE
DEUS VITAE
DIABOLO
DIGIMON
DIGIMON TAMERS
DIGIMON ZERO TWO
DOLL
DRAGON HUNTER
DRAGON KNIGHTS
DRAGON VOICE
DREAM SAGA
DUKLYON: CLAMP SCHOOL DEFENDERS
EERIE QUEERIE!
ERICA SAKURAZAWA: COLLECTED WORKS
ET CETERA
ETERNITY
EVIL'S RETURN
FAERIES' LANDING
FAKE
FLCL
FLOWER OF THE DEEP SLEEP
FORBIDDEN DANCE
FRUITS BASKET
G GUNDAM

GATEKEEPERS
GETBACKERS
GIRL GOT GAME
GIRLS EDUCATIONAL CHARTER
GRAVITATION
GTO
GUNDAM BLUE DESTINY
GUNDAM SEED ASTRAY
GUNDAM WING
GUNDAM WING: BATTLEFIELD OF PACIFISTS
GUNDAM WING: ENDLESS WALTZ
GUNDAM WING: THE LAST OUTPOST (G-UNIT)
GUYS' GUIDE TO GIRLS
HANDS OFF!
HAPPY MANIA
HARLEM BEAT
HYPER RUNE
I.N.V.U.
IMMORTAL RAIN
INITIAL D
INSTANT TEEN: JUST ADD NUTS
ISLAND
JING: KING OF BANDITS
JING: KING OF BANDITS - TWILIGHT TALES
JULINE
KARE KANO
KILL ME, KISS ME
KINDAICHI CASE FILES, THE
KING OF HELL
KODOCHA: SANA'S STAGE
LAMENT OF THE LAMB
LEGAL DRUG
LEGEND OF CHUN HYANG, THE
LES BIJOUX
LOVE HINA
LUPIN III
LUPIN III: WORLD'S MOST WANTED
MAGIC KNIGHT RAYEARTH I
MAGIC KNIGHT RAYEARTH II
MAHOROMATIC: AUTOMATIC MAIDEN
MAN OF MANY FACES
MARMALADE BOY
MARS
MARS: HORSE WITH NO NAME
MINK
MIRACLE GIRLS
MIYUKI-CHAN IN WONDERLAND
MODEL
MOURYOU KIDEN
MY LOVE
NECK AND NECK
ONE
ONE I LOVE, THE
PARADISE KISS
PARASYTE
PASSION FRUIT
PEACH GIRL
PEACH GIRL: CHANGE OF HEART

05.26.04T

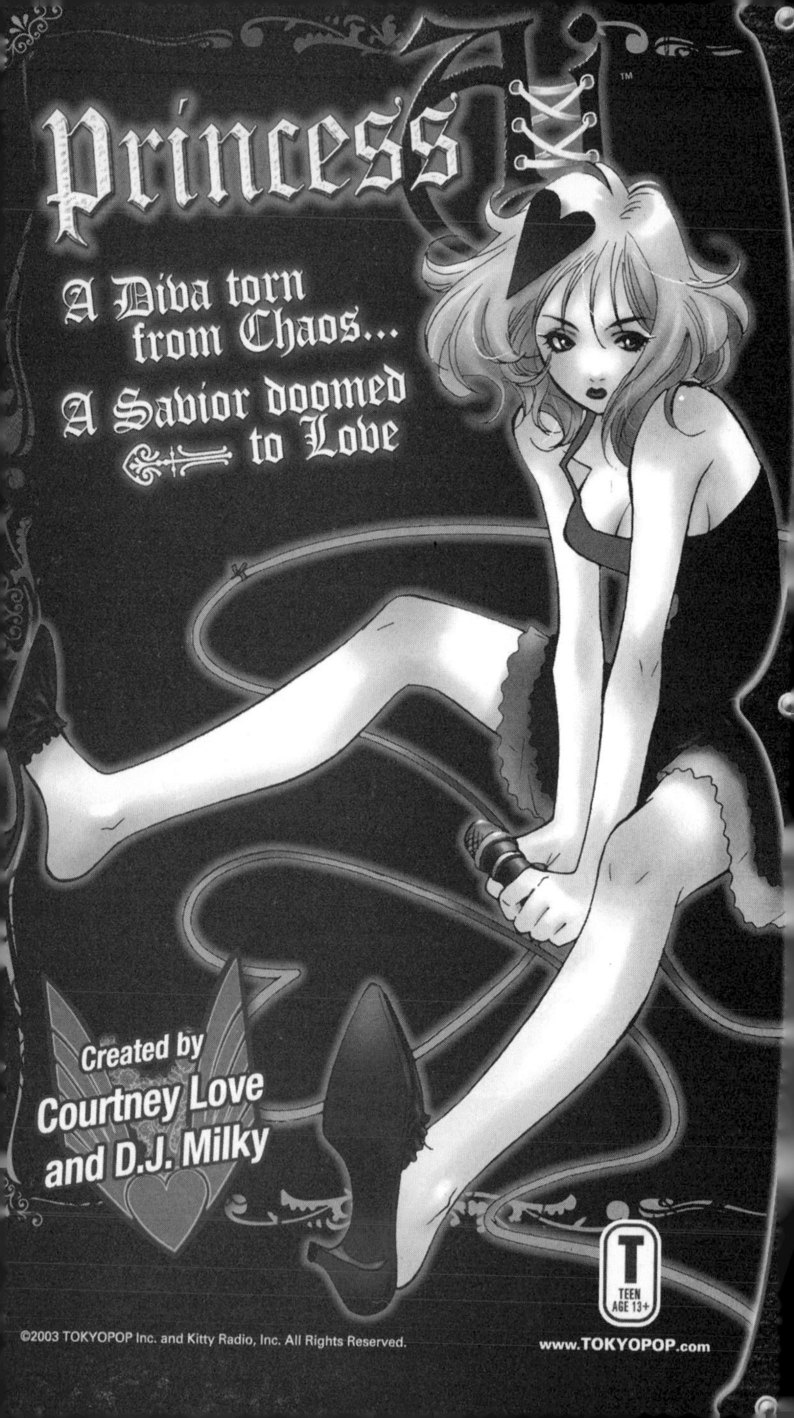
Princess Ai™
A Diva torn from Chaos...
A Savior doomed to Love
Created by
Courtney Love
and D.J. Milky
T
TEEN
AGE 13+
©2003 TOKYOPOP Inc. and Kitty Radio, Inc. All Rights Reserved.
www.TOKYOPOP.com

Blood, Sweat, and Gears.

B'TX

Available Now

©MASAMI KURUMADA 2004. ©2004 TOKYOPOP Inc. All rights reserved.

TOKYOPOP

T TEEN AGE 13+

TM

www.TOKYOPOP.com

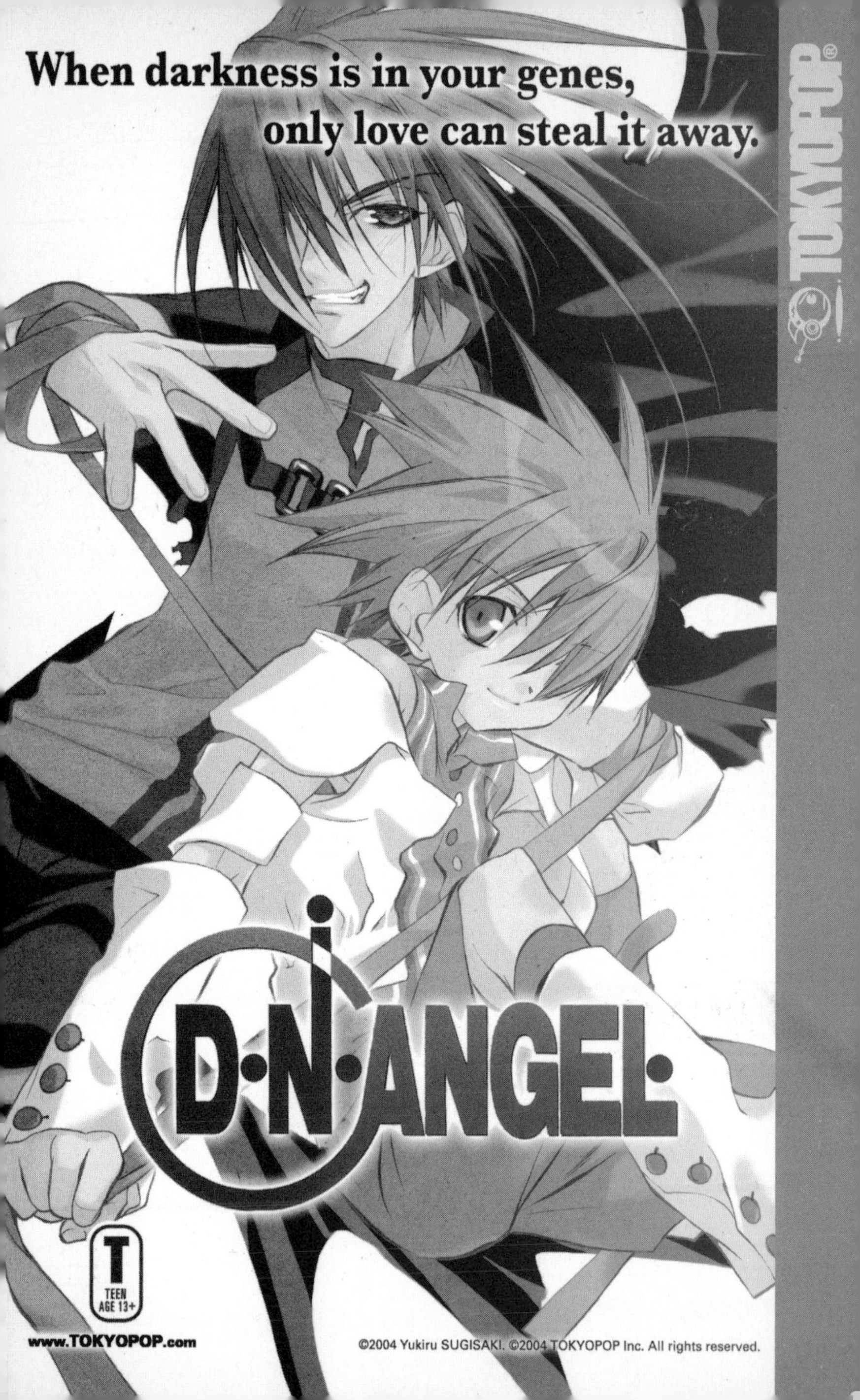
When darkness is in your genes,
only love can steal it away.
TOKYOPOP®
D•N•ANGEL
T
TEEN
AGE 13+
www.TOKYOPOP.com
©2004 Yukiru SUGISAKI. ©2004 TOKYOPOP Inc. All rights reserved.

The One I Love

watashi no suki na hito

FROM CLAMP
CREATORS OF
CHOBITS & TOKYO BABYLON

breathtaking stories
of love and romance

T
TEEN
AGE 13+

©1995 by CLAMP. ©2004 TOKYOPOP Inc. All Rights Reserved.

www.TOKYOPOP.com

Fruits Basket™

Life in the Sohma household can be a real zoo!

TEEN
AGE 13+

www.TOKYOPOP.com

©2003 Natsuki Takaya

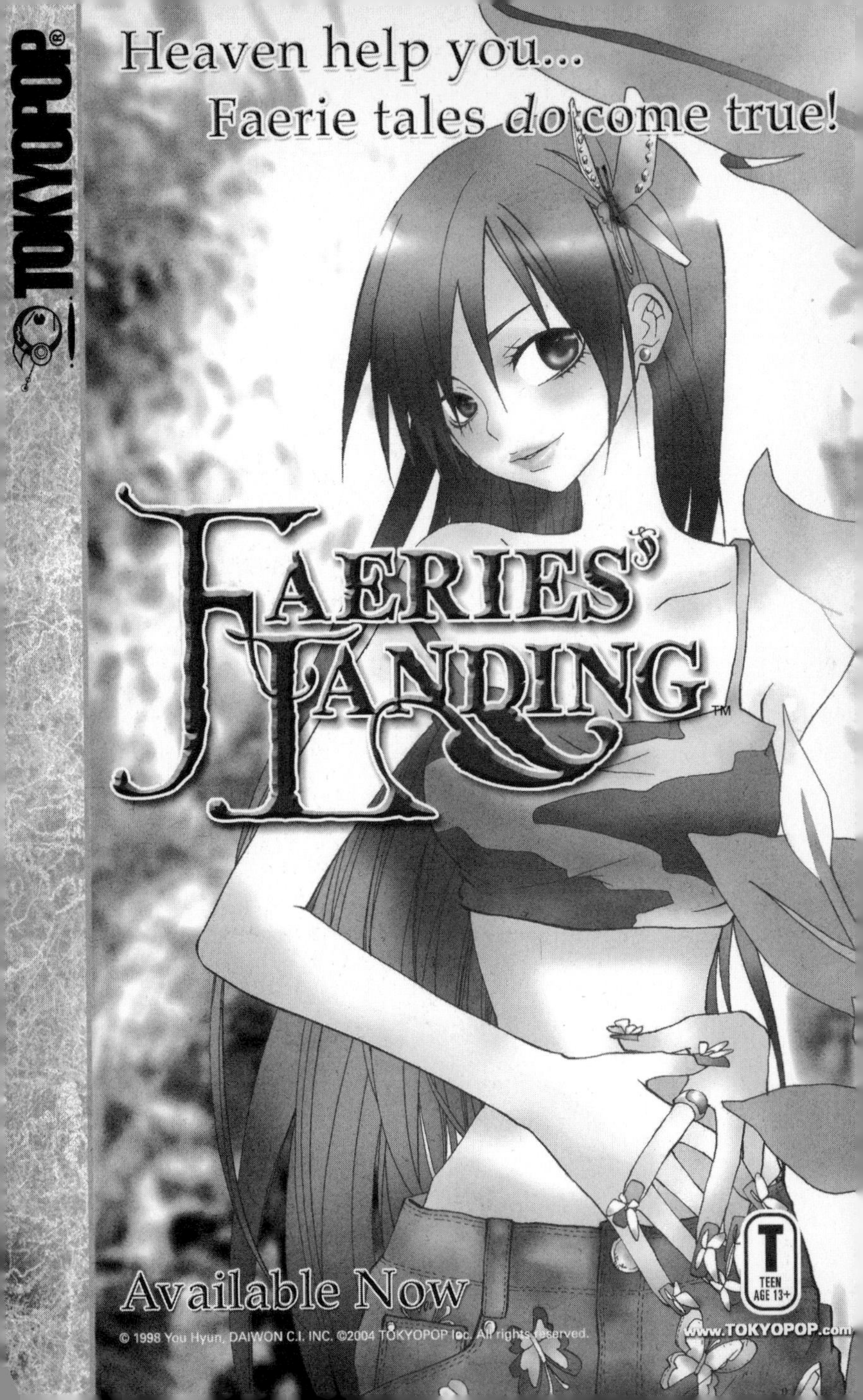
TOKYOPOP®
Heaven help you...
Faerie tales *do* come true!
FAERIES' LANDING™
Available Now
T TEEN AGE 13+
© 1998 You Hyun, DAIWON C.I. INC. ©2004 TOKYOPOP Inc. All rights reserved.
www.TOKYOPOP.com

CRESCENT MOON™

From the dark side
of the moon comes
a shining new star...

TEEN
AGE 13+

www.TOKYOPOP.com

©HARUKO IIDA ©RED ©2004 TOKYOPOP Inc.

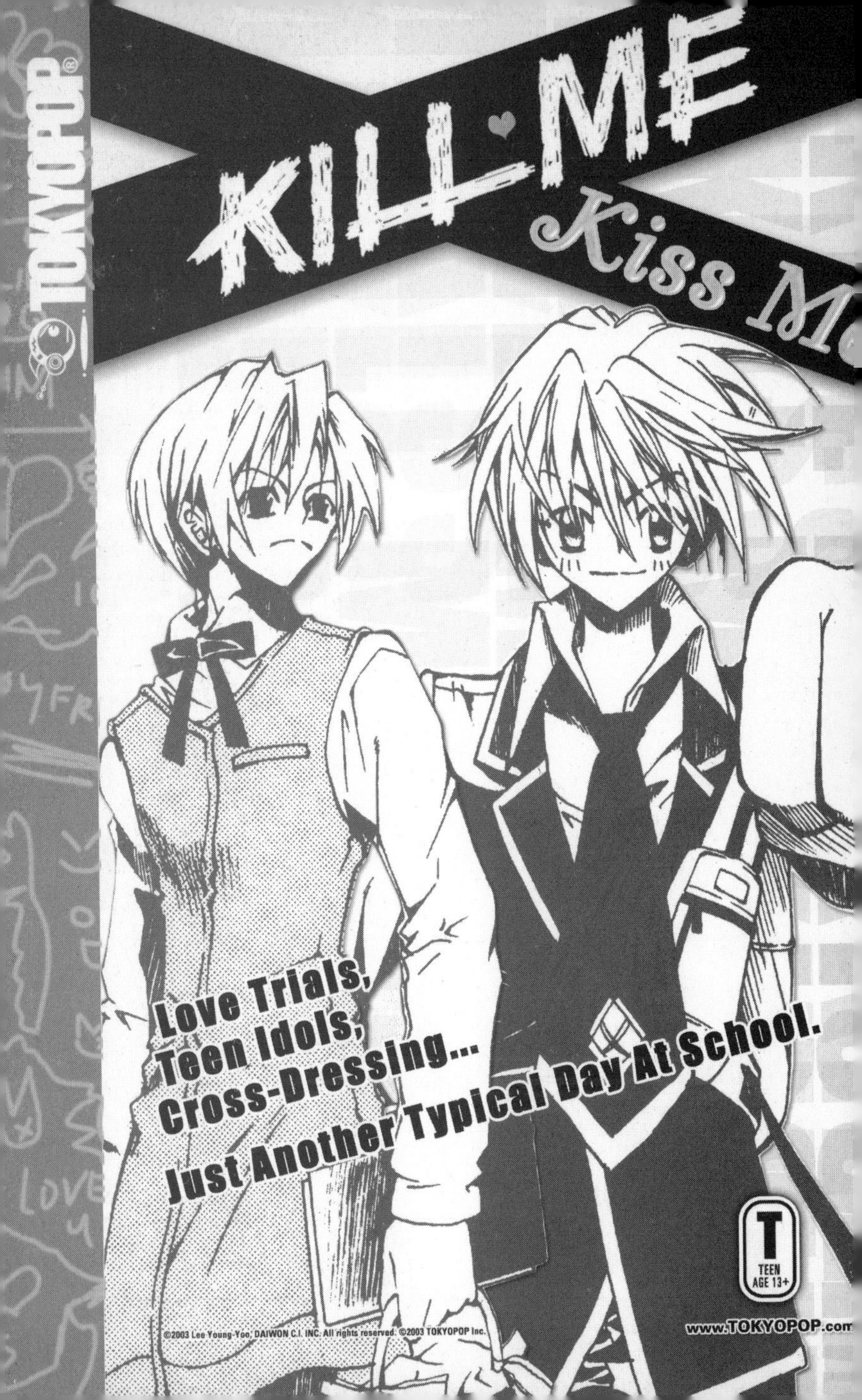
TOKYOPOP
KILL ME
Kiss Me
Love Trials,
Teen Idols,
Cross-Dressing...
Just Another Typical Day At School.
T
TEEN
AGE 13+
©2003 Lee Young-Yoo, DAIWON C.I. INC. All rights reserved. ©2003 TOKYOPOP Inc.
www.TOKYOPOP.com

STOP!

This is the back of the book.
You wouldn't want to spoil a great ending!

This book is printed "manga-style," in the authentic Japanese right-to-left format. Since none of the artwork has been flipped or altered, readers get to experience the story just as the creator intended. You've been asking for it, so TOKYOPOP® delivered: authentic, hot-off-the-press, and far more fun!

DIRECTIONS

If this is your first time reading manga-style, here's a quick guide to help you understand how it works.

It's easy... just start in the top right panel and follow the numbers. Have fun, and look for more 100% authentic manga from TOKYOPOP®!

AUTHENTIC MANGA